LEGAL PROTECTION OF CHILDREN AGAINST SEXUAL EXPLOITATION IN TAIWAN

TO MY FAMILIES

Legal Protection of Children Against Sexual Exploitation in Taiwan

A Socio-Legal Perspective

AMY H.L. SHEE 施慧玲
Associate Professor of Law
National Chung-Cheng University
Taiwan, ROC

Routledge
Taylor & Francis Group
LONDON AND NEW YORK

First published 1998 by Dartmouth and Ashgate Publishing

Reissued 2018 by Routledge
2 Park Square, Milton Park, Abingdon, Oxon, OX14 4RN
711 Third Avenue, New York, NY I 0017, USA

Routledge is an imprint of the Taylor & Francis Group, an informa business

A Library of Congress record exists under LC control number: 97038122

ISBN 13: 978-1-138-33523-3 (hbk)
ISBN 13: 978-1-138-33524-0 (pbk)
ISBN 13: 978-0-429-44390-9 (ebk)

Contents

List of Abbreviations

CCF	Chinese Children's Foundation
CCRP	The Code of Criminal Procedure
CCVP	The Code of Civil Procedure
CRC	Criminal Code
CVC	Civil Code
CWL	Child Welfare Law
CWLF	Child Welfare League Foundation
ECPAT (International)	International Campaign to End Child Prostitution in Asian Tourism
ECPAT (Taiwan)	End Child Prostitution Association Taiwan
GOH	Garden of Hope Foundation
HLMRF	Hsing Ling Medical Research Foundation
ICCB	International Catholic Child Bureau
JWL	Juvenile Welfare Law
KTPAI（VTCC）	Taipei Municipal Kuang Tze Po Ai Institution Vocational Training and Counselling Centre for Distressed Women
LGDJC	Law Governing the Disposition of Juvenile Cases
NGO	Non-Governmental Organisation
PRC	People's Republic of China
RGP	Regulations Governing Prostitution
RGSEE	Regulations Governing Special Entertainment Establishment
ROC	Republic of China
RP	Rainbow Project
SOML	Social Order Maintenance Law
TBA	Taipei Bar Association
TWRA	Taiwan Women Rescue Association (now TWRF)
TWRF	Taipei Women Rescue Foundation
UN	United Nations
WAF	Women Awakening Foundation
YLTTC	Taiwan Provincial Yunlin Technical Training Centre for Girls

Preface

I have had a special interest in child protection laws since I became a law student in October 1981. Unfortunately, children were only relevant in the study of law in *Taiwan* as a small part of the Family Law course, in which the concern was limited to parental rights over children. In other words, children were not discussed as legal subjects, so there was very little concern with children's rights in general or the role of the state and welfare authorities vis-a-vis that of the family. Later in the University of London LL.M. course, I was finally given the opportunity to study and write about children as the main concern of legal studies. It strengthened my intention to do a Ph.D. concerning child protection.

The period of M.Phil study at Warwick University from latter 1988 to early 1990 made me realise the importance of the practical operation of the law and I became attracted to socio-legal research. When my decision was made to study the newly discovered social problem of child prostitution for my Ph.D. degree, I returned to Taiwan and got myself involved in relevant activities concerning the issue. As I was able to devote full-time attention to conducting research, I was made responsible for leading certain parts of research projects including making proposals for the amendment of the divorce law and the child welfare law. My association with NGO leaders gave me the chance to participate in all sorts of social campaigns, especially those concerning women and children. I became involved in anti-child prostitution campaigns in September, 1990 when I joined the Taipei Bar Association (TBA) 14-month research project on the legislation for physical safety of women. It was during the course of research that I had full access to the problem of child prostitution and to those experts who worked on it.

As very little had been written on legal issues of child prostitution in *Taiwan*, I had to interview concerned professionals and activists in order to complete my Ph.D. thesis. Open-end questions were asked which required the interviewed persons to sum up from their past experiences and observations the main causes for the deterioration of child prostitution problems, the crucial obstacles in law enforcement, and their recommendations for changes in policy and practice. One unexpected information provided in the interviews was the reasons why legal reform became the main target of anti-child prostitution campaigns. Most interviewed professionals told me that from their experiences of being threatened by flesh traders, being ignored by the police and welfare authorities, and being unable to retain the custody of rescued children and to enforce effective rehabilitation programmes, they realised that in order to achieve their goals, more legal powers must be obtained through legislation. Their triumph in adding provisions to the 1989 Juvenile Welfare Law has been referred to as the landmark of NGO success. Since then, all concerned groups have concentrated on lobbying for legislation and their efforts have contributed to adding relevant provisions to the 1993 Child Welfare Law (Amendment) and finally the making of a specific law—the Law to Suppress Sexual Transactions Involving Children and Juveniles. Consequently, all the involved legal professionals, such as *Ms SHEN Mei Chen*, *Ms WANG Ching Feng*, and *Ms HUANG Yi Chun* of the Taipei Women Rescue Foundation, *Mr LIN Yung Sung* of the Garden of Hope Foundation and myself representing the End Child Prostitution Association Taiwan, became the leaders of social campaigns concerned with child prostitution.

The child prostitution problem started to be recognised as an international epidemic in 1990. The concerns for this 'modern form of slavery' accumulated to initiate the International Campaign to End Child Prostitution in Asian Tourism (ECPAT). My work as a legal advisor to the ECPAT-*Taiwan* Office provided me with unrestricted access to concerned professionals and activists including judges, lawyers, social workers, scholars, researchers, media reporters, and so forth. Besides, as one of the drafters of the TBA Child Welfare Law Bill, I obtained access to the ROC Legislative Yuan during the legislative process of the Law. From my association with some legislators and their assistants as well as my attendance at the readings of the Law, I was informed of the ways in which compromises were made between pressure groups, government officials, and the legislators. At the same time, my status as a Ph.D. student provided me with opportunities to learn from professional experts in this field. From constant discussions with them, I learnt to see the problems from various standpoints. As I had been given so many privileges to get to know the issue and to work on it, I felt that it was my responsibility as a legal researcher to conduct an analytical study to record and review the experiences of concerned professionals. So my Ph.D. thesis was completed on this base. Thanks to the encouragement of both my supervisor Professor Abdul Paliwala and the external oral examiner Dr.

Michael Palmer from the University of London, I contracted with the Dartmouth Publishing Company to publish my Ph.D. thesis. However, as a specific law was being made during those days, I considered it more appropriate to rewrite the thesis in order to make up-to-date analyses on ROC laws.

Since its discovery in 1987, the problem of child prostitution in *Taiwan* has been attracting concerns from religious groups, human rights and welfare organisations, the government as well as the public. For more than ten years now, experiences as well as problems have been accumulated but they have not resulted in any systematic socio-legal analysis. This book is therefore an attempt to examine the practice of ROC laws and corresponding measures on the basis of accumulated experiences of concerned professionals. Apart from the visits paid to professionals, information and materials were also collected with the help of library facilities available in *Taiwan*. Concerned governmental authorities, NGOs and individuals also provided me with data, statistics, cases and other useful materials.

A special remark has to be made concerning the reference to Court cases in this book. As pointed out by *Ms SHEN Mei Chen* (*SHEN*), under the case documentation system of the ROC Law Courts, it is extremely difficult for an individual researcher to collect enough cases concerning illegal prostitution for the purpose of systematic analyses. Very luckily, there was once an interested Criminal Court judge who managed to collect completed judgments (from indictment to final judgment) of ninety-five cases dating from 1981 to 1987 concerning illegal prostitution among which 23 cases involved children under 18. These cases have been summarised in the LL.M. dissertation of *SHEN*, which is the only available legal study of court cases concerning child prostitution in *Taiwan*. *SHEN*'s work will thus be the main reference for the analysis in chapter six on the application of the Criminal Code by the Criminal Courts.

During my involvement in anti-child prostitution campaigns, informal visits have been made to female children in rehabilitation centres and mid-way houses. However, no formal records were made during the visits mainly to avoid frightening and hurting the visited girls who did not want any of their trauma to be taken out of the centre/house by strangers. For the purpose of this book, interviews carried out by social workers who were familiar with the children are considered a more reliable source of reference, although I also made my own judgments and tried to avoid using social workers' observation which involved moral evaluation. Accounts given in published literature or during my interviews with concerned professionals will also be referred to support the arguments in this book.

Child prostitution has been recognised as a major social problem in modern capitalist Taiwan. It is now defined, both legally and socially, as a problem of 'sexual transactions involving children and juveniles', thus the issue of child abuse and sexual exploitation is submerged under other concerns. However, the main concern of this book is the protection of children from maltreatment, so related socio-legal measures will be examined by this parameter. During the social campaigns against child prostitution, structural problems such as police corruption, male sexual perversion, socio-economic inequality, and the maladjustment of aboriginal people in the modern Taiwanese society are subjugated to increasing criticism. Nevertheless, efforts to encounter any of them have had very limited accomplishment. This book intends to show that the functions of law in the prevention and treatment of the social problem of child prostitution cannot work as intended if those structural problems can not be properly tackled. Suggestions are also made to address the need to reconceptualise the problem in the analytical framework of child maltreatment and to recommend the direction for the reformation of policy and practice.

Acknowledgments

There are many people who have played a crucial part in the completion of this book. My most sincere gratitude and appreciation is owed to Professor Abdul Paliwala, whose patience, kindness, and intelligence have made invaluable contributions throughout my Ph.D. study at Warwick University, which produced the thesis that this book is based on. I am indebted to Abdul not only for his excellent supervision over my thesis writing but also for his generous help in the publication of this book.

Special thanks have to be given to Mr Joseph LIAO 廖建銘 in attending to my word processing queries. I am also indebted to my students and research assistants including Ms Grace TSAI 蔡穎芳, Ms Shih-Yi HUANG 黃仕儀 , Ms Sarah LI 李珮慈, Ms Vera CHANG 張純嘉, and Mr Chou-Chin YOU 游朝欽, as well as my colleagues at the Law School Professor Yi-Hsiung CHIANG 江義雄, Dr. Feng-Ming HAO 郝鳳鳴, Dr. Che-Sheng HSIEH 謝哲勝, Dr. Chin-Chin CHENG 鄭津津, Ms Chiou-Kuei WU 吳秋瑰 and Ms Fang-Ling HSU 許方玲 for their advice and supports. Further, I would like to express my admiration for the help of my friends in the field who have constantly supplied important information and materials for the use of my research, among them Legislators Mr. Chi-Chia LIN 林志嘉, Chu-Lan YEH 葉菊蘭, and Ms Chi-Ta HSIEH 謝啓大, Procurators Ms Pi-Yu TSAI 蔡碧玉and Ms Ling-Yu LIN 林玲玉; as well as TWRF Chairperson Ms Mei-Chen SHEN 沈美眞, ECPAT Chairperson Ms Ruth KAO 高李麗珍, ECPAT General Secretary Ms Li-Fen LI 李麗芬, and GOH Programme Director Mr Yi-Shih CHENG 鄭怡世 who have been most supportive. In addition, the supply of important international documents by ECPAT-International is equally acknowledged. Mention has also to be made for the special attention given by staffs of concerned NGOs to my inquiries.

Those who are dear to me and close to my heart have provided me with indispensable backup. My parents Justice Wen-Zen SHEE 施文仁 and Mrs. Su-Mei HONG-SHEE 施洪淑美 have constantly given me intellectual stimulation in their legal expertise and provided me with both material and mental support. My mother-in-law Mrs. Su-Chen PAN-KAO 高潘淑貞 is always prepared to comfort my distress and to care for my health. My younger brother Mr Chi-Yau SHEE 施繼堯 and his bride-to-be Ms Mei-Huei HUANG 黃美惠 have been guiding me through the reading of Japanese material. My youngest brother Dr. Victor SHEE 施繼顯 who teaches computer science at the Nottingham Trent University constantly passes on his concern and support through international phone calls.

The final words of the acknowledgments are to be dedicated to my husband Dr. Bernard Y. KAO 高玉泉, who is also an associate professor of law in Taiwan. For the past 16 years, Bernard has taken the roles of my university classmate, my best friend, my trusted advisor, my respected colleague in the law profession and my most devoted partner in marriage. The completion of this book would have been impossible without Bernard's affectionate encouragement and generous back-up.

Amy Huey-Ling SHEE 施慧玲
Department and Graduate School of Law,
National Chung-Cheng University,
Chai-Yi, Taiwan.

May 11, 1997
The Chinese Mother's Day

1 INTRODUCTION

Child prostitution[1] is part of the Chinese Han cultural history. Chinese laws have long prohibited selling children into prostitution, but the practice was tolerated for the survival of poor families. At the same time, prostitution was seen as a device to maintain the stability of well-off Chinese families.[2] Frequenting prostitution was never subjected to state regulation. Neither was the miserable lives of the children in prostitution a philanthropic concern. Instead, under the patronage of Chinese patriarchy, the sexually exploited children were kept in prostitution and thought of as 'bad' girls (women) for the preservation of the cult of 'good' women and girls.[3]

After the establishment of the Republic of China (ROC) in 1911, modern legal reforms were carried out to wipe out 'bad' Chinese traditions including the practice of child prostitution. The 1930 Civil Code provides for the suspension of parental rights. Under the 1928 Criminal Code, the exploitative parents as well as all other procurers, brothel-keepers and pimps can be charged with the offences against the family, against personal liberty or against social morals; and the customer may also be punished for committing unlawful sex with children under the age of 16.[4] When the Nationalist government retreated to *Taiwan* in 1949, the ROC Constitution and other basic laws were also brought to be implemented on the island. And in order to sustain the ROC on *Taiwan* against the People's Republic of China, a martial law (state of siege) was declared.[5] Since then, the people have been mobilised to build *Taiwan* under government-led modernisation programmes, which are based on Western capitalist models.

ROC policies have been aimed to show ROC's determination to become a devoted and 'good' member of international society by signing international documents, as well as to achieve modern law reforms by imitating laws from developed countries. As a result, it became a state policy to prohibit prostitution after the ROC government signed the United Nations Convention for the Suppression of the Traffic in Persons and the Exploitation of the Prostitution of Others (1949). The United Nations Declaration of the Rights of the Child (1959) resulted in the first ROC social legislation -- the 1973 Child Welfare Law. Even the United Nations

Convention on the Rights of the Child (1989)[6], to which the ROC is not eligible to be a signatory, has triggered the amendment of the Child Welfare Law in 1993.[7] When social problems were recognised to demand legal reform, legislative principles were taken from foreign laws. On the other hand, a developing welfare state has gradually replaced traditional functions of the Chinese families in the upbringing and discipline of children.[8]

Modernisation also led to social and political changes. Industrialisation has brought about migration, urbanisation, and nuclearisation of families. The nuclear family is now organised around young children, and the extended family is declining, especially in urban areas.[9] The Western concept of childhood[10] has also contributed to the social as well as legal construction of children as a separated group. Not only has modern public and private schooling been developed and strengthened, available governmental and voluntary welfare services for children are also augmented and multiplied. All these changes have facilitated the development of an interventionist welfare state as well as child protection legislation and measures in recent years. Besides, children also became major clients of philanthropic organisations. Moreover, owing to the accelerated democratisation process since the late 1980s, pressure groups have also been allowed to campaign for disadvantaged social groups including children, and more governmental measures and legislation have been consequent upon these campaigns.

It was against this background that the practice of child prostitution was finally found intolerable in modern Taiwanese society. Several concerned groups, mainly the Christian philanthropists, initiated the first wave of the anti-child-prostitution campaigns[11] with *the HUA HSI Street* demonstration held on January 10, 1987. The existence of child prostitution was then gradually recognised as a social problem through a series of child-saving activities organised by organisations (NGOs) concerned with the protection of women and children. At first, the problem was publicised with stories of the sold female children and their miserable lives in prostitution. The practice was defined as 'traffic in persons and forcing good girls into prostitution (*mai mai jen kou, pi liang wei chang 買賣人口，逼良爲娼*) '.[12] The public was informed of the inhuman practice of child prostitution and there was a social demand that these girls must be rescued from a situation resembling slavery.[13] The issue of socio-economic inequality was also addressed to emphasize the vulnerability of certain inferior groups -- the aboriginal and/or poor families. It was urged that in the modern, Han-dominated, capitalist society, these disadvantaged families were prone to be exploited.

The first wave of social campaigns succeeded in achieving three main results. First, it obtained the recognition of child prostitution as a serious social problem which demanded specific state measures. Second, it constructed the facts of the problem as the maltreatment of female children of disadvantaged families within an exploitative social-structural context. Third, it resulted in not only anxiety of professional experts, media reporters and the public, but also an immediate response from the government. However, the first mistake was also made: these sold children were named 'girl prostitutes'.[14] Besides, although some structural problems were criticised, no constructive proposals were made for policy changes.[15] All that was asked for was 'to rescue girl prostitutes'.

The government responded to these NGO campaigns with a police administrative project -- the 'Decent Society Campaign'[16], which involved constant police raids on the prostitution industry searching for 'girl prostitutes' under 16.[17] Since then, this phenomenon of the commercial sexual exploitation of children had been referred to as the 'girl prostitution problem (*chu chi wen ti* 雛妓問題) ' not only officially but also among activists, concerned professionals, and the public, and it was only until recently that the problem involving boys became a new concern. Moreover, although the main aim of the police project was to answer to the NGO demand 'to rescue girl prostitutes (*chiu yuan chu chi* 救援雛妓)', it was officially pronounced as 'to raid on girl prostitutes (*chu ti chu chi* 取締雛妓)'. Concerned NGOs would expect that the girls be treated as victims and all perpetrators including the customers be arrested and prosecuted according to applicable laws. However, the assigned job for the police was to crack down on illegal prostitution involving underage girls. So the girls were taken to the police station and questioned as 'unlicensed prostitutes'. After a file was made, the child victim was disposed of as an underage 'illegal prostitute'. Therefore, she was either returned to her parents for discipline or referred to the juvenile justice system for correction. The police record also showed a significant number of criminal suspects being arrested, but none of the customers were ever charged in the Criminal Court.

Within a short period of time, the police raids located a significant number of 'girl prostitutes', then the girls themselves became the centre of professional vigilance. First, the girls have to be protected from being taken back into the flesh market, so they must be kept in a well-guarded institution. Second, concerned professionals soon diagnosed the moral danger and sexual deviance of the 'girl prostitutes', so specific counselling and skill-training programmes were designed for their rehabilitation. This means that the campaigns against the inhuman practice of child prostitution actually resulted in treatment measures concentrating on the incarceration and discipline of the child victims. And the 'girl prostitution problem' has become a problem of 'illegal prostitution involving underage girls' rather than 'traffic in persons and forcing good girls into prostitution'.

When experiences accumulated, more problems were identified in association with the 'girl prostitution problem'. Statistics showed that the police were only able to locate annually on average about 200 'girl prostitutes', whilst concerned NGOs estimated a number of at least 40,000 to 60,000 girls under 16 in prostitution. The NGOs also claimed that 90% of the girls have fallen back to prostitution after rehabilitation. Besides, it was found that a growing number of children from well-to-do families were earning their pocket money by offering sexual services; while on the other hand, some run-away boys were found to offer sexual services to older men for food and money. Moreover, as the flesh trade became extremely lucrative, it attracted the involvement of various business interests as well as the patronage of not only organised mobsters but also local politicians and police officers. The ineffectiveness of rescue and rehabilitation, and the involvement of male as well as female children in all kinds of sex-related services were indicated as the 'deterioration' of the ‘child prostitution problem （*tung chi wen ti* 童妓問題）'.

On the other hand, there were also defects found in governmental and non-governmental social and legal measures. Responses from activists, social workers, police officers, welfare authorities, legislators, politicians, lawyers, judges, media reporters, and the public were extremely diverse. Some involved children might be subjected to exuberant vigilance of the idealist do-gooders, but some others might still be despised as 'bad' girls and abandoned to prostitution by law enforcers. Practising lawyers might be eager to ensure the termination of all exploitative parent-child relationship through Civil Court proceedings, while the Criminal Court would release the parents back to attend other children of the family.

A second wave of social campaigns was thus directed against this deteriorated child prostitution problem. Many factors were claimed by various pressure groups to be responsible for the deterioration. They included collusion of police officers and local politicians in the operation of illegal prostitution, ineffectiveness of rehabilitation programmes, inappropriateness of aboriginal development policies, and more recently, the failure of the state measures on prostitution control, selective and distorted application of laws by their enforcers, and social tolerance towards the pervert male sexual preference for 'tender and clean flesh'. As NGOs had organised themselves and became powerful pressure groups with the support of the media, professional experts, a few legislators, and some government officials, various social and legal measures were consequently implemented to respond to NGO urges. With the help of concerned legislators and media reporters, pressure groups have exercised significant influences in relevant law-makings. But new laws do not necessarily change the practices of police officers or Court judges, who have the discretion to dispose of cases with their legal knowledge and according to the laws they deem appropriate.

The second wave of anti-child-prostitution campaigns resulted in the recognition of the changing nature of the problem and the devotion of more resources to inter-disciplinary work. Government-sponsored social educational programmes have since then been organised for aboriginal peoples and school children. Past failure of rehabilitation was subjected to professional evaluation, and government-financed NGO plans have been initiated to establish loving and educational long-term mid-way houses. Administrative projects are taken to strengthen the discipline of police officers as well as the training of social workers. Legislative efforts have been led to the imposition of heavy and specific punishment on the customers as well as the procurers, pimps, and brothel-keepers involved in child prostitution. Helped by concerted efforts of all concerned professionals, the 'Law to Suppress Sexual Transactions Involving Children and Juveniles' was promulgated by the ROC President on August 11, 1995. The Law marked the success of NGOs concerned with child prostitution to demand a specific law governing prevention and treatment of the problem in their hands.

The new Law has been in practice for nearly twenty-two months at the completion of this book. As the Law requires the 'competent authority', namely, the Ministry of the Interior, as well as other 'relevant authorities' including those responsible for the administration of justice, education, health and hygiene, national defense, information, economics and public transportation to undertake specified measures within a prescribed period of time, not only the welfare administrators but also the police, the procurators, and the Government Information Office have devoted substantial efforts in the implementation of this Law.

This book examines the process of discovery and recognition of child prostitution as a social problem and the divergent ways by which people with different responsibilities and power have responded to it. Through this examination, one will see the dynamic interaction between the practice of child prostitution and the exercise of relevant socio-legal measures. Past efforts have contributed to several administrative, legislative, and social changes. State policies on prostitution control and the development of welfare state mechanisms for child protection have also moved against the practice of child prostitution. However, this book intends to show the inappropriateness of current socio-legal measures regardless of all the efforts. It is argued that in order to manage the problem appropriately, new efforts have to be made to reformulate policy and practice.

In other words, current socio-legal measures in relation to child prostitution have to be both modified and strengthened. First, child prostitution must be defined as a problem of child maltreatment and be explained within the exploitative social framework of patriarchy and modern capitalist consumerism which subjugated children of disadvantaged families to exploitation. Therefore, there is not only a need for decisive action and a sensitive response to help alleviate individual and family sufferings, but the problem also has to be tackled at its structural level by mitigating the social, economic and cultural conditions associated with the maltreatment. Statutory intervention has to be supplemented with long-term socio-educational services for the children and their families as well as the customers and the conniving public. More attention should be concentrated on improving the implementation of existing laws through inter-agency and inter-disciplinary cooperation. Apart from punishment and treatment, more resources should be channeled to preventive programmes so as to eradicate the problem from its root.

NOTES

[1] The term 'child prostitution' in this book denotes the social practice of involving female and male children under the age of 18 in all forms of prostitution. The child victim provides for sex-related service in exchange of money and the kind and the perpetrators benefit materially or physically from this commercial sexual exploitation of children. As the victims in *Taiwan* are mainly female, the term 'girl prostitution' is occasionally used instead of child prostitution. Although this book considers the term 'sexual exploitation of children' more appropriate to describe the social epidemic, though the commonly adopted term 'girl prostitution' or more recently 'child prostitution' is also used for practical convenience. It

will be urged throughout this book that the social practice of child prostitution should be redefined as a form of child maltreatment happening within the context of an overall exploitative social framework in the modern capitalist society of *Taiwan*.

[2] See chapter three for relevant discussions on the Chinese families.

[3] See chapters two and three for relevant discussions on the 'good/bad' dichotomy.

[4] See chapters six for relevant laws.

[5] The state of 'martial law' in the ROC is, in fact, similar to a 'state of siege' in civil law countries and is different from the concept of martial law in common law countries. The difference lies essentially in the divergent attitudes between the common and civil law systems toward the origin of this emergency measure. The 'martial law' emphasizes the suspension of normal rules of law, whereas 'state of siege' emphasises the emergency as an effective threat against public safety and order. Under the ROC 'martial law', the civil and military powers within the government work side by side in a spirit of cooperation and do not have to be substituted one for the other, as is the case in a common law country. Besides, the executive and/or the legislature in civil law countries has the final word as to whether an emergency situation has arisen, while the courts will assume this function under common law. For details, see Rossiter,C.L., Constitutional Dictatorship, 1948:86-87 (Princeton University Press, Princeton, N.J.). See also Chiu & Fa,1984:645.

[6] For a detailed introduction to the Convention, see Detrick,S. (ed.) -- The United Nations Convention on the Rights of the Child (Martinus Nijhoff, Dordrecht, 1992); and The UN Centre for Human Rights -- Human Rights Fact Sheets, No.10: The Rights of the Child (UN Office, Geneva).

[7] See chapter five for the relationship between these international instruments and relevant ROC laws.

[8] See chapter five for the legislative changes.

[9] For an introduction to the development of the Taiwanese family, see Shee,A.,1994: Appendix XI.

[10] For discussions on the Western concept and development of childhood, see Aries,1962; De Mause,1974,1992; Jenks,1992; Shorter,1976; Thane,1981.

[11] For the first wave of the campaigns, the concern for children were confined to the female ones who were found to have been sold into prostitution by parents from poor aboriginal areas to big cities.

[12] In principle, this book adopts the Wade System, which is commonly used in *Taiwan*, to translate the Mandarin phonetic symbols. An exception is made when a cited person/author/organisation has translated his/her/its name using another System.

[13] See chapter four for detailed discussions on the social campaigns since 1987.

[14] The term 'prostitution-involved children\girls' or 'sexually exploited children\girls' is preferred in this book to 'girl\child prostitutes' which has been generally used in *Taiwan*.

[15] In fact, most of the campaign leaders were also involved in anti-government campaigns, and they raised the structural problems mainly to embarrass the authorities and to hold the government solely responsible for solving the problems.

[16] See chapter four for details.

[17] This threshold was chosen because under the ROC Criminal Code. any sexual contact

with a child under 16 is penalised. See Huang,Y.C.,1991a.

2 SOCIO-LEGAL PERSPECTIVE ON CHILD PROSTITUTION

One critical barrier to theorising the socio-legal issues pertaining to child prostitution is the unavailability of an established analytical framework. Analyses of and responses to socio-legal issues in *Taiwan* have always been based on comparative studies among advanced countries (such as northern/western European countries, the USA, and Japan), which have provided learning models for policy makers, academics, and practitioners of all disciplines. Unfortunately, the existence of child prostitution in *Taiwan* is a unique phenomenon among modern capitalist societies. Suffering from the lack of appropriate learning models, this problem in *Taiwan* became theorised within the available analytical frameworks concerning family dysfunction, illegal prostitution, or juvenile delinquency. And in each framework, child protection is subjected to other priorities in both policy and practice.

Recently, the grave increase in the magnitude of child prostitution[1], including girls and boys, in certain Asian countries has accumulated enough global attention and outrage to gather concerned professionals and non-governmental organisations (NGOs) from both the North and the South to launch an International Campaign to End Child Prostitution in Asian Tourism (ECPAT).[2] Through the years since 1991, numerous reports, books, and conference papers have been published to support the Campaign. Consequently, the child prostitution epidemic in Asian countries (including *Taiwan*) also becomes a newly developed field of socio-legal studies.

A specific contribution of this Campaign is that 'children' are put at the top of all considerations (Shubert,1992:20), and child prostitution is harshly condemned as 'a modern form of slavery' (ICCB,1991:13; K. Srisang, 1991a:19). Efforts are also devoted to search for the structural (cultural, social, political and economic) factors leading to child prostitution. However, most of the literature so far is written from activists' perspective. Besides, the problem is seen as part of the corrupt impact of foreign tourism on child prostitution[3] and criticisms are mostly targeted at paedophilia activities organised by white men, and the conspiracy of national governments in the exploitation of women and children (Host Committee, 1996ab). As will be shown in chapter three, the epidemic in *Taiwan* is of a more complex and yet distinctive nature.

Bearing the disadvantages of the past socio-legal studies pertaining to child prostitution in *Taiwan*, this chapter attempts to develop an analytical framework within which the problem may be theorised as an entity, and child protection be taken as the core concern in policy and practice. It first depicts the problem in the traditional definition as an issue of family dysfunction, of illegal prostitution, and of juvenile delinquency. It also makes an investigation and examination in order to explore the reason why the epidemic of child prostitution is being inappropriately tackled.

The following section summarises past governmental and professional responses to the problems of child prostitution in *Taiwan*. It describes the process from discovery to legislation which led to the management of recognised problems in a 'three-compound matrix' -- child abuse, illegal prostitution, and juvenile delinquency -- and concludes that within this matrix the child victims have been misplaced in the whole process of problem management on both treatment and prevention. The conclusion thus suggests an analytical framework for this book which takes 'the maltreatment of children in an exploitative social framework' as the perspective to be taken for the management of child prostitution.

Conventional Socio-Legal Perspectives on Child Prostitution

This section examines the inappropriateness of responding to child prostitution in *Taiwan* as a problem of family dysfunction, of illegal prostitution, and of juvenile delinquency. It attempts to show the possible pitfalls of a fragmentary approach to the problem and of current socio-legal measures which focus only on the individual behaviour defined as 'deviant', while ignoring the necessity of attacking the cultural, social, economic and political conditions associated with the identified 'deviance'.[4]

Functionalist responses to abusing families Campaigners against the practice of child prostitution often concentrate their attention on the problems of the family. It is often maintained as a fact that the family as a basic social institution should carry out its functions including production, maintenance, education, socialisation, companionship, and moral support. However, it is also recognised that, in reality, not all families are able to perform the functions in the way that is generally expected by society. So violence towards and exploitation of children may take place. Parents selling children directly into prostitution is one extreme example. Research findings conclude that child prostitution is a direct result of maladjustment, disorganisation and breakdown of the family.[5] Thus, in order to prevent children falling into the flesh market, focus has to be placed on activities and laws for promoting the family as a basic social unit to provide for a loving and warm shelter for its children (ECPAT,1991:21) (*GOH,1992; TWRF,1991,1992*).

However, when the campaign advocates speak of promoting the family, they seldom question the nature of this 'family'[6], nor are there debates over the appropriateness of state measures. It seems that this family has to perform its expected social role of nurturance.[7] Thus, once the family abandons a child into prostitution, very few prevention and treatment programmes would be aimed at the assurance or reassurance of a nurturing native family for the child. Instead, the native family is deemed to have failed totally in nurturing the child victim, so state intervention in severe forms are justified in the management of the case. However, after the child victim is taken away from the family, this family will then be preserved as the nurturing family for other children until abuse or exploitation happens again.

On the other hand, campaigners seem to have seen no difficulties in promoting 'the family' as well as ensuring 'the best interests of the child' or 'child protection'. Debates over the possibilities of the conflicting interests between children and their parents have never been duly listened to. This deafness is possibly intentional. For the campaigners, the guiding principle of all activities is that 'children come first' (O'Grady, 1991), thus interests of the parents presumably come later. On the other hand, it is of course not in the interests of children to allow their involvement in any form of prostitution. Furthermore, as it is strongly urged that 'child prostitution is one of the worst contemporary forms of slavery' (ICCB;1991:13; Srisang, K.1991a:5), the interests of parents in enslaving their children are totally rejected.

It seems that the family is naturally bestowed with nurturing functions, so selling or abandoning children into prostitution will be, in D.H.J. Morgan's terms, the worst of the 'dysfunctions' of the family.[8] Applying Morgan's functionalist analysis, most families will perform the child-rearing duties properly and only in exceptional cases that parents would sell or conspire to sell their children into the flesh market. This problem may be alleviated by measures such as injunctions or removing children from the family.

Morgan's 'contradiction'[9] analysis is also useful in detecting problems of the functionalist approach. According to Morgan, 'dysfunction' has the implication that its occurrence is an abnormal situation and it is assumed that this dysfunction can be ameliorated or cured by imposing certain measures. But the 'contradiction' thesis does not make such assumption. It considers sexual exploitation of children by parents a product of the family system itself. Weaker members such as women and children are destined to be sacrificed for the benefits of the family (Barrett & McIntosh,1982; Engels,1891).[10] In the case of child prostitution, this destiny-oriented 'contradiction' thesis may well depict the Chinese patriarchal family.

As will be described later, under the tenets of Confucianism, unreserved obedience is demanded of a child to his father, and a subject to his ruler. This family ethic of 'filial piety' has been promoted to ensure the absolute authority of the family head and, more importantly, the ruler over others. Within the family, the patriarchal Confucian tenet has been transformed into the primary rationale for parental exploitation of children, especially the female ones.[11] However, this view which challenges the base of the family has never survived in the political debates dominated by the 'Right' as is the case in *Taiwan*. Further, as the development of the ROC welfare state is at its primitive stage, the 'functions' of the family in nurturing and socialising children cannot be denied.

Thus, the functionalist view is widely shared among policy makers, activists, and practitioners in *Taiwan*. However, the derived responses to child prostitution are taken in an extreme form. Families involved in child prostitution are identified as extremely abnormal and statutory intervention is used to terminate parental rights, to sever the involved children from all family ties, and less vigorously, to convict the exploitative parents. In other words, once a child is sold by her\his parents, the family is diagnosed as 'permanently dysfunctional' for the child, thus she\he is removed in the name of her\his protection. But on the other hand, the exploitation is taken as a single exceptional event. Thus the family is still expected to carry out its functions and is promoted as other 'normal' families. No special preventive measures at the individual or the structural level are taken for the protection of other children of the family. Moreover, the ROC Criminal Courts are often prepared to suspend the sentence pronounced for the parent offenders on the ground that there are other children to be reared.

'Policing' of the abusive families It is generally agreed that 'selling children into prostitution' is the most heinous form of child abuse (*Cheng,R.L.,1986*; *TMSB,1990a*), and thus state intervention into the

abusing families is most justified for the protection of children (O'Grady,1992a; Srisang,K.,1991a). This perspective can induce pitfalls in both prevention and treatment. In practice, the abusing family becomes the centre of state censure and social services are directed at segregating the abused child from her\his family. Legal sanctions are exhausted to punish the exploitative parents. But no measures are taken to offset the socio-structural inclination to sexual exploitation of children suffered by the family.

In other words, it is the 'individual patterns of behaviour, individual personalities and family relationships which are seen as central and not the economic and socio-cultural processes which direct and mediate such patterns of behaviour' (Parton,1985:175). Consequently, state regulations may tighten around the identified abusing family but fail to control the responsible environmental and social situation. On the other hand, the narrow definition of 'child abuse' in the confinement of the family fails to recognise the whole process of victimisation that the child experiences before, in, and after prostitution.

When dealing with child prostitution as a dysfunction of the family, it is often seen as an individual pathology of an abnormal family, and remedies are sought by correcting the exploitative behaviour of the individual abuser for the single event . Even if the dysfunction is seen in radical criticism as a by-product of the capitalist family system within which the weaker members (women and children) are destined to be suppressed and exploited, state intervention may still be called upon as a means of protecting its weaker members before the ideal of systematic reconstruction of the family may be realised (Barrett & McIntosh,1987:43-81).[12] On the other hand, when a conservative view of the family[13] is taken and intervention is limited to the most narrowly defined grounds, selling children would be one of the most serious case justifying 'authoritative, swift, and decisive' intervention (Goldstein, Freud & Solnit,1980:73). Families involved in child prostitution are by all definitions subjected to coercive intervention which often results in the severance of the child victim from all family ties .

Since *Taiwan* underwent the industrialisation process based on Western models, there have been a series of reshaping of Chinese families through the development of the welfare state.[14] Fitting into J. Donzelot's Foucaultian analysis, the old authoritarian, patriarchal family is being replaced by a 'policed'[15] family, in which many functions previously residing in the father as the head of the household are being usurped by the state (Donzelot,1980:6-7; Parton, 1991). When internal family decisions conflicted with the outside expectation of society as to how children should be brought up, the welfare state arose in the name of child protection to safeguard the normative family life (Chunn,1988:137-138).

The manner and extent of state intervention have changed over time in Western societies. The modern liberal state was aware of its responsibilities for children while respecting parental rights and duties of child-rearing. The dilemma was solved by allowing the state to intervene into childrearing with compulsory measures only when families were considered to have failed. Ostensibly this has remained the solution, though its interpretation has shifted through time first to render state agencies broader and broader discretion authorised by law, which has recently taken a more cautious view in empowering its agencies (Parton,1991:194-195).[16]

The growth of the welfare state creates a disciplinary society as described by M. Foucault (1977,1979). He identified that the new knowledge (e.g. medicine, pedagogics, epidemiology, etc.) developed in the twentieth century have created new fields of exploration and brought with them new modes of surveillance and regulation of the population. This new mode of regulation, the mechanism of discipline, is 'a closely linked grid of disciplinary coercion whose purpose is in fact to assure the coercion of this same social body' (Gordon,1980:106).

Within the disciplinary society, the state developed a preventive social welfare role, which always holds in readiness the coercive intervention carried out by disciplinary mechanisms if surveillance is resisted or there is an obvious lack of compliance to the new moral standards of family or parental behaviour (Parton,1985:38). Thus, the 'family' to be promoted is that which is willing to be incorporated into the 'policing' programmes and to assume their expected functions of child-rearing.

However, whilst alliances are established between the functioning/ deserving families and social services, the extremely abusing families become subjected to coercive statutory intervention, which, in the case of child prostitution, means the permanent termination of parent-child relationship. In a Chinese society where family ties still represent every individual's identification and where children are 'normally' nurtured in the state-promoted functioning families, these victims of parental abuse are further deprived of their entitlement to live as a 'normal' child in his\her own family.

On the other hand, it is pointed out that the rise of the welfare state was characterised by a widespread adoption of the middle-class family pattern (Donzolot,1980; Lasch,1979; Poster,1978; Zaretsky,1982). Enforced by the state with its laws, the families have been reshaped towards one end, but without success. It is urged that as the law prefers the middle-class family life, the Western welfare state can actually become a 'tutelary authority' which tightens around the family of lower socio-economic strata (Donzelot,1980:90-93). This is especially true in the case of child prostitution, as the poor family is among the most vulnerable groups who incline to sell or abandon children into the flesh market.

It will be demonstrated in chapter five that the policing of the Chinese family under the ROC welfare state remains at the stage of preserving the traditionalist 'private' family culture and promoting the family functions of nurturance and socialisation. Only in exceptional cases does the state provide welfare services for troubled families. The state does not 'intervene' in family relationships unless grave hardship, violence, abuse or exploitation takes place. On the other hand, however, when the state does intervene, welfare officers tend to judge families by 'middle-class' standards. And punitive measures are imposed on those who are not performing their expected social roles. Parents who are not able to provide 'good' parenting would be deprived of their parental rights through Court proceedings. Minor children who are diagnosed as being in behavioral delinquency or in moral danger would be subjected to legal discipline. There is hardly any welfare services available for troubled or vulnerable families as a whole in order to prevent its dysfunction.

It may be criticised that the welfare state will tighten around disadvantaged families and hinder the civil rights of parents. But if the preservation of the Chinese patriarchal 'private' family would lead to abandoning young children into prostitution, then the advancement of 'policing' and 'welfare' of the family by the state should be recommended. Although past experiences have shown that reinforcement of the child care system may result in over-intervention, this risk of state tutelage may be moderated by a well regulated and constantly monitored administration of the welfare system.

An Issue of Illegal Prostitution

Child-prostitution and prostitution control Very frequently, the involvement of minor children in commercial sex is discussed as a fragment of illegal prostitution.[17] Within this line of discussion, controversies have been centered on the modes of prostitution control[18]: criminalisation, legalisation, or decriminalisation. The 'criminalisation' school argues that in order to prevent forced or underage prostitution, commercial sex should be totally outlawed (*Shen,M.C.,1989,1990*).

Proponents for 'legalisation' consider that the existence of prostitution is a natural and unavoidable social phenomenon, but its practice should be subjected to state censor so as to maintain social order and prevent sexual exploitation (*Tang,S.P. et al.,1983*). The 'decriminalisation' advocates urge for the economic/civil rights to work as prostitutes and maintain that legal measures should be rendered to protect their working interests (*Huang,S.L.,1990*).

The suppression of all forms of prostitution has been a moral principle for some international and national legislation. This moral legalism is, however, challenged by theoretical as well as practical difficulties (Tong,1984:39-43).[19] Thus criminalisation is giving way to regulation (Foucault,1979:4), whilst various legal sanctions are imposed on those who threaten the public health and/or disturb the social order (Adams,1993; Smart,1989:94; Walkowitz,1980). The policing of prostitution has thus been referred to as an instrument to control women's sexuality (Brown,1992:49; Snare,1993:11; Stewart,1993:234-235). The predominant view of recent prostitution research in the Western world[20] has thus attacked prostitution law as the legal recognition of patriarchal rights over female sexuality (Adams,1993:295-297; MacKinnon,1982:644; Naffine,1990:9). Abolition of prostitution laws (decriminalisation) is therefore justified by the urge for equal legal, economic, and civil rights of women (Adams,1993:298; Edwards,1992:151-152; McLeod,1982:119-146; Richards,1982:84).

When child prostitution is caught in the debates over the social problems of prostitution, the element of child abuse and exploitation becomes submerged in the issues of public health, of social order, and of gender oppression. Under the law, the child victims suffer the existing stigma and vigilance imposed on women and women's bodies, and even further. If prostitution is criminalised, the exploited children are despised as illegal prostitutes. Under prostitution control regulations, children cannot be legally registered and are subjected to concealed exploitation. Decriminalisation will not solve the problem, either. It may increase sexual exploitation of minors in prostitution (Tong,1984:60).[21] In other words, criminal law is still necessary in preventing exploitation, but criminalisation of prostitution is not the solution. In order to control child prostitution, specific socio-economic and legal strategies have to be coordinated to develop both therapeutic and preventive measures targeting at the abuse and exploitation of children in the flesh trade.

Minor children in prostitution control laws Historical studies on the history of sexuality in Western and Chinese civilisation have observed that sex was a taboo both in knowledge and in actuality. Sex became justified only when it was performed in a private domain for achieving the purpose of producing the next generation of the family (Baker,1979:36; Levy,1949:86; Yang,1959:57). When legitimate sexuality was only permitted within the family for reproduction, prostitution was taken as a 'concession' which society was forced to make for the practice of 'illegitimate sexuality' from which male sexual desires and needs for affectionate love could be satisfied (Chen,K.C.,1986; Foucault,1979).

The 'concession' was not equally made to women (Fernandez-Magno,1987; Stewart,1993). Within a patriarchal system dominated by men, a good women/bad women dichotomy is established -- the good women meet men's need for nurturers, whilst the bad women meet men's need for sexual objects (MacKinnon,1987; McCaghy,1990). In order to preserve the chastity of the 'good' women, the practice of 'illegitimate sexuality' was thus allowed among men and the 'bad' women (Tong,1984:38). Thus, the primary function of prostitution has been to uphold the double standard placed on female sexuality (Ennew,1986; Matsui,1991). The sexuality of 'good' women only served the purpose of reproduction, so male sexual desires were to be satisfied by consuming the services offered by 'bad' women in sex-related professions. Without prostitution, the preservation of the 'good women' would have been impossible.[22]

Under the good/bad dichotomy, the social value of 'female virginity' became vital in the determination of the place of an unmarried woman. Still in many societies once a girl is sexually experienced, she is referred to as 'damaged goods' and are sometimes forced socially into prostitution (S.Srisang,1991:38-39) (*Huang,Y.C.,1991a*). It is observed that in most societies, the moral weight of boy's virginity and girl's are seen differently. There is an age-old prejudice among Asian countries that 'boys lose nothing' through being sexually active, while 'girls become spoiled goods' once she is deflowered (De Leon,1991:88) .[23]

The good/bad dichotomy was also constructed into legal discourses. What then became illegitimate under the law was the female non-marital commercial sexuality but not that of men. It was condemned as socially deviant for it had offended social order, endangered public health, and corrupted the youth, which then resulted in legal control over prostitution.[24] By legislation, the 'commercial sex' was regulated, while in real life, prostitution was classified as 'deviant' or 'immoral' and singled out from the normal bounds of acceptable society (Smart,1981,1989:94). It is the commercial sexual service that has been put under the scrutiny of state regulations, while the consumers are not regulated by law

(McLeod,1982:91-96). When the problem of child prostitution is tackled within this framework, the bias in prostitution control policies will unavoidably hinder the development and implementation of child protection law, both in treatment and prevention of the problem.

Within the institution of prostitution, the law punishes no consumer. Thus laws against statutory rape and relevant sexual assault and indecency based on the age of consent are hardly enforced within this institution. Further, the law often requires the child to prove that she\he has been the 'innocent child' whom the law is to protect. It is also difficult for 'buying sex from children' to become a specified offence for it has always been the 'selling' part that the law used to regulate. On the other hand, what is under legal control is the commercial sexual service offered by prostitutes. Unless the law specifically exempt children under certain age from punishment and recognise their victimisation in flesh trade, the prostitution-involved children will be subjected to the same legal sanctions against illegal prostitutes, which, in practice, means legal control over their bodies and mentality but not over those of their exploiters.

In addition, during the process of legal treatment, children often suffer the stigma of adult prostitutes. Child protection law has long aimed at preserving the 'innocence of children' (May,1973). As the prostitution-involved girls are referred to as 'damaged goods' and their innocence can never be restored, their social as well as legal status as a child is often deprived of -- they are in many ways treated as adult yet illegal prostitutes. Further, under prostitution control laws, children are 'illegal prostitutes', and thus they are not subjected to health control measures provided by law, especially the compulsory examination and treatment of sexually transmitted diseases including AIDS. All sorts of societal restriction on childhood sexuality have made children ineligible for public contraception or abortion services. Thus, their protection under the law is further jeopardised for being an 'illegal prostitute'.

An Issue of Juvenile Delinquency

Problems of the labelling process Under the legal discourses of social work in *Taiwan*, prostitution-involved children have been classified into 'forced' and 'voluntary', though recently this classification has been increasingly questioned. The 'forced' are those who were sold into the flesh market, and they receive more social and legal sympathy and protection. All others are loosely labelled 'the voluntary', and they are subjected to measures designed to correct their delinquency

(*TWRF,1991,1992*; *Wang & Wang,1992*). The distinction between the labels is 'whether the child intended to become a prostitute'. However, if one looks more carefully into the backgrounds of the 'voluntary' cases, there are full of reluctance and coercion behind this 'intention'. Furthermore, within the current labelling system, the child has to prove herself\himself to be the 'forced' victim, failing which she\he will be categorised as 'voluntary'.[25] In other words, a prostitution-involved child is not presumed 'innocent' in practice.

The original purpose of the labelling process was to divert treatment of juvenile victims from the jurisdiction of the Juvenile Court into the newly developed welfare system. Concerned professionals carefully studied the controversial philosophies of justice and welfare[26] and drew a line between pre-prostitution and after-prostitution delinquency. Those who were sold and forced into prostitution would be received into the welfare system for the treatment of the undesirable results of prostitution. Others who were labelled 'voluntary' would be referred to the Juvenile Court because of their sexual promiscuity or moral danger which made them act out.

The labelling process might be an useful reference for designing client-amicable treatment programmes, but the backfires it caused were destructive. Numerous case studies concluded that many of the 'voluntary' child prostitutes actually came from multidimensional involuntary backgrounds including familial abuse, economic deprivation, and social maladjustment.[27] Case studies in *Taiwan*[28] have indicated that many child prostitution victims were identified as belonging to the 'voluntary' group. Some agreed to be sold under the pressure of huge family debts, failure to repay which would endanger family security. Some were taken to the brothel voluntarily in order to save a sister from being sold. Some had lost their virginity and considered themselves 'used and damaged goods' to be dumped in the flesh market. Some were filial children who wanted to share parents' financial burdens by earning quick money, and some others were eldest sisters who felt responsible for paying the living and schooling expenses for younger siblings, thus connived with the family decision to trade their bodies. Social workers also urge that once involved in prostitution, there is no easy way out. Continuation of strong economic motivation, pimp-control, loneliness for love and care, drug addiction, fear of losing peer group relationship, pressure from their family, harassment by or hostility from the police, the conventional family and school, and society as a whole have all contributed to reinforce the children's self concept as 'outsiders' and make them remain where they are, or fall back into prostitution once and once again (David,1971:311; John Passion,1992:1,4;

Lowen,1978:3) (*Chen,YingChen,1992:3-5*). So the distinction between the 'forced' and the 'voluntary' may become blurred in practical terms. After undergoing the assimilation process of becoming money-making machines, the 'forced' character of a child victim may no be easily detected.

Inappropriateness of the juvenile justice system In Western literature, the form of child prostitution under discussion is predominantly the non-sold one. In this line of discussion, it is generally presupposed that a child first became a 'problematic' or 'delinquent' juvenile, then acted out promiscuously, and finally fell into prostitution. So child prostitution became one of the most difficult problems to be tackled within the juvenile justice system (Conway,1977; Elliott,1988:7; Humphries,1981).[29] It is criticised that the juvenile justice system, lacking an adequate treatment model for adolescents who act out sexually, often refers to them as 'incorrigible', 'delinquent', or 'out of control' and commits them to institutions where they receive rehabilitation for sexual deviance (Lowen,1978:1). Thus, no matter what has made them fall into prostitution, it is the law and legal process that impose on them the attributes of 'juvenile prostitutes' and make it even more exhausting for them to leave prostitution and become 'good' girls\boys again.

These socially and economically deprived children, when taken out of prostitution and received into legal disposition, are labeled 'sexually delinquent' (Elliott,1988:7). Within the welfare ideology of the juvenile court, this delinquency is seen as symptomatic of an underlying disorder (Morris,1983:126) -- becoming a professional prostitute -- and the task of the juvenile court is to facilitate and legitimate the early recognition, assessment and treatment of that disorder along with other agencies of what J. Donzelot calls 'the tutelary complex' (1979:96).[30] The major task of the juvenile justice system and its related disciplines is not that of the correction of the specific infractions of legal codes, but with what M. Foucault (1979) calls 'normalisation'[31] -- the control not only of behaviour but also of attitudes, values and self-images (Hall,1980:39-40; Thorpe,D.,1983:79-80). By subjecting a group of youth in moral danger to new modes of disciplinary control, the juvenile justice system has been criticised to have overlooked the social, economic and environmental circumstances within which the delinquency is produced (Asquith,1983; Gale, Naffine & Wundersitz,1993). It is stressed that delinquency prevention and treatment need to encompass not only the individual factors associated with delinquency but the institutional and structural factors as well (Friday,1983).

However, the juvenile justice system has never developed a treatment (or preventive) programme which looks at the sexual deviancy of prostitution-involved children in broad familial and social contexts. Consequently, the best endeavour to divert children from the stigmatising treatment for adult prostitutes 'merely created other (less visible) stigmatising agencies and processes which in turn have exacerbated the problems they were designed to solve' (Sarri,1983:71). As will be shown in chapter six, the good intention of social workers to keep the child victims out of prostitution has very often turned out to be mere imposition of a sense of shame, but as the social-structural disadvantages faced by those children were not removed, they often fell back to prostitution knowing the social stigma attached to it.

Current Responses to Child-Prostitution: the 'Three-Compound Matrix'

From Discovery to Legislation

When child prostitution was discovered and campaigned against in *Taiwan* in 1987, it was the 'slavery of female children' which dominated all public attention (*Chen, YingChen,1992*; *Tseng & Chun,1987*). The activists allied with the mass media reported the miserable lives of sold children in prostitution.[32] Concerted efforts were devoted to the rescue of these innocent children from sexual exploitation. However, after the rescue work was done, responses to the problem started to be expressed in a different tone -- the resulting sexual deviance of the children became the main concern.

Consequently, control measures were not directed at dealing with child prostitution as a crime against children in which procurers (including parents), pimps/brothel keepers, and customers are punished as 'the perpetrators' and the involved children are protected and treated as 'the victims'. Instead, 'selling children' and 'child prostitution' was seen as an age-old problem which had already been condemned in the criminal laws, and what was defined as a new threat to the social order deserving attention was an emerging group of sexually delinquent juveniles (*Hsu,C.L.,1988,1989*; *Yin,C.C.,1987*).[33]

The children became subjected to moral vigilance. They were incarcerated with other illegal prostitutes (*Hsu,C.L.,1988*; *Wu,H.Y.,1990*). Activists and the newly emerged social workers endeavoured to separate treatment of these children from other prostitutes by identifying specific characteristics of them and the factors leading to their prostitution (*Chen,H.N.,1992*; *Chen,YiChen,1991*; *Wang,I.,1992ac*; *Wu,T.L.,1987*). But then the rehabilitation programmes still aimed at saving the girls from their diagnosed 'moral danger' instead of removing their socio-economic disadvantages. At the same time, when the Western welfare state was promoted to deal with the newly recognised child abuse problems, the same approach was invoked by child savers to define child prostitution as the most atrocious form of parental abuse in order to justify the immediate and permanent termination of the parent-child relationship under the law (*Wang,C.F.,1992ab*; *Wang & Shen,1991*). Since then, the treatment in 'a social welfare point of view' has been coached in child-saving languages (*Pai,H.H.,1992*).

The 'rescue and protection network' was thus formulated to manage the problem (*Chen,M.L.,1991c*; *Wu,H.Y.,1991*). Specialist squads in the police force were designated to locate underage prostitutes, and as soon as a girl was rescued, voluntary lawyers were responsible for obtaining a quick Court ruling to transfer the custody right over this girl to eligible welfare organisations who would see to the moral transformation and skill-training of her (*Chen,M.L.,1992*; *Hong,W.W.,1991b*; *Huang,Y.C.,1991a*; *TMSB,1990a*). On the other hand, the perpetrators remained under the old control contrivances, in which child prostitution was connived more than denounced. The surveillance provided by the newly developed disciplinary mechanisms was confined to regulating the lives of the rescued children with a legally prescribed period of 'rehabilitation' (*Hong,W.W.,1992*; *GOH,1992*; *TWRF,1991,1992*).

As activists and social workers started to see the facts that only a marginal proportion of prostitution-involved children could be received into the care of social workers and most rehabilitative measures had proved to be ineffective in preventing the girls from falling back to the flesh markets[34], increasing attacks were being made on governmental failures in prostitution control. The moral legalists urge that because the state was not determined to abolish prostitution, the exploitation of young children existed under the veil of statutory tolerance towards the practice of commercial sex (*Huang,S.L.,1990*; *Shen,M.C.,1989,1990*). The involved lawyers and judges criticised the criminal justice system which made it almost impossible to prosecute and thus the perpetrators are left out there to take more victims (*Cheng & Fan-Chang,1990*; *Chung,K.M.,1991*; *Lin,Y.S.,1992*; *Wang,T.S. et al.,1989*). These concerns on prevention led to lobbying for legislation against perpetrators of child prostitution with special focus on the customers (*Chen,C.H.,1993*; *Chen,M.L.,1991a*; *Hsieh,Y.W.,1991a*; *Lin,Y.S.,1993ab*; *Wang,I.,1993*), which finally resulted in the birth of the Law to Suppress Sexual Transactions Involving Children and Juveniles in August 1995. However, most of the attention of this Law is concentrated on the rescue and treatment of the involved children, and though for the first time in the ROC law, all perpetrators of child prostitution are sanctioned with specific punishments, the customers are still subjected to comparatively lenient penalties.

Misplaced children in the 'Three-Compound Matrix'

Over the years of socio-legal experiments and reflection under the lead of concerned professionals, child prostitution has been recognised and constructed in a '**three-compound matrix**'[35] -- family dysfunction, illegal prostitution, and juvenile delinquency -- within which an involved child receive distinctive treatment depending on her\his label as an 'abused child', an 'underage prostitute', or a 'delinquent'.

Under the present socio-legal environment, the victimisation of children in prostitution is hardly envisaged in the 'three-compound matrix'. Selling of children into prostitution is the most serious and heinous form of family dysfunction in both social and legal terms. Thus paternalist state intervention into abusive families is promoted as unproblematic. The extreme form of intervention -- termination of parent-child relationship is executed without considering the wishes of a child. But on the other hand, no preventive measures are taken to protect other children of the same family.

Under a vague and hypocritical prostitution policy of 'short-term regulation and long-term abolition'[36], state control over the practice of illegal prostitution as a whole has been ineffectual. Numerous studies have stated the vulnerability of young children (especially the female ones) to the exploitation of commercial sex, but the social and legal policies on prostitution have never been amended for their redress. Case studies unanimously present the 'fact' that the prolonged victimisation of the sold children in prostitution is easily transformed into delinquency (*Chen,H.N.,1992*; *Hsu,C.L.,1988*; *Wang,I.,1992c*; *Yin,C.C.,1993*). Thus when the victims were finally rescued, they fit easily into the 'child-saving' discourses and their moral discipline becomes subjected to increasing legal scrutiny.

In Search of A Research Framework

The above two sections have explored the inappropriateness of the existing 'three-compound matrix' which fails to investigate the nature of child prostitution and respond to the victimisation of children in the process. An attempt is thus made in this final section to search for an analytical framework in which the vulnerability of children (especially the female ones) may be recognised in the structural context of *Taiwan* and their victimisation can be taken as the core concern. Under this framework of analyses, child prostitution will be defined as a socio-legal problem of child abuse and sexual exploitation in which child maltreatment will be the core concern.

Reconceptualising the Problem: An Issue of Child Maltreatment

A broad definition of child maltreatment In defining child abuse, D.G. Gill criticised traditional definitions which see child maltreatment as occurring and having its primary genesis within families.[37] He argues that any act of commission or omission by individuals, institutions or the whole society, together with their resultant conditions which 'deprive children of equal rights and liberties, and/or interfere with their optimal development, constitute, by definition, abusive or neglectful acts or conditions' (Gil,1975, quoted at Parton,1985:167-168).

It is useful to employ this definition by which the whole process of child prostitution can be identified as the 'abusive conditions'. The interaction between the abusive family and the prostitution industry takes place within the context of an overall exploitative social framework. The process may commence in an abusing or neglecting family, carried on in the exploitative prostitution industry, and although statutory intervention may interrupt this maltreatment, the process does not end until the child is no longer subjected to the exploitation.

Charges of exploitation and abuses If child prostitution is taken as a form of child maltreatment, who would then be identified as the perpetrators? The parents or other abusive\neglective caretakers are first in the list and no doubts have ever been raised against it. As to the prostitution operators, their contribution in keeping the 'women's oldest profession'[38] is often more appreciated than they are despised for exploiting young girls, and now including boys. What accusation can be leveled against the customers? Apart from being attached a blurry label of 'paedophiles'[39], very few sanctions are imposed on them. The parents (and other caretakers) are condemned because they sell their own children, which is the most abusive parental behaviour identified in *Taiwan* (*Cheng,R.L.,1986*), or connive in the prostitution of their children. But the offences involved in profiting from or consuming in child prostitution needs more clarification.

Exploitation, in internationally adopted definitions, is referred to in connection with a third party, who profits from the use of labour in particular forms of servitude.[40] And in terms of sexual exploitation, the reference clearly includes the employment of children in prostitution and the like.[41] The term child sexploitation is employed mainly to condemn adults who use children in sexual poses and acts for commercial benefit[42], or it may also be used to include acts of those who do so for their own sexual gratification (Baker,1980:292).[43]

Some may argue that children are potentially sexual and they should be granted the right to express their sexuality, develop sexual desire, and acquire sexual behaviour (Jackson,1982:24; Martinson,1976:489-490 & Langfeldt,1979:496, quoted at Ennew,1986:46-47). Some others may urge for children their right to choose what they want (Holt,1975; Hoyles,1979; Farson,1978), which may include the right to work as a prostitute (Lieberman,1973). However, in *Taiwan* children are under adult domination, child labour is prone to be exploited, involvement in prostitution is considered a disgrace, a child who has lost her\his expected 'innocence' by trading sex is discriminated against, and field work has concluded that childhood experiences in prostitution are detrimental to the optimal physical and mental development of children. It may thus be well justified to charge all operators and customers with the offences of sexual exploitation and abuse in the name of child protection disregarding possible suppression of the alleged 'children's rights'.

Managing the Problem in Its Structural Context: Discerning the Power of Exploitation

In responding to the problems involved in child prostitution, it has been the labeled individual deviant behaviour that is under the vigilance of the emerging 'disciplinary mechanisms'[44] operated by the recently developed 'therapeutic state'.[45] The approach has proven itself to be exhausting not only in child protection but also in the control of the prostitution industry involving children. No matter whether child prostitution is dealt with in which part of the 'three-compound matrix', it is important to explain the problem in its structural context. Numerous studies have pointed out that the problem of family dysfunction, of sexual exploitation in prostitution, or of juvenile delinquency is actually a structural one and it has to be attacked at that level (Arnold,1978; ECPAT, 1996; Korbin,1981; Morris et al.,1980,1983,1987; Su, 1995; Tong,1984).

Recent analyses on the epidemic of Asian child prostitution have systematically identified the structural problem of child prostitution -- the suppression of the powerless by the powerful. This suppression may be imposed by one individual on another or others, but the interaction is determined in a power structure within which individual behaviour is channeled to bring about consequences.[46]

There is something beyond the individual power which has supported and perpetuated the institution of child prostitution -- the power which has led to the failure of positive laws in controlling or correcting individual behaviour. Under this power, individuals have acted collectively in violation of the laws they are obliged to follow. Those who can manipulate the power are allied to those who support or tolerate the manipulation, and together they surrender the most powerless to exploitation.

Patriarchal power It is traditionally urged that powerful men and fathers enjoy superior and dominant socio-economic status and, as a result of their corrupt use of power, the powerless women and children are forced into an inferior and subordinate position prone to be exploited. Observations directed at the child prostitution practice in Asia have, however, explored the problem beyond the confinement of sexuality and maintain that it is far too simplistic to indicate the connotations of 'the powerful' and 'the powerless' as 'men-fathers' and 'women-children'. Researchers urge that it was the perpetuation of the patriarchal culture that placed not only women but also children in a position of subservience to male dominance.[47] Under this patriarchal structure, women as well as children are men's property, and thus, subject to men's exploitation (Athamesara,1991:91; de Leon,1991:88; Maurer,1991:99).

A general argument is that it is the patriarchal system and sexist attitude within which the sexual exploitation of women and children in prostitution has its origin (Athamesara,1991:91; Matsui,1991:101; Maurer,1991:99). When prostitution became culturally accepted and socially tolerated, women and children under the control of patriarchy are to sacrifice for the sake of the family,[48] and thus girls and boys[49] of deprived families become a ready prey for pimps and child-traffickers (Suresh,1991:65; Muntarbhorn,1991:69).

So the problem is now seen beyond the inequality between men and women, beyond the dominance of 'the powerful men-fathers' over 'the powerless women-children'. It is the misuse of power under the auspices of the patriarchal system which focuses the most helpless to be subjected to exploitation. In other words, there are both patriarchal men and women who may abuse their power and subject the powerless children to sexual abuse and exploitation.. As an eminent researcher and organiser of ECPAT -- Mrs. S.Srisang has pointed out:

> '[P]rostitution is a form of exploitation and oppression, done by the powerful to the powerless. This exploitation is both pervasive and systemic. Although both men and women are involved on either side of the exploitation equation, it is the patriarchal values and structures which undergird and perpetuate prostitution, including prostitution of children.' (S.Srisang,1991:37)

Economic-political power When discussing the proliferation of sex industry involving children in Asian tourism, Professor P. Wasi made the following observations:

> 'Disparities in economic development both within countries and between countries has divided people into those who have buying power and those who have no such choices. The buying power is so great and the limitation of choices is so extreme that those with buying power can buy anything, including the bodies and souls of people who have no choices.' (Wasi,1991:26)

Globally speaking, prostitution involving women and children is now regarded as a phenomenon resulting from the unjust economic imbalance between the rich North and the poor South (Matsui, 1991:101). In the poor countries, the sex industry has been initiated, maintained, and promoted by a marketing system and mechanism imposed by or transferred from the rich through tourism promotion and development plans. These growth-oriented economic development plans not only failed to solve the problems of national economics and mass poverty but also subject the people to foreign exploitation through tourism (Majgull,A.,1996; S.Srisang,1991).

At the national level, the unbalanced development and uneven distribution of wealth has enlarged gaps between the rich and the poor.[50] Moreover, the fact that the destitute always assume a disadvantageous status in the evaluation of priorities in national decision-making further makes poverty unbearable (Kent,1991:74).[51] The poor, particularly women and children, are relegated to the lowest socio-economic strata and have suffered most from these glaring inequalities (S.Srisang,1991:38). As a result, in the poor regions of a country, children are sold by their parents on a regular basis (Wasi,1991:27). The run-away or street children are organised or have organised themselves to serve local or foreign sexual demands (Host Committee, 1996ab, K.Srisang,1991a; O'Grady,1992ab).

In countries whose annual revenue depends mainly on tourism, it is not surprising to see a government policy which criminalises child prostitution while benefiting from it. Being fully engaged in the implementation of certain economic development scenarios initiated and supported by the First World, the state is widely criticised for having 'lost its political will and national pride to defend and fight for the rights of its own subjects and prosecute offenders of children' (De Leon,1991:87).

Apart from the state interests in conniving at the operation of child prostitution, it is observed that the lucrative sex industries in Asian countries have been supported and guarded by those who have control over the profit made therein -- organised mobsters, corrupted policemen and officials, local politicians who have a share in the sex service industry, or even the parents (Mutukumara,1992; S.Srisang,1991; Taliercio,C.,1996) (*Chen, YingChen,1992; Chu,H.Y.,1992; Ho,C.W.,1992; Pan,W.K.,1992; Chi,H.J.,1996f*).

The culture of silence and subservience accumulated through colonisation or resulting from suppressive national development policy towards the aborigines is also identified to be contributing to the vulnerability of certain disadvantaged groups.[52] It is a commonplace observation that colonisation of most Asian countries by the West has brought about some crucial effects on the development of child-sex industry (Richie,D.,1994). Consequently, 'long and continuing colonisation or oppression has made the assets, properties, qualities, and culture of the oppressor attractive to the oppressed' (De Leon,1991:88). A similar phenomenon is also present among the aboriginal tribes in *Taiwan* where the Chinese Han culture generally supersedes the indigenous heritage.[53]

Power of exploitation in the structural context Within a power structure, the powerful men now joined by women dominate over sexuality of the powerless, and the reinforcement of the patriarchal culture in the adverse economic and political environments places women and children of underprivileged origin (deflowered, destitute, unskilled, aboriginal, or colonised, etc.) in the front line of male sexual exploitation (Chutikul,1992). Recent studies on Asian child prostitution problem have come to the conclusion that, in the context of a capitalist society, the power of patriarchal dominance coupled by market forces of consumerism has further disadvantaged the position of women and children and made them more vulnerable to sexual exploitation in prostitution (ECTWT,1991; Healy,M.A.,1995,1996; McLeod,1982; O'Grady,1992).

Given the structural nature of the problem, it becomes obvious why child prostitution has been rampantly deteriorating under the structural power of what R. Tong called 'capitalist-patriarchy' (Tong,1984:60). Originally, the exploitation involved only the powerless daughter of a destitute family and a patriarchal figure of the traditional family who had the power of disposition over her body. But today, it can be found in many countries that the exploitation of children in prostitution has become a multimillion dollar industry (Densen-Gerber & Hutchinson,1978:317). And not only the organised mobsters (Baker,1980:297) but also the law enforcers, the politicians, and even the government (Muntarbhorn,1991:69) have all joined to strengthen the exploitation chain and directly benefit from the flesh trade. It is under this power structure that children (in the case of *Taiwan*) of disadvantaged families become easy prey.

Selling a child may be identified as a most outrageous 'dysfunction' of the family, but responding to it by severing the child from all family ties often results in 'punishing the victims'. The same consequence also befalls when the resulting undesirable (or 'deviant' in professional definition) mentality and behaviour of the exploited child are not understood at the level of social deprivation. However, such views are at most maintained as campaign discourses in *Taiwan*. Throughout this book, it is to be shown that the failures of the modern ROC law and its regulatory mechanisms in protecting children from sexual exploitation has been built upon a misplaced focus of policy and practice on wrong individuals and on wrong legal and social strategies.

NOTES

[1] It was reported at a news conference held in Jakarta on June 21, 1994 by the UNICEF (United Nations Children's Fund) that according to its annual Progress of Nations publication, '[r]ecent estimates suggest at least one million children are involved in prostitution... in Asian countries'. The numbers involved nationally are Taiwan: 100,000; India: 300,000; Thailand: 100,000; the Philippines: 100,000, Vietnam: 40,000; Sri Lanka: 30,000; China: almost 10,000. See The China Post on June 22, 1994, p.1; and *The Central Daily* (international edition) on June 23, 1994, p.7; *The Liberty Times* on June 22, 1994, p.6 & p.7.

[2] The ECPAT Campaign completed its first phase of three years from 1991 to 1993. After undergoing evaluations on the past performance, the Executive Committee decided that the Campaign would be extended for another three years from 1994 to 1996 (the special edition of the ECPAT Newsletter, placing issue number 9, July, 1993). The Campaign was completed by the World Congress Against Commercial Sexual Exploitation of Children held at Stockholm from August 27 to 31, 1996 (Host Committee, 1996ab).

[3] According to the aforementioned UNICEF report, '[m]any factors are driving the trade, including economic desperation. But in the age of cheap travel, more and more "tourists" and businessmen from the industrialised nations are seeking out child prostitutes... Many travel because there is less risk of enclosure and jail, or in the hope that sex with young children means less risk of AIDS'. See The China Post on June 22, 1994, p.1.

[4] The following analysis will draw upon ideas developed in the sociology of deviance and social problems, which question the terms like 'deviant' and ask 'deviant to whom?' or 'deviant from what?'. Such a skeptical view on the examination of the social problem of child prostitution is found useful in supporting the arguments of this book.

[5] See Hew,1992:27; ICCB,1992:8-11; Srisang,S.,1991:42-43; De Leon et al.,1991:55-56; De Leon,1991:88; Suresh,1991:65; Walz,1992:18; and *Chen,H.N.,1992*; *Hsu,C.L., 1988,1989*; *Huang,Y.C.,1991a*; *Wang,T.S.,et al.,1989*; *Wu,T.L.,1987*; *Yin,C.C.;1987, 1991,1993*; *Yin,C.C. et al.,1993*. See also the girl prostitution profiles provided in Shee,A.,1994:Appendix VI.

[6] For the controversies surrounding concepts and definitions of 'the family', see Aries,1962; Barrett & McIntosh,1987; Laslett,1982; Mount,1982; Smelser,1982. The general argument is that there have always been different types of family (extended, joint, conjugal, etc.) for different classes (Aries, Laslett, Smelser) and there is an increasing diversity of family types, including one parent, single-person, communal, and homosexual households (Barrett & McIntosh).

[7] As the presented facts in Asian countries mostly involve parents as the perpetrators, an equation in reference is generally made between 'the exploitative parents' and 'the exploitative family'. So it is the nuclear family unit composed of a married couple and their minor children that is in question. However, functions of the traditional extended family are often mentioned, especially in Taiwan. Some consider restoring the power of the extended family over its nuclear unit so that parents do not dispose of their children without restraint, while some others support the development of a protectionist welfare state (managed by a modern court and empowered professionals) to substitute the declining extended family.

[8] See Morgan,1975:47-54,92-96 and Morgan,1985:280-286.

[9] The word 'contradiction' is defined as 'experience of simultaneous affirmation and negation within the system in respect of an issue'. See Morgan,1975:96-97.

[10] Seeing the problem in this way, efforts in treatment and prevention will have to rest on fundamental changes in the family system.

[11] The observations made from an anthropological study on a Taiwanese farm family conducted by M. Wolf entitled 'The House of Lim' may help to explain this point.

[12] Barrett & McIntosh suggest that the family is not necessarily for the benefit of its weaker members such as women and children. In their terms, the 'anti-social family' inflicts

hardship and suffering on its members, which partly explains state intervention as a means of protecting its weaker members. See Barrett & McIntosh,1987:43-81.

[13] Arguments and recommendations for the protection of family privacy by limiting state intervention in cases of child abuse and neglect are expressed in the books by Goldstein, Freud, & Solnit -- Beyond the Best Interests of the Child (1973), and Before the Best Interests of the Child (1980). Similar statements are made in the book Justice for Children (1980), in which Morris, Giller, Szwed & Geach suggest a series of principles which they believe will greatly reduce the number of cases coming to court, provide a higher quality of care and protection to children brought to court and generally improve the nature of state intervention in families.

[14] Many Western sociologists have attempted to describe the rise and development of the welfare state in the European community as a response to development problems arising from industrialisation and urbanisation in the late 19th and 20th centuries. The Keynesians (the most popular school in Taiwan), for example, conclude that the welfare state is an answer to problems of changing working conditions, a highly differentiated social structure, and economic inequality and insecurity. So state provision of welfare services in industrial societies is an inevitable process and a 'functional prerequisite' for social integration and organic solidarity. It is under this rationale that some policy advisors and academics in Taiwan maintain that the welfare state must be actively developed to cope with the social problems resulting from industrialisation and urbanisation. See Li,K.T.,1988:1-2; and *Chu,M.L.,1990; Hsieh,M.E.,1990; Kuo,C.C.,1990; Li,.C.Y.,1988; Li,Y.C.,1990; Lin,C.Y., 1990; Lin,W.Y.,1990; Pai,H.H.,1973; Tsai,H.C.,1990; Tsai,W.H.,1990.*

[15] According to M. Foucault quoted by J. Donzelot in his analytical book of 'The Policing of Families', the term 'policing' encompasses all the methods for developing the quality of the population and the strength of the nation. The purpose of policing is to ensure the good fortune of the state through the wisdom of its regulations, and to augment its forces and its power to the limits of its capacity. The science of policing consists, therefore, in regulating everything that relates to the present condition of society, in strengthening and improving it, in seeing that all things contribute to the welfare of the members that compose it. The aim of policing is to make everything that composes the state serve to strengthen and increase its power, and likewise serve the public welfare.

[16] There has recently been a roll-back of this coercive intervention into the family in the English child protection law -- The Children Act 1989 -- as a result of the Cleveland Crisis. The message conveyed in this Act has also been passed on to the legislature in Taiwan. When the ROC Child Welfare Law (Amendment) 1993 was in its legislative process, some parts of the aforementioned Cleveland Report were briefly translated by a research team supported by the Taipei Bar Association (TBA) and organised by me. As will be seen in chapter five, the most controversial debate during the legislative process was that of coercive state intervention into the family. The Cleveland Report was quoted to remind the danger of giving too much power to social workers. For a better understanding of the Cleveland crisis, see Lord Justice Butler-Sloss (ed.) -- Report of the Inquiry into Child Abuse in Cleveland 1987 (1988). For introductions to the principles governing the

relationship between the state and the family in the 1989 Children Act, see Allen,1990; Alston, et al.,1992; Bridge, et al.,1990; Freeman,1992a.

[17] The concept of 'prostitution' is used to indicate 'a transaction where at least two trading parties buy and respectively sell sexual acts' (Jarvinen,1993:16). According to M. Jarvinen, '[t]he phenomenon of prostitution has traditionally been considered as difficult to define. The most important criterion used to define prostitution (in functional and other literature) has been *commerciality*. For a sexual relation to be called prostitution, the carnal knowledge must be linked to remuneration, in money or other forms. Another criterion often used in definitions of prostitution is that of *promiscuity*: the sexual transaction is not supposed to be unique in the sense that the seller only has one customer. A third criterion is *non-selectivity*: the prostitute is not assumed to choose her customers; all men who can and are willing to pay are serviced. A forth criterion is *temporariness*: the sexual transaction should not be a part of a long-term social relation. And a fifth criterion is *emotional indifference*: the prostitution relationship is to be impersonal and neutral. See Jarvinen,1993:24-25.

[18] The concept of 'prostitution control' refers to 'those formal and informal measures which target the parties involved in the transactions (prostitutes, customers, procurers) for the purpose of combating prostitution or channeling it into socially acceptable forms'. See Jarvinen,1993:16.

[19] It is widely urged that in modern democratic societies, the involvement of two consenting adults in commercial sex is maintained as a 'private' matter deserving no state censure (Rosenbleet & Puriente,1973:373; Tong,1984:56; Wolfenden Committee,1957). On the other hand, prostitution is still practised and socially tolerated as 'women's oldest profession' (Jarvinen,1993:17), the eradication of which is conceived as impossible. Thus the suppression legislation often fails in its enforcement (Tong,1984:43).

[20] Much of the new prostitution research in the western world has been feminist-oriented. See Snare,1993:9.

[21] In R. Tong's words, 'decriminalisation will not help these girls achieve autonomy unless it is accompanied by extralegal remedies in the form of needed social services and by laws that prohibit the sexual exploitation of minors' (Tong,1984:60).

[22] Prostitution was thus regarded by society as a better alternative to slavery and rape. See Bullough,1987:296.

[23] All these phenomena articulate culture's celebration of the 'good' woman and the condemnation of the 'bad' women in terms of female sexuality. See Tong,1984:193.

[24] In Western civilisation, this process was accelerated by the power of professional knowledge.

[25] See chapter six for further discussions.

[26] For discussions on the philosophical debates concerning juvenile justice, see Atkinson,1993b; Laster,1993; Naffine,1993; Pratt,1993; Seymour,1993.

[27] They often performed unsatisfactorily in the school and had a bad peer relationship. Those who were dissatisfied with their family life might become runaways. (Hilton,1971:32) Those coming from lower socio-economic status and/or disorganised families would seek to achieve economic and social status through economic independence, relationship with a

mother role (pimp/brothel-keeper), and peer acceptance through prostitution. Case studies also indicated a group of 'middle-class' prostitution-involved juveniles. They did not depend financially on prostitution. Ackerman (1969:49) identified sexual acting-out by middle-class girls as part of a broader pattern of revolt against authority (Lowen,1978:2). Adolescent girls traded their sex occasionally to express their reaction against over control by parents or to fulfill their desire to break certain social norms and become 'deviant' (Davis,1971:297-324). Adventure and independence provide another motivating factor for entering prostitution (James,1978:28). For those adolescents whose physical or emotional necessities of life have been denied or provided on an inconsistent basis, prostitution provides an obvious way to obtain self-sufficiency, a sense of power, and self-determination (James,1978:8). Social workers in Taiwan found that some girls actually came from a family with prostitution history (*Hwang,Y.C.,1991:3*). On the other hand, poor children in the third world countries were often abandoned and became street children who finally learned to trade sex (Bruce,1991:30). Generally speaking, money and material goods are the primary motivating factor for entering into prostitution (James,1974, 1978; Pomeroy,1965:175 & Esselstyn,1968:125, quoted at Lowen,1978:2). See Benjamin & Masters,1964:106; Deisher et al.,1969; Esselstyn,1968 & Greenwald,1971 quoted at Lowen,1978:3; Hilton,1971:32; James,1978:23,34; Lowen,1978:1 for discussions.

[28] Available case studies in *Taiwan* have concentrated on the psychology of sold girls. Research on the girls who act out themselves is still primitive as concerned professionals are inexperienced in dealing with such girls and much is learnt from the West. In comparison, Western literature, as shown above, has provided numerous case studies which conclude the motivating factors for children or juveniles themselves to enter, remain in, or fall back to prostitution.

[29] Female sexual delinquency is perceived as different from, and worse than, male delinquency. Female sexual delinquency is conceived as 'far more profoundly self-destructive and irreversible in its corrosive consequences' than male delinquency. See Blos,1969:109 and Friedman,1969:113, quoted at Elliott,1988:7.

[30] In J. Donzelot's words, '[t]here is a *dematerialisation of the offence* which places the minor in a mechanism of interminable investigation, of perpetual judgment. The break between the investigation and the decision is obliterated. The spirit of the laws... requires that more consideration be given to the symptomal value of the actions of which the minor is accused, to what they reveal concerning his temperament and the value of his native milieu, than to their materiality. The investigation is meant to serve more as a means of access to the minor's personality than as a means of establishing the facts' (1979:110-111, emphasis is in the original).

[31] M. Foucault claims that the techniques of the nineteenth-century penitentiary 'established a slow, continuous, imperceptible graduation that made it possible to pass naturally from disorder to offence and back, from a transgression of the law to a slight departure from a rule, an average, a demand, a norm' (1979:298-300).

[32] See the collection of newspaper reports provided in *Chao,K.C.,1988*.

[33] See chapter five for detailed discussions.

[34] See chapter four for relevant figures and discussions.

[35] This 'three-compound matrix' is, in my definition, a syndication of the above-mentioned three facets of the recognised problem of child prostitution in Taiwan.

[36] See chapter six for the ROC prostitution policy and relevant prostitution control laws.

[37] D.G. Gil defines child abuse as: 'inflicted gaps or deficits between circumstances of living which would facilitate the optimum development of children, to which they should be entitled, and their actual circumstances, irrespective of the sources or agents of the deficit' (Gil,1975, quoted at Parton,1985:167).

[38] It should also be reminded that sold female children have always played an essential role in the long history of this women's oldest profession.

[39] Paedophiles are those adults whose sexual preference is for children (Baker,1980:293). While some medical definitions described paedophiles as those for whom 'a pre-pubescent child is necessary for sexual gratification' (Websters Medical Dictionary), most now leave the question of puberty on one side and describe paedophilia as a 'sexual orientation of adults toward children' (Oxford Companion to Medicine) (O'Grady,1992:143-144). For more information, see Ennew,1986:50-52; O'Grady,1992a:Ch.4; Power,1977; Rossman, 1979:216,1980.

[40] Article 10:3 of the International Covenant on Economic, Social and Cultural Rights states that 'children and young persons should be protected form economic and social exploitation. Their employment in work harmful to their morals or health or dangerous to life or likely to hamper their normal development should be punished by law'. If this type of approach is implied when the sexual exploitation of children is discussed, then the reference is clearly the employment of children in prostitution and pornography. See Ennew,1986:41-42.

[41] It excludes other types of sexual contact between adults and children, however unpleasant these might be. See Ennew,1986:41-42.

[42] Recent studies on child prostitution refer to the sexual exploitation of minors as involving adults using children as prostitutes and as subjects in pornographic materials for commercial profit. See Baker,1980; Densen-Gerber & Hutchinson,1978; ICCB,1991; O'Grady,1992a.

[43] For further discussions, see Jones,D.P.H. and Melbourne McGraw,J., 'Reliable and Fictitious Accounts of Sexual Abuse to Children', Journal of Interpersonal Violence,2(1): 27-45,1987.

[44] This is a term adopted in J. Foucault's writings, quoted and discussed at Smart,1989:6-9; Gordon,1980:106-107; Taylor,1986:75.

[45] This is a term adopted in C. Lasch's book -- Heaven in a Heartless World, quoted and discussed at Freeman,1983:76-77.

[46] Definitions of 'power' are legion. To the extent that there is any commonly accepted formulation, power is understood as concerned with 'the bringing about of consequences'. For introductory discussions on the concept of power, see Dahl,196; Foucault,1980; Lukes,1976; Philp,1985; Russell,1938.

[47] There is no unified definition of patriarchy. In this book, a broad definition made by K. Millett is adopted with some modification: the principle of patriarchy will be defined as two fold: the powerful (male now joined by female) shall dominate the powerless, the elder shall dominate the younger. See Millett,1977:25.

[48] Under the veil of the Chinese Confucius teachings of 'filial piety', female children became more inclined to be sacrificed for the survival of a destitute family.
[49] According to national surveys released in the first ECPAT international consultation meeting held in Bangkok during May 1-5, 1990, the proportions of female and male children involved in child prostitution are as follows: In the Philippines, it was estimated that boys account for 60% of the children involved in prostitution and girls for 40%. In Thailand, among the many hundreds of thousands of Thai children caught in prostitution, most of them are girls, although the number of boys appears to be growing. In contrast, when child prostitution is referred in Sri Lanka, it really means boy prostitution. See the national reports in Srisang,K.,1991a. See also O'Grady,1992a:137-142.
[50] Prostitution tends to be symptomatic of economic inequality rather than uniform poverty in a society (Bullough,1987:296).
[51] In the aforementioned ECPAT 1990 international consultation meeting, Professor G. Kent argued that the real problem associated with sexual exploitation of children in Asia is not national poverty, but national priorities. He said, '[c]ontrary to common assumptions, poor countries, like poor people, do have money. Poor countries are not uniformly poor; most have a middle class and a wealthy elite. They all manage to muster sufficient food and medical services for the wealthy. Soldiers do not go hungry. But most countries spend very little on children. Poverty is their explanation but even very poor countries seem to find money for monuments and armaments. The limited allocation of national resources to serving the interests of children is due more to the ways in which available funds are allocated than to the absolute shortage of funds' (Kent,1991:74).
[52] See Chen,H.H.,1986; De Leon,1991:88; Kao,R.,1988,1991; Lin,M.J.,1989; TWRF, 1991; and *Chen, YingChen,1992*; *Hsu,M.C.,1991ab*; *Hsu,M.C.& Chu,H.Y.,1992*; *Lin,M.J., 1989*; *RP.1988*; *Wang,T.S.,et al.,1989*.
[53] See chapter three for elaboration.

3 STRUCTURAL CONTEXT OF CHILD PROSTITUTION

The review of literature in chapter two highlighted the power relations involved in the exploitation of children from disadvantaged families. This enables a better understanding of the nature of child prostitution in its structural context.[1] It also reveals the pitfalls of tackling the problem at an individual level. In order to facilitate the exploration of those pitfalls in later chapters, this chapter intends to elucidate the nature of child prostitution in *Taiwan* by reviewing research findings and case studies done by concerned professionals. It first describes the origins of the practice in the prostitution industry and the Chinese patriarchal family. With this background information, it will then become clear why certain groups of families and their children are predisposed to act as the suppliers of child prostitution, and how the customers manage to provide themselves with justifications or excuses for their behaviour. Some profiles of child prostitution which are summed up from social work cases are finally presented to depict the current exploitation chain in which vulnerable children are caught.

Evolution of the Prostitution Industry

Origins in Chinese History

The existence of prostitution in China can be traced for more than 2600 years (*Cheng & Fang-Chang,1990:6*). From 610 B.C. of the Feudal Era (1122 B.C. - 221 B.C.) to the imperial Chinese dynasties (221 B.C. - 1911 A.D.), the institution of prostitution had been initiated by the state to meet the sexual needs of traveling merchants, then the '*ying chi* 營妓' -- the barrack prostitutes were introduced into the army for those who did not have wives, and gradually, other types of prostitutes including the '*yueh chi* 樂妓' -- the music prostitutes, the '*chia chi* 家妓' -- the family prostitutes, and the '*kuan chi* 官妓' -- the official prostitutes[2] (the courtesan) were recruited to serve the rich, the privileged, the noble, the royal as well as the emperor himself. In the late 19th and early 20th centuries when Western hegemony intruded China, Chinese young women also became the 'beautiful merchandise' to meet the exotic demand (Gronewold,S.,1982).

Young girls were in great demand because of preference towards pure, virginal sex (Gronewold,S.,1982:44). There was a widespread Chinese belief that having sex with young girls, particularly virgins, will make a man younger and healthier. The false belief is called '*tsai yin pu yang* 採陰補陽', literally means to complement the '*yang* 陽' (the male) with the '*yin* 陰' (the female).[3] The phrase was derived from the philosophical thinking of Taoism but was misinterpreted by many as to mean 'virgin sex or underage sex can cure men's weakness' (Wang,I.,1992:44; *Chaing, H.S., 1994*).

Developments on Taiwan

Compared to the Chinese mainland, the recorded prostitution history of *Taiwan* commenced very recently (*Hsieh,K.,1972*; *Shen,M.C.,1990*; *Sun,T.W.,1980*). It is said that after *Taiwan* became a territory of CH'ING China, increasing numbers of south-east Chinese merchants came to *Taiwan* to do business. In the late 18th century, the island population began to concentrate in a few offshore cities as the mainland-island trade became intensive (*Shen,M.C.,1989:47-48*). The Chinese merchants brought about their wealth along with their urge for sexual gratification. In response, there emerged girlie restaurants (*chiu chia* 酒家) in most of the main ports alongside the western coast of *Taiwan*. Flesh markets flourished. Some of the noisy red-light districts from those days are still operating today (Chen,H.H.,1986:126).

The island prostitution industry was further strengthened during the colonial period. During the 51 years of Japanese rule, prostitution was encouraged and regulated in *Taiwan* by the colonial government as one of the means to ease tensions between the ruler and the ruled. Apart from regimented brothels and girlie restaurants in officially authorised special entertainment areas such as *the PEI TOU SPA* (*pei tou wen chuen* 北投溫泉),[4] American bars also began to operate in the late 1920s, which turned out to be houses of lewdness or prostitution in reality. Hence, before the ROC government regained control over *Taiwan*, the island had become notorious for its debauchery which attracted local consumers as well as exotic sex travellers.

In 1945, the *CHIANG Kai Shek* government sent officials to operate the *Taiwan* Provincial Government. The women's emancipation movement, which had started in Mainland China in the early 1920s, also influenced legal reforms against the practice of prostitution in *Taiwan*. A prohibition order was promulgated as part of the ROC anti-prostitution policy. But the order was never truly implemented. It was recognised that those who came from China were soldiers who had fought for their country for many years and were thus described as 'hungry for food and sex'. So prostitution was tolerated for practical reasons.[5] As a result, a temporary order to regulate prostitution was announced. The aim was to control the prostitution affected population in the hope that it would be gradually swept away from society. However, the result was that prostitution became socially institutionalised and finally grew out of legal control. In every big city there were at least one or two red-light districts (official or unofficial) full of girlie restaurants and brothels.

From 1962 to 1971, *Taiwan* underwent an economic transformation from an agricultural society to an industrial one. The old girlie restaurants were replaced by Western dancing halls, tea houses, and American bars. Hotels in *the PEI TOU SPA* area became the most popular holiday resort for American soldiers. During the 1960s and the 1970s, the number of prostitutes increased to meet the demands of American soldiers of local US military bases and those who came from the Vietnam battlefield to *Taiwan* for vacations.[6] The epidemic development of the prostitution business finally became notorious internationally. On December 22, 1967, photos of two naked prostitutes with American soldiers in a hot spring bath at *the PEI TOU SPA* were published in the TIME magazine under the title of 'The *Taiwan* Particular'. As a result, *Taiwan* suddenly became a sexual paradise for foreign tourists, especially the Japanese (*Hsieh,K.,1972:151-152*; *Shen,M.C.,1989:51*).[7]

Then the transition period for the Taiwanese society arrived. Industrialisation invited mass migration of the rural population to the cities. Modern buildings and flats gradually replaced the old Chinese houses. The traditional Chinese ethics were eroded but a new social order had not yet been established.[8] It was said that the Taiwanese society gradually took on an overwhelming spirit of worshipping wealth and searching for profits (Branegan,J.,1990:50-51). Poverty is generally regarded as more disgraceful than prostitution[9], especially among people of lower socio-economic strata (Chen,H.H.,1986:129).

Gradually, the essence of low wage but long working hours made factory work less desirable for many young girls and their families (Diamond,N.,1975,1979; Li,K.T.,1985). With the incitement of big and easy money offered by cunning procurers, the flesh market was able to recruit a satisfactory number of 'clean' virginal prostitutes from remote villages and aboriginal tribes. *Taiwan* suddenly became the amusement park for local as well as foreign men to satisfy their sexual gratification (*Cheng & Fan-Chang,1990:7*). A series of governmental orders were announced in an attempt to control the local illicit sexual practice, but these have proved futile. On the other hand, the government continued to tolerate and connive in sex tourism for the sake of earning foreign currency.

The situation met its turning point between 1972 and 1980, during which *Taiwan* underwent another economic take-off (Liu,A.P.L.,1982). As the industrialisation process was successfully accelerated and foreign trade had continuously brought about rapidly growing export surpluses, the government decided to undertake major national construction projects and economic development plans (Chung,L.J.,1989:261-267). On the other hand, US withdrawal from Vietnam in 1975 reduced the demand for prostitution service from American soldiers. Moreover, following the US government's decision to sever the diplomatic relationship with the ROC in 1979, the US Army Base and military consultants were completely withdrawn from *Taiwan*. On the other hand, Japanese tourists began to move their sex trips to South and South-East Asian countries such as India, Sri Lanka, Vietnam, and Thailand, whose governments were eager to accumulate foreign exchange through mass tourism (*Cheng & Fan-Chang,1990:8*).

Then the ROC government started to review its past failure in controlling the practice of prostitution and decided to initiate a series of 'purity society campaigns'. Three measures were thus taken to combat the flood of sex business. First in 1974, a new law was passed to levy heavy business tax against the so-called 'special entertainment establishments (*te chung ying yeh 特種營業*)' including girlie restaurants, American bars, massage parlours, coffee/tea houses, and the like. However, the result was that those who could not afford paying taxes went underground and survived in other forms (*Liu,Y.M.,1976a:50-59*; *Shen,M.C.,1989:34*). Brothel-keepers became hotel managers. Call girls became available in most hotels, motels and the like. Girlie restaurants changed their official registration into snack bars, ice and fruit houses, and normal restaurants. Peep shows began to appear in small cinemas. Illegal dancing halls found their new operational bases at the top or the cellar of huge buildings. And many luxurious Western restaurants were actually a combination of girlie house, dancing hall and night club for illegal sexual practice.

Another measure taken at the same time was to outlaw lustful massage parlours. So during that period, the illegal business was apparently extinguished, while in reality, thousands of those 'massage girls' transferred their work to the so-called 'luxurious high-class barber saloons' and brought their illicit practice to the originally legal barber shops. These 'barbers' also offered massage service. Consequently, the blind people who were doing traditional massage as a living could not compete with those young beautiful massage girls who also offered negotiable sexual services (*Shen,M.C.,1989:50*).

Finally, helped by a moralist social movement against sex tourism, the aforementioned most disreputable red light district for foreign customers -- *the PEI TOU SPA* -- was abolished by the *Taipei* City Council in November 1979 (*Shen,M.C.,1989:51*). Unfortunately, what the government did was simply to sweep away the disorderly houses from *the PEI TOU SPA* without taking good care of those who had been making their living in it.[10] Nor were the operators or pimps arrested and punished. In other words, the institution remained intact though in another form. As a result, many prostitution operators, pimps and prostitutes themselves went underground to join the operation of girlie houses which appeared as Chinese, Western, or Japanese restaurants (Kao,R.,1991:61).

Between 1981 and 1986, there was an economic recession in *Taiwan* which split the prostitution business into two classes. On the one hand, the parvenus who emerged during the prosperity could still afford to enjoy their lives in lavish brothels and girlie restaurants, which operated under the disguise of clubs, recreation centres, hotels, massage saloons, etc.. On the other hand, a large number of unemployed young girls with unsatisfactory education or qualification entered into all kinds of flesh markets. They filled the demands of those low-income workers and bankrupt businessmen with low prices.

The economy of *Taiwan* recovered after 1986. The price of real estates went high. The stock exchange flourished in an unprecedented way. Mark Six lottery was introduced from *Hong Kong* and became popular. The whole island was corrupted by the game of money. Much wealth was undoubtedly used to support all sorts of businesses involving prostitution and the like. The lust problem in *Taiwan* became even more disturbing with the engagement of numerous young girls from all social strata in the flesh market, first the local ones, then those from the Chinese mainland, Thailand, and the Philippines also joined in (*TWRF,1989ab,1990*). In the past few years, prostitution also became a desirable profession for young men in Taiwan. Numerous media reports have explored the facts that the male prostitution industry is flourishing helped by sufficient inflows of supply and demand. More and more young men, including students and university graduates, consider it acceptable to earn quick money by offering sex-related services. The male prostitutes are generally referred to as 'cowboys (*niu lang* 牛郎)'. Their customers are mainly women, but if the consideration is fair, male customers will also be accepted.[11]

Once in a while now, the lust problem is mentioned as the core issue of political debates, yet the solutions have always been restricted to the mouth-talk level and no action followed. Everybody seems to be content with the situation of keeping the issue as an topic for moral debates and occasionally the target for political criticism while election is under stake.

Summary

For more than twenty five centuries now, the Chinese dynasties have witnessed the waxing and waning of the prostitution institution. Although prostitution had been legally prohibited during certain periods, due to societal tolerance as well as loose implementation of laws, the institution never died (*Shen,1990:41-58*; *Sun,1980:32-42*). This is easy to understand, for there were always tremendous demands from those who were politically or economically in power, and as will be shown later, the supply was mostly filled by those from the most vulnerable groups of lower socio-economic strata.

It is said that prostitution has deeply rooted itself in Chinese culture and has become an integral evil of Chinese society which can not be eliminated (*Ho,C.W.,1992; Pan,W.K,1992; Shen,M.C,1989*). Development of modern capitalism and its mechanisms have further 'modernised' this social evil. Operators from all social strata are joined by providers as well as consumers of both sexes from various age groups to luxuriate the flesh markets. Governmental control measures were not able to eradicate prostitution, although they have moved the operation of the industry into new directions.

Origins of Child prostitution in Chinese Families

Children under Patriarchal Exploitation

The traditional Chinese family is patrilineal and patriarchal. The tenets of Confucianism[12] deliberately set up and guarded family relationships on a unique generation-age-sex hierarchy. Under the hierarchy, the oldest male family member from the highest generation rules supreme. 'Filial piety' was proclaimed by Confucius as 'the root of all virtue'.[13] Under his teachings, unreserved obedience and devotion was demanded of a child to his parent (father), of the younger to the older, and of the subject to the ruler.[14]

Confucianism made a strong effort to put parental authority on the basis of genuine respect and love and to eliminate fear and compulsion in relations between children and parents. Parents' love for their children was also stressed[15], but parents' obligations toward their children were considered much less essential than children's obligation toward their parents. Parents were legally empowered to dispose of their children, but only in the interests of the family (Lang,O.,1946:331-332). However, when this tenet was transformed into social practice, it became the ready excuse for parental exploitation of children.

Apart from 'filial piety', the exploitation was further facilitated by the misinterpretation of the Chinese ethic of 'self-sacrifice'. In Chinese tradition, social harmony was maintained by a strong moral rule of mutual consideration and the 'denial of self' (Kim,H.I.,1981:118). Those with lower social/familial status were always expected to deny their personal advantages in order to secure the benefits of the superior. The sacrifice was considered a 'duty' of the inferior. This moral ethic has contributed to mitigate the 'force' involved in the parental exploitation of children.

The status of Chinese women started to deteriorate in the late feudal period (1027-256 B.C.) and continued under the Imperial rule (256 B.C.-1911 A.D.). Not only did the traditional Chinese philosophy provide a theory of women's inferiority which gave ideological justification of her lower status in society as well as in the Imperial Codes, but the most popular Chinese religions -- Buddhism and Taoism -- also stressed women's inferiority and helped to perpetuate it (Lang,O.,1946:43,332) (*Liu,L.C.,1977*). Consequently, women had extremely subordinate status in the Chinese patriarchal family and within the generation-age hierarchy the young female children became most vulnerable to suppression and exploitation (Lang,O.,1946:24; Wong,A.K.,1979:252).[16]

The killing of baby girls was not uncommon among poor people.[17] Although the Imperial laws forbade selling of children, it was widely practised among desperate families with social condemnation (Baker,H.D.R.,1979:7-8,40-42; Lang,O.,1946:259,332). Marriages were arranged to serve the purpose of procreation. Concubinage and prostitution offered alternatives for men to satisfy their desire for love and companionship. Those who assumed the responsibilities of producing heirs were entitled to be treated as 'good women', while the sold female children were to play the role of 'bad women' in order to meet the culturally celebrated sexual gratification of men (Baker,1979:36; Levy,1949:86; Yang,1959:57).

Families Providing for 'Supply' and 'Demand'

The practice of prostitution in general and child prostitution in particular can both find their root causes in the traditional Chinese families. Miserable lives of sold female children in prostitution, concubinage, and the like have been well documented in historical and anthropological books as well as novels, poems and all sorts of Chinese literature including the modern ones. Husbands and mature sons were very often encouraged by family members to frequent prostitution. This created a supply and demand market relationship between the prostitution industry and the families as shown in the following figure.

FAMILY	FAMILY
/	\
female children	husbands / sons
|	|
supply	***demand***
|	|

PROSTITUTION

Under the customs and laws of the Chinese Empire, imbued with the spirit of Confucianism,[18] the father and the husband were given enormous power and superior status comparable to the *Pater Familias* in Republican Rome (Lang,O,1968:26). Being the inferior members of the family, women and children were to be sacrificed when a family was under economic stress. A female child -- the daughter -- of a desperate family had been especially vulnerable to socially sanctioned practices of infanticide, abandonment, and selling children to become servants, concubines and prostitutes (Baker,1979:7-8; Leslie,1973:94; Levy,1949:69). Some other poor parents might choose to marry out daughters as child brides or to take in young girls as foster daughter-in-laws for economic reasons (Lang,1946:126-127; Wolf,1968,1970,1974).[19]

Under the Chinese patriarchal system, the sexual role of the so-called '*liang cha fu nu* 良家婦女 (women of good families, women with respectable characters[20])' was to produce a male successor. Men, married or unmarried, were allowed, if not encouraged, to satisfy their sexual desire by visiting brothels where they paid money in return for sexual service of the 'bad women' -- prostitutes. The traditional Chinese marriages were arranged and romantic love was not an essential part of marital life. It was feared that the men's romantic disappointment would become a disruptive factor in the institution of arranged marriage from which the stability of the traditional patriarchal family drew much of its strength. In order to remedy the suppression of romantic love by arranged marriage, prostitution was seen as a device to maintain the stability of traditional marriages.

Resort to prostitution was regarded as an acceptable means of escaping from distant or inimical marriages. It was neither uncommon nor considered particularly reprehensible, except when carried to the point of financially ruining the family (Baker,1979:36; Yang,1959:57). On the other hand, as pre-marital carnal relationship was forbidden for girls, young men were encouraged to look for sexual gratification in prostitution (Levy,1949:86).

Summary

Chinese patriarchal families did not only act as a main supplier of prostitutes but also created great demand. Husband and sons of better-off families were allowed to frequent prostitution as far as the family foundation was not threatened. It was through the practice of prostitution that not only the virtue of women of good family but also familial harmony were preserved. On the other hand, female children were prone to be sold into prostitution for the survival or benefit of the family. Under the moral ethics of 'filial piety' and 'self-sacrifice', the practice was justified with no resistance. This supply and demand relationship between the Chinese families and prostitution may help understand part of the cultural background of child prostitution currently practised in *Taiwan*.

Disadvantageous and Vulnerable Families in Taiwan

Causality and Vulnerability

When talking of causes which lead parents to sell their children into the flesh markets, there is a tendency to attribute the existence and proliferation of the sex industry involving children only or mainly to economic reasons.[21] However, many families in the face of hardship and desperate social and economic conditions would never send their children out onto the streets or into brothels to trade their sex, or make deals with the traffickers disregarding what would become of the child later, or pretend not knowing what sort of well-paid jobs could be offered to their young charming but unskilled children. In the slums of the aboriginal areas, a remarkable proportion of children become involved in prostitution or other indecent jobs, but many others do not.

Thus, before discussing the causes of child prostitution, it must be first made clear that there is no direct causal link between poverty (or other factors enumerated afterwards) and the sexploitation. The 'causes' would only make certain disadvantageous groups in society the most vulnerable prey for sexual exploitation. This vulnerability may be offset by certain favourable factors such as affectionate parents, high family pride, strong family ties, and so forth. On the other hand, one single cause would not normally lead to child prostitution. As will be shown in the later section of 'child prostitution profiles', studies of social work cases reveal that the road to prostitution is far from straightforward. The ready-to-blame causes in every case profile may only be the trigger or a 'scapegoat'. The real causes have always been much more profound, complicated and deep-rooted in culture and society.

Apart from poverty, recent research has indicated other leading factors in child prostitution. The personal and familial ones are (1) neglecting, abusive, disorganised, or broken families, maladjusted parent-child relationship; (2) control of patriarchal power and authority over women and children, misinterpretation of the traditional ethics of 'filial piety' and 'self-sacrifice'; (3) male sexual perversion, female sexual subordination, maladjustment of male-female relationship in modern egalitarian society; (4) decline of the extended family; (5) unhealthy neighbourhoods; (6) inadequate education, low levels of intelligence, ignorance of sexual matters, unskilled female labour; and a whole combination of personal, familial and environmental factors.[22]

The societal, economic and political factors include (1) breakdown of social ties and traditional social orders; (2) widespread dislocation of rural population, migration, the pressure of urbanisation, and unemployment; (3) the attractions of Western consumerism and the promotion of commercialistic values and life patterns; (4) the presence of American military bases and the government's active promotion of the tourism industry; and (5) colonialism resulting in a 'colonial mentality' which degrades ones' own culture as inferior while worships Western religion and social teachings.[23] All the above factors have contributed to the vulnerability of certain disadvantaged families in contemporary *Taiwan*.

Children of Vulnerable Families

In *Taiwan*, there are two groups of children who are especially vulnerable to the flesh trade. They are, as identified by some eminent Taiwanese professionals: aboriginal girls and children of troubled families.[24]

The first group is indigenous girls, especially those who have beautiful faces and charming figures.[25] From the statistics shown in chapter four, one can see the high proportion of underage female prostitutes who were sold or lured out from aboriginal tribes or villages.[26] Earlier observations often mistakenly assumed that the aborigines had a promiscuous sexual tradition, but this has been strongly rebutted by recent historical and empirical research (Chen,H.H.,1986:133) (*Chu,H.Y.,1991*; *Li,Y.Y.,1991*; *Tseng,S.M. et al.,1992*; *Yin,C.C.,1987*). Careful studies of indigenous peoples and their cultures pointed out that there was not a prostitution tradition in any aboriginal tribe. Illicit sex was harshly prohibited.[27] It was the intrusion of Westernised Chinese Han culture with its values that resulted in the cultural changes among the aborigines (Hsu,M.T.,1982,1987,1991; Wang,I.S.,1980).

Researchers of the ten indigenous tribes[28] located in *Taiwan*'s mountain areas have come to the conclusion that as a result of the inappropriate aboriginal policy carried out by the ROC government which considered the Han culture and civilisation superior and dominant, the young generations of aborigines now choose to forfeit their own traditional ethics and values while pursuing the modern Westernised city life (*Hsu,M.C.,1991ab*). The Han ideologies and living styles have become preferable to them. Many young girls have refused to marry their tribe boys but became the brides of old Chinese men (*Hsu & Chu,1992*).

As the aborigines are comparatively poorer than the Han people, and they do not have the Han saving habit, when they have access to the more luxurious living styles of the Han, or when they are in need of money to pay for food and drinks,[29] destitute parents become vulnerable to the flesh traders who offer their unskilled children well-paid jobs in the city. In the beginning, the parents did not know what would become of their children. Later, more and more children came back with enough money to rebuild the family houses and the parents were made proud of their children among the poor neighbourhood. Other families became envious and followed suit. Recently, young girls have started to join their friends or act out themselves with or without the knowledge of their neglecting parents (*Chen,M.L,1996; Lin,M.J.,1989;TWRF,1992;Wang,Y.H.1993b,1996b*).

So, in the first place it was economic necessity which led the parents to give away their children. Most of the aborigines were not well-educated, so when sex traders were accompanied by local gentry, school teachers, civil servants, or local influential politicians to persuade the parents to sell their children, they could hardly resist. As more and more children left and returned, parents started to realise what their children had been involved in, and many regretted it. However, the wealth brought in by the daughter's sacrifice was praised by relatives and neighbours (*GOH,1992*; *RP,1988*; *TWRF,1989*).

Gradually, parents learned to rebuild their family pride on lavishness and vanity. More and more new Western brick houses were being built and decorated. Now not only are parents openly contracting with sex dealers and pimps, but more and more young girls look upon prostitution as an acceptable alternative to start their career (*Chen,M.L.,1995*; *Chiou,C.J.,1996; TWRF,1991*). Sociologists have noticed the breakdown of traditional social values and mores among aboriginal people which upheld strict sex taboos (Chen,H.H.,1986:133) (*Li,Y.Y.,1982*[30]). Consequently, a new culture of 'structuralised and generalised female prostitution' has emerged (*Wang,T.C. et al.,1989; Hu,S.H.,1996*).

The children of troubled families are the other high-risk group. Here the 'troubled families' include those whose financial situation is marginal, the education standard is low, the family ties are weak, or simply the parents are too busy (*Hong,W.H.,1995; Shen,M.C.,1990*).[31] Many studies have concluded that these vulnerable families are much more likely to have connection with prostitution and crimes (*Chen,H.N.,1992*; *Lin,C.H.,1988*; *TWRF,1992; Wang,S.N.,1997; Wu,H.Y.,1990; Yin,C.C.,1991*).

It is mentioned above that those who live below the poverty line will find it harder to resist the temptation of easy money. Especially when the family encounters grave hardship such as family debts accumulated from expensive medical expenses,[32] or drinking and gambling, the family inclines to give away a child to whoever is willing to pay; and very often, the elder child who has just finished her\his primary school or junior high may start the first job in prostitution or the like. Once a child comes under the discipline of a pimp/brothel-keeper, she\he will undergo a thorough physical as well as psychological reform to make her\him a capable prostitute. Consequently, many children, though forced to trade their sex in the beginning, would choose to remain in it even after the family debts have been repaid.

The poor families usually have a low education standard. The parents are unskilled and some mothers might have once been prostitutes themselves. It is commonly found that these parents do not, or are not able to, pay appropriate attention to their children's school or family education as will be expected from normative families. As a result, children from such families tend to perform unsatisfactorily in the school, play truant on a regular basis, and quit their studies even before they complete the national compulsory education.[33]

Without proper family and school education, the children cannot undergo appropriate socialisation processes. Nor can they acquire sufficient knowledge and skills to compete at the workplace. As a result, both the parents and the child become easy prey to the outside world. Neighbours' new houses, friends' beautiful dresses, procurers' tempting instigation, all are in unbearable contrast with the distressful family situation. The ignorant but greedy parents, the naive and neglected children, coupled by the tricky and pitiless traffickers, procurers, pimps, brothel-keepers, and customers, together they supply and operate the million-dollar business of the flesh trade in *Taiwan*.

Weak family ties also play a crucial role in leading children into indecent jobs. The typical characteristics of such families include the presence of abusive or neglecting parents, broken marriage of the parents, absence of one parent and involvement of another sex partner of the other parent, which result in disharmonious or remote parent-child relationship, and delinquent or rebellious juvenile behaviour. Case studies found that underage prostitutes hardly came from an intact family of well-cultivated parents and affectionate parent-child relationship (*Chen,H.N.,1992*; *Liu,Y.M.,1976a*; *Shen,M.C.,1989*; *Sun,T.W.,1980*; *Wang & Wang,1992*; *Wang,S.R.,1984*; *Wu,T.L.,1987*). However, it is also observed that in the present consumerism-oriented Taiwanese society, parents tend to express their love for children in terms of material supplies. Many busy parents are extremely surprised to be informed of the fact that their beloved children have been involved in sex deals for extra pocket money (*Chen,C.M.,1995; Chen,M.L.,1996; Huang,Y.C.,1991a*; *Yin,C.C.,1991*).

Apart from the above two vulnerable social groups, it is worth mentioning that, historically speaking, adopted children have long been an easy prey for family exploitation. It was reported that during the 1950s and the 1960s, adopted children constituted approximately 20% to 25% of sold-prostitution population in *Taiwan* (*RCCI,1967:183,194-195,209*). It is believed that since the 'Campaign for the Protection of Adopted Children in Taiwan' was launched in 1951, the number of sexually exploited adopted children has been dropping. However, the five sold-prostitution cases dealt with by the TWRF from 1987 to 1989 all involved adopted children (*Shen,M.C.,1990:112*). More recent study findings also place adoption as one of the negative elements of child prostitution (*GOH,1996b*). Case studies revealed three most possible routines for adopted children to be sold into prostitution.

First, the adoptive mother could be a retired prostitute herself and the reason why she adopted a child was to prostitute her. Second, a married couple did not have offspring and adopted a child[34], but later a family crisis appeared so the parents sell the child into prostitution. And third, a single mother[35] married a man who adopted her child after the marriage, then the mother died and the adoptive/step father conspired with his new partner and forced the child into prostitution. Generally speaking, an adoptive child has assumed an inferior status in Chinese families. Whenever someone has to be sacrificed for the benefit of the family or the parents, the adoptive child may still be first in line (*Shen,M.C.,1990:113*).

The Customers

It was said that under the traditional patriarchal system, men of the Chinese families were given the 'entitlement' to paid sex. Prostitution was justified for the maintenance of arranged marriages. In contrast, the modern Chinese marriage in *Taiwan* is based on romantic love, and family opinions are playing a declining role in mate-choosing. Divorce is legally discouraged but the law can no longer lock a determined couple in a dead marriage. Besides, more and more women have chosen to emancipate themselves in pre-marital or extra-marital carnal relationships. The traditional excuses for frequenting prostitution seem to be disappearing. However, the modern capitalist-patriarchal men have provided themselves with more warrants to demand exotic youth flesh. Moreover, this 'entitlement' to paid sex is now equally shared by modern patriarchal women.

Those Who Frequent Prostitution

According to a government survey carried out in 1983, among 925 men interviewed, more than half of them had experience of frequenting sex-related service establishments, over 80% of the latter visited prostitutes with companions and 34.12% of them did it on a regular basis (*Tang,S.P. et al.,1983*). The excuses or motivations given were, first, for the sake of successful business meetings (33.13%), second, out of curiosity (20%), third, for entertainment (18.45), fourth, looking for excitement (11.18%), fifth, for sexual needs (12.34%), and last, to make up for unsatisfactory marital sex (2.15). So one can see that nowadays most men do not buy sex only to meet their sexual needs (*Cheng,Z.H. et al.,1990:33-34*). There are no available figures concerning female customers. According to the aforementioned media reports, women who frequented male prostitution may belong to four main categories: first is the female prostitutes who demand the power of control in sexual relationship; second is the lonely wives of busy or impotent husbands who need physical as well as psychological comforts; third is the so-called single nobility (*tan shen kuei tsu* 單身貴族) who chose not to marry while having sexual needs to be attended to; and finally is the emancipated women who enjoy male sexual service under her disposal.

Those Who Especially Prefer Under-Age and/or Virgin Sex

It is reported that some men in *Taiwan* prefer underage prostitutes with various incentives including, first, passion for a pretty, young, and clean virgin -- for many men such girls may only be made available in the flesh market; second, superstition that youthful prostitution provides 'safer' and 'more healthy' sex, especially the virgin one;[36] third, curiosity for something different -- having sex with a very young girl is a curious adventure for men;[37] fourth, desire for an easily manipulated sex partner -- for those who do not have enough confidence in handling mature women, young girls are less experienced and easier to handle and control; and fifth, pressure from business partners or peer groups -- many men found it difficult to resist the encouragement of friends (Cheng & Fan-Chang,1990:34; Wang,I.,1992:1-2).

Among the customers there may appear paedophiles or pederasts (ephebophiles) who are sexually attracted by children or young boys. Western literature has identified organised child-sex pursuers.[38] In *Taiwan*, no paedophiles or the like have ever been identified yet. However, the major reason is not that there are none, but because no such research has ever been done on sex consumers. Before a careful and professional survey can be carried out, one may keep the suspicion in mind that if there are men who would buy sex from an 8-year-old girl[39] or from boys under the age of 12,[40] there might have been a noticeable number of undisclosed paedophiles or pederasts in *Taiwan*. Recently, cases involving boy prostitutes have also been reported occasionally, but no information has been given concerning the customers except that female customers normally require for older boys (17 or 18 years old, for example), while male customers may demand for boys of all age groups ranging from 7 to 18 (*Chiou, Y.C., 1995; Chou, J.T., 1996a*).

Sex Tourism[41]

In 1984, a research programme was carried out to look at, *inter alia*, the influence of the Japanese sex tourists to *Taiwan*. It was found that Japanese made up 52% of all foreign tourists, of whom 81.18% were male visitors.[42] It was estimated that an overwhelming majority of these Japanese men paid visits to the 'special entertainment areas'.[43] It was stated that their impetus was two-fold. Japan has long been a patriarchal society which was strongly influenced by Confucian thought and the traditional Chinese morality which strictly emphasized female chastity while tolerating the male pursuit of sex pleasure in prostitution. This is manifested in the habit of Japanese men gathering with friends after work and enjoying a good time at locales of sex entertainment, and returning home very late.

Unfortunately for *Taiwan*, prostitution was outlawed by the Japanese government in 1957. And the Japanese wealthy men with old habits started to rebuild their sex paradise in another Confucian society, *Taiwan* -- Japan's ex-colony. With the similar cultural background, Japanese men felt at home in *Taiwan*. By coming to *Taiwan*, they could leave behind social and legal restraints, and in the role of an economic master, they enjoyed unlimited exercise of male domination through collective sexual adventure abroad.

There is now a growing panic that Western paedophiles may have landed on *Taiwan*.[44] These men used to spend holidays in south Asia, mainly Thailand and the Philippines. According to concerned professionals, paedophilia tourists coming from Western developed countries preferred buying sex from Asian children because (1) Asian children are more obedient, and (2) Asian children have smooth skin and looked younger and pure (O'Grady,1992:55-76; Ruff,1992:35-38). When travelling abroad, the social and legal control of ones' own country was removed and foreign laws did not especially forbid sexual exploitation of children, thus those sexually pervert men were further encouraged to play their role of 'Uncle Sam' (*Liao,P.I.,1996*).

Profiles of Prostitution-Involved Children[45]

In this section, information derived from available research findings and case studies will be summarised to help understand the operation of the child prostitution institution in *Taiwan*. There are first some terms used in this book needing special definitions. The subject of concern in this book is the child[46] victim who will generally be referred to as 'prostitution-involved children\girls' instead of 'child\girl prostitutes' as are generally referred to in Chinese literature.[47] Although the involved children are predominantly the female ones, the word 'child' or 'children' is preferred to girl\girls[48] to emphasise the theme of this book that they should be protected as all other abused and exploited children, and their social label as prostitutes and delinquents should be removed. The perpetrators may include parent figures,[49] other procurers, perpetrators of sex industry,[50] and customers.[51] The term 'child prostitution'[52] is employed to denote the social practice of involvement of children under 18 in the prostitution industry, the operation of which has been increasingly lucrative owing to as well as resulting in direct and indirect patronage of politically, economically, and socially powerful people.

My discussions will commence with the illegal but socially binding sales contract made between parent figure(s) and procurer(s) which results in committing a female child[53] (the child) to sex-related business. Knowledge of the consequences of this contract -- prostitution -- by the parent figure(s) or the child herself is not essential; instead, ignorance, negligence, or recklessness may be present. Force or coercion is not necessarily involved; in fact, although consent of the child may facilitate the agreement-making, absence of this consent would not impede the final decision-making or its fulfilment. On the other hand, the immediate or subsequent financial benefits generated from this body contract are under the disposal of involved perpetrators, though the child may be given a nominal share.[54] After the deal is made, the child will be taken directly or indirectly into prostitution, in which customers pay the operators in exchange for her sexual services.[55]

Beneficiaries of the Exploitation

Those who benefit from child prostitution may include the exploitative parents, the procurers,[56] the traffickers (the brokers), the pimps, the brothel-keepers, and the customers. Their roles may overlap in some cases. Newspapers and magazines are notorious for profiting from the advertisements of prostitution recruitment under the disguise of 'well-paid non-skilled jobs' (*Chi,H.J.,1995c,1996c; TWRF,1995a*). It is also well known that corrupt government officials, especially the police, are willing to turn a blind eye towards the practice of child prostitution. Besides, local politicians and well-off businessmen are very often the underground bosses of special entertainment establishments (De Leon,1991:88)(*Chi,H.J.,1996f*).

The government may also benefit indirectly when the country is fully promoting its economic development by tolerating selling the physical beauty of the country while ignoring or acquiescing in the nexus of tourism and child prostitution (S.Srisang,1991:38; Muntarbhorn,1991:69, Suresh,1991:65). In *Taiwan*, it is pointed out that all those who benefit from the deal have now formed a strong network for exploiting powerless children (*Chen,YingChen,1992; Chu,H.Y,1992; Hu,S.H.,1996; Pan,W.K., 1992*).

Paths to Flesh Markets

There are direct and indirect routes for children to enter the flesh market. On the one hand, a child may be sold by parent figures or others into brothels and the like, or she herself may make her own a deal with a pimp. If a child is considered too young to start working, she will be put under 'apprenticeship' during which she is taught various skills to please customers as well as receives injections to build up her body. Moreover, in order to control the children and make them profit-making machines, the pimp or the brothel-keeper will use all sorts of measures, involving force or inducements, to reform the mentality of the children.

On the other hand, a child may gradually fall into prostitution. A stereotype case history given by social workers in *Taiwan* is:

> 'It is difficult to say who sold her into prostitution, or whether she was sold/forced[57] at all. Very often the parents signed a contract for the child to work in the city for good money. She might start being a waitress in a bar, later the boss would offer her an extra job of serving male customers wine and spirit; once she became popular, the boss might arrange for her

to reserve exclusive service for specific customers and drink with them; then on a special occasion, she might be encouraged by the boss and agree to go out with a rich customer after work, and finally end up in bed whether with or without her consent. Once 'the first time' took place, the second time and many times afterwards followed, then she became one of them (girl prostitutes). As time went by, she started to gain experiences at all sorts of sex-related service establishments. Many such girls, after obtaining enough experience, also act as procurers, pimps or brothel-keepers themselves.'[58]

Body Contracts

The contracts for bodies may be for life or for a specified period of time. There is considerable disparity in cost. The price of a virgin sold for life will be at the top of the list. It may range from N.T.$400,000 to N.T.$1,000,000[59] depending on the beauty and age of the children. For those who are contracted on an annual basis, the prices range from N.T.$100,000 to N.T.$400,000. If a children has lost her virginity before being sold, the price may tumble dramatically. The main reason is that virgin sex has a very high market value in *Taiwan*. The generally agreed bottom line for the first night of prostitution was N.T.$10,000, and for a virgin, the price may go up three to five times. When there is a scarcity of supply, a determined rich man may be willing to pay ten times the said price for a virgin night.

The sale contract is not legally enforceable, but it is socially executed in the institutionalised exploitation chain of the prostitution industry (*Pan, W.K., 1992:1-2*). Once a body contract is made, force by all means -- fraud, thread, coercion -- is employed to ensure the procurement of a body as specified in the deal. Therefore, when the sold daughter escapes or she is rescued, another daughter may have to be taken to fill the vacancy or the parent contractor(s)' lives will be threatened. But no matter whether the vacancy can be filled by another daughter of the family or not, the first escaped/rescued one may still be taken back once she is found or when she is no longer under legal protection.[60]

Brothels and Special Entertainment Establishments

Apart from being accommodated in licensed or unlicensed brothels, prostitution-involved children can also be found through/in the following variety of special entertainment establishments (*Chen,M.L.,1996; Huang,Y.C.,,1991a; Li,C.W.,1995; Wang & Wang,1992*):

1. Girlie restaurants (the Chinese version of Japanese geisha houses), special houses;
2. Call girl stations, tour guide centres, or other escort services;
3. Hotels, motels, hostels, bungalows, guest houses;
4. Massage parlours, barber shops, sauna saloons;
5. Night clubs, dancing halls, discotheques, or other leisure centres such as KTV and MTV shops;
6. Restaurants, coffee shops, tea houses, cocktail lounges, pubs, and all kinds of bars.

It should be reminded that the above are only those which were mentioned in past studies in *Taiwan*. As a matter of fact, it is possible to locate prostitution-involved children in all sorts of new entertainment settings and leisure centres (*Chen,C.M.,1995; Chu,H.Y.,1992*; *Ho,C.W.,1992*; *Huang,Y.C.,1991ab; Wang,Y.H.,1996b*).

Means of Pimp/Brothel Control over Children

Pimps/brothel-keepers used to reform and control girls with physical punishment and threats to the lives of their parents and families. However, 'modern' pimps/brothel-keepers have learnt less coercive tricks to soothe the tension between the exploiter and the exploited. According to a considerable number of children interviewed by professionals, pimps and brothel-keepers make them feel at home. More care and affection are given in brothels than in their own families. Apart from emotional support, the girls also enjoy luxurious lives (*Liu,1976a; Shen,1989; Wang & Wang,1992*).

Most pimps/brothel-keepers allow intimate association among girls under their control. Beside the company of peer friends, many girls are also given handsome 'boyfriends' and 'bodyguards' who are actually bouncers employed by the pimp/brothel-keeper. These young gangsters accompany the girls whenever they leave the brothel and/or work out. The young couples normally dress very well and travel around by taxi. Their expenses are deducted from the money the children can earn for themselves. As a result, the girls are always in debt to the pimp/brothel-keeper.

Another reason that may cause the endless indebtedness of the girls is drugs. Girls are often given drugs and many become drug addicts. Besides, if a girl is infected with sexually transmitted diseases or gets pregnant, she has to suffer a loss of income, and she will have to borrow from the pimp/brothel-keeper to cover the costs of medical treatment and abortion. Some pimps/brothel-keepers even require the children to pay for their losses during her absence from work.

For a child who has joined the flesh market without telling her family (that is those who work on a part-time basis), the pimp/brothel-keeper may threaten to disclose her situation to the family, the school, or the boyfriend if she has one.

Consequently, many 'forced' ones become 'voluntary' sooner or later. When taken to the police, many children are unwilling to reveal the fact that they were forcibly sold into prostitution. As a matter of fact, many children told the social workers that they were very well treated in the brothels. Some even regarded the brothel as a 'loving family' and the bouncers as 'nice and generous boyfriends'. Many of them thus refuse to give evidence against the pimps/brothel-keepers and the bouncers.[61]

Deals Per Day and Profits Made

Recent figures showed that call girls went out to meet customers on an average of 10 to 20 times every day. Those who worked in a brothel had to receive on average 20 to 30 customers per day. The highest number ever reported was 89 per day (*Shee,1992:9*). A call-girl was paid more than N.T.$1,000 every time, out of which she may get a one-third to one-half share. Customers visiting brothels had to pay N.T.$400 to N.T.$500 for every 'period' -- 15 minutes, from which the girl could share from N.T.$10 to half of the total payment. Virgin sex would cost a lot more as mentioned above. Street children[62] who served the needs of old men were said to have been paid NT$300 to NT$800 depending on the customers (*Chou,J.T.,1996a; Chiou,Y.C.,1995*).

Case studies have never estimated the respective earnings of the children, their families and the operators involved in various sorts of child prostitution. But it is a tenable conclusion that the profit made therein is much bigger than all other legal business so as to involve not only mobsters, but also local politicians and police officers (*Pan,W.K.,1992:2*; *Wang,I.,1992:45*).

Effects of Prostitution on Children

What comes to mind immediately and readily is that prostitution is psychologically detrimental to the children. The children involved in prostitution are traumatised for life (Coombs,1974; Muntarbhorn,1991:69-70). In the short term, they suffer from the fear of disclosure, of further violation, fear of being blamed and for complicity, anger at being violated and abused and loss of family love and caring. Escape is found through retreating into drugs, through denial and through silence (De Leon,1991:87). Case studies have concluded that humiliating experiences have in the long term pushed the children to a loss of self respect, low self-esteem, sense of self-blame, guilt, shame, psychiatric illness and disturbed behaviour including maltreatment of their own children (Hiew,1992:29). Depression is a constant part of their existence, even to the point of suicide (Chutikul,1991:86). Other research findings suggest the possibility of sexually abused or exploited children descending into alcoholism, psychopath or schizophrenia.[63]

In rehabilitation centres, the psychological and behavioral problems commonly found in prostitution-involved children in *Taiwan* include being suicidal, emotionally unstable, timid, and lack of confidence. They possess low self-esteem and tend to fail in keeping promises. Besides, they always make excuses for their wrong-doings. The worst thing is that the prostitution experience may have altered the value system of a children to the point that psychological rehabilitation is virtually impossible.[64]

These children have physical problems, too. Those who are injected with hormone before puberty became shorter in height compared to normal children. In addition, due to early sexual exposure and contraception, many children have all sorts of gynecological problems. A few of them even underwent unskillful abortion and became barren. Recent reports have posed evidence of the prostitution-involved children's exposure to severe health hazards (Hiew,1992:29)(*Wang,Y.H.,1993a*). Some of them are infected with venereal diseases or other sexually transmitted diseases. Multiple infections lower their immune system to fight off other contagion. Concerned professionals conclude that the brothel has become the probable source of HIV transmission and prostitutes of the youngest age group have the highest risk of contamination (Belton,D.,1992) (*Wang,Y.H.,1993a*).

Apart from suffering from physical disabilities, prostitution-involved children may also face other difficulties as summed up from research findings of concerned professionals (*Chen,H.N.,1992; Chiou,I.N.,1993; Jen,I.A.,1996; Lai,W.C.,1995; Tang,L.C.,1996; Wang,Y.H.,1996ac*):

Difficulties of family reunification If the child, for any reason, leaves the pimp/brothel control before she fulfills the contract made by her family, it is unlikely that the family will open its arms to welcome her, for the family financial situation may be further worsened once she stops working. On the other hand, the family may have to face harassment and threats from the contracting pimp/brothel-keepers and associated gangsters. Many children realise that their return would not do any good to the family, nor to herself, so choose not to return home.

For those girls who had bad parent-child relationship before entering prostitution, family reunification is nearly impossible without appropriate professional assistance.[65] Some parents are ashamed of a prostitution-involved daughter (though they have never been equally ashamed of the money she sent back home) and refuse to take her back. Some girls are considered so promiscuous or incorrigible that the parents prefer to forfeit her custody.

Difficulties of continuing education There are no special education programmes available for the rehabilitated children. Especially when a child suspended her study before completing national compulsory education, as most of the children did, it is understandable that a normal school will give all possible excuses to decline her application for enrolment once their prostitution history becomes known to the school. On the other hand, many children have been absent from school for many years, so it is very hard to find a suitable course or grade for them to continue their study.

Difficulties of 'reincarnation' As mentioned before, it is found by involved professionals that the children in rehabilitation centres possess a twisted value system and living habits which are difficult to correct. They are accustomed to make use of their body and earn easy money. Their lives were once full of excitement and indulgence. They may have been alcoholics or drug abusers. They are mostly unskilled and not well-educated. It is a commonplace frustration of social workers to see a child fall back to prostitution because she can not find a well-paid job as expected or because she finds the new job too boring.

It is also a shared problem among the children that they find it difficult to establish peer relationships with children of the same age. Very often they feel wary and rejected among peer groups. But what is more detrimental is the social estrangement of 'bad' children. Parents do not want their children to mingle with 'bad children'. Teachers are afraid that admissions of these 'promiscuous' or 'delinquent' children may bring reverse influence on other students. A child with a record of 'prostitution' is refused by managers of workplace with the same reasons given to those with criminal records. Moreover, professionals always have a confused feeling towards prostitution-involved children and their families. They urge the illegality and inhumanity of the practice of child prostitution but very often they also blame the wrong people. Generally speaking, society rarely gives support to the maltreated children and their families.

Concluding Remarks

History seems to have secured the prosperity of the child prostitution industry. Within the interminable patriarchal system, the sexuality of 'bad' (in the sense of morality) but 'clean' (in the sense of body) children has been constructed to serve the patriarchal 'entitlement' to exotic desires. Commercial sex is not only to satisfy sexual 'needs' of men but also to improve their strength as a dominant '*yang*'. Consequently, there remains a high demand for young, especially clean virginal, female child in prostitution. Families of low socio-economic strata become vulnerable to the lucrative temptation of selling children into prostitution. The capitalist society of *Taiwan* also nourishes an institutionalised exploitation chain within which the powerful prostitution industry keeps expanding and numerous young children are sold as objects.

The historical analyses of this chapter points out two distinctive traits of child prostitution in *Taiwan*. First, the strength of the prostitution industry to survive and evolve in a different era reveals its strong cultural roots in Chinese society. Filial piety, family ties, moral standards regarding sexuality, patriarchal authority, and even sacrifice of the individual for the family, all helped to sustain this old vice institution, though on the face of it, they were the cornerstones of traditional society. In other words, Chinese culture did not overtly support child prostitution, but it laid down the soil bed for this modernised institution to grow into part of the Taiwanese society.

Second, modernisation introduced by Western capitalism and its institutional designs -- including its economic and legal systems -- did not solve the problem of prostitution, but has instead contributed to its expansion and institutionalisation including that involving child victims and female consumers. Certain groups of people with strong economic motives organised themselves and systematically recruited children to this old industry.

Satirically, they run the industry and protect themselves with a sense of modern law, particularly the contract law: children are sold by their parents (sales contract), customers buy their services from the pimps/brothel-keepers (service contract), and the sold children are regarded as private properties of the brothels (ownership). It does not matter that the state refuses to enforce these contracts as they are *malum in se*. What matters is that the involved people -- the exploiter as well as the exploited -- believe and maintain that these contracts must be honoured and fulfilled. So the industry is 'modernised' as well.

Child prostitution as an institution today is fundamentally caused by the interplay of the old cultural heritage and modern capitalism developed in *Taiwan*. The problem has a distinctive structural context with Chinese traits. It is therefore not something that can be easily removed by transplantation of foreign positive laws or regulatory mechanisms. On the other hand, the modern ROC law in *Taiwan* has functioned with a specific nature created to respond to its unique political, economic and social situations. As a result, ROC law has had limited controls over the practice of child prostitution.

NOTES

[1] This 'structural context' involves the cultural, social, economic, political and legal factors.

[2] This is the Chinese version of the Japanese 'geisha', the Greek 'hetaira', or the French 'cocotte'. See Bullough & Bullough,1987:293.

[3] According to S. Gronewold, '[t]o the Chinese male, men existed as part of the great chain linking home to the state. Just as *yin* had become subordinate to *yang*, women had become appendages to men' (Gronewold,S.,1982:44).

[4] *PEI TOU* (*北投*) was a quiet, elegant resort area near the *Taipei* city famous for its hot springs. The Japanese developed it as a very typical Japanese hot spring resort, where customers were entertained in *tatami* rooms by geisha performers. Emperor *Hirihito* once visited there and *kamikaze* pilots were served there before their suicidal missions during World War II. See Chen,H.H.,1986:126.

[5] It should also be noted that as the 1945 ROC government on *Taiwan* led by *CHEN Yi* was notorious for its brutal rule which actually resulted in the '228 incident' which happened on February 28, 1947, the government was too busy to deal with political rebellions, and of course, the symbolic prostitution prohibition law was easily forgotten.

[6] It is estimated that in the late 1960s, there were approximately 3,000 American soldiers coming to Taiwan for sex pleasure every month. See Liao,B.Y.,1985.

[7] According to a social survey published by the Asian Church Women's Conference (ACWC), during the decades immediately following World War II, 80% of the tourists were

Japanese. It is said that 90% of the Japanese tourists were men and the purpose of their tour to *Taiwan* was mainly for sex pleasure. Besides, official statistics of late 1980s showed that there were around 700,000 Japanese tourists travelling to Taiwan every year which constituted half of *Taiwan*'s foreign-tourist population. More than 80% of them were male, most of who aged between 30 to 59. The period of their staying was usually four days (three nights) or five days (four nights). Most of the tour-agencies interviewed said that these tourists generally spent on average two nights in buying sex pleasure. For details, see Chen,H.H.,1986; Kao,R.,1991:60-61.

[8] E. Durkheim described a similar condition of Western societies in the late 19th century when people were caught up in the rapid changes caused by industrialisation which took place too fast for easy adjustment. The people then were forced out of the stability of the village social system and the support of family, friends, and tradition, forced to cope with new complex urban environments. In this situation the old rules lost their salience, but not enough time had elapsed for new norms and traditions to develop. See Bullough & Bullough,1987:300.

[9] Many social science researchers have attributed the rampage of prostitution in Taiwan to the declining of social moral standing to the extent that people laugh at those who are poor but not those who are prostitutes (*hsiao pin pu hsiao chang* 笑貧不笑娼). See *Cheng & Fan-Chang,1990:7.*

[10] At that time the average monthly income for a *PEI TOU* prostitute was N.T.$30,000, while those who accepted government retraining and joined the normal labour market would receive a wage between N.T.$5,000 to N.T.$6,000 (1 English Sterling Pounds is approximately 40 NT$). As a result, only 15 *PEI TOU* prostitutes accepted government retraining. The others, 500 at least, went underground and most of them flowed into the *CHUNG SHAN North Road* (中山北路) red-light district where more than half of special entertainment establishments (totally 2,500 in number) in the *Taipei* city were located. See Chen,H.H.,1986:126-128.

[11] For the most recent and detailed media reports on male prostitution, see *The United Evenings* on May 22 (p.3) and May 23 (p.5).

[12] Confucianism was established as the official ideology in the early Han Dynasty (202 B.C. - 220 A.D.) and since then Confucianism has been a dominant force of Chinese civilisation. See Chen,F.T.,1946; Chen & Hou,1990; Chiu & Fa,1984:608; Nivison & Wright,1959; Shaw,W.,1981; Yang,C.S.,1988.

[13] See Legge,J. (trans.) -- Sacred Books of the East, Book III: The *Hsiao Ching* (Classic of Filial Piety), p.466, quoted at Lang,O.,1946:10.

[14] Of the 'five most important human relationships' urged by Confucius, three are family relationships: father-son, husband-wife, and elder brother-younger brother, all built on relations of domination and subordination. Last comes friendship, which forms the transition from family life to public life. What is on top of these four relationships is that between the ruler and the official, which crown the successful work of the family and insures peace in the state (Lang,1946:10). The strengthening of the family ties was meant primarily as a means of strengthening the state. When there were contradictions between the family and the state, Confucius and his disciples subordinated the interests of the family to

those of the state. So when the duties of a good son and family member were in conflict with the duties of a good citizen, a man owed his filial piety and royalty first to the state (Lang,O.1946:333).

[15] Although Confucian teachings concentrated on regulating the father-son relationship with the family, Chinese parents gave preference to the children of the sex different from their own. The warmest relations in the family were those not mentioned by Confucius as being the most important: the relations of mother and son and of father and daughter. See Lang,O.,1946:24-31.

[16] However, women of unusual attractiveness and with power did enjoy good treatment and often achieved dominant positions in the family. See Lang,O.,1946:333.

[17] It was urged that infanticide in China, as in Greece, in Rome, and in medieval Europe, was caused not by lack of parental affection but by poverty and starvation. It persisted there longer than in other civilised societies only because China's standard of living lagged behind that of European countries. See Lang,O.,1946:47.

[18] For introduction to the cult of Chinese Confucianism, see Chen & Hou,1990; Cheng,F.T.,1946; Lee & Lai,1984; Nivison & Wright,1959; Shaw,W.,1981; Yang,C.S., 1988.

[19] Even a little lucky girl in a noble family could not escape the torture of widely practised foot-binding. See Lang,1946:45.

[20] And the term '*lian chia fu nu*' still remains in the ROC Criminal Code. See chapter six for relevant discussions.

[21] Among ECPAT talks, poverty is the most readily identified root cause of child prostitution. See Bruce,1991:30; De Leon, et al.,1991:55-56; ICCB,1991:9-10; Kent,1991:74-75; Seneviratne,et al.,1991:48; S.Srisang,1991:42.

[22] See Bullough,1987:297; Hew,1992:29; Klanprasert,1992; and *Chen,H.N.,1992*; *Chen,YiChen,1991*; *Hsu,C.L.,1989*; *Huang,Y.C.,1991a*; *TWRF,1991*; *Tseng & Chun,1987*; *Wu,H.Y.,1990*.

[23] See Bruce,1991:31; Hew,1992:27; ICCB,1992:8-11; Srisang,S.,1991:42-43; The Host Committee,1996: Part I & Part II; De Leon et al.,1991:55-56; de Leon,1991:88; Suresh,1991:65; Walz,1992:18; and *Liau,B.Y.,1985*; *Lin,M.R.,1989*; *Wang,T.S. et al.,1989*; *Yin,C.C. et al.,1993*.

[24] For studies concerning the families involved in child-prostitution, see *Chen,C.,1988*; *Chen,H.N.,1992*; *Chen,C.M.,1995*; *Chen,M.L.,1991a,1996*; *Chen,Y.C.,1991*; *Cheng,Z.H. et al.,1990*; *Chu,H.Y.,1991,1993*; *GOH,1992*; *Hong,W.W.,1991ab,1992,1995*; *Hsieh,K.,1972*; *Hsu,C.L.,1988,1989*; *Huang,Y.C.,1991ab*; *Kao,R.,1991:60*; *Li,C.W.,1995*; *Li,T.C.,1992*; *Li,Y.Y.,1991*; *Liau,B.Y.,1985*; *Liu,Y.M.,1976ab*; *Shee,A.,1992*; *Shen,M.C.,1990:109-114*; *Sun,T.W.,1980*; *Tang,S.P.,et al.,1983*; *TMKTPAI,1990*; *TMSWB,1990*; *TWRF,1990, 1991,1992*; *Tseng,S.M. et al.,1992*; *Wang,I.,1992c*; *Wang,I. et al.,1992*; *Wang,S.R.,1984*; *Wang,T.C. et al.,1989*; *Wu,H.Y.,1990,1991*; *Yin,C.C.,1987,1993*. This section is a summary of these research findings.

[25] According to information provided by researchers (*Wang,S.Z.,1984:60-61*) and concerned professionals (*Shen,M.C.,1990:110*), of the nine major aboriginal tribes in *Taiwan*, the

TAYAL girls are most welcomed and attractive to sex traders because, compared to girls of other tribes, they are considered beautiful and the colour of their skin is fairer.

[26] It was reported that in the *HSIU LIN* County (*秀林鄉*) aboriginal village, 53% of women were sold into prostitution, and many of them chose to stay on even when they were free to go. A field study carried out in *the HUA HSI Street* brothels also showed that aborigines constituted 60% of the prostitutes working therein. See *Shen,M.C.,1990:110-111.*

[27] Sanctions imposed upon offenders of sexual mores include beaten to death, driven out of the family, ostracised for life, sex organs cut off, stripped naked and exposed to public view, the promiscuous couple tied to tree, exposed to the public, the girl banned from taking part in sacred ceremonies, denied right to wear certain items, and door posters of man's home torn down. See Chen,H.H.,1986:132-133.

[28] They are AMI, BUNAN, LUKAI, PAIWAN, PUYMUA, SAISIAT, TAYAL, TOROKO, TSOU, YAMI. Among them TAYAL has the worst record in girl prostitution. AMI, BUNAN, and PAIWAN are also at the top of the list. Nearly no prostitution-involved girls have ever been found from PUYMUA and SAISIAT who are located at much remote areas having little contacts with the HAN Chinese. See TWRF,1991:1, Chen,H.H.,1986:132.

[29] Generally speaking, indigenous peoples in *Taiwan* are very fond of drinking. There is a large number of alcoholics among the aboriginal peoples.

[30] It was stated that if the aboriginal prostitution problem cannot be properly tackled, 'the traditional social structure and ethical norms of aboriginal society will collapse totally'.

[31] These are also the generally recognised characteristics of the aboriginal families.

[32] The ROC social welfare service does not cover all the medical expenses for those who live under the poverty line. When there is a member in such families (especially the breadwinner) needs intensive medical treatment, the families always end up in debts, which they can not repay. Experienced social workers told me that many cases they dealt with before involved such families. According to them, when such families needed urgent money, they went for usury because it was impossible to borrow money from the bank without a mortgage. It was out of the question that they would be able to repay the usury debts unless 'money fell down from the heaven'. Often very soon after the family member had went through the treatment, the lender came for money. These usury lenders were normally accompanied by mobsters who threatened the family with violence. And the family would been paid constant visits until the debts were repaid. Then prostitution of daughters (or in absence of daughters, wives) became the most visible, if not the only, solution.

[33] According to Article 21 of the ROC Constitution and the corresponding national education regulations, every child in Taiwan shall at least receive 9 years' school education including 6 years in the primary school and 3 years in the junior high. Unfortunately, enforcement of the national education has witnessed failures in rural and mountain areas. Concerned professionals generally attribute the aboriginal girl prostitution problem to this failure of the ROC education system. See *Shee,A.,1992:16.*

[34] In *Taiwan*, there are always more girls than boys available for adoption. Adoption of a boy may be time-consuming and it normally costs a lot more money.

[35] She could be unmarried, divorced or widowed.

[36] There is a demand for young girls because men are afraid of contracting sexually transmitted diseases. In order to lessen the chances of infection, many customers will pay a very high price for disease-free, that is, pure virginal, prostitutes. On the other hand, the customary belief in the therapeutic function of virgin sex is still pervasive in contemporary Taiwan. See Bullough & Bullough,1987:266; *ECPAT,1995c,1997ab; Wang,I.,1992:44.*
[37] Men satiated with or not aroused by ordinary sexual activities have looked for variety. With wives who were usually sexually conservative, these variety-seekers found it difficult to satisfy their sexual needs at home and turned to the fee-for-service system of satisfaction. Sometimes wives, even if they had the desire to do so, could not have satisfied their spouses' sexual desires as evidenced by the nineteenth-century taste of many upper-class Englishmen for deflowering young virgins. See Bullough & Bullough,1987:294.
[38] According to the international coordinator of ECPAT R. O'Grady, '[m]ost of the major paedophile organisations operating around the world have become known through court cases. Despite their secrecy, some information can be obtained from police files and from documents of the main paedophile organisations, particularly in the United States. These include: 1. The North American Man/Boy Love Association (NAMBLE): USA; 2. The Rene Guyon Society (RGS): USA; 3. The Lewis Carroll Collector's Guild: USA; 4. The Howard Nichols Society: USA, Western Europe, Australia, Canada, New Zealand and Japan; 5. The Paedophile Information Exchange (PIE): Europe; 6. The Stichting Paidika Foundation: Netherlands; 7. Australian Paedophile Support Group (BLAZE): Australia, USA'. For further information, see O'Grady,1992a:57-61.
[39] According to the Taipei Women Rescue Foundation (TWRF), the youngest prostitution-involved girl they had counselled till January 1996 was 8 years old (TWRF, 1996); while the *Hua-Lien* Good Shepherd Sisters Centre reported that the youngest victim treated in their centre aged only 7 and half. See *The China Times* on January 25, 1996.
[40] It was reported recently that some runaway boys were found to be soliciting in the most noisy shopping areas in *Taipei*. Their customers were mostly 'middle-aged and old men'. See relevant reports in *The China Evenings* on May 20, 1992; *The Liberty Times* on May 21, 1992; *The United Daily* on July 15, 1996; *The United Evenings* on May22, 1997.
[41] The following description is based on the findings provided in ACWC,1985; ECPAT,1992; ECTWT,1991; ICCB,1992; O'Grady,1992:55-77; Chen,H.H.,1986:127-130; *ECPAT,1994,1995de; Hsiao,H.C.,1996; Kang & Shee, 1995; Li,L.F.,1996a; Shee,A., 1995;Wang,I.,992:43-44; Wei,H.C.,1996; Yeh,T.H.,1996.*
[42] The statistics released from the research findings are as follows: 1. Number of Japanese visitors to Taiwan 1984: 636,744; 2. Purpose of trip: 87.7% listed 'tourism'; 3. Sex ratio: Male 81.18% (in 1979 it was 94%); 4. Profession: businessmen, salesmen, office workers 70%; 5. Age: 30-39 -- 23.75; 40-49 -- 27.5%; 50-59 -- 22.0%; 6. Length of stay: 4 days/3 nights 42.9%; 5 days/4 nights 16.2%; 7. Came directly from Japan: 89.2%; 8. Returned directly to Japan: 92.6%. The researchers were told during interviews with travel agents that most Japanese tourists preferred a standard 4 days/3 nights package tour. The majority of the package tours allowed the tourists to spend two nights in sexual activity. The most common format was for the travel agent to bus the group to a club or a cabaret, where they enjoyed a few drinks and picked out their escort girls, for which they paid a fee of at least

30,000 Japanese Yen (about US$125). They then left for a day of sightseeing. About 11 at night the girl they picked came to join them at the hotel. The fee paid was split three ways, among the travel agent, the club owner, and the girl. See Chen,H.H.,1986.

[43] This was defined in the research as 'the officially authorised red-light districts'.

[44] Now the notorious AIDS problem in Thailand has become a fatal retardation to girl-sex pursuers. Besides, the Philippines has passed a special law against child sexual exploitation in prostitution on June 17, 1992 (Philippine Republic Act No 7610. It is predictable that many paedophiles are going to be (or have been) discouraged from visiting the two countries. And if special measures are not taken to safeguard Taiwan, it is feared that Taiwan will soon become a popular destination for Western sex tourists. See ECPAT Newsletter, No.9 (special edition), p.6 for the new Philippine law.

[45] This section will be a summary of the research findings of the following studies on prostitution-involved children (mainly girls): ACWC,1986:73-76; Kao,R.,1991:61-62; Wang,C.F.,1988:1; *and Chen,C.,1988; Chen,C.M.,1995; Chen,C.T.,1996; Chen,H.N.,1992; Chen,M.L.,1991a,1995,1996; Chen,Y.C.,1991; Chen & Cheng,1994; Cheng,I.S.,1993; Cheng,Z.H.,et al.,1990; Chi,H.J.,1996eg; Ching,W.,1992; Chiou, C.J.,1996; Chiou,Y.C., 1995; Chou,J.T.,1996a; Chu,H.Y.,1991,1993; GOH,1992,1996b; Hong,W.W.,1991ab,1992; Hsieh,K.,1972; Hsu,C.L.,1988,1989; Hong,W.H.,1995; Huang,S.L.,1995; Huang,Y.C., 1991ab; Li,C.W.,1995; Li,T.C.,1992; Li,Y.Y.,1991; Liau,B.Y.,1985; Liu,Y.M.,1976ab; Shen,M.C.,1990:59-66; Shee,A.,1991:9,1992; Sun,T.W.,1980; Tang,S.P.,et al.,1983; TMKTPAI,1990; TMSWB,1990; TWRF,1990,1991,1992,1994a,1996; Tseng,S.M.et al.,1992; Wang,I.,1992c; Wang,I.et al.,1992; Wang,S.R.,1984; Wang,T.C.et al.,1989; Wang,Y.H., 1992,1996b; Wu,H.Y.,1990:5-14,1991; Yin,C.C.,1987,1993; Yin,C.C.et al.,1993.*

[46] The United Nations Convention on the Rights of the Child accepts 18 years as the threshold of adulthood. The international Labour Organisation (ILO) with its concern for labour laws including child-labour says that the minimum age for work should be 15 years (reducible to 14 years in some situations). Several NGOs including the International Campaign to End Child Prostitution in Asian Tourism (ECPAT) describes a child as under the age of 16 years. The age when childhood ends varies from one culture to another (O'Grady,1992a:143). Legal definitions of 'children' follow different lines depending on purposes of the law. According the ROC Civil Code, the age of majority is 20 and all minor children are subjected to the care of their legal guardians (generally the parents). In other laws, the lines are drawn at 12 for child welfare laws, between 12 and 18 for juvenile welfare and delinquency laws, at 14 for criminal responsibility, at 15 for national education and child labour laws, at 16 for the age of consent, and at 18 or 20 for prostitution license. This thesis does not intend to define a 'child' by a certain age. Instead, the definition a 'child' depends on the specific law discussed, as the aim of this thesis is to show the failures of various ROC laws in the protection of children.

[47] There has been a debate over the use of the term 'child prostitutes' or 'girl prostitutes'. Since in most human societies prostitution is socially degraded and in many countries it is not legal, the use of the term(s) may identify the child with the 'violator' or 'criminal' instead of the 'victim'. The recent International Campaign to End Child Prostitution in Asian Tourism (ECPAT) suggested that the term 'prostituted child' or 'prostituted girl' would be

more accurate (O'Grady,1992a:143). In this thesis, I choose to employ a more objective term 'prostitution-involved children' used by M.J.Seng in his empirical study of the causal relationship between child sexual abuse and adolescent prostitution (Seng,1989:666). Thus, minor girls in prostitution who had the experience of being sold by parent figures will be generally referred to as 'prostitution-involved girl(s)' or simply as 'the girls'.

48 However, the child is referred as 'she' in order to coincide with the fact. Besides, the word girl\girls will occasionally used for the convenience of expression.

49 The term 'parent figure' is preferred in referring to the family perpetrators involved in sold-daughter-prostitution to 'parents' or 'the family', which are generally used in relevant literature. A 'parent figure' denotes a person who is in control (absolutely or partially) of family decision-making concerning the disposition of female children. As shown in social work cases, the involved parent figure in a body contract can be a grandparent, an aunt, or (very occasionally) an elder sibling, so the term 'parents' is considered too narrow. On the other hand, although the daughters are sold out from the family by some family member(s), the body contract is often made without the knowledge or consent of certain family members. The description that 'children are sold by the family' may imply conspiracy of the sale by the family as a whole, which disregards the fact that the power of decision-making within a family is not equally shared even among adult members. Further, as will be discussed in chapter two, references to the exploitative family are not based on a unified concept of 'the family'. Thus 'parent figure' is adopted as it is more encompassing than 'the parents' and more specific than 'the family'.

50 The brothel-keepers include owners of sex-related special entertainment establishments, and their abettors.

51 The customers are the consumers of commercial sex who especially go for girl prostitution, or who just do not care how young their sexual objects are.

52 The word 'daughter' is used instead of 'girls' or 'minor children' to distinguish and emphasise the status of the sold girl in the family and the involvement of a parent figure in the sale.

53 All cases studied in *Taiwan* so far involved only female children.

54 A lump sum of cash is normally paid to the involved parent figure when the daughter is taken away, and the daughter may, though not often, get a nominal share of the money if she has been cooperative. This principle also works in prostitution. When the girl is performing sexual services as required, she is awarded a proportion of the operator's income derived from her service, starting from one-fortieth to two-fifths of what is paid by the customer depending on the relative status of the girl in the establishment.

55 If the girl is considered too young or too ignorant when sold, she may have to undergo an apprenticeship period during which all possible means (injection, rape, moral transformation, etc.) are employed to make her promiscuous and attractive. The girl may be put in some indecent jobs first, moved from one to another, and finally led into prostitution, during which the control over her sex service may have been transferred from one operator to another.

56 According to case studies, the procurers include the parent(s), other family members, [illegible] friends, divorced parents' cohabitees, relatives, local gentry, school teachers or head

masters, neighbours, boyfriends, classmates, bosses, colleagues or customers at workplace, rapists or other strangers.

[57] The ROC laws, the rehabilitation system, as well as field practitioners, all classify prostitution-involved girls into the 'forced' and the 'voluntary'. Although many concerned professionals have been strongly protesting against the classification, it is generally agreed that for the convenience of reference and for the sake of designing rehabilitation programmes, the classification should remain for practical purposes. Thus, the word 'voluntary' is used loosely in this chapter.

[58] This is a composite account based on four collective interviews with social workers of the Garden of Hope Foundation (GOH) on May 5, 1992, and April 25, 1997; the Taipei Women Rescue Foundation (TWRF) on May 6, 1992; and the End Child Prostitution Association on May 5, 1997.

[59] The exchange rate of NT$: English Sterling Pound is approximately 1:40.

[60] Under current juvenile delinquency laws, a rescued child may be kept under legal protection for at most two years in rehabilitation centres. After that, no follow-up service is provided and it is observed that the majority of the girls will fall back to prostitution either voluntarily or reluctantly. In practice, a critical proportion of rescued girls were not committed to rehabilitation centres and it was commonly expected that they would be taken back to meet the body contracts.

[61] The information in this section was obtained during my interviews with social workers in *Taiwan*. See Shee,A.,1994:Appendix X for the names of social workers interviewed.

[62] Recently a new form of child prostitution involving boys appeared among street children. According to newspapers such as *The China Evenings* on May 20, 1992 and *The Liberty Times* on May 21, 1992, these children normally gathered under the *Taipei* Grand Bridge (*tai pei ta chiao* 台北大橋) to wait for customers. See also *Chou,J.T.,1996a; Chiou,Y.C.,1995*; *Shee,A.,1992:21-22* .

[63] Researchers warned that the early sex experiences of boys might impede their normal sexual development and make them grow up becoming paedophiles themselves. (O'Grady,1992a:64) A study on male prostitution also found an association between prostitution and early homosexual seduction followed by a reward (Coombs,1974).

[64] Social workers in *Taiwan* generally attribute failures of rehabilitation to the 'fact' that the experiences in prostitution have transformed the value system and moral standards of a girl. In their interviews with girls in rehabilitation centres, they found a high proportion of girls taking prostitution as a visible living style. See *Chen,H.N.,1992*; *Wang & Wang,1992*.

[65] In fact, social workers in *Taiwan* have been very reluctant to work towards family reunification, which is generally considered more detrimental to the girls than helpful.

4 DISCOVERY OF AND REACTIONS TO THE SOCIAL PROBLEM

As shown in the previous chapter, the existence of child prostitution can be traced back to early Chinese history, and the Han culture has tolerated or even safeguarded its practice (*Hsieh,K.,1972:151-152*; *Shen,M.C.,1989: 50-52*). When *Taiwan* was linked to Chinese history, this Han culture was also implanted on the island, first to the Han-origin Plain inhabitants (Chen,H.H.,1986:126), and then to the Mountain aborigines eroding their traditional norms and values (Anti-Slavery,1997:29-48; Lin,Y.M-J,1989:37; Stainton,M.,1989c:46).

Although there was no lack of 'awareness' of this practice, child prostitution was not 'discovered' as a social problem which led to a 'moral panic'[1] until the late 1980s. People with diverse expertise and responsibilities defined and recognised involved problems and decided how the problems should be tackled. Academics, welfare professionals, activists, media reporters, police officers, administrative authorities, legislators, and the others, each made use of their power of doing 'something'. Their construction of the problem is based on their individual or group values as to what constitute healthy children, good women, caring family and decent society, and confront it for different purposes.

The main aim of this chapter is to describe the process of professional and governmental awareness and recognition of problems pertaining to child prostitution and their responses in confronting the resulting moral panic. The first section reviews available figures and statistics relating to the concerned problems in order to show the changing nature of the prostitution industry and the role of child prostitution in it. It will then be demonstrated how the phenomenon has come to be discovered and recognised as a social problem, and how different groups of people with direct or indirect decision-making powers have spoken for the 'truth'[2] of the problem and responded to it in diverse discourses before and after the making of a specific law to deal with child prostitution.

Evolving Nature of the Problem

In *Taiwan*, child prostitution denotes an social epidemic of evolving nature. It was first a 'girl prostitution problem (*chu chi wen ti* 雛妓問題)' which has been dealt with as an issue of under-age female prostitution. Recently, as the international campaign against the sexual exploitation of children in Asian tourism discovered the fact that young boys were also involved in prostitution, the media was motivated to search for 'evidence' in Taiwan. Some isolated cases involving boy prostitution have been reported as a result, thus certain concerned NGOs started to use the term 'child prostitution problem (*tung chi wen ti* 童妓問題) which included boys as possible victims. During the evolution of the problem, the 'moral panic' on the sexual exploitation of children has been gradually submerged by new concerns over the degenerate middle-class young girls, the wandering boy prostitutes, and the deteriorating lust problem in an economically prosperous society. This section illustrates such information with figures and statistics. It also shows the extent to which professionals and government authorities tried to construct the problem by employing or dismissing all sorts of figures.

It should be noted that although various statistics and figures are available for reference, most of them appear controversial. On the other hand, no systematic research has yet been conducted concerning boy prostitution. Past research findings have been conducted on the basis of various definitions of 'girl prostitution' regarding the age of the girl (under 16, 18 or 20), and forms of prostitution with a line drawn between 'forced' and 'voluntary'. Contentious as they may seem, a review of these statistics and figures is crucial in demonstrating how the problem has been depicted, recognised, and responded to.

Aboriginal Involvement

The initial focus of concern was on the inhuman sexual exploitation of disadvantaged aboriginal women and children.[3] The first organised social campaign was based on findings of an extensive survey conducted by the Rainbow Project (RP) beginning in October 1985 at *the HUA HSI Street*, the most well-known red-light district in *Taipei* (O'Grady,1992b:139[4]). Male researchers from the RP disguised themselves as customers and visited all the brothels known to them during September and October, 1985. As a result, 300 licensed and 800 illegal prostitutes were located. 63 % of the illegal ones were under the age of 18 and almost all of them were originally sold from aboriginal tribes and villages (Chen,H.H.,1986).[5]

Since then, research findings on the topic have constantly reported a remarkably high percentage of indigenous prostitution population of something between 20% and 60% depending on samples taken (*Chen,M.L.,1996; Chen,Y.C.,1990:7; Chu,H.Y.,1993; Hung,S.L.,1995; Hong,W.H.,1995; Li,C.W.,1995; Shen,M.C.,1990:110; Wang & Wang, 1992:21; Wang,S.R.,1984:31*). In view of the fact that the aboriginal population constitutes less than 2%[6] of the total inhabitants on *Taiwan* island, even 20% is a disturbing figure which deserves special attention. However, these figures alone were not enough to bring about a widely shared public concern in society without the media reports of the stylised and stereotyped miserable lives of the suicidal prostitution-involved children (*Tseng & Chun,1987:57-69*).

Debates Over Girl Prostitution Population

As early as in 1980, the Asian Women's Liberation released a research finding that there were 220,000 prostitutes in *Taiwan* which constituted 2.1% of the existing female population. Of this number, 40% (880,000) were claimed to be female children (girls) under the age of 18[7], most of them were aged between 12 and 17.[8] These are the earliest available figures concerning child prostitution in *Taiwan*, and were often quoted in later commentaries on the subject (*Chen,C.,1988:23*; *Ho,C.W.,1988:2*). However, the numbers did not attract public notice until 1992 when its accountability was doubted.

Police raiding brothels have routinely reported 50% to 100% of the rescued girls\women being under the age of 16 (Wang,C.F.,1990:4) (*Wang,C.F.,1992:6*).[9] A social survey conducted in 1987 by the Women Awakening Foundation indicated that there were approximately 70,000 to 100,000 prostitution-involved girls under 18 in *Taiwan.*[10] Other concerned professionals estimated a number of underage prostitutes (under 16) at something between 30,000 to 50,000.[11] At that time, these figures were cited by attending professionals and legislators in consultation meetings in order to call for social concerns, governmental measures and legislation.[12] Since then, the number of '100,000' has been loosely quoted to make criticism on the girl prostitution problem in *Taiwan* (*Chen,C.,1988:22*; *O'Grady,1992:139*; *Shee,A.,1992:9*; *Wang,C.F.,1988:2*; *Wang,C.F.,1992:6*; *Wang & Wang,1992:1*). Actually, before these figures were widely criticised to be excessive, many referred to the number '100,000' as a moderate estimation on the lower side.[13]

The most recent and carefully assessed figures were published by the Garden of Hope Foundation (GOH) in June, 1992 (*Wang & Wang, 1992*). The researchers first completed a list of legal and illegal special entertainment establishments nationwide according to official classifications, then interviewed 109 girls (aged between 13 and 18) in major rehabilitation centres. According to the past experiences of the interviewed girls, the researchers counted the average number of prostitution-involved girls in each special entertainment establishment. Multiplying the estimated number of girls under the age of 18 by the number of those listed establishments results in a figure of 72,000.[14]

When the figures of 100,000, 88,000 and 72,000 were announced in the ECPAT(Taiwan)[15] public hearing and the GOH public consultation meeting held in the ROC Legislative Yuan in June 1992,[16] they aroused serious public debates. All sorts of criticism against the abuse of figures, the unreliable sources of information, and the unscientific methodologies used appeared in newspapers[17] to protest against over-estimates of the child prostitution population in *Taiwan.*[18] Words of government officials, local politicians, and eminent researchers were quoted in the newspapers[19] to disqualify the accountability of the released figures.

Of all the authoritative statements, that of the Interior Minister, *Mr WU Po Hsiung*, was the most powerful and conclusive, for he was the most prominent government official who had been advocating and raising funds for campaigns against child prostitution. The word he chose to respond to the figures was 'impossible', because if there were so many 'girl prostitutes', 'how many customers do we need to balance the demand with the supply?'.[20] A female political leader and a member of the *Taipei* Municipal Council, *Ms CHEN Hsueh Fen*, urged that the artificially boosted figures had seriously disgraced Taiwanese women. Her view was shared by an active female ROC legislator, *Ms HONG Hsiu Chu*, who condemned the exaggerated figures for leading to the social humiliation of the great majority of 'pure and innocent girls' who were not prostitutes.

The Head of the Department of Sociology of the National Taiwan University, *Professor CHAN Huo Cheng*, was sceptical about the figures on the ground that 'there should not be so many "girl prostitutes" in a healthy society'. He maintained, with his expertise in sociology, that the social values in *Taiwan* had not been distorted to the extent that 100,000 customers frequented girl prostitution every day.[21] A leading researcher in prostitution problems, *Dr. HO Chung Wen*, cautioned that the report of such high figures may bring about more 'curious' customers and increase the demand for youth flesh.

In short, the figures of 72,000, 88,000 and 100,000 were rejected as they were 'unscientific', 'exaggerated' and 'sensational'. They were criticised as having 'aggravated social discrimination against women', 'misled social recognition towards a problem at the expenses of the dignity of a predominant majority of innocent girls' and 'degraded the international image of *Taiwan*'. The governmental and professional 'authorities' quoted in the newspapers all urged that the concerned voluntary organisations should not have 'deliberately' over-estimated the scale of girl prostitution in order to provoke social and governmental concerns.

The credibility of the figure of '100,000' was questioned again when the UNICEF (United Nations Children's Fund) reported in its 1993/94 annual 'Progress of Nations' publication[22] that in *Taiwan* there were 100,000 children in prostitution.[23] The responses of both the government and the concerned NGOs to the UNICEF figure were that 'it is not the fact', although there remained a big gap between the 'right' figures claimed by each side. Government officials urged in media interviews that there were at most 3,000 prostitution-involved children in *Taiwan*.[24] On the other hand, the GOH modified their earlier estimation of 72,000 and claimed that 'there were about 40,000 to 60,000 children working as prostitutes in *Taiwan*'.[25]

In my observation, the wide discrepancy between the government and the NGO figures was caused by two reasons. First, the definition of 'prostitution' is different. The government figure refers to girls in professional prostitution involving sexual intercourse, while NGOs are generally concerned with all children who offer sex-related services (not necessarily sexual intercourse) for money and the kind. So the NGO figure is definitely much higher than the other.

Second, there exists tendencies of the government to dampen and the NGOs to exaggerate the prevalence and seriousness of a social problem. Official statistics show that the police found on average 200 prostitution-involved girls every year.[26] Thus the NGOs' five-digital figures are certainly unacceptable to the government which has been praised and proud of its achievement in modernisation and economic development. The existence of child prostitution on a big scale is definitely a dishonourable fact which is difficult to accept. On the other hand, NGOs are inclined to quote or report appalling figures in order to attract public concern, to pressure the government, and to demand more power for concerned professionals. Nevertheless, since the NGO estimation being widely questioned and the number of 100,000 being announced by the

UNICEF to embarrass Taiwan, NGOs seem to have given up this 'appalling figure strategy'. Thus, estimations concerning the child(girl) prostitution population has not appeared as a main issue in NGO public announcements ever since.

Changing Nature of the Problem

Age of first involvement is declining According to the Taipei Women Rescue Foundation (TWRF), among the 430 cases coming to their attention between 1987 and March 1991, in 2.1% of the cases, the first prostitution experience took place before 12, 12.8% between 12 and 14, 22.2% between 14 and 16, 3.3% between 16 and 18, 22.8% unknown, a total of 77% fell into prostitution before the age of 18, the youngest being 8. And the average first-involvement age declined from 15.5 in 1987 to 13.7 in 1991 (rough estimation).[27] Among the 109 girls in major rehabilitation centres interviewed by researchers of the Garden of Hope (GOH) during February 1991 and May 1992, 3.7% first entered prostitution before the age of 12, 24.7% between 12 and 14, 44% between 14 and 16, 25.7% between 16 and 18, 1.8% unknown. Comparing these figures to the TWRF ones taken before March 1991, one can see the first-entry age has been on the decrease.

Number of 'voluntary' and 'well-to-do' children is increasing Recently, social workers and other professionals have noticed gradual diversification of the forms of child involvement in prostitution. It was reported that more and more of those who were sold did not come from a poor family (*Chen,C.M.,1995; Chen,M.L.,1996; Chu,H.Y.,1993; Huang,Y.C.,1991b*): many parents (or parent figures) started to trade their children with procurers and use their earnings to construct a new brick house, buy modern consumer goods, and build family pride on vanity.

Newspapers also reported a group of 'part-time child prostitutes' who are primary and high school students aged between 10 to 17. In 1991, a local council member accused of a 'fact' that there was a problematic class of a private senior high school in *Taichung Hsien (台中縣)* in which among the 40 girl students, more than 20 of them were working as 'part-time' prostitutes earning their pocket money. Some secret informer also pointed out that in order to promote the lucrative girl prostitution business stressing 'pretty, pure (*ching chun* 清純) and young (*yu chih* 幼齒)', some prostitution operators approached the school managers to negotiate 'wholesales' of the student ID cards at the price of N.T.$ 15,000 each.[28] In

1992, after a school teacher in the *Pintung Area (屏東地區)* reported to the Hsing Ling Medical Research Foundation (HLMRF) of her worry that 10 out of 50 student in her class were earning pocket money by offering sexual service,[29] an active female legislator, *Ms YEH Chu Lan*, also openly criticised in the Legislative Yuan of the existence of 'self-organised school girls making collective profits from offering sexual services' (*GOH, 1992:20*).[30]

The number of 'voluntary child prostitutes' is also increasing. According to the aforementioned research findings of *Ms HUANG Sue Ling*,[31] among the child prostitution population, the proportions of children being sold (forced) and those acting out themselves (voluntary) were getting nearer and nearer.[32] Besides, a survey conducted in the governmental rehabilitation centre -- the Taipei Municipal Kuang Tzu Po Ai Institution (KTPAI) also confirmed the findings. According to KTPAI, among the 104 prostitution-involved girls received into the institution between February 1989 and November 1990, not only 64.47% among the girls in care was classified as 'voluntary' (not sold), but 82.89% of them were from well-to-do families (*hsiao kang chia ting 小康家庭*).[33] In the past couple of years, as the voluntary/forced classification of child victims has been widely criticised for it disregarding the 'involuntary' family and social backgrounds of the 'voluntary', statistics of this kind have since not been announced in public, though social workers still express occasionally their regrets and say something like 'there are less and less "forced" children to be rescued and protected'.[34]

There are street and school boys offering sexual services In 1992 when ECAPT(Taiwan) reported through the media on the exploitation of young boys in other Asian countries, a series of newspaper reports on the discovery of prostitution-involved boys in *Taipei* also attracted temporary public concern. Teenage boys were seen soliciting in busy shopping areas, billiard shops and the like (*Shee,A.,1992:19-22*). However, as no social survey was conducted to estimate the scale of this new form of child prostitution and no striking figures or accounts on this problem were made available to the media. Since then, social concerns over these boys faded away despite occasional media reports of individual cases.[35] In 1995, ECPAT (End Child Prostitution Association Taiwan) launched a reaching out programme to help run-away children, one of the aims being to obtain more understanding on the nature and scale of the boy-prostitution problem. However, information collected so far has not been enough for a systematic research (*Chou,J.T.,1996a*). Recently, high school boys have been cautioned by the police for being involved in prostitution as 'cowboys'.

According to media reports, many of these 'part-time boy prostitutes' were from middle-class or well-to-do families and their parents had no knowledge at all as to their 'after-school activities'. Most of these children were found in big cities like *Taipei* and *Kaohsiung* where luxury lives are very much worshipped.[36]

Types of sex-related business settings are multiplied During interviews with girls in the care of rehabilitation centres, researchers also recorded that the types of establishments involving underage sex services have multiplied (*Chen,H.N.,1992; Chen,M.L.,1996; Li,C.W.,1995; Wang & Wang,1992*; *Yin,C.C.,1993*). And their deception techniques for recruiting children from the aforementioned vulnerable groups (indigenous and troubled families) and means of controlling them have become more and more sophisticated. Further, their new disguises under all kinds of entertainment settings can always help make their ways through legal loopholes (*Wang & Wang,1992; Li,C.W.,1995; Li,L.F.,1996b*). It is also widely accepted without surprise or resistance that more and more organised mobsters, policemen, and local politicians are involved in the operation of illegal prostitution in all forms (*Chen,YingChen,1992*; *Chen,M.L.,1991b; Chi, H.J.,1996f; Pan,W.K.,1992; Wang,I.,1992b).*

Discovery and Recognition of the Problems

Introduction

In 1986, a social survey was conducted in *Taiwan* by *Mr CHENG Rey Long* (*CHENG*) under the title of 'Assessment of the Seriousness of Child Abuse' (*Cheng,R.L.,1986*). It was concluded that among the 92 forms of familial child abuse listed by *CHENG* ranging from physical, sexual, emotional abuse to neglect and improper discipline,[37] 'selling daughters into prostitution' was chosen by the surveyed people as the most intolerable parental behaviour and the most serious form of child abuse currently practised in *Taiwan*. However, this awareness of the existence of child prostitution and social loathing towards it did not result in a 'moral panic' until concerned activists initiated large-scale social campaigns in 1987 against the prostitution of young girls sold from families of inferior socio-economic strata -- the aboriginal and/or the destitute (*Tseng & Chun,1987:118*). This first wave of anti-child-prostitution campaigns achieved the recognition of child prostitution as a social problem caused by structural inequality.

Later in the early 1990s, another moral panic erupted as the concerned professionals reported a rapidly growing number of girls, first from the poor, then from all other socio-economic strata, were lured (instead of 'sold') into all sorts of entertainment business ending up in prostitution (*TWRF,1991,1992*). The previous moral panic was directed against the inhuman exploitation ('slavery' in activists' terms) of young children in the flesh trade and the problem was defined as 'traffic in persons and forcing good girls into prostitution (*mai mai jen kou, pi liang wei chang* 買賣人口，逼良爲娼)'. With the newly identified group of 'voluntary girl prostitutes of well-to-do families', the threat became the degenerate youth and their sexual deviance (*Yin,C.C., et al.,1993*). In comparison, the finding of 'boy-prostitutes' does not receive equivalent attention as there have only been isolated cases reported once every couple of years and such a low profile cannot attract collective media or NGO attention.

Helped by a 'Campaign to End Child Prostitution in Taiwan' initiated by concerned NGOs in June 1992, the evil of the paedophile perceived in Western societies became a new focus of media attention and professional attacks.[38] It fuelled the 'discovery' of a group of 'sexually pervert men' among child prostitution customers. However, compared to the earlier discovered threats of sexual exploitation (the operators) or sexual deviance (the children), the sexual perversion of customers seems to arouse a much restricted moral panic shared only among activists.

Thus the main concern in the second wave of anti-child-prostitution campaigns has been the child prostitution problem involving an unbearable number of lured youth not only from the poor, but increasingly from the well-to-do families, and it involves not only girls but also boys. The worries are further intensified by the awareness that prostitution of all kinds is becoming part of organised business settings. The inhuman practice of child prostitution is still under constant attack. However, as will be shown later, efforts in the 1990s are mainly devoted to work on new measures performing new tasks -- first to rehabilitate the sexually delinquent juveniles and to halt the deterioration of the lust problems, and more recently, to develop a protection-oriented and unified system of treatment, to intensify legal responsibilities of government authorities, and to strengthen legal sanctions against all perpetrators.

Main Concerns in the First Wave of Anti-Child-Prostitution Campaigns

In the late 1930s, enthusiastic Christian men and women started to go into the deep uncivilised mountain area to preach and console the aboriginal people who had been deprived of their land and dignity under Japanese colonisation (Stainton,M.,1989c:43-44) (*Hsu & Chu,1992:46-47*). After 1945, *Taiwan* was returned to the Chinese government but since then the mountain peoples have been made 'a disadvantaged ethnic subculture' in the Chinese society of *Taiwan* (Stainton,M.,1989c:44). With great efforts devoted to the care of the social minorities, Christianity spread rapidly, and most of the aboriginal tribes in *Taiwan* became Christian before the 1980s (Lin,Y.M-J,1989:19).

Although development of the aborigines was never a concern of the CH'ING or the Japanese governments, their potential for acting as suppliers of prostitution markets was subjected to exploitation (Kao,R.,1991:60). When the ROC government started to make and enforce aboriginal development plans through tourism promotion in the 1960s, the 'mountain flowers'[39] also became profitable goods to be traded off (Lin,Y.M-J,1989:33). With an established alliance between procurers and the bribed powerful people within tribes, more and more daughters were quietly sold directly or indirectly into the flesh markets (Lin,Y.M-J,1989:20). Local priests heard rumours about it but people refused to disclose any information when making Sunday confessions. Owing to a persistent woman minister, *Ms LIAU Bi Ying*, and her assistants, there finally accumulated enough suspicion that flesh trades on a large scale were taking place among some aboriginal tribes.[40]

As a result, the first non-governmental organisation (NGO) working on the problem of child prostitution, the Rainbow Project (RP), was established in 1986 by the above group of committed Christian activists as they found the practice of child prostitution intolerable (*Kao,R.,1991:61*). Helped by some primitive studies, they established a fact that families of inferior socio-economic strata -- the aboriginal and the destitute -- were prone to sell children into prostitution in the Han-dominated, capitalist Taiwanese society. In order to initiate a campaign against the practice, the RP associated with the Women Awakening Foundation and other interested professionals. Together they launched a large scale demonstration on January 10, 1987 at the most notorious red-light district -- *the HUA HSI Street* (*Tseng & Chun,1987:55*).

In this first wave of social campaigns, the problem under attack was 'traffic in persons and forcing good girls into prostitution'. As the RP was a support group for indigenous people, and their surveys indicated that '40%

of the prostitutes in *the HUA HSI Street* were sold from certain aboriginal tribes, despite the fact that the aboriginal people only constitute 1.72% of the island population'[41] (*Liau,B.Y.,1985* quoted at *Wang & Wang,1992:2*). It was claimed that the problem has resulted from the socio-economic inferiority of the indigenous people resulting from inappropriate state policies for aboriginal development.

The Second Wave of Anti-Child-Prostitution Campaigns

Before 1990, calls for social concern and state intervention were directed at the rescue and treatment of the 'sold' aboriginal girls. However, in the late 1980s, concerned professionals started to detect an increasing number of non-sold girls, though it remained individual suspicion derived from daily experiences (*Chen,M.L.,1991b:10*). On December 19, 1990, a Ph.D. student researching on the social phenomenon of girl prostitution in *Taiwan*, *Ms HUANG Su Ling* (*HUANG*), was invited by the Taipei Women Rescue Foundation (TWRF) to give a speech on her research findings. An analysis of all the cases *HUANG* collected in *Taiwan* during 1990 found that the number of 'voluntary girl prostitutes' had increased dramatically in the past couple of years to the extent that the numbers of 'sold/forced' and 'non-sold/voluntary' were becoming even.[42]

The message conveyed by *HUANG* was immediately accepted among concerned NGOs as a 'fact', as it conformed earlier observations shared among social workers. Worries towards this newly discovered group of 'voluntary girl prostitutes' were intensified by the aforementioned figures[43] released by the Taipei Municipal Kuang Tzu Po Ai Institution (KTPAI), which confirmed that a high proportion of the involved children in rehabilitation had fallen into prostitution 'voluntarily' (not sold). Besides, 'poverty' was no longer the main cause of child prostitution. On the other hand, it was also found that a considerable number of girls did not have negative feelings towards prostitution and earning 'immoral earnings' (*Hsu,C.L.,1988*). It was also estimated by the TWRF that 90% of girls fell back to prostitution after rehabilitation (*Chen,M.L.,1991b*).

In 1991, a branch office of the International Campaign to End Child Prostitution in Asian Tourism (ECPAT International) was established in *Taiwan* under the name of ECPAT-Taiwan. The main function of ECPAT-Taiwan is, as manifested in its title, to campaign against the practice of child prostitution in *Taiwan*. To start the Campaign, a Public Hearing was held on June 9, 1992 and a collection of research materials (*Shee,A.,1992*)[44] was widely distributed to concerned media reporters,

NGOs, individual researchers, law enforcers, legislators, and governmental apparatus. The information given in the materials attracted wide media attention. Helped by the intensive reports in newspapers of the following two weeks, the public was warned of the internationally organised 'Western' paedophiles and informed of the structural conspiracy towards the practice of child prostitution in Asian tourism.[45]

So all of a sudden, it was discovered by journalists that a group of teenage street boys are making their living by offering sexual service to the 'middle or old aged men' with 'pervert sexual orientation'.[46] It was also widely condemned that *Taiwan* is 'exporting' a huge number of customers to contribute to the deteriorating child prostitution problem in some South Asian countries.[47] When asked to comment on the corrupt officials in other Asian countries, the Interior Minister, *Mr WU Po Hsiung*, spoke openly of the bribed police in *Taiwan* by saying that 'everybody knows where to find the girl prostitutes except the police themselves'.[48]

On June 13, 1992, another public consultation meeting was held in the Legislative Yuan by the Garden of Hope Foundation (GOH) entitled 'Consultation on the Prevention and Treatment of Girl Prostitution'. Authorities in the fields of law, sociology and social work, religion, and politics were invited to deliver speeches. Governmental authorities, local politicians, NGO representatives, researchers, and social workers who attended the meeting expressed their concerns with their conceived 'truth'[49] of the problems (*GOH,1992*).

Generally speaking, there were four alleged 'truths' of the child prostitution problem during June 1992 which were constructed through media reports. First, it was a deteriorating social problem involving more and more lured girls and boys from families of all social strata.[50] Second, current rescue and treatment programmes had been ineffective in preventing children from falling back to prostitution.[51] Third, the corrupt policemen/politicians and the incapable officials/social workers were both responsible for the perpetuation and strengthening of the 'prostitution exploitation network'. (*GOH,1992:2,4,11*) And fourth, the customers of child prostitution were sexually pervert and should be subjected to harsh social condemnation and legal punishment. (*GOH,1992:1,9,16,24-25*)

New concerns over the deteriorated child prostitution problems were raised recently when cases involving 'part-time youth cowboys' were reported by the media. The moral panic of concerned NGOs, professionals, and the public has been expressed in all directions by criticisms against the sexually degenerate youth, the indulgence of juveniles in material lives, the worsening lust problem, the dysfunctioning family, the loose education system, and even the consumerism-oriented state economic policy.[52]

Responses to the Social Problem

Introduction

A social problem is a phenomenon which is defined by a considerable number of persons as a deviation from some social norms or values which they cherish; and the phenomenon is alleged to be incompatible with the values of a significant number of people who agree that action is needed to alter the situation (Fuller & Myers, Rubington & Weinberg, quoted at Parton,1985:6-7).[53] The allegation is crucial not only in determining whether and how a phenomenon is defined as a problem but also as to what is seen as appropriate to do about it. And these allegations, when made by the people who have the power or the authority in defining the problem, may result in changes in policy and practice.

Child prostitution in *Taiwan* was discovered as a public problem through allegations made by professional campaigners. Helped by continuous activities reported by the media, the practice aroused governmental and public concerns. Experts of social and legal disciplines were asked for their opinions. With their ability to create and influence the public definition of a problem, these experts 'shaped' the facts in various ways according to their assumptions and values (Gusfield,1975:290[54]). In other words, the facts of social problems are socially constructed, and responses to tackle the recognised problems depend on how they are defined and what are identified as 'deviant' (Parton,1985:9).

On its discovery in 1987, child prostitution was defined as a 'girl prostitution problem (*chu chi wen ti 雛妓問題*)'. The first large-scale social campaign -- *the HUA HSI Street* demonstration -- informed the public of a simple fact: many female children were sold into prostitution and their lives were miserable. The urged solution was straightforward: those girls must be rescued. This urge was met with social consensus and the police authority was pressured to take effective action. So a 'Decent Society Campaign (*cheng feng chuan an 正風專案* ' was initiated and enforced with constant police raids on illegal prostitution. Perpetrators (except the customers) were arrested and punished according to relevant criminal or police offence laws. But the police did not know how to dispose of the rescued children, except to send them to the public rehabilitation centres[55] -- the KTPAI and the YLTTC as they did to other illegal prostitutes.

The Christian women and lawyers who were involved in the campaign started to establish links with police stations, procurators' offices, public rehabilitation centres, and welfare authorities. Several NGOs were established to help in rescue and treatment including the Rainbow Project (RP), the Garden of Hope Foundation (GOH), the Taipei Women Rescue Foundation (TWRF), the Christian Good Shepherd Sisters Centre (CGSS), and later joined by the Catholic Good Shepherd Sisters Foundation (GSS). As a result of activists' efforts, a rescue and treatment network was set up, first in *Taipei* then in other cities. Over the years, this network has been strengthened with more legal power, more governmental and private resources, and more interdisciplinary and inter-agency collaborations.

On the other hand, however, as experiences accumulated and new problems kept arising, the 'girl prostitution problem' became no longer a simple fact of sold-daughters being maltreated in prostitution as presented on its discovery. For the record of the Decent Society Campaign, the police successfully arrested traffickers, procurers, pimps and brothel-keepers, whose ugly villain faces were shown to the public through media reports. Then these perpetrators were disposed of with routine legal procedures for offenders of illegal prostitution. Apart from a heavier workload for the police and the Courts, there were no problems encountered.

However, protection and treatment of the rescued children posed a problem, and more problems followed. These children were 'rescued' because their suffering in the flesh markets was conceived to be worse than slavery. But after the rescue, their accommodation became a problem. This first problem was responded with the designation of special areas in the KTPAI and the YLTTC for the protection and treatment of police-rescued prostitution-involved female children. Also, some private mid-way houses were established to accommodate the girls who escaped from prostitution and came for help.

Treatment in the first couple of years explored other problems. Social workers found that treatment programmes were not effective in correcting the moral and sexual deviance of the children as 90% of them were reported to have fallen back to prostitution. This worry was intensified by other reported figures which showed an increasing number of non-sold (voluntary) prostitution-involved children, among who some actually took part-time prostitution as a viable way of earning pocket money and some others were runaway boys. Concerned professionals have been distraught for developing appropriate and effective rehabilitation programmes for the 'voluntary girl prostitutes'; while on the other hand, it is even more distressing to work on the establishment of a rehabilitation centre for the 'boy prostitutes'. Thus, it is generally recognised that the child prostitution problem has been deteriorating and something more must be done about it. However, in all the 'facts' which define the problems, the systematic maltreatment of children has not yet been clearly articulated. Neither is victimisation of children at the centre of socio-legal concerns.

Responses Before the Making of A Specific Law

Police reactions to social campaigns The *HUA HSI Street* demonstration against the practice of child prostitution led by the Rainbow Project resulted in extensive media concerns. Many case histories were published under false names (*Chen,YiChen,1989*). All of a sudden, demands for governmental measures sprang up from every corner of society. In response, the National Police Administration launched a 'Decent Society Campaign (*cheng fong chuan an* 正風專案) ' on March 1, 1987, vigorously cracking down on flesh traders and prostitution-involved girls under the age of 16 (*Wang,C.F.,1990:3*).[56] A considerable number of procurers and brothel-keepers were arrested and prosecuted.[57] The immediate governmental actions and the effectiveness of the Campaign in the following months were applauded by the public and concerned professionals.

The police were assigned to play the hero in the 'Decent Society Campaign'. Under the Campaign, the police authorities located 574 prostitution-involved girls, 842 procurers, and 18,572 brothel-keepers, pimps, and their abettors during the first 10 months (March to December 1987). In the following years, however, the number of cases in the Police records fell gradually. During the year of 1988, the number of found prostitution-involved-girls dropped to 210. In 1989, 159 girls were located. And the numbers further fell to 145 in 1990 and finally to 89 in 1991 despite the efforts of a newly organised Rescue Team.[58]

In the next years, the police were often embarrassed with their 'dropping numbers' (*Huang,Y.C.,1991a*, quoted at *Shee,1992:17*). In order to improve the ineffectiveness of the Decent Society Campaign, a 'Juvenile Prostitutes Rescue Team' was recruited in July 1990 under the supervision of 'The *Taipei* Police Squad for Juvenile Cases'.[59] In the first several months, the number of arrested prostitution-involved girls was significantly increased. However, as time went by, the number tumbled again (*Huang,Y.C.,1991a:20-23*; *Li,M.C.,1992:1*). Consequently, the total number of located prostitution-involved girls (under the age of 16) under the Campaign from 1987 to 1991 (nearly 5 years) was only 1,177.[60]

Over the years, police corruption has been accused of contributing to the deterioration of child prostitution problems, and more and more social pressure is accumulated to require a reform in the police force.[61] The

Central Police Administration finally announced an internal 'Regulation Governing the Police Merits and Demerits in Relation to the management of Girl Prostitution Cases' in April 1993. This Regulation has tightened around the police themselves by giving strong incentives to raid on illegal prostitution in the jurisdiction areas of other police stations. If a prostitution-involved child is found in area 'X' by a police of another jurisdiction area 'Y', then all policemen of the 'X' station will be recorded a demerit, whilst the 'Y' police will be recorded a merit.[62]

The Regulation itself received considerable resentment in the police force and it was not widely welcomed by concerned professionals nor the public. Most policemen would not intervene into the affairs of other jurisdiction areas to give their colleagues hard time. Experienced professionals urged that the structural corruption in the police force was historical and a reform project as to what the Regulation proposed could only cause splits among policemen, and it could be expected that very soon, all would learn to cover up for their colleagues instead of making an embarrassing image of 'the police' in public.[63]

In order to fight against the unreasonable and impractical Regulation, the police for the first time attacked other structural problems through the media. All of a sudden, representatives of the police force started to quote other authorities and talk about the need to tackle child prostitution from its structural causes: erosion of traditional ethics, social tolerance, family breakdown, economic inequality, commercialism, and so on.[64] They also urged the 'truth' that the present police force is not powerful enough to encounter the institutionalised prostitution industry which had been managed as an enterprise with the most modern techniques and technologies. Moreover, they alleged that the job of the police was no longer to rescue the sold helpless children, to enlighten the ignorant aboriginal parents, or to prosecute individual operators -- the problems were bigger than what the police could handle -- the degenerate and promiscuous youth, the irresponsible families and parents, the pervert customers, and the well-guarded prostitution industry.[65] This reflection from the police has been welcomed by concerned NGOs and often quoted in their activities. During the legislative lobbying for the Law to Suppress Sexual Transactions Involving Children and Juveniles, the police definition of the 'truth' of the problem was transformed into powerful arguments not only for the imposition of heavy punishment on all child prostitution perpetrators, but also for the provision of prevention programmes of moral education for society, families and their children (*Chi.H.J.,1996f; GOH,1996c; Lin,Y.S.,1993abc*).

Governmental involvement in prevention and treatment programmes In contrast to the active involvement of NGOs in the responses to child prostitution, the welfare authorities reacted passively at the supervision level (*Pai,H.H.,1973:6, 1992:40-41*). In principle, 'sexual exploitation of children in prostitution' is included in the official definition of 'child abuse/child maltreatment', which should have been the responsibility of the child protection unit of every welfare bureau or department (*TMSB,1990*). In dealing with child abuse, the welfare authorities in *Taiwan* have played a leading role in coordinating all available resources by assembling interdisciplinary teams of police, prosecutors, judges, and social workers, and involving all concerned voluntary groups in order to associate their expertise. However, this welfare service for maltreated children has never been extended to prostitution-involved children (and their families). Instead, it was considered more practical to classify the problem as 'women's affairs'. The unfortunate result was that all prostitution-involved children became treated as young prostitutes.

Before 1987, there existed two official rehabilitation centres which were established for the rehabilitation of illegal prostitutes (*Hsu,C.L.,1988:1*). The two rehabilitation centres, as shown in their names, 'The Taipei Municipal Kuang Tzu Po Ai Institution-- Vocational Training and Counseling Centre for Distressed Women (KTPAI-VTCC)' and 'The Taiwan Provincial Yunlin Technical Training Centre for Girls (YLTTC)', were designed to help the women and girls found in illegal prostitution in acquiring some skills in order to find socially acceptable jobs for 'good women'. All girls, disregarding their age and past experiences, are subjected to similar counselling and skill-training programmes aiming at their rehabilitation towards the same end -- keep them out of prostitution and become 'good women'.

On the demand of concerned NGOs in 1987, the treatment of prostitution-involved girls was added to the responsibilities of these two institutions: the KTPAI (VTCC) for girls located in *Taipei* area, and the YLTTC for those found in other parts of *Taiwan* (*Tsai,Y.Y.,1982:454*; *TWRF,1992:53-56*). As the 1989 Juvenile Welfare Law mandated a two-week observation period during which the girls will be categorised into 'voluntary' and 'forced', an observation centre was established in the KTPAI. After the observation, the 'voluntary' would be referred to the Juvenile Court and the 'forced' would stay in the KTPAI (VTCC), or be transferred to the YLTCC for rehabilitation.

Apart from financing and supervising the operation of the two rehabilitation centres, expertise was not developed among welfare officials and social workers. In general, the welfare authorities in *Taiwan* are both impotent in manpower and in knowledge. As a result, together with the KTPAI (VTCC), the YLTCC, the police and the judiciary, the welfare authorities were incorporated into the 'rescue networks' established by individual NGOs. (*Chen,M.L.,1991c*; *Hong,W.H.,1992*) In the rescue network, welfare authorities would only be called upon when their legal power is needed.[66] Occasionally, welfare authorities also gave research funding to private or NGO researchers in the field. (*Wang & Wang,1992:1*; *Yin,C.C. et al.,1993:1*) The aforementioned education programmes organised by the RP and the TWRF were also subsidised by government (TWRF,1991:1) (*RP,1988:1*; *Pai,H.H.,1992:41*). In a word, apart from a few limited passive governmental measures taken to deal with child prostitution in general, most prevention and treatment programmes were initiated and carried out by NGOs.

Developments of Non-Governmental Organisations (NGOs) A laborious task immediately encountering the pioneering Rainbow Project (RP) after the commencement of the Decent Society Campaign was the care and rehabilitation of the rescued girls, which was not a specialty of the police nor a specific concern of the then existing laws or welfare services. Legal aid provided by voluntary lawyers for the children was also lacking. In response to practical needs, the RP established temporary mid-way houses in March 1988 under the name of the 'Garden of Hope'[67] (GOH) to accommodate the girls and 'heal them with the Gospel of Christ'.[68] Besides, a lawyers' group was also recruited to offer free legal consultation and a Taiwan Women's Rescue Association (TWRA) was organised in December 1987 under the auspices of the RP.

Although the RP, the GOH and the TWRA were organised by the same group of activists, there was a clear division of labour among the three. The RP remained a Christian group working for the welfare and enlightenment of aboriginal people, the GOH offered rehabilitation services in mid-way houses, and the TWRA were responsible for the prosecution of involved perpetrators, mainly the parents. However, a bleak emerged between the RP and the TWRA as the lawyers of TWRA started to visit aboriginal tribes and find their own cases.[69] The TWRA finally re-organised itself and officially registered as the Taipei Women Rescue Foundation (TWRF) in December 1988, and it was no longer a Christian group. As the problem they were dealing with was defined as an 'underage female prostitution' problem, all of the three NGOs were categorised as 'women's groups'.

After the establishment of GOH and TWRA, the RP started to concentrate on prevention and education projects among aboriginal tribes.

A social education programme named 'The Flaming Blossom Project' was initiated by the RP in the summer of 1988 to prevent primary-school graduated girls from joining prostitution.[70] Besides, social workers of RP also visited the rural tribes 'to organise seminars and to inform aboriginal children and families about the realities of prostitution and the suffering in the brothels' (*Kao,R.,1991:62*). Since then, their work has been concentrated on conducting grassroots-programmes on aboriginal education of preventive nature.

The other Christian group -- GOH -- has developed the most well-organised and officially registered short-term as well as long-term mid-way houses which are subsidised by the *Taipei* Municipal government (*Wang & Wang,1992; Li,M.L.,1995,1996*). Under the successive leaderships of two whole-heatedly devoted Christian women, *Mrs. WANG Isa* and *Ms CHI Huey-Jong,* the GOH gradually took on a dominant role in the field. They also recruited a group of lawyers and become heavily involved in law reform lobbying as well as law enforcement programmes. The TWRF still considered itself to be a 'legal experts' group' and claimed its authority over all legal matters. The two presidents *Ms SHEN, Mei Chen* (1987-1989, 1993 onwards) and Ms *WANG Ching Feng* (1989-1993) were eminent and influential practising lawyers[71] as well as humanitarian moralists who strongly believed in legal justice and urged for the criminalisation of prostitution.

There were remarkable differences between the practice of GOH and TWRF. GOH was mainly working on treatment of the received girls with Christian education, while TWRF concentrated more on legal actions against perpetrators, especially the parents. GOH had its own lawyers, but they were generally only concerned with legally obtaining physical custody of the received girls in order to avoid outside disturbance during treatment. TWRF also had a mid-way house, but it was not well-equipped nor sufficiently-staffed. Thus, over the years, it has suffered serious loss of received girls for most of the them ran away after some time.[72] Recently since 1991, TWRF has been concerned with the growing number of 'voluntary girl prostitutes' and carried out a series of preventive educational programmes under the title of The Lily Project'(TWRF,1991) (*TWRF,1991, 1992,1993*).[73]

New Situations under the Specific Law

Making of the specific law The legislative climate in Taiwan since the lift of the martial law has developed a tendency of making specific laws to solve specific social problems claimed by interest groups. The Law to Suppress Sexual Transactions Involving Children and Juveniles is one good example. In fact, if the existing general laws can be properly enforced, there are enough laws to govern both punishment and treatment of child prostitution. However, the enforcers were either incapable or unwilling to prosecute the perpetrators; and the administrative authorities were unable to provide for pertinent protection and treatment measures. NGOs worked very hard, but they had to bear the sorrow of facing failures in rehabilitation and of witnessing the gradual deterioration of the problem in their hands. So after accumulating enough experiences in the field, the Garden of Hope Foundation (GOH) first proposed a specific law – the draft bill to the Girl Prostitution Treatment and Prevention Law (*Chu Chi Fang Chi Fa* 雛妓防治法) -- to solve the deteriorating problem in their hands.[74]

The GOH bill was welcomed by nearly all concerned NGOs including mainly the Rainbow Project (RP), the Good Shepherd Sisters Foundation (GSS), the End Child Prostitution Association Taiwan (ECPAT), and certain anti-prostitution groups like the Women Awakening Foundation and the Housewives Association (*GOH,1992bcd*). However, many 'legal experts' especially those in connection to the Taipei Women Rescue Foundation (TWRF) openly confronted such legislative lobbying. Their opposing arguments were mainly, first, the real problem which was in law implementation and not the law itself, and second, the ROC legislative order which would be disturbed by making too many specific laws (*Shen,M.C.,1995*). Disregarding such comments, GOH and their associates started to hold constant demonstration in front of the Legislative Yuan in the second half of 1992. AS GOH owned substantial media resources, reports concerning their actions appeared very frequently in not only newspapers and magazines, but also radio programmes and TV news. When social pressure accumulated, there appeared one, then a couple, then a dozen and more legislators who became willing to sign their names on the GOH bill. So finally the bill entered its legislative process under the name of legislator *Ms YEH Chu Lan*[75] (the YEH Bill), who had been fully supporting the GOH bill since its first drafting. Later, some KMT legislators such as *HUAN Chau Shuen* and *TING Shou Chung* also proposed their draft bills under the same title.[76] What is worth noticing is that there was no governmental draft bill proposed by the administrative authority of the child prostitution issue -- the Ministry of the Interior.

The YEH Bill faced very restricted challenges in its first reading, but it was jammed after the long queue of other draft bills to undergo its second reading. The concerned NGOs soon realised that they had to find some influential legislators of all parties in order to push the legislative process. Then they found legislator *Ms HSIEH Chi Ta* -- a leading female legislator of the New Party[77] who had been concerned with juvenile welfare legislation. HSIEH promised to make the Law pass as soon as possible if the GOH Bill could be properly amended and became a 'HSIEH Bill'. So a compromise was made and HSIEH assumed the leadership in the amendment of the GOH Bill. Long-hour meetings were held for more than 20 times within seven months and this time HSIEH was able to invite the legal experts and leaders of the TWRF to join.[78]

The HSIEH Bill was finally completed in the end of 1994 and in a couple of months, it went through its second reading, then its final reading and became a new Law in August 1995 right before the election season started.[79] NGOs all celebrated their triumph as they were not only empowered by the new Law in treatment matters, all concerned authorities were also imposed on certain legal duties to enforce the law of punishment and prevention. However, as no official opinion was ever sought from any concerned authority during the legislative process as to what had been commonly practised during other social legislative processes, there could be pitfalls in its implementation depending on the attitudes of law enforcers towards this Law.

Passive attitudes of law enforcers in implementation Under the new Law, certain administrative authorities are responsible to fulfil specified legal duties within prescribed periods of time. For instance, under Articles 11 to 13, the local authorities have to set up the Affectionate Care Centres, the Emergency Settlement Centres and the Temporary Settlement Centres for short-term treatment of the victims within six months after the Law is enacted; while the central authority has to build Mid-Way Schools for the continuing education of the victims within one year after the Law becomes effective. Now the time is due for all authorities, but no new buildings yet are assigned for the establishment of the above centres, and the first Mid-Way School is still at its planning stage. What has been done to fulfil their legal duties are to give new names specified by the Law to the old rehabilitation centres with a note saying that before there are enough resources to build up new centres, they will be the temporary 'Centres'; while the original functions of the centres will be augmented to fulfill their legal purposes (*Chen & Chuan et al.,1996; Chou,Y.Y.,1995; Li,T.C.,1996a*).

Take the Police Authority and the Central Procurator's Office for another example, they are abided by Articles 6 and 7 to establish Specialised Duty Squads and to set up national hot lines. Both authorities announced that they had accomplished their legal responsibilities.

However, what they have accomplished are simply to assign a police in each station and a procurator in each Procurator's Office to handle all child prostitution cases under their jurisdiction, but these 'specialised' law enforcers may also be assigned to handle other cases. On the other hand, there is a national hot line numbered 080-000-919 (080 is the common numbers for free phones; 000-919 is similar to the Mandarin pronunciation of *鈴鈴鈴、救一救* which may be literally translated as 'ring for rescue'). But as very few citizens know this number, it has been reported that most informers are still calling concerned NGOs for help (*Chen,C.D.,1996; Chou,P.J.,1996b*). Such passive attitudes of law enforcers have seriously hindered the prosperity of the Law in suppressing the social practice of child prostitution.

Changing orientation in NGO work Now the TWRF and the GOH remain the 'owners' of the child prostitution problem and have recently extended their concerns to child victims of sexual abuse (*GOH,1996,1996e; Su,H.T.,1997; Yeh,T.H.,1993*). The Child Welfare League Foundation and its associate NGOs still restrict themselves to dealing with child protection of sex-excluding nature. The Good Shepherd Sisters Foundation has in recent years actively involved in setting up rehabilitation programmes for girl victims of all forms of sexual abuse and exploitation (*GSS,1996*). NGOs of treatment orientation have gradually extended their attention to victims of sexual abuse. The GOH is now raising funds for establishing a 'Centre for the Treatment of Child Sexual Abuse', which is to serve the needs for victims of all forms of sexual exploitation and abuse (*Chi,H.J.,1997; Wang,Y.H.,1997*), though in recent years the GOH have established well-organised mid-way houses and follow-up programmes for victims of girl prostitution (*Chueh,H.C.,1995; GOH,1996d,1997; Lai,W.C.,1996; Li,M.L.,1995,1996; Lu,Y.H.,1995ab,1996*). The End Child Prostitution Association Taiwan (ECPAT) also redirect their attention from children's right issues to the 'Perfect Tourist Programme' and campaign for 'responsible tourism' which urges all tourists to refrain themselves from sex tours (*ECPAT,1997ab; Li,L.F.,1995c,1996c*). In treatment issues, ECPAT becomes the leading NGO to conduct reaching-out programmes for foreign girl prostitutes who are incarcerated in the 'Alien Detention Centre' as well as for prostitution-involved boys (*Chou,J.T.,1996a*). As far as prevention work is concerned, the Rainbow Project keeps their concentration in out-reaching preventive programmes designed especially for indigenous peoples. The GOH and TWRF have reinforced their preventive programmes through the media, and the ECPAT have carried out sex education programmes for primary and high schools (*ECPAT,1997ab;*

GOH,1996c; Li,C.W.,1995). In short, the new Law simply empowers NGOs to reinforce their programmes, but all NGOs have their own development policies which are rarely influenced by the new Law.

Concluding Remarks

A recurring theme in this book is that the social phenomenon of child prostitution existed throughout Chinese history, but it was not alleged to be a social problem until recently. On its discovery in 1987, child prostitution was first fostered by the activists as a most inhuman form of sexual exploitation committed against the helpless 'mountain flowers'. It was urged that the vulnerability of aboriginal tribes was caused by structural inequality and the inadequate government policies towards aboriginal people and tourism development were held responsible.

Helped by media reports of the miserable lives of prostituted female children, considerable social outrages against the practice was accumulated to the extent that the police department had to issue a special project to crack down on underage prostitution, though the structural problems were not recognised in official discourses. The police records immediately showed outstanding numbers of arrested exploiters and rescued girls. Then the social outrages were soothed and the campaigners became fully engaged in the resulting problem: management of the child victims.

In order to respond to practical needs, the activists became social workers and set up mid-way houses, offer legal aid, and started to assemble interdisciplinary teams of police, procurators and social workers. All attention became centred on the protection and rehabilitation of the rescued children. The newly organised group of social workers (Christian women and female lawyers) entangled themselves with the resulting 'moral danger' of the girls under their care. Thus the victims themselves became a new focus of surveillance and all rehabilitative measures were directed at the resulting delinquency. Such responses to the problem had a prolonged implication on policy and practice -- the moral danger and behavioural delinquency of the prostitution-involved children becoming fixed at the centre of all socio-legal concerns.

Therefore, unlike the moral panic[80] in late Victorian England which led to legislation reform criminalising the practice of underage prostitution[81] (Smart,1989:51-52), the anti-child-prostitution activities in *Taiwan* finally resulted in new laws of prevention and treatment directed at the surveillance of juveniles and children. As other juvenile problems deteriorated at the same time, and welfare discourses became dominant among professionals and decision-makers, a Juvenile Welfare Law was finally made in 1989.

Owing to vigorous lobbying of the activists, apart from making welfare services available to the prostituted children, innovative provisions concerning the legal suspension of parental rights and administrative punishments for child prostitution operators were incorporated into the Law. However, most of these laws were simply accessories to facilitate the moral vigilance over the juvenile victims. On the other hand, as the Law was only applicable to adolescents aged between 12 and 18, the involved child under 12 were left unattended until similar reform was made in the 1993 Child Welfare Law.[82] A specific law to govern the problem was then made in 1995 to deal with the child prostitution problem and to supersede applications of all other laws. However, as the new legislation was entitled 'The Law to Suppress Sexual Transactions Involving Children and Juveniles', the legal concern seems to be switched away from child protection under the Welfare Laws to the 'sexual transactions' in which children under 18 are involved.

As will be shown in the following chapters, when the problem of child prostitution is legally constructed, the subject of concern has not been the 'victimisation of children'. Therefore, although very few would disagree with the statement that 'child prostitution is the worst and most intolerable form of child abuse', the consequences of this abuse are seldom dealt with under the umbrella of the child protection system. And even where child protection laws do apply, the 'victim' status of a prostitution-involved child is undermined by a social as well as legal presumption that, consequent on the assimilation process she\he underwent in prostitution, the child is now sexually deviant and socially incorrigible.

NOTES

[1] S. Cohen (1973) has outlined the process of events which constitute a 'moral panic'. These are: a stage where a condition of group of persons becomes defined as a threat to the social order; the involvement of the mass media which presents the problem in stylish and stereotypical terms; the 'manning' of moral barricades by right-thinking people; the pronouncement of solution by experts; a means of coping evolves; the problem is seen as being solved or simply becomes submerged. See Cohen quoted at Smart,1989:51-52.

[2] The 'truth' concerned in this thesis refers to 'certain discourses which are claimed to speak the truth and thus can exercise power in a society that values this notion of truth' as defined by M. Foucault (Smart,1989:9). In using the concept of truth Foucault does not mean 'the ensemble of truths which are to be discovered and accepted' (Gordon,1980:132). On the

contrary Foucault uses it to refer to 'the ensemble of rules according to which the true and the false are separated and specific effects of power attached to the true' (Gordon,1980:132).

[3] See a special report in *The China Times* on December 14, 1986. It was the first time that a main newspaper in Taiwan seriously reported the 'fact' that a unbearable number of aboriginal young daughters were sold into prostitution leading a life 'worse than that of an American black slave'.

[4] See also *The China Times* on December 14, 1986.

[5] It was reported that 60% of the girls were sold out from a single aboriginal tribe: the TAYAL people. According to *Ms Liao, Bi Ying* (the Campaign leader), the main causes to the epidemic involvement of aboriginal peoples in sold-daughter-prostitution were their inferior social status in the Han-dominated society and their maladjustment to the modern capitalist economic structure. The distinctive vulnerability of the TAYAL people was due to the tourism promotion plans carried in their residence areas. See the report in *The China Times* on 14 December, 1986.

[6] It was officially reported as 1.75% in 1996. See Important Statistics of Interior Affairs published by the ROC Ministry of the Interior, 1996.

[7] According to the ROC Ministry of the Interior, the population of juveniles between 12 and 18 has been around 1 million and 1.1 million, and the population of children under the age of 12 is the equivalent.

[8] See Asian Women's Liberation, Vol.3, June 1980, quoted at O'Grady,1992a:139.

[9] For the police, under-age prostitutes refer to girls under 16, for having sexual relationship with girls under that age is criminal under the ROC law.

[10] The figures were first released in a consultation meeting held on February 8, 1987 in which legislators, concerned governmental officials, and scholars participated and called for social concern. See *The China Times* on February 9, 1987; *The Independent Evenings* on March 12, 1987.

[11] See statistics released in *The United Daily* on February 9, 1987.

[12] See *The China Times* on February 9, 1987; *The Independent Evenings* on March 12, 1987.

[13] See interview of *Ms WANG Ching Feng* (Chairperson of the TWRF) reported in *The United Evenings* on September 5, 1989. See also interview of *Dr. CHU Hai Yuan* (a research fellow of the ROC Academia Sinica) reported in *The China Evenings* on June 13, 1992.

[14] According to the Ministry of the Interior, the female population aged between 13 and 17 is around 110 million in 1992. See statistics released in *The People's Livelihood Daily* on June 21, 1992, p.15.

[15] ECPAT (Taiwan) denotes 'End Child Prostitution Association Taiwan' in this book.

[16] For papers delivered in the two meetings, see *Shee,A.1992* and *GOH,1992*.

[17] See, for example, *The People's Livelihood Daily* on June 21, 1992, p.15; *The China Times* on June 14, 1992, p.6; *The China Evenings* on June 13, 1992, p.7; The China Post on June 14, 1992.

[18] However, certain researchers and activists still argued that those figures were on the low side of the truth. 'A tip of the iceberg' is the general term used by those concerned

professionals. See the conference papers published in *GOH,1992*. See also *The China Evenings* on June 13, 1992, p.7.

[19] Professional and governmental responses to the released figures were later collected and reported by *The People's Livelihood Daily* on June 21, 1992.

[20] See *the People's Livelihood Daily* on June 21,1992.

[21] According to the 1992 *Taiwan-Fukien* Demographic Fact Book (Ministry of the Interior, ROC), the male population between the ages of 18 and 50 were approximately 4,700,000 in the end of 1991.

[22] The publication records various aspects of children's development throughout the world.

[23] According to *The Central Daily* (international edition) on June 23, 1994 (page 7), concerned agencies in Taiwan were not sure where the UNICEF got the figure. It was suspected that the figure was taken from the relevant report in the 'Asian Women Revolution' magazine. But I would presume that as the UNICEF has been heavily involved in the activities of ECPAT (International Campaign to End Child Prostitution in Asian Tourism), the figure must have been taken directly from ECPAT publications. For relevant figures in ECPAT publications, see O'Grady,1992a:139; ECPAT Newsletters; *Shee,A.,1992:9*.

[24] The ROC Ministry of the Interior stated that, in the past year, the police has located less than 300 prostitution-involved girls, and according to the police 'expert estimation', the number comprised approximately 10% of the total number. So 'there should be no more than 3,000 girls working in prostitution', said the police authority. See The China Post on June 22, 1994; and *The Central Daily* (international edition) on June 23, 1994; *The Liberty Times* on June 22, 1994.

[25] See The China Post on June 22, 1994, pages 1 & 2. See also GOH,1993.

[26] According to the Ministry of the Interior, the police has cracked down on an average of 200 prostitution-involved girls per year since March 1987. See The China Post on June 22, 1994; and *The Central Daily* (international edition) on June 23, 1994; *The Liberty Times* on June 22, 1994.

[27] See *The China Times* on June 19, 1992.

[28] See the report in *The Independent Evenings* on July 13, 1991.

[29] See interview of a research fellow of the HLMF, *Ms LIN Yen Ching*, reported in *The China Evenings* on April 27, 1992, p.7.

[30] See information given by *Ms YEH* in a press conference reported by *The China Evenings* on May 1, 1991.

[31] *Ms Huang* was a Ph.D. Candidate of Social Work in the University of Wisconsin (USA), who was writing a Ph.D. thesis on the prostitution problem in Taiwan.

[32] See interview of *Ms HUANG* reported in *The Independent Daily* on December 20, 1990.

[33] See report of the KTPAI survey findings in *The China Times* on December 13, 1990.

[34] In my association with concerned social workers, this kind of words are often heard. In fact, it can be observed from recent NGOs practice that they are re-channeling resources from treatment to prevention programmes, and for treatment programmes, attention is broadened to include all child victims of sexual abuse and assault.

[35] See, for example, *The Liberty Times* on April 1, 1993; *Chiou,Y.C.,1995*.

[36] See *The United Evenings* on May 22, 1997; *The People's Livelihood Daily* on May23, 1997.
[37] See *Cheng,R.L.,1986:169-172* for the list of the 92 forms of child abuse and the questionnaire.
[38] See mainly reports concerning 'Western paedophiles' in *Taiwan* newspapers dated from June 9,1992 to 15 June, 1992 including *The Central Daily, The China Times, The China Evenings, The Independent Daily, The Independent Evenings, The United Daily, the United Evenings*, and *The Liberty Daily*. For professional critiques, see conference papers included in *Shee,1992* and *Wang,I.,1992b*. See also *Chen,C.H.,1993*; *Lin,Y.S.,1993ab*; *Wang,I.,1993*.
[39] The term 'mountain flowers (*shan hua* 山花)' is generally used to denote the young girls of the indigenous mountain people.
[40] The above information was given by the then assistants of *Ms LIAU* who were involved in the operation of the Rainbow Project, including *Ms KUO Huey Ling*; *Ms LI Ming Yu*; and *Ms WANG Yu Lang*.
[41] According to *Ms LIAU Bi Ying*, the 1987 campaign leader, the TAYAL aboriginal people who were surrounded with tourism areas were most vulnerable to the exploitation of sold-daughter-prostitution. See the survey findings of the Rainbow Project (RP) reported in *The China Times* on December 14, 1986.
[42] See report in *The Independent Evenings* on December 20, 1990.
[43] See *The China Times* on December 13, 1990. For details of the research findings, see *Wu,H.Y.,1990*.
[44] Among the materials, there were the translated articles and statistics concerning the child (girls and boys) prostitution problems in Asian countries including Thailand, the Philippines, and Sri Lanka. Several introductory essays on the activities of the ECPAT-International and the ECPAT-Taiwan were also included. There are also summaries of research findings (including figures) on the child prostitution problem in *Taiwan*.
[45] See mainly *The China Times* on June 19,1992, p.14; *The Independent Evenings* on June 9, 1992, p.3.
[46] See mainly *The China Evenings* on May 20, 1992; and *The Liberty Times* on May 21, 1992.
[47] See mainly *The China Times* on June 10, 1992, p.14.
[48] See *The Independent Evenings* on June 9, 1992, p.3.
[49] It is the 'truth' in Faucault's terms as aforementioned.
[50] According to the figures released and emphasised in the GOH Consultation, there were at least 70,000 prostitution-involved girls under 18 among which 10,000 or more were 'forced'. See *The China Times* on June 14, 1992, p.6.
[51] According to the estimation of the then TWRF Executive Manager, *Ms CHEN Mei Ling*, 90 % of the girls fell back to prostitution after being rescued. See *The China Times* on June 14, 1992, p.6. Field experiences also revealed a high proportion of girls falling back to prostitution after rehabilitation (*Hsu,C.L.,1988*; *Cheng & Fan-Chang,1990*; *Tsai,Y.Y.,1992*; *Wang & Wang,1992*; *Yin,C.C. et al., 1993*).
[52] For relevant comments, see *The United Evenings* on May 22, 1997; *The People's Livelihood Daily* on May23, 1997.

[53] For further discussions, see Fuller & Myers,1941:320; Parton,1979:431-451; Rubington & Weinberg,1977; Waller,1936:922-933.
[54] In the words of J. Gusfield, '[a]t every stage in this process human choices of selection and interpretation operate. Events are given meaning, and assumptions and values guide the selection. Public "facts" are not like pebbles on the beach, lying in the sun and waiting to be seen. They must be picked, polished, shaped and packaged. Finally ready for display, they bear the marks of their shapers'.
[55] The two rehabilitation centres for illegal prostitutes were the Taipei Municipal Kuang Tze Po Ai Institution (KTPAI) -- the Vocational Training & Counselling Centre for Distressed Women (VTCC) and the Taiwan Provincial Yunlin Technical Training Centre for Girls (YLTTC).
[56] The target of this Campaign was girls involved in criminal prostitution, and as the age of consent is 16 under the Criminal Code, this age was chosen as the threshold for defining girl prostitution in the Campaign.
[57] The Campaign was cancelled in the end of 1991. According to the figures released by the National Police Administration (supplied on the demand of the ROC Legislative Yuan for the purposes of the ECPAT public hearing held on June 9, 1992), the numbers of arrested persons were as follows: (1) Procurers: 842 (March-December,1987)-> 175 (1988)-> 167 (1989)-> 126 (1990)-> 166 (1991). (2) Brothel-keepers, pimps, and abettors (bouncers, etc.): 16,572 (March-December 1987)-> 4,908 (1988)-> 2,255 (1989)-> 3,417 (1990)-> 3,744 (1991). No record is available as to how many were finally prosecuted and sentenced to prison by the Criminal Courts.
[58] See the police figures released in *The China Times* on June 10, 1992, p.14; *The Independent Evenings* on June 9, 1992, p.3. See also *Huang,Y.C.,1991:9.*
[59] There has not yet been similar police squad in other cities which is assigned to deal especially with the child prostitution problem.
[60] After 1991, the National Police Administration cancelled the Campaign. The Taipei Police Squad for Juvenile Cases is still responsible for girl prostitution cases but no more figures are made available to the public. According to the advisor to the Squad on girl prostitution matters, *Ms HUANG Yi Chun*, because of the unbearable embarrassments made in several public hearings during 1992 which claimed that there were between 72,000 and 100,000 prostitution-involved girls (under 18) in *Taiwan* and in comparison the police records (1177 in five years) was only 'a tip of the iceberg'.
[61] See the aforementioned first newspaper report of a interview of the Chairperson of the Rainbow Project (RP), *Mr SHANG Cheng Tsung*, in *The China Times* on December 14, 1986. According to *Mr SHANG*, the main cause of the serious child prostitution problem among aboriginal tribes was 'the involvement of local interest groups and organised mobsters, or even the local policemen and politicians acting as the procurers themselves'. For similar accusations, see *Chen,YingChen,1992:4*; *Chen,M.L.,1991b:11*; *GOH,1992:2,4, 11*; *Wang,I.,1992b:54*; and *The China Times* on April 3, 1993; *The United Daily* on April 5, 1993; *The Independent Evenings* on April 6, 1993.
[62] See *The Independent Evenings*, *The Liberty Times*, and *The United Daily* on April 6, 1993.

[63] See *The China Times* on April 3, 1993; *The United Daily* on April 5, 1993; *The Independent Evenings* on April 6, 1993; *The Liberty Times* and *The United Daily* on April 6, 1993.

[64] See chapters eight and nine for critiques on the overall absence of a structural policy approach in the management of the child prostitution problem in *Taiwan.*

[65] See interviews of policemen reported in *The Liberty Times* on March 31, April 1, 1993; *The China Daily* on April 1, April 6, 1993; *The China Times* on April 2, April 3, 1993; *The United Daily* on April 5, April 6, 1993; *The Independent Evenings* on April 6, 1993.

[66] For example, when individual NGOs need financial sponsorship to carry out their activities, the welfare authorities are legally empowered to allocate its welfare budget to promote appropriate prevention and treatment programmes.

[67] The GOH was officially registered in June 1989 in the name of the Garden of Hope Foundation as a juvenile welfare organisation according to the 1989 Juvenile Welfare Law (JWL). See the Garden of Hope Magazine, June 1989.

[68] See The pamphlet of the Rainbow Project (RP).

[69] Information given by *Ms KAO Huey Ling*, who was then a social worker of the RP, later a special reporter of the *Liberty Times* on aboriginal problems, and then a legislative assistant on social issues to several ROC legislators since 1990.

[70] In *Taiwan*, the flaming trees (*feng huang shu 鳳凰花*) always blossom prosperously in summer (May - July) with its shining orange flower petals scattered on the ground. It is at the same time that all primary schools hold graduation ceremony. Among aboriginal tribes, it was found that this celebration also brings about procurers to recruit the graduated girls into prostitution. 'The Flaming Blossom Project' was thus initiated and has been carried out among indigenous tribes in the beginning of every summer vocation since 1988.

[71] Neither of them is Christian. *Ms SHEN* is still a practising lawyer and also one of the main organisers of Buddhist Associations. *Ms WANG* became one of the members of the ROC Control Yuan in October 1993 and now back to practice law.

[72] The above information was given by social workers of ECPAT (*Ms LI Ming Yu*); RP (*Ms WANG Yu Lang*), GOH (*Ms WANG Yeh Hau & Mr CHENG Yi Shih*) and TWRF (*Ms CHEN May Ling & Ms HUANG Yi Chun*).

[73] For relevant information on the Lily Project (*pai ho chi hua 百合計畫*), see TWRF,1991; *TWRF,1991,1992.* Basically the Lily Project is a similar educational programme as the Flaming Blossom Project of the Rainbow Project, except that the work of Lily Project is not restricted to aboriginal areas.

[74] For introduction to the GOH bill, please see *Li,T.C.,1992; Lin,Y.S.,1993abc, 1995; Shen, M.C.,1995.*

[75] Ms YEH was (and still is) one of the leading female legislators of the strongest opposition party -- the Democratic Progressive Party.

[76] In fact, many of their provisions of the two KMT bills were copied from the GOH bill with some amendments. The only big difference was made in the TING Bill to 'punish' the 'voluntary girl prostitutes'. Obviously, TING had no understanding at all as to what was going on in the field.

[77] The New Party was (and still is) the second strongest political party on the opposition side.
[78] The TWRF and many legal experts finally made their compromise to join, because they all realised that the law was to be made disregarding their opposition, and if they joined the legislative process in time, they could prevent the Law being misled by non-lawyers.
[79] For introduction to the legislative process of the Law, see *Cheng,Y.S.,1993; Chi, H.J.,1993,1995d; Li,T.C.,1992; Lin,Y.S.,1993abc,1995; Shen,M.C.,1995; Wang,I.,1993.*
[80] According to C. Smart, all of the stages described by S. Cohen can be identified in the period leading up to the 1885 Act, although she also pointed out that child sexual abuse alone cannot be guaranteed to produce a moral panic. The concern over child sexual abuse in 1885 was further intensified by the worries of the working-class girls being 'ruined' by the degenerate aristocrat. For elaboration, see Smart,1989:51-52.
[81] The section of the 1885 Criminal Law Amendment Act which dealt with sexual abuse arose from a major moral panic about the sale of children into prostitution. The legislation raised the age of consent for girls from 13 to 16 years and imposed various penalties for procuring women and children and for abducting young women and heiresses. It also criminalised brothels and male homosexuality (Smart,1989:51). See further Bristow,1977; Criminal Law Revision Committee [England],1980,1982,1984; Gorham,1978; Home Office Policy Advisory Committee on sexual Offences [England],1979,1981; Howard League for Legal Reform,1985; Pearson,1972; Stafford,1964; Weeks,1981.
[82] The Law was a reforming legislation to respond to the recognised social problem of child abuse with a more interventionist welfare state.

5 POLICY AND LEGISLATIVE DEVELOPMENTS ON PROSTITUTION, FAMILY AND CHILDREN

The legal regulation of child prostitution has evolved dramatically from its discovery by the Christian humanitarians to legislative recognition as a result of lobbying by law and order pressure groups. As early as the birth of the modern ROC Criminal Code in 1935, both prostitution of children under 16 and sexual intercourse with children under the same age have been defined as criminal acts. The traffickers, the procurers, the pimps and the brothel-keepers can all be sentenced (at least theoretically) to prison for a maximum of ten years, and the involved parents or guardians are subjected to even harsher sanction. A customer is legally punishable if the child is under 16, and if he is charged with statutory rape (sexual intercourse with a girl under 14) the penalty is a maximum period of imprisonment for 20 years (minimum 5 years). However, under the vague ROC prostitution policy which has created legal loopholes for diverse forms of illegal prostitution to flourish and multiply, the application of the Criminal Code has been extremely restricted.

As law and order lobbying groups started to redirect attention from sexual exploitation to the discipline problems of involved children, they became unhappy with the Law Governing the Disposition of Juvenile Cases 1980. In the Law, 'habitual truancy or runaway', 'frequenting undesirable places' and 'drug abuse' were all identified as symptomatic actions of delinquency shared by the children. Thus child prostitution was constructed under the Law as a 'juvenile delinquency problem'. This approach met its turning point in latter 1980s when the emergence of a growing army of foreign-educated welfare professionals nurtured a welfare approach[1] to state intervention for child protection. Thus unlike the 1970s, when facing social problems caused by increasing degenerate youth, the new legislation became protection-oriented. It was manifested in the 1989 Juvenile Welfare Law which was framed in the language of welfarism and protection. Thanks to this Law, the prostitution-involved children of a 'forced' origin were removed from the jurisdiction of the punitive Juvenile Court and received into the arms of welfare professionals, and in order to facilitate their protection, the legal severance of the exploitative family bonds was made easy to obtain.

Although the ROC prostitution control policy was never strengthened to respond to underage prostitution problems, the welfare approach towards the family and its children has incidentally tightened around the sexual exploitation chain involving abusive parents and flesh trade operators. In both the 1989 Juvenile Welfare Law and the 1993 Child Welfare Law (Amendment), administrative punishments were made applicable to the parents as well as the operators. Under the welfare laws, the state's interests in the protection of children were gradually outweighing all other interests. Thus the parental rights which were cautiously guarded in the Civil Code are now under much more legal surveillance. The flesh trade operators who could easily survive in the loopholes of prostitution control regulations were then double-checked by welfare laws. The 1993 Child Welfare Law (Amendment) also provides for specific administrative punishment against customers who purchase sexual services from children under 12.[2]

However, this welfare law approach was replaced by a specific law approach by the making of the Law to Suppress Sexual Transactions Involving Children and Juveniles 1995. In formality, the Law was made to unify existing legislation and thus shall supersedes the application of all other relevant laws in child prostitution cases. In substance, the new Law not only provides for thorough measures for protection and treatment but also for specific administrative and criminal punishments for all legally defined perpetrators. Practically speaking, it solved certain old problems, though in ideological terms, the term 'sexual transactions' sounds disturbing as opposed to the urge to define child prostitution as a problem of child abuse and sexual exploitation.[3]

Obscure and Incompatible Prostitution Policies

Should the law criminalise, legalise or decriminalise prostitution?[4] The ROC decision-makers have never given a consistent answer. Since the dawn of the Republic of China, prostitution itself has never been a criminal activity under the law, although governments have tried several times without success to abolish the institution.

Policy of 'Short-Term Regulation and Long-Term Abolition'

In 1949, a 'Convention for the Suppression of the Traffic in Persons and the Exploitation of the Prostitution of Others'[5] was adopted by the United Nations General Assembly, which placed an obligation on governments to prohibit prostitution (Bullough,et al.,1987:287) (*Shen,M.C.,1990:131-133*). The ROC government signed the Convention and seemed determined to wipe out illicit sexual practice from *Taiwan*. However, in the name of meeting social needs, the decision-makers chose not to outlaw prostitution completely. In fact, apart from being a moral goal to be achieved in the future, the Convention has never been put to work due to practical difficulties which are deeply rooted in Chinese culture and society (*Liu,Y.M.,1976:60-62; Shen,M.C.,1989:272-273*).

After 1949, the ROC government announced successive central or local orders and decrees to abolish prostitution but it was finally agreed among the decision-makers that such a radical prostitution policy against a historically rooted social evil was bound to fail. Consequently, a concession[6] was made to use control and regulation of prostitution as a temporary measure in order that a total eradication would be achieved according to a planned agenda with dates for achieving the goal of 'short-term regulation and long-term abolition' (*Shen,M.C.,1989:32-49*). However, the planned time for abolition has been postponed to a certain date in the 1960s, then in the 1970s, and so on. Gradually, the urge for abolition faded away with failures in its implementation, and the 'date' for total abolition has finally disappeared without notice. Thus the 'total abolition' prostitution policy has given its way to 'control and regulation'.[7]

Although legal moralists have never given up imploring for the eradication of prostitution as a whole or the criminalisation of forced or underage prostitution in particular, the flesh trade institution has grown out of legal control.[8] Now law makers and enforcers have started to quote and agree on the argument that the institution of prostitution is 'a social sewage system which was an unpleasant mechanism but is necessary in order to keep society clean' (Ennew,1986:66-67) (*Chen,M.L,1991a:13-19*).

During the years, numerous administrative orders have been passed in order to regulate the so-called 'special entertainment establishments'[9] operating in an officially or unofficially designated 'special entertainment area' (Chen,H.H.,1986:128).[10] From time to time the government has shown its 'iron arm' in tackling the problems caused by prostitution and initiated short-term 'purity society campaigns'.[11] However, as described in chapters three and six, the measures taken (to levy high taxes, outlaw illicit massage parlours, abolish the internationally notorious *PEI TOU SPA* red light district, for example) were so inappropriate and ineffective as to redirect the practice of illegal prostitution into all sorts of legal entertainment business.[12]

Under the 'short-term regulation and long-term abolition' policy, prostitution became legally regulated under the 'Regulations Governing Prostitution'.[13] Thus unregulated prostitution, pimping or brothel-keeping does not constitute police or criminal offences. The Social Order Maintenance Law is only applied by the police to punish the prostitutes, pimps and brothel-keepers who are involved in unregistered prostitution. The Criminal Code does not penalise commercial sex either. Only those who have committed bigamy, offences against social morals, offenses against the family, or offences against personal liberty will be prosecuted under the Criminal Code.[14] Owing to the anti-child-prostitution movements since the late 1980s, there seemed to have emerged a legislative climate towards the penalisation of the customers and the recognition of the vulnerability and needs of women/child victims in prostitution, though the process is slow and full of disagreements and comprises.

Policy Implications of Related Legislation

Juvenile Welfare Law and Social Order Maintenance Law The first triumph of the anti-underage-prostitution movements was marked in the 1989 Juvenile Welfare Law (JWL), in which heavier administrative punishments (fines, suspension of business, or revocation of license) are provided, although a specified provision against the customers did not survive during the readings of the draft bill (*Chung,K.M.,1991:49*). The parents, adoptive parents, or other guardians (*de facto* or *de jure*) of a juvenile (12-18 years of age) who connive in or profit from the prostitution of their children can be subjected to heavy fines.[15] The business accommodating juvenile prostitution may be suspended, its license revoked, and a fine of up to NT$300,000[16] may be imposed (JWL:46-I).

These innovative provisions in the JWL were, however, no more than a legislative concession to the anti-child-prostitution campaigns. In other words, no basic policy on the control of prostitution were changed -- the needs of men to frequent prostitution was not legally rejected. Therefore, the majority of male legislators again conceded to the practice of the old evil during the readings of the 1991 Social Order Maintenance Law (SOML).[17]

As the Executive Yuan prepared the draft bill of this Law in February 1987, it accepted opinions from concerned professionals and pressure groups[18] that if the law was to punish the operators and workers of illegal prostitution, it must equally punish the customer (*Chen,M.L.,1991a*). However, when the draft bill was finally debated in January 1991, Article 90 which provided that 'those who frequent illegal prostitution should be punished with detention of not more than three days and imposition of a fine of less than N.T.$2,000 Yuan' became the centre of debates (*Chen,M.L.,1991a:13-19*). The male-dominated ROC Legislative Yuan voted by a great majority against Article 90 and it was erased without delay during the first reading for the following reasons:

1.The sexual needs of a single man should be understood.
2.The consuming of prostitution is one aspect of the Constitutional right to privacy in which the law should not intervene.
3.The act of frequenting prostitution itself does not sabotage the social order, and thus it should not be condemned in the 'Social Order Maintenance Law'.
4.It has been the ROC legal tradition not to punish prostitution customers, and therefore in order to ensure the consistency of legislative principles among laws, Article 90 should not be retained. (*The ROC Legislative Yuan*, quoted at *Chen,M.L.,1991a:14-15.*)

Previously, it was provided by Article 64-I(3) of the 1954 Police Offence Law (POL) that all the traffickers, brothel-keepers, pimps, prostitutes, and customers involved in illegal (not legally registered) prostitution were to be equally punished with detention of not more than seven days together with a fine of not more than 50 yuan. Now according to Article 84 of the newly enacted 1991 SOML, the seven-day administrative detention for pimping, soliciting and prostitution is reduced to three days[19] with a rise in fine up to N.T.$30,000. Illegal prostitutes who are cautioned for three or more times during one year may be committed to rehabilitation centres for not less than six months and not more than one year. But those who frequent illegal prostitution will not be subject to any punishment under the Law.

Child Welfare Law (Amendment) After their defeat in the Social Order Maintenance Law, the advocates of the anti-prostitution movements joined NGOs and professionals concerned in girl prostitution in the lobbying for the amendment of the out-dated 1973 Child Welfare Law (CWL). The results were constructive as far as the punishments against child prostitution are concerned. Now under the 1993 CWL (Amendment), the parents, adoptive parents, or other guardians (*de facto* or *de jure*) of a child who condone or abet the prostitution of their children can be fined up to NT$30,000 (CWL:45). The business accommodating child prostitution may be suspended or its license revoked, and a fine of up to NT$300,000 may be imposed (CWL:46-I).

The most distinctive provision of the 1993 CWL may be Article 46-II which, for the first time in the ROC law, explicitly imposes punishments on the customer of underage prostitution. It provides:

> 'Any person who conducts sexual transactions with a child (under 12) who has made a living by engaging in commercial sex or indecency, shall be subject to an administrative fine of not less than N.T.$30,000 and not more than N.T.$100,000. In addition, the violator's name shall be publicly announced; (II)
> The competent authority shall impose, or mandate other delegated organisations to impose, counseling education for not less than four hours on the violators specified in the preceding section. (III)'

If one takes the literal meaning of Article 46-II, then the provision only applies to cases in which the customer trades sexual service directly with a child, and the child must be one who has been making a living from offering sexual services. So, will the law punish those men who make payments to pimps/brothel-keepers or even to the parent(s) and have sex with children under their control? Or, if a man saw a child begging on the street and offered him money in exchange for his sexual service, should he be subject to punishment? No official reports had been made to examine the effects of the CWL in practice before its application in child prostitution cases was technically replaced by the 1995 Law to Suppress Sexual Transactions Involving Children and Juveniles.

It will be shown in chapter six that, before the 1995 Law was enforced, no customers had ever been brought to the Criminal Court for conducting unlawful sexual intercourse with children under 16, because frequenting underage prostitution was not considered criminal in police practice, and customers were generally not arrested during police raids. Thus it may be fair to presume that unless there can be an overall change in police practice, the effect of Article 46-II,III would be limited as it could be expected that only those police stations which had been incorporated into the NGO 'rescue, protection and treatment network' would implement the law, as was the case for the 1989 JWL.

The Law to Suppress Sexual Transactions Involving Children and Juveniles Despite the obscure prostitution control legislative policy, the ROC Legislature finally agreed with pressure groups to make specific law to deal with the child prostitution problem. The purpose of specific legislation is to unify and strengthen the existing applicable laws on protection, treatment and punishment. There are certainly practical merits of the Law. First, the issue of sexual transactions involving children under 18 is singled out from prostitution and defined as a legally sanctioned problem with specific legal effects on its treatment, punishment, and prevention disregarding whatever legislative policies towards prostitution control. Second, as the Law is directly dealing with the child prostitution problem, it has a clear definition of every single punishable act as well as who the perpetrators and the victims are, of the responsibilities every authority should take, of the rescue-protection-treatment process for the victim, and of specified punishments for all perpetrators. In other words, the Law unifies all civil, criminal, and administrative effects attributed to a child prostitution case in one single piece of legislation. However, as the title of this Law shows, legislative attention has been switched from 'child\juvenile welfare' to 'sexual transactions', thus the definition that child prostitution is a problem of child abuse and sexual exploitation is rejected.

Comment

The ROC government once seemed to be determined to abolish prostitution in order to meet international requirements, but the prostitution policy has gradually given way to accommodate the urge of male legislators in the apparent interests of 'social needs'. Coupled with the experience of malfunctions of anti-prostitution measures, decision-makers now restrict themselves to the control and regulation of the prostitution industry. Only certain acts involving prostitution are criminal and the administrative liability of illegal (unregistered) prostitution rests upon brothel-keepers, pimps, and prostitutes, but not the customers.

The message given during the reading of the Social Order Maintenance Law seemed to have suggested that the ROC legal policy on prostitution has been based on a recognition of the social (male) need to tolerate its practice. The state would thus allow the operation of a regulated prostitution industry and the law only punishes those operators who do not legally apply for a license to profit from prostitution or who for such purposes commit criminal offences. The Juvenile Welfare Law and the Child Welfare Law (Amendment) are two landmarks made in child protection legislation to include victims of underage prostitution. However, their applications in child prostitution cases are now replaced by the Law to Suppress Sexual Transactions Involving Children and Juveniles in social work practice.[20] This Law marked the first clear legislative intention towards prostitution involving children under 18, though it also recentred the legal attention from child protection to underage prostitution.

Conflicting Laws on the Family and Its Children

The Chinese Family Reshaped in the Modern Civil Code

When the ROC Civil Code was promulgated in 1931, it was an advanced law compared with the social conditions (Buxbaum,D.C.,1978abc; Chiu,V.Y.,1966; Riasanovsky,V.A.,1938). Helped by the family revolutions started on the Chinese mainland since the 1920s and continued in *Taiwan* after 1949, family relationships among the Han people have been reshaped to a very large extent towards the imported legal norms against the customary practice of arranged marriage, female suppression, and abuse of parental power (Hsieh,C.C.,1985; Spear,A.,1974; Tang,M.C.,1978).

Disregarding the fact that the modern Chinese law reforms under the Nationalist government (KMT) were based on Western legislation, it is worth noticing that its family law -- Book IV of the Civil Code (CVC) is entitled '*chin shu* 親屬', which is commonly translated as 'Family',[21] while the term literally means 'relatives'. The first chapter -- General Provision -- immediately define relatives as including lineal relatives by blood, collateral relatives by blood, and relatives by marriage (CVC:967-971), and in the third chapter an adoption system is added to provide the basis for regulating relationships between constructive relatives (CVC:1077-1083). So the subject which is to be governed by the ROC family law is still the traditional Chinese family which includes the whole kinship.

The basic ROC law concerning parent-child relationships is provided in chapter three: Parents and Children (*fu mu tzu nu* 父母子女) which governs adoption and the exercise or deprivation of parental rights and duties.[22] It is followed by a chapter four designated to regulate 'guardianship (*chien hu* 監護)'. In principle, parents are the statutory agents and natural guardian of their minor children[23] (CVC:1086); the separate property[24] of a minor child is legally managed by the parents (CVC:1086,1087); and both the parents shall jointly exercise the right and the duty to protect, educate,[25] and maintain their minor children unless it is otherwise provided by the law (CVC:1084). The rights are exercised by the parents together under the amended law of 1996[26] and by either parent if one of them cannot exercise such rights.[27] Where the parents cannot assume the duties jointly, they will have to be assumed by the parent who has the ability to do so (CVC:1089). Custody of children after divorce is dealt with in chapter two entitled 'marriage (*hun yin* 婚姻)'.[28] Under the newly amended Article 1055, custody of children after divorce may be arranged by the couple themselves or decided by the Court in the best interests of the child.[29]

Conflicts of interests between parents and children are legally recognised. But unlike Western laws which appoint welfare authorities and the Courts to supervise the exercise of parental rights, the Civil Code retains the traditional functions of the extended family in monitoring the operations of its nuclear units. When parents or guardians exercise their rights over children, their nearest ascendants (the grandparents of the children) or members of the family council[30] are authorised by law to correct such parents.[31] It is only when such correction is of no avail may a nearest ascendant or a family council member apply to the Court for a ruling in order to suspend parental rights in part or in total (CVC:1090). In cases where the Court has decided to suspend the rights of both parents, a guardian will be appointed by the Civil Court according to a legally specified order[32] ranging from grandparents, head of the house, paternal uncles to any person selected by the family council (CVC:1091,1094).

Thus it can be observed that as far as the parent-child relationship is concerned, the subject of concern in the Civil Code is the parents and the legal rights they may enjoy over their children, who then become the object of legal concern. As parents enjoy rights over their children, they are legally obliged to assume duties in order to carry out such rights (*Tai, Y.H., 1982:288*). When parents have failed to fulfil the duties or have abused their rights, the traditional power of the extended family to supervise and monitor its nuclear units and to correct the misuse of parental rights is now legally entrusted to the grandparents and a 'family council' as a legal obligation. It is only when the extended family has failed to fulfil such obligation are its members empowered to apply to the Court for reallocation of the guardianship of their children to the grandparents, the head of the family, a paternal uncle, or any person designated by the family council pursuant to Article 1094 of the Civil Code.

The Civil Code was first promulgated in 1931 as a means for modernisation. At that time, free marriages, sexual equality, and the Western concepts of parental rights as duty-rights shared between two parents which might finally be deprived through Court proceedings were foreign to the Chinese patriarchal family. However, during the forty years in which the Civil Code was applied to Taiwanese society, the family system had undergone tremendous evolution, thus the law was no longer able to cope with the new situation. On the contrary, the law in practice started to be reshaped by the family. In 1985, it was finally realised that the old 1931 law could no longer cope with new social conditions and an amendment was called upon. However, as the Civil Code was the basic law for family relations, there was also a strong moral commitment that the Chinese culture and historical heritage should not be abandoned and certain 'good custom' (such as the extended family support system) and 'Chinese ethics' (such as filial piety) should be further strengthened. Consequently, amendments were introduced to provide a compromise to maintain Chinese traditional ethics.[33]

As a result, the 1985 amended law keeps a hybrid family system which releases individuals from the authoritative control and discretionary power of the male family head, but not from the surveillance of the legal institution of the family council.[34] The obligation of parents to rear, educate and protect children and the right of the parents to impose necessary discipline on their children remain, while a provision was added to the effect that 'a child shall be filial and shall respect his parents' (CVC:1984).

It was commonly agreed that the Chinese extended family had declined and its traditional power over the nuclear units was on the wane.[35] On the other hand, as the extended family members no longer lived in the same neighbourhood, it was not easy to constitute a family council whenever problems emerged in one of the nuclear units. Many expected that, by the amendment, the supervision and monitoring functions of the extended family would be handed over to welfare authorities in cooperation with the Court. However, the legislators were not prepared to abandon the Chinese patriarchy to a foreign concept of state intervention. Thus when the amendment was passed in 1985, the family council remained intact. The argument was that the Civil Code was a fundamental law which should not undergo radical amendments (*ROC Legislative Yuan,1985*). The Chinese family should not only stay in the fundamental law, but also be supported by state measures.

The rise of the welfare state in the West also made its impact on the ROC social welfare planning (Li,K.T.,1988:1). It has been a state policy to emphasise the significant value of the Chinese family in the provision of welfare services, and it is officially urged that 'any welfare system, if it is to be successful, must be based on and must strengthen the family' (Li,K.T.,1988:4). Therefore, welfare services in *Taiwan* have been designed not to displace the traditional family support system, but to reinforce it. Consequently, the ROC family law (CVC:1114-1116) imposes on the extended family members (including the lineal relatives by blood, brothers and sisters) a mutual legal obligation to maintain one another.

Although the Civil Code still retains provisions governing the constitution of a 'family council' to fulfil some of the functions traditionally served by the extended family,[36] it is worth noticing that the role of the extended family is declining in recently promulgated welfare laws, and is gradually being replaced by the welfare state.[37] As an fact, it can be found that in the recent amendment of the custody law (CVC:1051&1055) as aforementioned, the Court is now taking the legal role to guard the best interests of the child. The amendment of the Book IV:Family is still carried on and expected to be completed by the end of 1998. It can be expected that as the amendment proceeds, more and more traditional power of the extended family will be taken over by the Court together with the welfare authorities in the name of child welfare and protection.

Children, Family and the State under Implanted Welfare Laws

Among the 175 provisions of the ROC Constitution, there is one article which is directly concerned with the welfare of children. Article 156 states, '(t)he State, in order to consolidate the foundation of national existence and development, shall protect motherhood and carry out a policy for the promotion of the welfare of women and children'.[38] Over the years, children have been portrayed in governmental propaganda as 'the future master of the nation'. Consequently, corresponding laws and measures were successively put into practice including population policy[39] and family planning programmes,[40] compulsory education regulations,[41] sanitation and medical care services for pregnant women and children, financial support for poor families with children,[42] and so on, all of which were based on the same ideology to ensure that every child would develop into a 'healthy and well-cultivated good citizen of the nation' (*Feng, Y., 1993:28; Ting, B.Y., 1987:160*).

When the Declaration of the Rights of the Child was adopted by the United Nations in 1959, the Republic of China was one of the original signatories. The Declaration was then brought back to the Department of Social Affairs (under the Executive Yuan), which was then planning to initiate social welfare legislation. As a result, a draft bill of the Child Welfare Law was prepared and proposed by the Executive Yuan to the Legislative Yuan in 1960. However, as it was the pioneer social welfare law made by the Nationalist (KMT) government, the following legislative process proved very controversial and underwent considerable debates. Consequently, the Bill was not passed and enacted until 1973 -- thirteen years after the draft was submitted to the Legislative Yuan.

The 1973 Child Welfare Law was intended to convince international society that the ROC legislation had complied with the UN Declaration and that the Nationalist (KMT) government on *Taiwan* was willing to carry out certain child and juvenile development programmes financially supported by the UNICEF. It did not signalise a real cognizance by the ROC decision-makers themselves that the rights of the child had to be materialised in law or that the protection of children from abuse and neglect had become so important as to deserve a specific law (*Chen,C.,1988:13-14*; *Feng,Y.et al.,1992:29-30*; *Ting,P.Y.,1987:160*).

Thus the law was only composed of thirty articles, most of which were superficially copied from Western laws without proper consideration of the substance of 'children's rights' and their corresponding welfare measures.[43] Evaluation reports conducted by experts so far have concluded that owing to lack of budget, qualified personnel, and appropriate facilities, the 1973 Child Welfare Law has never been whole-heartedly implemented (*Cheng,S.Y.,1990*; *Chou,C.C.,1986*; *Chou,C.O.,1991:1-25*; *Hsieh,Y.W.,1991a*).[44] As a result, under the seemingly progressive child welfare legislation, the patriarchy of the old Chinese family remained under the tutelage of the state, the purpose of whose 'intervention' is to ensure that the exercise of parental rights does not jeopardise 'the foundation of national existence and development' -- the children.

It should also be mentioned that, under this 1973 Law, the 'child' was defined as a person who had not reached the age of 12, and thus, the welfare of children aged between 12 and 18 should be provided by another law. Although a draft bill of the Juvenile Welfare Law was also prepared by the Executive Yuan in 1960, it was considered unnecessary to make two laws with similar contents at that stage of development (*Ting,T.Y.,1987:635-641*). The resolution was hence an Article appearing at the end of the 1973 Child Welfare Law stating: 'Before the promulgation of a Juvenile Welfare Law, this Law shall temporarily apply *mutatis mutandis* to adolescents aged between 12 and 18' (CWL:28).

Thus, the administration of juvenile welfare affairs had been governed by the 1973 Child Welfare Law until a Juvenile Welfare Law was finally passed in 1989. It shall however be noticed that although this 1989 Law is entitled 'welfare', the original intention was primarily to deal with the growing juvenile delinquency problems with protection-oriented measures (*Yang,K.S. et al.,1991:1*).[45] It was urged that rapid economic growth had resulted in the breakdown of traditional social orders and juvenile crimes and misbehaviour were one manifestation of social disorder. Welfare professionals thus allied with the law and order campaigners in the lobbying for preventive legislation (*Yang,K.S. et al.,1991:1-2,110*). On the other hand, social pressures have also mounted to make juvenile prostitution one of the paramount problems to be tackled by the law. Helped by enthusiastic lobbying of concerned NGOs,[46] the prevention and treatment of juvenile prostitution problems was legally dealt with by the Juvenile Welfare Law (*Hsu,C.L.,1989:82-84*; *Wang,C.F.,1992:13*; *Yang,K.S. et al.,1991:127-128*).

The Juvenile Welfare Law was thus the result of a combination of governmental determination to deal with juvenile delinquency problem with preventive measures and the NGO demands for new laws to tackle practical problems concerning forced-juvenile-prostitution. The basic rationale for legislation is to prevent the deterioration of social disorder by controlling degenerate youth. Consequently, instead of providing for the general welfare of adolescents as a whole, the law concentrates on rendering relieves and benefits to juveniles of troubled families or families tormented by their children (*Yang,K.S. et al.,1991:109-110*). The protective measures offered are designed to protect juveniles from abuse of others as much as from delinquency of their own.

After the promulgation of the Juvenile Welfare Law in 1989, the necessity of amending the out-of-date Child Welfare Law also drew the attention of decision-makers.[47] Helped by the adoption of the United Nations Convention on the Rights of the Child in 1989, the government was again motivated to make a law in line with 'world trends'.[48] The governmental draft bill for amendment was completed in early 1991 and sent to the Legislative Yuan. Although the bill had made big steps to adopt the 'best interests of children' principle, and the 'mandatory report system', and to provide for the qualifications and guarantee the legal status of social welfare professionals, it was criticised as being too conservative and not providing for a thorough child welfare system.

In response to this situation, a Child Welfare League (CELF) was established by committed legislators, eminent paediatricians, concerned social workers and a few lawyers for the purposes of proposing another draft bill to amend the Child Welfare Law (*CWLF,1991:2-3*). Again, their bill planned for a protection and welfare system based on the laws of foreign countries including Japan, Korea, the USA, England, Germany, France, and so on.[49] Some principles of the UN Convention were also emphasized and taken as guidelines.

Practical problems and suggestions were widely taken from social workers and paediatricians who had been urging for more power in dealing with child abuse cases while ignoring the danger of unguarded state intervention. Armed with Western welfare laws in their hands, child protection professionals made a statement that the traditional functions of the Chinese family are withering and all Western developed modern legislation has extended state intervention into family lives for the purpose of child protection. In the end, the bill adopted a foreign system but with certain amendments specifically to cope with local needs, which also constituted the main thrust of the CWLF bill -- that child protection professionals should be empowered to intervene in families and to remove a child whenever it was considered necessary without any court proceedings (*CWLF,1991:1-3*).

As soon as the Child Welfare League published their bill, a number of legal academics and practising lawyers decided to defend the legal doctrine that parental rights could only be suspended or deprived through court proceedings. It was urged that once social workers were over-empowered,[50] the normal operation of the existing legal system would be disturbed, and thus a research group financed by the Taipei Bar Association (TBA) and exercised by the Taipei Women Rescue Foundation (TWRF) also sent in a proposal for amendment to the Legislative Yuan before the other two bills went into legislative process in February 1992 (*TBA,1992:1-2*). One paramount principle urged by this group was that parental rights were legally bestowed and could not be interrupted by unguarded administrative authorities.

In addition, as this group of researchers were legal professionals who had also been much more involved in the management of child prostitution problems, their bill also consisted of more detailed provisions on the punishment of offenders and treatment of prostitution-involved children. Two significant provisions in the TBA bill were adopted in the final reading, both related to the punishment of child-sex customers. One is Article 46-II,III which imposes administrative punishment (fines) and treatment (counselling education) on the customers. The other is Article 43-II which empowers the welfare authority to file an independent complaint against any criminal offenders against children including the 'institution only upon complaint (*kao su nai lun 告訴乃論*)' offences.[51] Under this provision, any welfare authority may institute a case against a customer for statutory rape or criminal indecency without involving the child in the court proceedings.

As there had never been so many draft bills proposed for the amendment of any social welfare laws before, and all child welfare and protection experts and practitioners in *Taiwan* were involved in the making of one or more drafts, coupled with the fact that a young legislator, *Mr LIN, Chieh Chia,*[52] was determined to devote his political future to the promotion of child welfare, it was highly expected that the amendment would be a success. Unfortunately, however, the drafts were discussed in the Legislative Yuan over the year of 1992, and its progress was disrupted after the second reading by the general election. New legislators were elected in the beginning of 1993 and most of them were barely aware of the contents of the three bills. As a result, the new Child Welfare Law was passed and promulgated without the thorough consideration it deserved.

Generally speaking, the 1993 Child Welfare Law was a compromise between the requirements of child protection professionals who were eager to solve practical problems and claims of the legal professions who insisted that due legal process must be followed. It was also a hybrid of idealist measures derived from several foreign welfare systems balanced by solutions to local problems. The scale of provision of welfare services was also adjusted by the practical concerns of tight governmental budgets on social welfare. Although the names of the UN Declaration and Convention have been highlighted in the ROC child welfare legislation, the state's regulation of parental rights and child care is still legally expressed in terms of child-saving language rather than children's rights statements.

Despite some imperfections of the legislative processes of the 1989 Juvenile Welfare Law and the 1993 Child Welfare Law as observed above, the two laws not only strengthened the primitive 1973 Child Welfare Law (applied to both children and juveniles) by making it more effective but also significantly replaced the Chinese patriarchal family preserved by the Civil Code with a paternalist welfare state. The custody of children after divorce is no longer an ancillary matter in the contested divorce cases. The role of the family council in monitoring parental behaviour is also transferred to the Courts and the welfare authorities. Besides, a welfare authority or a procurator is legally empowered to require the Civil Court to appoint a pertinent guardian for a child of abusive, divorced or troubled families in the interests of the child disregarding Articles 1051, 1055 and 1094 of the Civil Code.

In contrast to the Civil Code (1931 & 1985 amendment) and the 1973 Child Welfare Law, the 1989 Juvenile Welfare Law and the 1993 Child Welfare Law (Amendment) have replaced the extended family with concerned welfare authorities and provided for detailed emergency protection and treatment measures.[53] Now in cases of parental abuse of rights, correction of parental behaviour by grandparents or the family council is no longer necessary. In fact, the family council has been abandoned by the law, and now not only the grandparents, but also the procurators, welfare authorities and government-appointed organisations are all legally entitled to apply to the court for an order to suspend parental rights. And when reallocating custody or guardianship of children, the court does not have to abide by the legal order provided in Article 1094 of the Civil Code and it may decide to give custody of a juvenile to a person who is in charge of a juvenile welfare authority or organisation or to any other pertinent person chosen by the court.

Further, an innovative legal principle was adopted in the 1993 Child Welfare Law -- the parameter of the first and paramount consideration of the best interests of the child. Article 4 of the Law states, '[w]hen child related matters are dealt with by governments of all levels and governmental as well as non-governmental institutions or organisations, the first consideration should be the best interest of the child; in addition, cases concerning children's protection, rescue and assistance shall be preferentially admitted and attended to'. Although this is only a moral principle, it is significant in terms of law as an instrument of education.

Comment

The 1973 Child Welfare Law was primarily window-dressing for international consumption. The effects of the Law on providing welfare for children were marginal. The 1989 Juvenile Welfare Law resulted from national clamour including the juvenile welfare professionals' law and order campaigns and the NGOs' anti-child-prostitution activities. The Law was to put pre-delinquents under legal vigilance. But this Law also labels the 'voluntary' prostitution-involved adolescents as 'sexually delinquent' and excludes them from welfare services. In other words, a group of 'voluntary' juvenile prostitutes is legally constructed (JWL:22).

The 1993 Child Welfare Law was a response to the professional call for state intervention into child abuse in the family. The anti-child-prostitution activists also proposed specific provisions for protection and treatment. It was convincingly urged that all prostitution-involved children are the victims of sexual exploitation and no professional authorities stated otherwise in the lobbying. As a result, two innovative legal truths were constructed in written laws. One is that no child under 12 is legally capable of making sex-related deals, so all prostitution-involved children are defined as victims to be protected with no exception; the other is that not only the exploitative parents and the operators but also the customers are offenders against child prostitution victims who should be subjected to both administrative and criminal punishments (CWL:43-48).

Generally speaking, the 1993 Child Welfare Law marked another big step towards the protection of children against prostitution. There are innovative provisions concerning protection of prostitution-involved children and punishments against the perpetrators. Besides, it was gradually recognised, at least among the concerned professionals, that the problem of child prostitution should be dealt with in child protection laws. However, these do not mean that the prevention and treatment of child prostitution has been transformed into an exclusive child protection issue.

During the legislative process of the 1993 Child Welfare Law, there were two main pressure groups involved in the lobbying, namely, the Child Welfare League (CWLF)[54] and the Taipei Women Rescue Foundation (TWRF), each being responsible for proposing one of the three draft bills.[55] An observation of the amended Child Welfare Law in comparison with the two bills will find that all provisions concerning child prostitution were taken from the TWRF bill, while welfare institution and administration parts of the Law were remade according to the model set up in the bill proposed by the CWLF. In fact, the TWRF joined the Child Welfare League in the lobbying not to urge that child prostitution was a child protection issue, but to make another piece-meal law covering their concern. If there had been a chance for a Women Welfare Law or a Prostitution Control Law to go through the legislation process, the TWRF would have assumed a more dominant role in the legislative process. And thus, when a specific law was finally made to deal exclusively with the problem in their hands, the concerned NGOs made no resistance to the title of the new piece of legislation being 'sexual transactions involving' instead of 'sexual abuse and exploitation of' children and juveniles.

Policy Implications in Legislation

Prostitution Control

The ROC prostitution policy has been by and large vague. Indeed, only a few people know what has been going on during the last three decades. In the first instance, the government, led by old KMT members and old bureaucrats with a strong sense of Chinese morality, condemned and thus attempted to ban prostitution with 'iron arms'. But very soon, prostitution was ironically tolerated for practical reasons. Later, the 1949 UN Convention revived the earlier determination. But again, as the policy-makers found that it was never possible to eliminate the thousand-year institution, they quietly and slowly changed their policy preferring instead to deal with it by regulation, hoping that at least such a social 'evil' would not spread or last long.

Therefore, after careful observation, one might be able to find that the ROC government has actually been tolerating, albeit reluctantly, the existence and operation of prostitution. This vague and expedient prostitution policy has not only confused the concerned authorities in implementation but also made it possible for the operation of forced and under-age prostitution to continue under the auspices of bribed and impotent officials. Under such an ambiguous policy, it would not be too difficult to imagine what the laws and enforcement might be like. Many of the laws were not only unenforceable in practice, but also self-contradictory, not to mention numerous pitfalls and defects in the provisions. The new Law to Suppress Sexual Transactions Involving Children and Juveniles 1995 marked the first clear legislative intention to outlaw underage and forced prostitution. However, application of the Law has been despised by certain law enforcers who confine the definition of 'sexual transactions' to flesh deals made in sex-related establishments.

Child Welfare and the Family

With regard to the law-making process of child welfare laws, it might be an amazing thing to note that it was mainly a work of translation. Before the lifting of the martial law (state of siege) on July 1, 1987, all legislation was government initiated. It was a legislative tradition that relevant foreign laws would first be translated, published, and distributed among the legislators as if they represented 'modern' laws that every modern legislation should copy from. Afterwards, when legislation started to be made through pressure groups lobbying, the tradition of 'copying from foreign laws' was followed, although some room was made to accommodate local solutions.

During the legislative process of recent welfare laws, most legislators simply cannibalized all proposed welfare systems in their files to make a law which, in their opinion, will follow the contemporary 'world trends' as well as solve local problems in Chinese ways. The result of such a blind imitation was that problems of enforcement and the inconsistency between the general law (the Civil Code) and the specific law (the

Child/Juvenile Welfare Laws) were never a consideration during the legislative process. The relationship between law and society was nothing but a myth, for the laws were developing in a directionless way. On the other hand, when local solutions were made into some provisions in the new legislation, they often conflicted with other provisions of foreign origins.

Such a process of legislation, of course, filled with possible pitfalls. First, modern progressive national laws have been made more for political reasons than to respond to the need to solve local social problems. Therefore, in order to initiate legislation, local problems must be presented to the legislators by powerful pressure groups in a form which they will appreciate. Second, the stage of legal development and the legal environment in *Taiwan* are generally ignored during the legislation process. Third, the functions of foreign laws in solving historically rooted local problems are not evaluated, and very often, foreign laws are copied as if they are panaceas with no side effects. Fourth, contents of international or foreign laws are translated into Chinese and copied without knowing their original legal intentions and environments. Fifth, lobbying from pressure groups can always add provisions to a new law which aim at solving local problems without considering their incompatibilities with other parts of the law or in the current legal and administrative systems. And finally, it seems that the purpose of legislation can be to make a beautiful black-letter law but not necessarily to ensure its actual implementation.

One might ask, why then did the government waste so many resources in making such impracticable laws if it did not really mean to? The answer is that the policy-makers did care about all the legislation, but that the motivation behind was more political than legal or social. Many laws were passed to respond to local political demands. The alliance established between concerned professionals and legislators has since the 1980s facilitated the making of social laws. However, the paramount objective of the legislative process was to pass a law rather than to solve social problems. Further, the alleged social problem was often very different from the discovered one.

Consequently, it is not uncommon to see such laws consist of incompatible or conflicting provisions. Some other laws were made to impress international society, hence improve the image of the ROC government. For a government which has been de-recognised by most of the countries on earth, international image is precious. This explains in part why laws on paper are always better than laws in action, and that laws are made according to international standards or requirements regardless of the actual national needs.

On the other hand, social laws have been on the periphery of legislation. In order to ensure national survival, the government has vigorously carried out a series of economic plans and actively initiated corresponding economic legislation. It cannot be denied that a crucial factor which has contributed to the successful story of the '*Taiwan* miracle' was the up-dated and effectively enforced economic laws made under a unified state economic policy. In contrast, although there have been new laws made to deal with the problem of child prostitution, many of the laws were not initiated for the purposes of child protection. Further, these laws are piece-meal in their form and scattered under the umbrella of inconstant policies regarding prostitution on the one hand and the family and children on the other.

On the part of the government, initiation of this social legislation was primarily for political purposes. Over the years, concerned professionals have learned to take advantage of the governmental or legislative concerns and pushed for child protection legislation. But many of their efforts were like painting the grass green while leaving its roots rotten. In the next two chapters, the substance and enforcement of these laws concerning the punishment, treatment, and prevention of child prostitution will be discussed. Through the evaluation of these laws as practised in Chinese culture and Taiwanese society, it will become clear that without a total system reform directed at the structural origins of the problem, piecemeal legal reforms can never generate green grass.

Concluding Remarks

In view of the historical developments of ROC legislative policies and regulations concerning prostitution, family relationships, and welfare services for children and juveniles, it becomes clear why the law has been unable to deal with the social problem of child prostitution properly. Under the vague prostitution policy, child prostitution is hidden under the sewage of unregistered but flourishing flesh markets. The laws governing family relationships and welfare services for children of the family take different views on abused children and prostitution-involved children. In contrast to an abused child, the prostitution-involved child is totally severed from her\his family and the treatment programmes are designed for the correction of the resulting delinquency.

If child prostitution could be defined as child abuse and neglect, welfare services would be delivered to the family as a whole. Yet, the present laws find it much easier to subject the involved child to institutional treatment and turn a blind eye to other children of the family. On the other hand, if child prostitution could be defined as a problem of child protection, its solution would not have to be found in prostitution control. But the most recent specific law to deal with child prostitution problem fixes the nature of the problem as 'sexual transactions', which makes it an issue of underage prostitution. Thus loopholes in prostitution control legislation have in turn nurtured the practice of illegal prostitution including that involving children. If child prostitution could be identified as a problem of child abuse and sexual exploitation, then no child could be legally eligible to make sexual transactions. So the perpetrators should all be punished for their acts of abuse and sexual exploitation of children, while the involved children should all be legally treated as victims of maltreatment disregarding their social labels as 'forced' or 'voluntary'.

NOTES

[1] 'The welfare approach', as defined by M. King, 'is founded upon an ethos of enlightened concern arising from advances in the behavioural sciences which supposedly enable experts to assess and meet the needs of children and thus entitle them to take or influence a wide range of decisions over what should happen to children who, for one reason or another, come to the attention of state authorities'. See King,M.,1981b:105.

[2] This has been the first and only ROC law which makes the act of purchasing sexual services from children a specific offence. Its effect in practice has not yet been examined officially. It is my presumption that unless the police would change their practice and refer the customers found in police raids to competent welfare authorities for punishment, the effect of this law will be limited.

[3] Detailed discussions of all these laws will be presented in the following chapters.

[4] For theoretical arguments for criminalisation, legalisation, or decriminalisation of prostitution, see Howard League for Legal Reform,1985:196-210; McLeod,1982:91-118; Richards,1982; Sion,1977; Smart,90-113; Tong,1984:37-64. See also relevant analyses in chapter two.

[5] See Yearbook of the United Nations 1948-1949, published by Columbia University Press in cooperation with the United Nations, New York, p.613.

[6] As what has happened in Western societies, such concessions were made to accommodate illegitimate sexuality (the legitimate sexuality being confined into the home bedrooms). Prostitution was thus not prohibited by the penal law. Rather, control regulations were

made to govern the profits made therein and to prevent possible danger caused by illicit sexual acts involved (Foucault,1979:2; McLeod,1982:92-118; Smart,1989:94). But the difference made by the ROC prostitution policy is that this 'concession' was not made to accommodate illegitimate sexuality, but rather to mitigate the difficulties of halting the practice of prostitution instantly.

[7] In fact, the suppression of all forms of prostitution has been a moral principle for some international and national legislation. This moral legalism is, however, challenged by theoretical as well as practical difficulties. On the one hand, it is widely urged that in modern societies, the involvement of two consenting adults in commercial sex is a 'private' matter and should not be subjected to state censure (Rosenbleet & Puriente,1973:373; Tong,1984:56). On the other hand, prostitution is maintained as the 'women's oldest profession' (Jarvinen,1993:17), the abolition of which is conceived as impossible. Thus the suppression legislation often fails and replaced by regulation and control, whilst legal sanctions are imposed on those who threaten the public health and/or disturb the social order (Smart,1989;94; Tong,1984:43). However, as the law often only regulates the activities of women prostitutes, it is criticised, especially among feminists, that the policing of prostitution has functioned as an instrument to control women's sexuality (Adams,1993:298; Edwards,1992:151-152; McLeod,1982:119-146; Richards,1982:84). See also relevant analysis in chapter two.

[8] See relevant discussions in chapters three and six.

[9] The special entertainment establishment (*to chung ying yeh* 特種營業) is a general official term for all business settings which offer sex-related services including brothels, call-girl stations, massage parlours, sauna saloons, dancing halls, bars, tea houses, and so on. See chapter six for relevant discussions.

[10] This special entertainment area (*to chung ying yeh chu* 特種營業區) is the official title of a red-light district.

[11] See chapter four for relevant measures taken for carrying out Campaigns during the 1970s.

[12] See discussions and critiques of prostitution control laws and measures in chapters four and six.

[13] See chapter six for introduction to the Regulations.

[14] For details, see chapter six.

[15] According to JWL:28, the maximum fine for condonation is approximately 75 pounds sterling, the fine being up to three times if such parent figures take part in the sexual exploitation.

[16] The current exchange rate between English Pound Sterling and NT$ is approximately 1:40.

[17] Under the martial law pronounced on *Taiwan* since 1949, there was a Police Offence Law to govern administrative punishment which could be imposed by the police on violators of social order. As the martial law was lifted in 1987, the Police Offence Law should also be abolished. Thus a draft bill of the Social Order Maintenance Law was also prepared to replace the Police Offence Law. However, before the Social Order Maintenance Law was passed and enacted in 1991, the Police Offence Law had been in use.

[18] Those who were involved in the lobby included (in alphabetical order) the Garden of Hope Foundation, the Rainbow Project, the Taipei Women Rescue Foundation, the Women Awakening Foundation, and individual supporters from all professions.

[19] This reduction was due to the fact that the martial law had been lifted and people's Constitutional right not to be detained by the police for more than 72 hours was thus restored.

[20] Authorities as well as NGOs have taken the Law as a specific law to be applied in all child prostitution cases in their hands. However, as will be discussed later in this book, certain leading procurators in this field are now determined to exclude the application of the Law on customers when a case involves statutory rape or criminal indecency against children under 16.

[21] See Liu,J.C. et al.,1991:293-340.

[22] These parental rights and duties may be slightly different from those of the common law. See Maidment,S.,1984:23.

[23] According to the CVC, majority begins with the completion of the twentieth year of age (CVC:12). A minor who is under seven has no disposing capacity, and an unmarried minor who is over seven has a limited disposing capacity under the law (CVC:13). For the making or receiving of a declaration of intention, a person of no disposing capacity is represented by the statutory agent (CVC:76), and when a person of limited disposing capacity is to make a legally valid declaration of intention, the approval of the statutory agent is essential (CVC:77). A unilateral act of the minor or a contract made by him/her without such approval of the statutory agent is void (CVC:78 & 79). For concluding a valid marriage, consent of the statutory agent must be obtained (CVC:974, 981, 989 & 990), and by concluding a valid marriage, the same consent is also essential on divorce (CVC:1049). Besides, the consent is required for the adoption and termination of adoption of a minor (CVC:1079 & 1080).

[24] According to CVC:1087, property which accrues to minor children by inheritance, gift or other gratuitous title constitutes their separate property.

[25] A parent may, within the limit of necessity, inflict punishments upon his children (CVC:1085).

[26] Under the old Article 1089, the rights were to be exercised by the father alone if the parents are not in agreement. This Article was declared unconstitutional (against the principle of sexual equality) by Interpretation No.365 of the Grand Justice Council made in September 1994. The Interpretation further mandated the law to be amended in two years time to comply with the principles of not only sexual equality but also the best interests of the child. Now under the 1996 amended Article 1089 of the Civil Code, parental rights are equally shared by parents during the marriage, and shall disagreements arise between parents as to important matters concerning child-rearing, a petition may be made to require for a Court decision.

[27] According to Supreme Court Precedent No.415 of 1973, such disabilities of exercising parental rights include disability *de jure* and disabilities *de facto*. When parental rights are legally suspended under CVC:1090, the parent(s) will be disabled *de jure* in exercising his/her parental rights until he/she successfully resumes such rights through pertinent court

proceedings. And where a parent is imprisoned for three years or becomes insane or otherwise hospitalised for a period of time, then he/she is disabled *de facto*. But if there are merely difficulties in exercising the rights, for example, a mother with full-time job who has to entrust her child to a child-minder, such parent cannot be alleged under CVC:1089 to be unable to exercise the parental rights. See *Tao,P.C.,et al.,1991:373.*

[28] The Chapter is divided into five Sections, namely, betrothal (*hun yueh 婚約*), conclusion of marriage (*chieh hun 結婚*), efficacy of marriage (*hun yin chih p'u tung hsiao li 婚姻之普通效力*), matrimonial property regimes (*fu chi chai chan chih 夫妻財產制*), and divorce (*li hun 離婚*). Custody of children after divorce is dealt with in the final Section.

[29] Husband and wife may effect a extra-judicial divorce themselves where they mutually consent to it (CVC:1049). Under the old Article 1051, if parents divorce by mutual consent , the legal principle is that custody of children rests with the father unless it is otherwise agreed upon, in which case the mother may enjoy the sole custody instead. According to CVC:1052, either spouse may apply to the court for a divorce provided that one of the legal conditions enumerated in the Article exists. And under the old Article 1055, the father will in principle assume the sole custody of the children unless an otherwise agreement was made between the couple, or an otherwise judgment was made by the Court for the interests of the child. No matter whether the custody disputes are settled extra-judicially or in Court, a non-custodial parent is deemed under the law to be temporarily unable to exercise or assume parental rights and duties. According to the Supreme Court Precedent No.1398 of 1973, which is still followed by all Civil Courts in *Taiwan*, the non-custodial parent does not lose the right of custody over children in such cases. According to CVC:1051 & 1055, the custody rights of this parent is only temporarily suspended after divorce and such parental rights can be reassumed when the custodian parent is proven to have abused his/her rights or when the custodian parent dies (*Tao,P.C. et al.,1991:363-366*).

[30] 'Family council' is a traditional concept which has been retained by the modern Chinese Law and been given a statutory form. For the composition and operation of the family council, see Shee,A.,1994:Appendix I: CVC: Book Four: Chapter VII.

[31] Under the law, parents may not in the exercise of their rights endanger the person or the property of the child. They are obliged to fulfil their duties with respect to maintenance and education of their children; in case that they do not exercise rights or assume duties properly, the nearest ascendants as well as the family council may correct them by an admonition or a warning. It has legal significance, for according to a binding Supreme Court Precedent No. 1194 of 1954, the correction is an essential preliminary to the initiation of a court proceeding for suspending parental rights. In other words, the complaint(s) has to prove that the alleged parent has abused his/her rights and the correction has been carried out in vain. See *Tao,P.C. et al.,1991:373.*

[32] This order has been set aside by the 1989 JWL:9 and the 1993 CWL:40.

[33] For example, the original CVC:1084 provides, '[p]arents have the right and the duty to protect, educate and maintain their minor children'. And when the law was amended in 1985, there was a strong feeling among the legislators that the 'good' Chinese traditional ethic of filial piety is waning among the Chinese society in Taiwan, so a new section I was

added to CVC:1084 which reads, '[a] child shall be filial and respectful to his parents'. See Appendix I: CVC: 1084.

[34] Chapters VI and VII of the CVC: Book Four are entitled 'Household' and 'Family Council'. For the text of these two chapters, see Liu,J.C. et al.,1991:332-335.

[35] See the specific reports on 'The structure and nature of families in Taiwan are changing', by *Ms Chang, Chuen Hua*. The four reports were originally published by *The China Times*. *The Central Daily* (international edition) collected the reports and published them with further comments. See *The Central Daily* on February 1, 1994, p.7.

[36] For example, according to CVC:1090, where the parents have abused their rights over their children, their nearest ascendants or the family council may correct them, and where such correction is of no avail, they may apply to the court for an order suspending parental rights in part or in total.

[37] For example, CVC:1094 provides, 'when both parents can not exercise the rights nor assume the duties in regard to a minor child, or where the parents die without appointing any guardian by a will, the guardian is determined by the following order: 1. grandparents living in the same household with the minor; 2. head of the house; 3. grandparents not living in the same household with the minor; 4. paternal uncle, 5. a person selected by the family council'. But according to JWL:23, when appointing a guardian for a juvenile, the court may now exclude the application of the said CVC:1094 and reallocate custody of a juvenile to a representative of the social welfare authority or any other juvenile welfare body, or any other pertinent persons.

[38] This concern for children under the ROC welfare policy may be allied to what the Western theorists Dingwall, Eekelaar and Murray called a 'national investment' view of children. (Dingwall, Eekelaar & Murry, 1983:217-221; Dingwall & Eekelaar,1984:106-107).

[39] Here the term population policy refers to government regulations and programmes designed to change the growth rate of the population. Family Planning, as the major policy instrument, is used interchangeably with population policy. See Lee,K.T.,1988:68.

[40] The first unofficial family planning programme emerged in 1963, which was officially adopted in 1968 by promulgation of the Regulations Governing the Implementation of Family Planning in Taiwan. Under the programme, every married couple is encouraged to have not more than two children, and in achieving that, birth control services are offered at low prices. For more information on the family planning programmes and practices in Taiwan, see Chang, Freedman, & Sun,1981; Freedman & Takeshita,1969; Lee,K.T.,1988.

[41] The national compulsory education in *Taiwan* under the Nationalist government had been six years in the elementary school until 1967 when the Executive Yuan passed and announced a 'Principles for the Implementation of Nine-Year National Education'. This administrative law was further ratified by the 1979 National Education Law to the effect that, starting from 1968 in *Taiwan* and *Kingmon* (another island which is under the physical control of ROC) areas, children aged between 6 and 15 shall receive compulsory education for six years in the elementary/primary school and three years in the junior high school. See *Hsieh,Y.W.,1987:224*; *Ting,P.Y.,1975:611*.

[42] Both of these are provided in the Child Welfare Law and relevant administrative laws. See *Hsieh,Y.W.,1987:140-195*.

[43] In fact, before the promulgation of the 1993 CWL, child welfare affairs had been administered by a branch of the Social Bureau (*Taipei* and *Kaohsiung* Municipalities) or the Social Department (*Taiwan* Province) together with welfare affairs of the aged, the disabled, juveniles, and women.

[44] There was no specified central or local child welfare budget. In *Taipei*, there were only three child welfare officers, who were responsible for all child welfare affairs, and the situation became worse in other cities. Further, there was no public emergency protection centre to accommodate abused children.

[45] The most serious problem to be tackled then was drug-abuse and arms-fighting among school children. Such cases used to be dealt with by the Law Governing the Disposition of Juvenile Cases (LGDJC). It was felt that the law could no longer cope with troubled adolescents for it did not provide for preventive and welfare-oriented measures.

[46] It is worth mentioning that NGO lobbying only commenced after the second reading of the JWL Bill. According to *Ms WANG, Ching Feng*, the chairperson of the Taipei Women Rescue Foundation (TWRF), '[o]n November 8, 1988, the TWRF united all concerned NGOs and marched to the Legislative Yuan to petition for the inclusion of related provisions in the welfare law'. She told the newspaper interviewer: '[w]e made emergency rescue of the Juvenile Welfare Law after its second reading. And because we acted in time, the Juvenile Welfare Law finally incorporated our proposals concerning the protection and care of prostitution-involved girls'. See *The United Daily* on September 5, 1989, p.12.

[47] Before January 1989, the 1973 CWL had been providing for welfare measures to children under the age of 18. When the JWL was enforced in January 1989, it took over the jurisdiction over children between the ages of 12 and 18. It was once considered during the amendment of the CWL during late 1992 and early 1993 that a new CWL shall be made to replace both the 1973 CWL and the 1989 JWL in order to save resources and to catch up with the world trend (*Feng,Y. et al.,1993:7*). However, it was finally decided that juvenile and child affairs were of different nature and should be governed by two sets of laws, measures and personnel.

[48] Although the ROC cannot sign or ratify any UN Convention, the government still make national laws to respond to every new UN legislation in order to show its determination to rejoin international society.

[49] What they did with the foreign laws were to print out a Chinese translation of every law and distributed them to the members. Certain committed members would study and choose those laws which were considered appropriate. Meetings were then held to discuss proposals made by the members in order to decide which laws were to be selected.

[50] It was felt that if social workers were suddenly given too much power without proper professional training and legal education, it was possible that more power would be invoked to intervene in normal family life than to protect children in danger. See similar argument and controversy made in the Cleveland Report (Butler-Sloss,1988); Parton,1985,1991.

[51] Under the CRC, there are several offences which may only be prosecuted if the case is initiated in the Criminal Court by a private complaint. For example, in order to charge customers of underage prostitution (girls under 16), a private compliant has to be filed by or on behalf of the involved girl. See chapter six for discussions of relevant laws.

[52] *Mr LIN* is also the founder and the president of the Child Welfare League Foundation (CWLF).

[53] Corresponding administrative Regulations and Rules have been announced successively to regulate the establishment and operation of public and private child and juvenile welfare measures and facilities.

[54] The Child Welfare League was officially registered later as the Child Welfare League Foundation in January,1993.

[55] The third bill was proposed by the Executive Yuan, which was the main bill to be read by the legislators. The other two bills were affixed for reference, but the Law was actually amended more in line with these two bills than with the governmental bill.

6 LEGAL CONTROLS OVER CHILD PROSTITUTION UNDER GENERAL LAWS

A major argument for the making of a specific law to replace all the existing general laws was that the existing laws were unable to manage the child prostitution problem. The underage flesh markets prospered under the dysfunction of prostitution control regulations. Perpetrators escaped from the loopholes of the Criminal Code and the Social Order Maintenance Law. Victims rescued from but then abandoned back to sex-related business settings by the same bunch of treatment legislation including the Civil Code, the Child Welfare Law, the Juvenile Welfare Law and the Law Governing the Disposition of Juvenile Cases. However, many others argued against the making of a specific law, because in their observation, the mismanagement resulted from the failures of law enforcement and not the insufficiency of law provisions. Before presenting the new specific law, it is worth reviewing the failures of relevant general laws in order to examine the accomplishments of the specific law.

Legal Construction of Illegal Prostitution

ROC Prostitution Control Regulations

As discussed in chapter five, the ROC state government has adhered to the moral goal of the total abolition of prostitution in *Taiwan* since 1945. Several Prostitution Prohibition Orders[1] were successively pronounced by the *Taiwan* Provincial Government (1945-1949) to ban the practice of commercial sex but all failed. After the ROC central government moved to *Taiwan* (1949), the state started to regulate the so-called 'special girlie restaurants (*to chung chiu chia* 特種酒家) ' (left behind by the Japanese), in order to meet the practical needs of society and, in particular, of those single men who followed the ROC army to *Taiwan* (*Chen,P.H.,1970:145*).

In 1949 the ROC government signed the 'UN Convention for the Suppression of the Traffic in Persons and the Exploitation of the Prostitution of Others'. The Convention then became the best weapon of the moralists to attack the illicit practice of the 'special girlie restaurants' (*Hsieh,K.:160-161*). After chronic debates among decision-makers as to how to counterbalance the conflicts between the state policy of prostitution suppression and male 'needs' in society, a practical solution was adopted. Total abolition remained the final goal, while the mandatory approach adopted by the central government to achieve this goal was not the criminalisation of prostitution, but to passively allow local governments to make their own laws to regulate the practice of prostitution under a hypocritical guideline -- 'short-term regulation and long-term abolition' (*Chen,P.H.,1970:145-148*; *Shen,M.C.,1989:32-33*).

As a result, the first *Taiwan* provincial 'Regulations Governing Prostitution (RGP)' was pronounced in 1956 to legalise 'public prostitution (*kung chang* 公娼)'. It was governed under the rationale that not only the practice of prostitution was culturally rooted, there were also practical needs in society, thus prostitution had to be regulated in ways which would lead to total abolition. Over the years, the RGP was constantly amended and/or supplemented by other governmental orders/decrees. Several means were employed successively, and a new one was always adopted to supplement the ineffective old one.

It started with regulation of red-light districts, licensing public brothels/public prostitutes, and giving registered prostitutes incentives to join rehabilitation programmes in order to help them take 'moral' jobs, the official slang being 'abolition through regulation (*yu chin yu kuan* 寓禁於管)' since the late 1950s (*Shen,M.C.,1989:33*). In the early 1960s, abolition became a symbolic goal. The RGP was amended and supplemented by several governmental orders in order to tighten up legal control over registered prostitution and to prohibit unregistered prostitution (*Liu,Y.M.,1972:40-41*).

From 1968 to the early 1970s, the ROC government initiated three 'purity society campaigns' against the deteriorating prostitution problems including that involving under-age girls (*Shen,M.C.,1989:34*). Three new sets of the 'Regulations Governing Prostitution' were enacted by the local governments of the *Taiwan* Province (April 6, 1973), the *Taipei* Municipality (June 27, 1973) and the *Kaohsiung* Municipality (June 21, 1982) in order to help wipe out illegal prostitution. In reality, however, the hypocritical state prostitution policy of 'short-term regulation and long-term abolition' has not only failed the goal of eliminating prostitution but contributed to its illegal practice in all sorts of entertainment establishments in addition to legal and illegal brothels (*Lin,Y.M.,1976:50; Shen,M.C.,1989:36,114-117*).

The state finally decided to supplement the 'abolition through regulation' prostitution policy with a new idea -- 'abolition through taxation (*yu chin yu cheng* 寓禁於征)'. Governmental Orders/Decrees were thus issued in 1974 to charge high license fees and levy six-times the original business tax on all special entertainment establishments.[2] The result was that many legally registered girlie restaurants, American bars, night clubs, girlie coffee/tea houses and massage parlours chose to close down, while the underground flesh markets kept recruiting more illegal operators and workers (*Liu,Y.M.,1976:58-59*).

As mentioned in chapter five, owing to the report of 'The *Taiwan* Particular' in the TIME Magazine on December 22, 1967, and a series of moralist social movements, a *Taipei* Governmental Order was finally announced on October 28, 1977, which mandated the abolition of the most notorious red-light district -- *the PEI TOU SPA* in two years' time. It was reported by the then *Taipei* Municipal Government that on October 29, 1979, prostitution became extinguished within *the PEI TOU SPA* district.[3] However, it was also observed that most of the exiled operators and prostitutes simply joined the business settings which accommodated illegal prostitution (Chen,H.H.,1986:128) (*Kao,R.,1991:61*).

In view of the failures, three sets of the 'Regulations Governing Special Entertainment Establishments' were successively announced by the local governments of the *Taiwan* Province (January,31), the *Taipei* Municipality (October,24) and the *Kaohsiung* Municipality (July,31) in 1986 (*Shen,M.C.,1989:35*). And since then, the basic legal principle in practice has been two-fold: on the one hand, to strengthen the regulation of existing legal public brothels and other special entertainment establishments and to prohibit all governmental authorities[4] to license new brothels; and on the other hand, to confine the practice of legally-registered prostitutes to those public brothels (*Shen,M.C.,1989:32-42*).

Despite all the efforts made in pronouncing new governmental regulations and orders, the practice of illegal prostitution became so endemic that an unbearable number of young girls were sold or forced into the flesh markets, which finally triggered the first wave of the moralist movement against child prostitution. As a result of vigorous lobbying of concerned NGOs and a close relationship established between concerned professionals and the legislators, the vulnerability of underage children was recognised in the making of the 1989 Juvenile Welfare Law and the 1993 Child Welfare Law.

Children under 18 years of age were then singled out for specific protection against sexual exploitation in prostitution under national laws. Under the two Welfare Laws, the welfare authorities are not only legally empowered to impose administrative fines on violators, but also entitled to obtain legal guardianship of the victim through court proceedings and act on behalf of the child to institute a case in the Criminal Court against the perpetrators.

Conflicts between National and Local Laws

An indispensable side effect of the vague and hypocritical prostitution policy is that local laws -- Regulations Governing Prostitution (RGP) -- actually conflicted either with the contents or the spirit of relevant national laws including police offence laws and criminal laws.

Conflicting police offence laws and the 'Regulations Governing Prostitution' Under the Police Offence Law (POL) which is now replaced by the Social Order Maintenance Law (SOML), prostitution has been illegal since 1945. So no public prostitution should have been allowed by any local laws. However, in order to accommodate practical needs and to redress the failures of strict prostitution policy, the RGP was made by local governments to legalise the practice of registered prostitutes in licensed brothels. According to Articles 116, 170 and 172 of the ROC Constitution, these laws made by local governments which are in contradiction with the national laws should have been declared null and void. However, the validity of the RGP has never been questioned in the Council of Grand Justices (*ta fa kuan huei yi* 大法官會議) and thus remains intact. Therefore in practice, public prostitution is legally operated by local governments according to the Regulations Governing Prostitution, and only those who have violated such regulations are subjected to the punishment of police offence laws and criminal laws.

Contradictions in the application of the Criminal Code Under Article 231 of the Criminal Code (CRC), it is a felony to induce or retain 'a female person of respectable character'[5] in order to involve her in commercial sex. This Article was made in 1935 and has never been amended. The basic legislative intention was to prevent women from joining prostitution in the hope that there would be no prostitutes when the then practising ones finally retired (*Tao,P.C. et al.,1991:857*). However, the local laws allow a woman over 18/20 years of age to apply for a prostitution license. Thus in order to avoid criminal punishment, the brothel-keepers only have to ensure the registration of all employed prostitutes according to the Regulations Governing Prostitution before they are charged with the CRC:231 offences.

According to Article 239 of the Criminal Code, the wife of a married customer can file a private complaint to charge both the husband and the prostitute(s) of adultery, and both of them can be sentenced to imprisonment for a maximum of one year. Thus it is a principle of the national law that all extra-marital sexual relationships constitute a criminal offence, although a spouse has the right to withhold prosecution. But the Regulations Governing Prostitution do not prohibit the admission of married men into brothels.[6] The Regulations have thus been accused of abetting in the commission of adultery (*Shen,M.C.,1989:113*).

Administrative Offences[7]

Those who are involved in the operation and consumption of illegal prostitution may be subjected to administrative punishments for committing police offences, for violating governmental regulations governing the operation of public brothels or special entertainment establishments, or for offending welfare laws of special protection for juveniles/children.

Relevant national laws concerning prostitution control include the Social Order Maintenance Law (police offence laws), the Criminal Code, and certain provisions in the Juvenile/Child Welfare Laws. The registration/licensing, operation, and taxation of public brothels/public prostitutes and special entertainment business settings are subjected to the administration of local governments according to the 'Regulations Governing Prostitution' or the 'Regulations Governing Special Entertainment Establishments'.

National Laws Theoretically speaking, prostitution itself has been illegal under the ROC police offence laws. Under Article 64-I of the Police Offence Law (POL), those who were involved in commercial sex including the prostitutes, the pimps, the brothel-keepers, and the customers, could all be subjected to administrative punishment of detention/compulsory labour (maximum seven days) or fines. After the Social Order Maintenance Law (SOML) was promulgated in 1991 to replace the POL[8], now the police offences of commercial prostitution, pimping, brothel-keeping in the POL remain in the SOML, though the latter provides for much heavier administrative fines of maximum N.T.$30,000 (SOML:80 & 81).[9] However, frequenting unregistered prostitution is no longer a police offence under the SOML.

According to the 1973 Child Welfare Law (CWL), those who profited from child prostitution should be liable for an administrative fine of maximum N.T.$25,000.[10] (CWL:18,20,26) And under the 1989 Juvenile Welfare Law (JWL), such fine is raised up to maximum N.T.$75,000, and in addition, the violator's name will be publicly announced (JWL:21-III & 28-II). However, no provisions are available for imposing administrative punishment on customers of juvenile prostitution.

The 1993 CWL has now brought about some innovative administrative punishments against both the operators and consumers. For those who profit from child prostitution (including the parents), an administrative fine of maximum N.T.$120,000 may be imposed (CWL:26,44-II), and the welfare authority should order the parent to attend family and parenting education and counselling for a period of not less than four hours (CWL:48). Those business holders who employ or allow children to work in prostitution can be fined maximum N.T.$300,000, their names announced publicly, and if the violation is grave or the violator is a persistent offender, then the business setting may be ordered to close down and the license may also be repealed (CWL:46-I). And most importantly, a provision was added to empower welfare authorities to impose on the customers of child prostitution an administrative fine of maximum N.T.$100,000, to announce the violator's name publicly and to order him to attend counseling education for not less than four hours (CWL:48-II,III).

Local Laws Despite the illegality imposed by various national laws on prostitution as enumerated above, all the past or existing 'Regulations Governing Prostitution (RGP)' have allowed the practice of commercial sex under the regulation of local governments (the *Taiwan* Province and the *Taipei/Kaohsiung* Municipalities) (*Shen,M.C.,1989:36-39*). Under the RGP, any woman over 18 in the *Taiwan* Province can apply to the police authority to register as a public prostitute. The regulation is stricter in the *Taipei* and *Kaohsiung* Municipalities: the age limit is raised to 20 and a woman can only apply for a license to practice prostitution through a legally registered brothel.

Some general principles may be summed up from these three sets of the RGP. First, commercial sex can only be legally practised by registered prostitutes in legal brothels. Second, no exploitation[11] or other illegal practice against the criminal laws is allowed. And third, brothels can only practise legally if they are registered under the first sets of the RGP pronounced in 1973 (*Taiwan*, *Taipei*) and 1982 (*Kaohsiung*); besides, the licensed brothels can not move or expand, and cannot be leased or transferred by sale, bestowal or succession (*Shen,M.C.,1989:38-39*).

The three sets of the 'Regulations Governing Special Entertainment Establishments (RGSEE)' were pronounced in 1985 to offset the illegal practice of commercial sex in legally licensed business settings such as dancing halls, girlie restaurants, American bars, coffee/tea houses, and hotels/motels. Apart from charging expensive annual license fees[12] on the existing registered ones, the RGSEE also prohibits the licensing of new special entertainment establishments. Prostitution constitutes a violation of the terms of the license with the penalties of revocation and confiscation of earnings. The licensing authority is also required to inform the police of any suspected criminal offences (*Shen,M.C.,1989:41-42*).

Criminal Code Offences[13]

Relevant Offences Provided in the Criminal Code There are a number of provisions in the ROC Criminal Code which provide penalties for prostitution-related offences. However, these laws leave significant loopholes which, in practice, make it possible for some perpetrators of child prostitution to avoid criminal punishment. This sub-section introduces relevant provisions in the Criminal Code in order to facilitate later examinations. They include the laws governing 'offences against social morals'(CRC:221, 224, 227, 231, 232, 233), 'offences against the family' (CRC:240, 241, 243), 'offences against personal liberty' (CRC:296, 298, 300, 302, 304), and 'offences causing bodily harm' (CRC:286).

A comparative study among the relevant Articles is made in the following table. The table is divided into four columns: the first column numerates the Article of the Criminal Code (CRC); the second column indicates the constituent elements of the offence punished by the Article; the third column shows the recommended tariff of basic punishment[14] including imprisonment and fine; and the forth column specifies whether or not prosecution against the offence can be initiated only upon private complaint[15] (IOUC).

Article of CRC	Criminal Offence (constituent elements)	Criminal Punishment	IOUC
§231(I)	for the purpose of gain induce or retain a **female person of respectable character**[16] to have carnal relations[17] with a third person	imprisonment: not more than three years + fine: not more than 500 yuan[18]	no
§231(II)	for the purpose of gain cause a person to commit an indecent act[19]	same as §231(I)	no
§231(III)	make the commission of §231(I) or (II) an occupation	imprisonment: not more than five years + fine: not more than 1,000 yuan	no
§232	commit §231(I) against a person subject to ones supervision because of family or other guardian relations	imprisonment: not more than five years + fine: not more than 1,000 yuan	no
§233	induce a person under the age of 16 to submit to an indecent act or carnal relations	imprisonment: not more then five years	no
§240(I)	abduct a person under the age of 20 from the family or from another who has supervision right[20]	imprisonment: not more than three years	no
§240(III)	commit §240(I) for the purposes of gain or further causing the abducted person to submit to an indecent act or carnal relations	imprisonment: not more than 5 years + fine: not more than 1,000 yuan	no

§241(I)	forcibly abduct[21] a person under the age of 20 from her family or from another who has supervision right over her	imprisonment: not less than one and not more than seven years	
§241(II)	commit §241(I) for the purposes of gain or further causing the abducted person to submit to an indecent act or carnal relations	imprisonment: not less than three years and not more than ten years	no
§241(III)	abduction with consent of a person under the age of 16 shall be considered to have committed forcible abduction	same as §241(I) or §241(II)	no
§243(I)	receive, harbour or conceal an abducted person specified in §2240 or §241 for the purposes of gain or further causing the abducted person to submit to an indecent act or carnal relations	imprisonment: not less than six months and not more than five years + fine: not more than 500 yuan	no
§296	enslave a person or place a person in a position without freedom similar to slavery	imprisonment: not less than one and not more than seven years	no
§298(II)	forcibly abduct a **female person** for the purpose of gain or to cause her to submit to an indecent act or carnal relations	imprisonment: not less than one and not more than seven years + fine: not more than 1,000 yuan	yes
§300(I)	receive, harbour or conceal a forcibly abducted **female person** specified in §298 for the purposes of gain or further causing the abducted person to submit to an indecent act or carnal relations	imprisonment: not less than six months and not more than five years + fine: not more than 500 yuan	no

§302	detain a person without authority or deprive a person of freedom of movement by other illegal means	imprisonment: not more than five years; detention; fine: not more than 300 yuan	no
§304	cause a person to do a thing which the person has no obligation to do by means of violence or threats, or prevent a person from doing a thing which the person has the right to do	imprisonment: not more than three years; detention; fine: not more than 300 yuan	no
§221(I)	rape: render resistance impossible and thus impose carnal relations on a **female person** by using violence or threats, administrating drugs, inducing hypnosis, or by other means	imprisonment: not less than five years	yes
§221(II)	statutory rape[22]: has carnal relations with a **female person** under the age of 14	same as §221(I)	yes
§224(I)	indecent assault: render resistance impossible and thus impose indecent acts on a person by using violence or threats, administrating drugs, inducing hypnosis, or by other means	imprisonment: not more than seven years	yes
§224(II)	commit an indecent act against a person under the age of 14	same as §224(I)	yes
§227(I)	has carnal relations with a **female person** between the ages of 14 and 16	imprisonment: not less than one and not more than seven years	yes
§227(II)	commit an indecent act against a person between the ages of 14 and 16	imprisonment: not more than five years	yes
§286(I)	maltreating a person under 16 or by other means impairing the natural development of the body of such person	imprisonment: not more than five years; detention; fine: not more than 500 yuan	no

§286(II)	for the purpose of gain committing an offence specified in §286(I)	imprisonment: not less than five years; fine: not more than 1,000 yuan	no

Although there are various provisions in the Criminal Code applicable to child prostitution cases, not a single one of them actually coincided with the exact offences. Concerned law professionals in *Taiwan* have found it difficult to apply correct or appropriate laws to cases of this kind. Studies on past ROC Criminal Court cases have shown disparities in the applications of laws (*Shen,M.C.,1989*).

In theory, if the victim is abducted from her\his custodian\guardian, provisions concerning **offences against the family** will be applied to the procurers and the brothel-keepers (CRC:240, 241, 243-I). If no such supervision rights have been infringed, but a forcible abduction is committed, then the **offences against personal liberty** (CRC:298-II, 300-I) may be charged by a private complaint (CRC:308). Otherwise, provisions governing **offences against social morals** can be availed of to prosecute the procurers in cases where the victim is a female person of 'respectable character' (CRC:231, 232) or is under the age of 16 (CRC:233). Alternatively, all perpetrators may be charged with **offences against personal liberty** involving slavery, illegal detention or forcing others to act (CRC:302, 304) or **offences causing bodily harm** involving impeding development of the victim (CRC:286).

The Criminal Code also contains two offences of unlawful sexual intercourse with young persons, namely, statutory rape committed against a girl under the age of 14, and having carnal relations with a girl aged between 14 and 16. So the age of 16 is what is commonly referred to as the 'age of consent'.[23] Thus those who conduct sexual intercourse with a girl under the age of 16 should be prosecuted with sex offences under the Criminal Code. To establish whether a man is guilty of either of these offences, consent on the part of the girl is irrelevant. And as the policy of the law is to protect young girls,[24] mistakenly believing that the girl is over 14 or over 16 is no defense, although in practice, the conviction rests on recklessness.[25] If the victim is a boy under 16 or an indecent act is committed against a girl under 16, the perpetrator may be charged with offences of criminal indecency (CRC:224II, 227II). However, all these sexual offences may only be prosecuted upon private complaints (CRC:236).

So the Criminal Code seems to have provided for the punishment of all perpetrators including the procurers, the pimps\brothel-keepers, and the customers of child prostitution. However, as a result of the selective application of law by law enforcers, some relevant provisions have never been considered applicable in practice. One is CRC:296[26] -- offences of slavery. Another is CRC:286[27] -- offences of impeding the natural development of children under 16. And the others are CRC:221, 224, 227 -- offences of having unlawful sexual relations with children under 16.

During the making of the Criminal Code, child prostitution was considered a social evil to be criminalised. In the early draft bills of the Criminal Code, there were specific offences of traffic in persons, sale of children by parents, sale of wives by husband, and sale of minors by guardians. All these offences were finally incorporated into a catch-all provision against slavery (*Tao,O.C. et al.,1991:857*). Therefore, one of the leading criminal law professor in *Taiwan*, Professor *HAN Chung Mo*, maintains that it was the legislative intention of the Criminal Code that 'child prostitution' shall be punished as an offence of slavery[28], which is now provided in CRC:296 (*Han,C.M.,1980:366-367*). But case studies have concluded that, in practice, CRC:231, 232, 233 are applied instead of CRC:296, for the judiciary adopts a rather strict and narrow definition of 'slavery' (*Shen,M.C.,1989:136-137*).

It is generally observed that as a result of the experiences in prostitution, the natural development of children is seriously hindered.[29] *SHEN Mei Chen* (*SHEN*) therefore argues that CRC:286-II should be applied to punish those who prostitute children under 16 (*Shen,M.C.,1989:146-147*). However, the issue brought before the Courts is the criminal act involving the operation of illegal prostitution but not the victimisation of children, thus the fact that children's natural development is casually impaired has never been the concern of the Court. Further, as pointed out by *SHEN*, if CRC:286-II is applied, the perpetrators will be subjected to a minimum sentence of five years imprisonment. Compared to other relevant offences, this punishment is so severe that no Court would consider it appropriate to apply the provision to child prostitution cases (*Shen,M.C.,1989:146*).

Theoretically speaking, the consumer of child prostitution, generally referred to as the customers in this book, is liable for sexual offences against social morals. He can be charged under CRC:221-II with statutory rape if the girl victim is under 14. In cases where the victims are aged between 14 and 16, CRC:227-I also punishes the customer for committing unlawful sexual intercourse. When indecent acts are committed rather than sexual intercourse, CRC:224-I (victims under 14) and CRC:227-II (victims between 14 & 16) should apply. All these are severe crimes with heavy basic punishment. The law (CRC:236), however, provides that no such case can be heard before the Criminal Court without a private complaint. In practice, there have been no known cases in which such customer is prosecuted or charged under these provisions (*Shen,1989:143-144*).

Application of the Criminal Code in Child Prostitution Cases[30] According to Article 1 of the ROC Criminal Code (CRC), the modern concept of '*nulla poena sine lege* (no person shall be punished except in pursuance of a statute which fixes a penalty for a certain criminal behaviour)' is the guiding principle for imposing penal punishments on criminal offenders. If an act does not tally with the constituent elements (*ko cheng yao chien 構成要件*) of a specified criminal offence, it is not punishable under the law even if the act is most heinous and morally condemnable (*Shen,1989:149*).

Therefore, in order to charge any perpetrator of an offence, all the 'constituent elements' legally specified for that offence must be fulfilled. Take CRC:231-I, for instance, it provides that a person who for the purpose of profit-making induces or retains 'a woman of respectable character' to have sexual intercourse with a third person shall be punished by the law. Thus in practice, if a girl was sold by *brothel-keeper A* to *brothel-keeper B*, then *B* cannot be charged with CRC:231-I, for the procured girl was already involved in prostitution and by the definition of the Criminal Courts she was no longer 'a woman with respectable character' (*Shen, M.C.,1989:191-192*).

For each of the criminal offences specified in the CRC, a recommended tariff of basic punishments is affixed. The penalty finally pronounced by the Court may however be increased or decreased under certain circumstances specified in the CRC.[31] The final sentence can also be increased by applying specific articles in the Child Welfare Law (when the victim is under 12).

The act or acts of a perpetrator may commit more than one criminal offence specified in the CRC. The governing principles can be best explained by an example of a person who abducts an 18-year-old girl with her consent, then detains her by force, and finally rapes her. The involved offences provided by the CRC include abduction (CRC:240: maximum three years), illegal detention (CRC:302: maximum five years), and rape

(CRC:221: minimum five years). The offender may be charged with one, two or three of the offences depending on his *mens rea* (intention). If he intends to rape the girl, while abduction and detention are the means adopted to obtain rape, the Court will only impose the punishment prescribed for the most severe crime -- rape. (CRC:55) If the offender has three separate intentions to abduct, to detain, and then to rape the girl, he will be found guilty of all the three offences. The Court will first pronounce the penalty for each offence, then combine all the penalties to make the final sentence, but this cannot exceed 20 years (CRC:50 & 51). It is also possible that the offender first abducts the girl for other purposes, but later he detains her for the purpose of rape. Then he will be guilty of abduction and rape.

On the other hand, when an offender is brought to the Court for a single criminal act, more than one provision of the CRC may become applicable. For example, a procurer who bought a 13-year-old girl from her mother without the consent of the father may be charged with CRC:231 (maximum three years) and CRC:233 (maximum five years) or CRC:241(III) (maximum ten years). According to the CRC, the court should apply the CRC with the most severe punishment -- CRC:241-III (CRC:55).

Under the ROC criminal justice system, a procurator[32] should investigate all suspected crimes in order to decide whether to file a public prosecution in the Criminal Court. But if the committed offence can only be prosecuted upon private complaint, the perpetrator(s) will not face the Court unless a case is legally initiated by or on behalf of the victim. There are two kinds of relevant offences which may only be prosecuted if private complaints are brought to the Criminal Court according to CRC:308 and CRC:236.[33]

One is the forcible abduction of women specified in CRC:298-II. It may be applied against the procurers, and if no private complaints have been filed, the Court may apply other relevant provisions such as CRC:231, 232, 233, 240, 241 to convict the perpetrators. The other is unlawful sexual relations with children under 16. Under CRC:221, 224, 227, customers may be charged with offences of rape, statutory rape or indecency. But if no private case is filed, no customers can be punished under the CRC.

The perpetrators involved in a child prostitution case include the parent figure, the procurer, the pimp\brothel-keeper, and the customer. It was explained earlier that though the customer can theoretically be prosecuted with sex offences, no such cases have been brought to trial. Besides, the Court of final instance has never convicted any perpetrator of the offence of slavery or of impeding the natural development of children. The following analyses sum up the ways that the Court of final instance interpreted and applied relevant provisions of the Criminal Code.[34] In principle, the laws applied to individual offenders including the parent figures, other procurers and pimps\brothel-keepers are as follows:

a. THE PARENT FIGURE (PF): A PF offender may be prosecuted with an **offence against the family** or an **offence against personal liberty** depending on whether or not the offender is a sole custodian/guardian. In cases where a daughter is sold by a custodial PF without the consent of the other custodian, the PF is charged with abduction (CRC:240-III) or forcible abduction (CRC:241-II,III) -- both are offences against the family -- depending on whether a valid consent of the girl is obtained.[35] When the PF sells the daughter by means of violence, threat, or fraud, he may also be held guilty of the CRC:298-II forcible abduction -- an offence against personal liberty -- upon a private complaint.[36] In all other cases, the PF can be prosecuted with **offences against social morals** if the involved girl is a woman of respectable character (CRC:232) or is under the age of 16 when she is sold (CRC:233).[37]

b. THE PROCURER AND THE PIMP\BROTHEL-KEEPER:[38] The offender who abducts a girl from her custodian(s) is responsible for the **offence against the family** under CRC:240-III or CRC:241-II,III, the application of which is the same as that for a parent offender. Otherwise, the procurer may be held guilty of the **offence against social morals** according to CRC:233 if the victim is under 16, or CRC:231 if the victim is of respectable character.[39] And if a private complaint is brought to the court, the procurer can also be punished for the **offence against personal liberty** (forcible abduction) under CRC:298-II.[40]

A brothel-keeper who receives, harbours or conceals an abducted person specified in CRC:240,241 or CRC:298 can be punished under CRC:243-I (**offences against the family**) or CRC:300-I (**offences against personal liberty**).[41] But if a brothel-keeper is found guilty of procurement, he/she will only be punished for the more severe offences of CRC:240, 241, 298.[42] Besides, the brothel-employed bouncers who are responsible for restricting the freedom of the girls are liable for the offence of illegal detention provided in CRC:302-I.[43]

In two of the studied cases, the offenders were prosecuted under CRC:296.[44] However, in both cases, the Courts of final instance held that neither selling daughters into prostitution nor procurement/brothel-keeping is an offence of slavery. In addition, according to CRC:286, the Criminal Court can imprison those who, for the purpose of gain, maltreat a child under 16 and as a result (or by other means) impair the natural development of such child. The impossible penalty is 'imprisonment for not less than five years (not more than 15 years)'. However, it was said that the Court would not apply CRC:286 because the offence involved a very heavy basic punishment, which is considered by the Courts to be excessive (*Shen,M.C.,1989:146*). This reveals general judicial attitudes that the harm done to a prostitution-involved girl by the perpetrators is not the crucial issue in criminal prosecution.

The imposed punishments

a. THE PARENT FIGURE: Among the 23 Court cases studied by *SHEN Mei Chen*,[45] two parent figures were convicted by CRC:298-II (maximum seven - minimum one year) in the case *SHEN-6*, which was initiated by a private complaint. One was an adoptive grandparent who not only prostituted his 11-year-old adopted granddaughter in his hotel but also procured another 13-year-old girl. The Court thus imposed a severe penalty of seven years. The offending father of the sold 13-year-old girl was sentenced to imprisonment for three years and six months.[46] Compared to this case, the Courts imposed very lenient punishments on parent offenders in other studied cases.

Three cases were decided according to CRC:241-III,II (maximum ten - minimum three years). Although no 'extenuating circumstances' were mentioned in the judgments, the final sentences were the minimum 'three years' imprisonment' for two mothers and the slightly heavier 'three years and six months' imprisonment' for an adoptive father. In all other cases, CRC:232 (maximum five years - minimum two months) was applied. The final imposed basic penalties ranged from 10 months,[47] one year,[48] one year and two months,[49] one year and six months[50] to two years [51].

Apart from the general leniency in imposing punishment, two Courts also decided to suspend the execution of the pronounced sentences according to CRC:74 on the grounds that the parents were 'ignorant aboriginal people with financial difficulties' and there were 'tender children back home for them to take care of'. As a result, five parents/adoptive parents were released subjected to the supervision of the Court for five years.

b. THE PROCURER AND THE PIMP\BROTHEL-KEEPER: Among the 23 cases studied, the general thread observed in the imposition of punishment on the procurers, pimps, brothel-keepers and their abettors by the Courts of final instance was that of leniency (*Shen,M.C.,1989:192*). For those who were convicted of **offences against social morals** with basic punishment of maximum three-year (CRC:231-I) or five-year imprisonment (CRC:231-III,233), the average final sentence was less than one year. For those who were charged with **offences against the family** with basic punishment of three to ten years (CRC:241-II,III), no one was sentenced to imprisonment for more than three years and six months.

Comments Three comments may be made from the above case study.[52] The selective application of laws by the Courts pose two main problems. It was observed that the Courts had deliberately evaded the application of certain relevant provisions. Although there were relevant provisions in the CRC which could be applied to punish slavery (CRC:296) and child maltreatment (CRC:286), the ROC Criminal Courts have generally considered them unsuitable or irrelevant in child prostitution cases.

Despite the fact that it was the legal intention of CRC:296 to punish perpetrators of child prostitution with the offence of slavery, the Courts have held that the girl victims were not subjected to a circumstance which was as unbearable and inhuman as 'slavery'. On the other hand, child prostitution cases were dealt with as an issue of illegal prostitution. Therefore, criminal justice was held to punish those who had committed offences of illegal prostitution. Under this rationale, the harm caused to the victim became an irrelevant issue. Besides, it was also a legal tradition that customers who pay for commercial sex were not subjected to criminal punishment.

As a result, those who had sexually exploited and abused underage children were never punished for maltreating children, which involve more severe offences than the provisions applied in practice. In addition, when several Articles of the Criminal Code were pertinent in a case, the Court inclined to apply the provision with a less severe offence. Moreover, as the application of the laws in child prostitution cases was complicated and confusing in practice, it was not uncommon for a Court to apply inappropriate or even wrong provisions.

Apart from the fact that the Courts tended to chose to prosecute offenders of girl prostitution with less severe offences, the imposition of sentences was generally lenient compared to the recommended tariffs of basic punishment. As indicated above, the perpetrators were usually punished with a sentence which was not much more than the minimum basic punishment. The punishment for offending parents were often decreased further, for under the perception of the Courts, those parents who would sell their daughters into prostitution shared certain common traits -- ignorance and poverty (*Wang,T.S. et al.,1989:358*). And it was held that the law should be more sympathetic with these socially and financially disadvantaged people. Besides, the Courts also considered the responsibility of these parents towards other children and is reluctant to lock them away from the family.

Deficiency in the Implementation of General Penal Laws

Obstacles in Enforcing the State Prostitution Policy

The obstacles in the implementation of laws against the practice of illegal prostitution emerged mainly as a result of the vague and hypocritical 'short-term regulation and long-term abolition' prostitution policy, which has formed a vicious circle of societal tolerance and official indifference towards the deterioration of the problem. The continuous failures of law have been manifested by the retreat of the state control policy from abolition to regulation, and from actively eliminating vice business settings to passively restricting the practice of unregistered prostitution. It was because of these failures that the practice of child prostitution became rampant. In order to explain the ineffectiveness of laws in protecting girls from prostitution, it is useful to sum up some general obstacles in the implementation of prostitution control laws.

Incompetence of government authorities The successive regulations and laws of contradictory contents have confused administrative authorities who generally suffer from lack of appropriate legal discipline. Thus there may be no enforcement because the authority does not know the existence of a law, or distorted application of laws because of misunderstanding, imprudence, or other incapability of the enforcers (*Shen,M.C.,1989:119*).

Coalition between local politicians, policemen, and prostitution operators Among speeches in all consultation meetings and conferences concerning child prostitution in Asian countries, 'police corruption' and 'involvement of local politicians (council members)' have been mentioned as the main hindrance to be removed (Srisang,1991a; O'Grady,1992b; Host Committee, 1996ab) (*GOH,1992; Li,C.W.,1995; Lin,S.F.,1996; RP;1988; Shee,A.,1992; TMSB,1990b; TWRF,1991,1992,1996*). According to the conclusion of an official research report published by the *Taipei* Municipal Government (*Tang,S.P. et al.,1983*), illegal prostitution is mostly operated under the guard of organised mobsters with the patronage of some local politicians and policemen.[53] There is a widespread belief that many politicians and policemen are local law makers and enforcers during their office hours, while after work, they may also be leaders of organised mobsters, co-operators of unregistered brothels, or regular visitors of illegal prostitution.[54]

Societal conspiracy According to the above mentioned research of the *Taipei* Municipal Government, 54% of men over 20 had experienced commercial sex, 64% of whom described themselves as 'frequent visitors/buyers', that is, 37.26% of men over 20 -- 488812 in number -- in *Taipei* (1982) visited prostitution on a regular basis (*Tang,S.P. et al.,1983:46-52*). How were the consumers informed of the locations of vice business? 37% were supplied the information by relatives and friends, and another 29.26% knew it from reading newspapers and magazines (*Tang,S.P. et al.,1983:46-52*). What did the citizens think of prostitution? Most did not deny its existence, while urging the restriction of its practice to officially regulated areas (60.75%) or supporting the high taxation policy (13.33%). In comparison, there were only 19.25% in agreement with total abolition.

Legislative tolerance towards consumers The consumers of all forms of prostitution are traditionally exempted from legal responsibilities under general laws. As shown in chapter four, the message conveyed in the readings of the Social Order Maintenance Law (1991) has made it clear that it is not in line with the ROC legislative principle to punish customers of illegal prostitution. Although an exception has been made in the recent 1993 Child Welfare Law to provide for some specific administrative punishments for child-sex customers (CRC:46), no basic legal policy has been changed in the Criminal Code.

In fact, any legislative amendment concerning the age of consent will be irrelevant in the practice of ROC laws if a specific offence is not added to punish customers of illegal prostitution. In the past, customers have never been caught for committing carnal relations or other indecent acts against the girls under the age of consent (16 years) according to Articles 221-II, 224, and 227 of the Criminal Code. Concerned professionals in *Taiwan* have provided three reasons for the failures in the prosecution of customers.[55]

First, illegal brothels are generally well-guarded and during police raids, there are 'backdoors' for the customers to escape from the spot. Second, for the police, frequenting illegal prostitution is at most a police offence instead of a criminal offence. And third, the girls and their families would not suffer further humiliation by taking the customers to Court. Consequently, although the customers can, in theory, be punished for conducting unlawful sexual intercourse with girls under 16, it is not considered criminal in practice to purchase sexual services of any kind.

Indifference of law enforcers towards involved crimes The operators and consumers of illegal prostitution who are arrested by the police can first be imposed administrative detention and fines according to the administrative laws governing police offences. If one is suspected of having committed an offence which is subject to public prosecution, the police should also transfer the case to the procurator's office. Various governmental authorities are legally empowered to impose administrative fines, confiscate the illegal earnings, or revoke the license of registered brothels or other special entertainment establishments; in addition thereto, the authorities should also inform the police or the procurator's office of suspected police offences or crimes.

Unfortunately, law enforcers seldom take the initiative to inform on the involved criminal suspects. Administrative authorities only restrict themselves to the 'administration' of illegal prostitution, namely, revoking licenses, imposing fines, and confiscating immoral earnings and leave everything concerning criminal offences to the police. As for the police, illegal prostitution is normally dealt with as a commission of police offences rather than crimes.[56]

Taint of Administrative Laws Disregarding the changing legal measures adopted in the past to offset the problems caused by vice business, the ROC laws have always restricted the practice of commercial sex to officially registered brothels and there are strict rules governing the management of such brothels. Nevertheless, according to the observation of *SHEN*, a review of past official and unofficial statistics and data showed that although the number of officially registered brothels had been declining, more and more entertainment business settings were getting involved in the operation of illegal prostitution, especially the forced and the underage ones (*Shen,M.C.,1989:50-55*).

The enforcement of administrative laws including the regulations over the registration and management of brothels and other special entertainment establishments and the sanctions on violators did not therefore subject the operation of vice business to legal control. On the contrary, it contributed to the prosperity of an illegal prostitution industry. After studying the corrupted practices of commercial sex under the ROC prostitution policies and laws, *SHEN Mei Chen* pointed out that:

> 'The basic aim of prostitution control regulations was to restrict the undesirable expansion of the prostitution industry, to prohibit exploitation, to maintain the hygiene standard, and to wipe out illegal prostitution. However, not only have the laws failed the regulation purposes, the industry is now a haunt of crimes... Forced and underage prostitutes are detained in the backrooms of legal brothels/special entertainment establishments... Gangsters are employed as guards to avoid escapes of the girls, to maintain orders in the business, and to act as required during police raids... The police are bribed to cover the illegal practice... There remains a high demand for young flesh, and illegal child prostitution provides for many people's livelihood including that of the Mafia, the gangsters, or even local politicians... (translation from Chinese)'. (*Shen,M.C.,1989:52-56*)

Frailty of Penal Laws There are many relevant provisions in the Criminal Code (CRC) which can be applied to convict the procurers, the brothel-keepers/pimps, and the customers of child prostitution. However, each provision is affixed with certain conditions (constituent elements) for the establishment of a specific offence. It is only when the victim was under 16 when an offence was committed that the law punishes all involved perpetrators. CRC:233 can be applied indiscriminatorily to all procurers and pimps\brothel-keepers. The customers may be charged under CRC:221-II, 224, 227 if a case is initiated by a private complaint.

If the victim is over 16, no criminal charges can be brought against the customers unless a 'rape' case is initiated by or on behalf of a girl victim (CRC:221-I, 236). Other perpetrators can only be punished if the victim is

a woman of respectable character (CRC:231, 232: offences against social morals), if certain supervision rights have been infringed (CRC:240, 241, 243: offences against the family), or if a private complaint is filed against a forcible abduction (CRC:298, 230: offences against personal liberty).

Consequently, the application of the law imposes strict responsibility on the girls to prove themselves to be 'the victim'. A customer will not be charged with statutory rape once a girl has appeared to have completed her age of 14 unless it can be proven that the offender has made it impossible for her to resist sexual intercourse.[57] And once it is proved that the woman was a prostitute when the concerned offence was committed, none of the perpetrators can be convicted of such **offences against social morals**.[58] On the other hand, in order to punish an offender involved in flesh contracts, it must be proved that the perpetrator has committed one specific offence provided by the law. If an abduction is committed against a guardian of the girl, a public prosecution may be filed to convict the perpetrators with **offences against the family** according to CRC:240, 241, 243-I. But the conviction of such offences depends on the existence of a guardian. On the other hand, if a private complaint is filed against forcible abduction, CRC:298-II and CRC:301-I may be availed of to convict **offences against personal liberty**. However, prostitution-involved children and their families seldom choose to confront the possible humiliation to be faced during Court Proceedings (*Shen,M.C.,185*).

Thus once a child over 16 is procured for the second time, it becomes extremely difficult for the Criminal Code to convict any of the first or later perpetrators. On the one hand, it is practically impossible for the child -- the sole witness -- to identify or inform on the first (or previous) offenders. On the other hand, those immediate perpetrators who are arrested with the victim can always spare themselves criminal punishment through the legal loopholes. There is no **offence against social morals**, for the child was over 16 (CRC:233) or a girl had lost her claim of 'respectable character' (CRC:231,232). There is no **offence against the family**, for the child was not abducted from her\his legal guardians (CRC:240,241,243). And it was not a forcible abduction -- an **offence against personal liberty** (CRC:298-II,230-I), for a child who is already in prostitution cannot be 'abducted'.

The conviction of a criminal offence depends very much on the attitude of the police, the procurators, and the judges. Although there are certain loopholes in the Criminal Code (CRC), all perpetrators can be brought to court and sentenced with harsh punishments if the law enforcers could take an active role in the conviction. To take an extreme example, if CRC:296 (**offences of slavery**) and CRC:286 (**offences of impairing the natural development of children under 16**) could be considered applicable, there would be no 'loopholes' in the Criminal Code.

In practice, however, the enforcers have constructed the crimes involving child prostitution into less severe offences or even no offence. The crucial reasons that CRC:296 and CRC:286 were not applied are that 'slavery' was deemed too serious a crime to convict the perpetrators and those who prostitute children were not considered so heinous as to deserve a **minimum** punishment of five years' imprisonment. So the procurators and the judges have carefully selected other provisions of less serious crimes with less severe punishments in order to construct child prostitution into the Criminal Code.

On the other hand, consuming is not constructed as part of the crime. The police would not even try to arrest customers of child prostitution. Actually it is generally held by the law enforcers that frequenting illegal prostitution is at most an immoral act against social orders. And if the Social Order Maintenance Law has considered it to be no offence, it is definitely not the principle of the Criminal Code to punish it.

Relevant General Laws for Protection and Treatment

In the protection and treatment of child prostitution victims, two main measures under general laws (mainly the Civil Code, the Child Welfare Law, the Juvenile Welfare Law, and the Law Governing the Disposition of Juvenile Cases)[59] may be involved. First, the immediate cutting off of the sexual exploitation by rescue and protection, which may involve dismantlement of the illegal business setting, conviction of the perpetrators, and severance of exploitative parental control. Second, treatment of the child for the undesirable consequence of her\his victimisation through a rehabilitation process, which may be accomplished by provision of counselling, schooling, and skills-training.

Measures taken may be criminal, civil, or administrative in nature[60] and the respective governing laws can be contradictory in purpose. In practice, it is sometimes controversial as to who is to be protected -- the child, the family or society, how the children are to be treated -- as victims, delinquents or offenders, and what is to be done to the child's family tie --

severance, surveillance or reinforcement. In implementation, the police and the Courts may appear to be too tough and are unable to attend to the needs of the child and the family, while the welfare authority or organisations are too powerless to deal with the ferocious prostitution industry.

It was indicated above that the ROC laws and their enforcement have been unable to control the deterioration of the problems of illegal prostitution. The exploitation chain is getting stronger and taking in more daughters of vulnerable families. For the past years, NGOs have been devoted to set up rescue and treatment networks incorporating governmental agencies. Despite the decision-makers and the legislators' reluctance to tighten up the prostitution policy for the purpose of child protection, more laws with corresponding measures are made and provided for the treatment of prostitution-involved children.

It was reported by the ROC Ministry of the Interior that the police cracked down on illegal prostitution and find an average of 200 children under 16 annually, and the government estimated that there were at most 3,000 prostitution-involved children in *Taiwan.*[61] However, the number released by NGOs and individual researchers went as high as 10,000 as indicated in chapter four. Although concerned professionals tended to over-estimate the scale of the problem in order to attract concerns, it may be a safe observation that the legally provided rescue and treatment measures have affected only a very limited proportion of the child victims.

Calls to reinforce police raids on illegal prostitution are often made by the NGOs through the help of the media. And when public concerns accumulated to the extent that the government is pressured to take action, the NGO requests are normally responded to with a short-term administrative project like the 'Decent Society Campaign'. Experiences show that the number of rescued or arrested girls will suddenly go high in the following month which always soothes public as well as professional criticisms. Then the number drops without being noticed until the next NGO complains.[62] This section intends to concentrate on the effects of rescue and treatment on the children who are given a chance through the help of law to rid themselves of the exploitation chain. It discusses when and how the measures are taken under the ROC general laws and why most children will fall back to prostitution despite all the legal efforts.

The basic law governing parent-child relationship is the Civil Code. The 1989 Juvenile Welfare Law and the 1993 Child Welfare Law (Amendment) provide new rules for the special protection of children against parental abuse.[63] These laws have set aside the application of the Civil Code to children under 18 according to the 'specific law supersedes general law' principle.[64]

Custody and Guardianship[65] *of the Girls* Under the Civil Code (CVC), parents are the natural guardians who have legal rights and duties to maintain, educate, and protect their minor children (CVC:1084). When parents abuse their rights, the grandparents or members of the family council may correct them, but if such correction is of no avail, the same people can then apply to the Court for a ruling suspending or terminating such parental rights (CVC:1090). When both parents are deprived of their legal rights, the Court should at the same time appoint a guardian for a minor child (CVC:1091). The guardian can only be chosen from the extended family and be determined by the following order: first, the grandparents living in the same household with the minor; second, head of the house; third, grandparents not living in the same household with the minor; fourth, paternal uncles; and fifth, the person selected by the family council (CVC:1094).

Although the functions of the extended family as above mentioned are still retained by the Civil Code, they are being gradually taken over by the emerging welfare state. The welfare approach has been adopted in special legislation concerning children under 18 as manifested by the 1989 Juvenile Welfare Law (JWL) and the 1993 Child Welfare Law (CWL). Thus the above Civil Code rules concerning the suspension of parental rights and the reallocation of guardianship for children under 18 have been replaced.

Now in cases concerning children under the age of 18, correction of the extended family is no longer essential and in a case of child abuse and neglect of any kind, procurators, welfare authorities or NGOs, as well as the grandparents may apply to the Court for suspension or termination of parental rights and for appointing another appropriate guardian. When appointing such a guardian, the Court may disregard Article 1094 of the Civil Code and designate a head official of the welfare authority, a chairperson/director of a registered juvenile welfare organisation, or any other pertinent person to be the legal guardian of a child (JWL:23-II; CWL:40).

Protection and Treatment Measures Three sets of laws are relevant in the protection and treatment of prostitution-involved girls under the Juvenile Welfare Law (JWL) and the Child Welfare Law (CWL). First, all children under 12 as well as those adolescents between 12 and 18 who were sold into prostitution are legally constructed as 'the victims' who are to receive welfare services (JWL:22, CWL:37). Second, the juvenile girls who were not sold are to be referred to the Juvenile Court (JWL:22) and the 1980 Law Governing the Disposition of Juvenile Cases (LGDJC:3) will be applied by the Court to judge their delinquent behaviour. Third, unregistered prostitutes over 18 are offenders of police offences. If such girls are found to be involved in habitual prostitution, they will be charged with a police offence and committed to a 'special training institution' according to the Social Order Maintenance Law (SOML:80).

Before the 1989 Juvenile Welfare Law (JWL) and the 1993 Child Welfare Law (CWL) were enacted, there were no specific laws governing the treatment of prostitution-involved girls. In order to meet practical needs, the concerned professionals diagnosed the 'sexual deviance' shared among all prostitution-involved girls and persuaded the police to transfer such cases to the Juvenile Court.[66] The Court often committed these girls to governmental rehabilitation centres according to the Law Governing the Disposition of Juvenile Cases (LGDJC).[67] Now under the 1989 JWL (Article 22-III), only the girls who have violated Article 3 of the LGDJC will be referred to the Juvenile Court.

According to Article 3 of LGDJC, there are two cases under the jurisdiction of the Juvenile Court, viz., first, where the conduct of a juvenile violates any criminal law or statutes; and second, where a juvenile is in one of the following situations having the possibility to commit a crime -- (1) associating with habitual criminals; (2) frequenting places where juveniles' presence is prohibited; (3) constantly playing truant or running away from home; (4) participation in gang activities; (5) carrying a lethal weapon without a justifiable reason; (6) habitual violation of police offence laws or constantly loitering at midnight;[68] or (7) drug abuse.[69]

So the Juvenile Court is in charge of juvenile criminals and juvenile delinquents, who, without proper discipline, are in danger of committing crimes in the future. Under the Juvenile Welfare Law as well as the 'Regulations Governing Prostitution and Special Entertainment Establishments', all business settings offering sexual services are 'places where juveniles' presence is prohibited'. The above Article 3-II(2) of the LGDJC is thus, by judicial explanation, applied to prostitution-involved girls who 'frequent' (but are not sold into) such prohibited places.

As soon as a case is under the jurisdiction of the Juvenile Court, a commissioned probation officer will start the investigation under the supervision of the commissioned judge (LGDJC:19). At the same time, the Court may make an order placing the juvenile under the supervision of his/her statutory agents, members of the extended family, a probation officer, or any other suitable person, or it may order to keep the juvenile under the custody of the Juvenile Observation Centre for not more than one month if the former measures are deemed inadvisable (LGDJC:26).

After completing the investigation, the probation officer should submit a report together with his/her opinion to the Court (LGDJC:19) and on the basis of this report the Court may decide to announce commencement of a trial against the juvenile (LGDJC:30) or to announce a judgment of non-trial of the case (LGDJC:28). The Court may also hold that the offence committed by the juvenile is of a trivial nature and issue a Court ruling of non-trial but render simultaneously an instruction that the statutory agent or guardian of the juvenile must exercise stricter discipline over him/her (LGDJC:29).

Hearings of the Juvenile Court are not open to the public, but relatives, school teachers, social workers and other suitable persons may obtain permissions from the Court to attend (LGDJC:34). After the hearing, if the Court finds that the juvenile has committed grave criminal offences such as murder, rape, etc.,[70] the Court should issue a ruling to transfer the case to the competent procurator's office (LGDJC:40). Otherwise the court should announce its own decision to put the juvenile under reformatory measures or to release him/her.

The reformatory measures that may be imposed upon a juvenile offender include: first, in addition to being reprimanded in court, the juvenile should also receive vocational guidance and counselling when needed; second, to be placed on probation; and third, to be committed to a reformatory educational institution for reformatory education. Besides, an additional measure may also be decreed to commit the juvenile to an appropriate institution for compulsory treatment if he/she is a drug abuser or for medical treatment if he/she is suffering from physical or mental deficiency (LGDJC:42).

For the first group, the Court will call the parents and require them to impose good discipline over the juvenile after the court releases him/her. Those who are placed on probation will also return home and the commissioned probation officer will set a schedule for the juvenile to attend the meetings in the probation office. The reformatory education is carried out by public Reformatory Educational Institutions. They are closed well-guarded institutions. A juvenile offender may be detained in the institution for not more than three years (LGDJC:53) and after that he/she will be returned to the family.

According to interviewed social workers, and the chief judge of the Juvenile Court *Ms CHEN Meng Ying*, a prostitution-involved child will not be committed to reformatory education solely because of her\his involvement in prostitution. It is more likely that she\he is placed under probation if the Court has doubts on the competence of the parents. Otherwise, the commissioned judge will normally call upon the parents and require their strict disciplining of their child.

There was wide criticism, especially among concerned professionals, that measures provided by the Law Governing the Disposition of Juvenile Cases were punishment-oriented. Many urged that sold juveniles should not be treated under the same law as delinquent adolescent offenders. Owing to their vigorous lobbying, special rules for dealing with juvenile victims of forced prostitution were finally set up by the Juvenile Welfare Law (JWL) in January 1989. Under this Law, there is a new legal routine for the disposition of juvenile prostitution cases alongside the old one. The legal rules are:

a. REPORT AND RESPONSE: Whenever a juvenile is found in prostitution and the like, the case shall be immediately reported to the competent welfare authority, the police, or the concerned juvenile welfare organisations (JWL:22-I). The police or the juvenile welfare organisations, after receiving such reports, should notice the competent welfare authority and act immediately for rescue and emergency protection. When encountering difficulties, the case should be handled under the supervision of the competent authority, and the police as well as the juvenile welfare organisations should provide necessary assistance for the authority (JWL:22-II).

b. OBSERVATION: Whenever a prostitution-involved juvenile is rescued, arrested, or received by the police or other authorities, she\he should be referred to the competent welfare authority for observation of two weeks to one month. During the period, assigned social workers will look into the reasons why the girls fell into and remained in prostitution (JWL:22-III).

c. CATEGORISATION: A report will be made after the observation as to whether the juvenile has offended Article 3 of the LGDJC or otherwise (JWL:22-III). In professional definitions, those juveniles who acted out themselves are labelled 'voluntary'. Their cases belong to the 'LGDJC:3 category', which means the juveniles should be referred to the Juvenile

Court for their delinquency. Others are categorised as 'forced' and remain under the disposition of welfare authorities.

d. THE 'VOLUNTARY' CASES: In such cases, the Juvenile Court should look into the situation of the case and make a ruling according to the aforementioned rules of the Law Governing the Disposition of Juvenile Cases, which may result in returning the juvenile to her\his statutory agents (normally the parents), placing her\him on probation, or committing her\him to a reformatory institution, or otherwise choose to apply the Juvenile Welfare Law (JWL:22-III) and render custody of the juvenile to a pertinent welfare authority or juvenile welfare organisation. The authority may then commit her to a rehabilitation centre where she\he will receive counselling and guidance education and necessary medical treatment[71] for not less than six months and not more than two years (JWL:22-IV,V).

e. THE 'FORCED' ONES: A line is drawn between whether the perpetrators are the guardian(s) or not. If, according to the observation report, there is a fit statutory agent who was not involved in the deal, then the juvenile should be returned to such a person. If the report shows that the juvenile was forced into prostitution by her\his statutory agent(s), then the welfare authority is responsible for providing for protection and placement services (JWL:9-II), during which period[72] the authority is legally bestowed the guardianship[73] of the juvenile (JWL:9-III). This authority can decide whether to put her\him in a short-term counseling centre or in a public or private short-term mid-way house (*TWRF,1992:56*).

During the period of protection and placement, the authority may choose to achieve family reunification for the juvenile[74] or to apply to the Civil Court for termination of adoption or of parental rights and reallocation of guardianship to the authority (JWL:23-II). If the latter is followed and the Court appoints the welfare authority to be the new guardian, then this authority has the legal responsibility to arrange for adoption, schooling, skills-training, or job placement for the juvenile (*TWRF,1992:53*).

After February 1993, children under the age of 12 are now governed by the Child Welfare Law (CWL). Similar provisions concerning child prostitution of the Juvenile Welfare Law (JWL) are inserted into the Amendment including report (CWL:35-I), emergency protection (CWL:35-II), reallocation of guardianship (CWL:40), and treatment (CWL:37). The law has, however, abandoned the classification process so no prostitution-involved children under 12 will be labelled 'voluntary'. Now a child found in sex-related services will still go through the observation period for two to four weeks during which competent authority will decide whether there is a need to commit her\him to special educational centres for a period of six months to two years (CWL:37-II). If not, she\he will either be returned to the statutory agent(s) or be sent to appropriate foster homes or child welfare institutions. In addition, custody of children may also be reallocated according to the same regulation as provided by the JWL (CWL:40).

Police Offence Laws Under police offence laws, illegal prostitutes are defined as 'offenders of social orders'. Under the 1991 Social Order Maintenance Law (SOML),[75] the police are given the discretion to impose administrative punishments on the offenders including detention of maximum three days, a fine of not more than N.T.$30,000 (approximately £750). In addition, a habitual offender who has been caught in illegal prostitution three times during the past one year should be committed to a rehabilitation centre for counselling and skills-training for a period of minimum six months and maximum two years (SOML:80). As children under 18 are dealt with under juvenile and child laws, the police only apply the SOML when the arrested prostitution-involved juvenile is 18 or older.

Application of Laws on Prevention and Treatment

Relevant Agencies The relevant agencies involved in the protection and treatment of prostitution-involved children include the police, the welfare authorities, and the concerned non governmental organisations (NGOs).

Generally speaking, the police are in the first line to dispose of a case involving sold-daughter-prostitution. When receiving information or reports, the police may commence the rescue work after obtaining a warrant from the competent Procurator's Office. A commissioned procurator may also instruct the police to raid suspected brothels or special entertainment establishments.[76] All found prostitution-involved girls should be brought to the police station. After 1989, it is mandated by the welfare laws that cases involving children under 18 should be immediately referred to welfare authorities. Others can be disposed of according to police offence laws.

At present, there is no specialist police to deal with child victims in general nor are there female police especially designated to question or interrogate prostitution-involved children. Since the 1980s, there have been more and more special police squads operating in big cities for cracking down on girl (later including boy) prostitution. But their emphasis is still on raiding crimes and arresting criminal suspects. On most occasions, the rescued children are often only attended to when their testimony against criminal suspects is requested and when a file has to be made for further reference or to close the case. Generally speaking, the job of the police is not to care for the needs of victims of crime.

There are welfare authorities on all administrative levels of the ROC government within which specific department or personnel is assigned to look after the needs of children. At the central government level, the Social Department of the Ministry of the Interior is responsible for the formulation and drafting of social welfare policies and laws. At the municipal level, both *Taipei* and the *Kaohsiung* Municipalities have Social Bureaus. Apart from the two municipalities, there are social affairs bureaus or sections in the city or county governments under the supervision of the Department of Social Affairs of the *Taiwan* Provincial Government (Chung & Hsieh,1989:349-363).[77] Due to increased demand and insufficiency of trained social workers, the government has encouraged the establishment of private institutions since the 1980s, especially those concerning child prostitution (*Chou,Y.Y.,1995; Pai,H.H.,1992*).

After the child prostitution problem was discovered in 1987, the *Taipei* Municipal Social Welfare Bureau passively assigned its Women Service Centre (the Southern *Taipei* Branch) to be the governmental authority to supervise the operation of concerned NGOs. When NGO activities started to penetrate into other parts of *Taiwan* in 1989 after the promulgation of the Juvenile Welfare Law, the *Taiwan* Provincial Social Department and the *Kaohsiung* Social Bureau also added 'prevention and treatment of child prostitution' on to their list of 'social service affairs'.

Governmental roles in the prevention and treatment of child prostitution have mostly involved supervision over NGO activities, except that two official rehabilitation centres have been assigned for observation, short-term and long-term treatment of involved child victims: The Taipei Municipal Kuang Tzu Po Ai Institution (KTPAI) -- Vocational Training & Counseling Centre for Distressed Women (VTCC) for children located in *Taipei* area, and the Taiwan Provincial Yunlin Technical Training Centre for Girls (YLTTC) for those found in other parts of *Taiwan*. Now, in a case concerning abused or neglected children under 18, the person in charge of a welfare authority may also be entrusted with the temporary physical custody or permanent guardianship of the child.[78]

Generally speaking, welfare authorities are too powerless when encountering the prostitution industry or even exploitative parents, thus their success always relies upon efficient police intervention. Apart from the police force, welfare authorities are also in great need of professional help. During the whole process of protection and treatment, expertise, manpower, and facilities are very often obtained from concerned professionals or NGOs.

Under the 1989 Juvenile Welfare Law, NGOs are divided into two groups. If an NGO is legally registered with the welfare authority according to the 'Standard of the Establishment of Juvenile Welfare Organisations', its operation is subsidised and monitored by the juvenile welfare authority. Among the five main NGOs introduced in chapter four, namely, the Rainbow Project (RP), the Garden of Hope Foundation (GOH), the Taipei Women Rescue Foundation (TWRF), the Good Shepherd Sisters Foundation (GSS) and the End Child Prostitution Association Taiwan (ECPAT), the latter four are now 'juvenile welfare organisation'. The RP remains an aboriginal development organisation but it is not legally registered for political reasons.

From the discovery of the child prostitution problem to its specific legislation, the NGOs have always played a leading role in all activities. As a result of their hardy assertion and determined actions, they are not only empowered by welfare laws but also relied upon by the authorities and trusted by the public. Over the years, the NGOs have achieved good access to the public through the media and successfully aroused moral panics over the 'problems' defined by them. Although the police or the welfare authorities often do not respond to the problems in the ways required by NGOs, certain measures are always taken as considered appropriate by the authorities.

Protection and Treatment before January 1989 Before the Juvenile Welfare Law was enacted in January 1989, juvenile prostitution cases could be dealt with through various routines under the discretion of the authorities in charge. Relevant provisions in the 1954 Police Offence Law (POL), the 1980 Law Governing the Disposition of Juvenile Cases (LGDJC), or the 1973 Child Welfare Law (CWL) were applied selectively.

The police were normally involved in nearly all cases of rescue or capture, who would deal with the case without informing the welfare authorities. Every commissioned police officer might deal with such cases according to his/her own experiences and training. After certain administrative procedures such as making deposition and records, the police could choose to release the girl on caution, to impose administrative punishments according to the POL, and/or to transfer the case to the Juvenile Court according to the LGDJC.

Except for those cases in which the juvenile indicated that she\he was forced into prostitution by the guardians (statutory agents), the routine police work was to locate and return the juvenile to the guardians or any family member named by her\him. By so doing, the police could simply file the case and save the trouble of doing otherwise. If the juvenile was aged between 12 and 18, the LGDJC would generally be applied. According to LGDJC:3, an adolescent who has frequented places where a juvenile's presence is prohibited such as sexual service establishments is presumed to be in danger of committing a crime, and thus is subject to the jurisdiction of the Juvenile Court. Therefore, a prostitution-involved juvenile could also be disposed of under this provision provided that the commissioned police had knowledge of this law and had time for all the paper work.

Since 1987, when the government announced a 'Decent Society Campaign', several concerned NGOs have been making efforts to establish rescue and protection networks. They first approached police stations and juvenile squads responsible for certain areas where the practice of underage prostitution prevailed, then offered expertise on child counseling, aboriginal issues, and police legal education. The NGOs also appealed to welfare authorities in *Taipei* Municipality for allocating the responsibility of dealing with child prostitution affairs to specifically designated personnel.

As a result, before it actually became law, the Women Service Centre (the Southern *Taipei* Branch) of the *Taipei* Municipal Social Bureau and the concerned NGOs would be given information on cases from some connected police stations who were willing to help. However, it should be noticed that without the auspices of law, such a rescue and protection network could only rely on the benevolence of certain police officers. Thus only a few police stations in the *Taipei* were involved, and all other parts of *Taiwan* were left unattended.

In contrast, if a case was first brought to the attention of NGOs or welfare authorities, less punishment-oriented and more protection measures would be taken according to the Child Welfare Law. However, until 1989 when the Juvenile Welfare Law was enacted, welfare authorities were not legally empowered to retain children under their protection without obtaining a Court ruling to suspend parental rights and to assume custody of the child through complicated and time-consuming Court proceedings. As a result, child victims were often taken back by their exploitative parents or escaped from rehabilitation centres without trace. The welfare measures were also hampered by the fact that the establishment of the child protection system was incomplete and both expertise and facilities were lacking. So even if NGOs managed to hide some girls under their temporary protection, there were no long-term plans for rehabilitation, re-education, and re-training.

After 1989 Both preventive and therapeutic measures are provided by the 1989 Juvenile Welfare Law (*Chen,M.Y.,1990*), which are followed by the 1993 Child Welfare Law (Amendment) (*Hsieh,Y.W.,1993*). Under the laws, children under 18 are prohibited to enter certain entertainment establishments, or to have access to pornographic films and publications. Obligations are now imposed on parents and guardians to restrain their children from certain misbehaviour such as smoking, drug abuse, and access to pornographic materials and establishments. The violators are subjected to specific administrative punishments as well as heavier criminal punishment where they have also violated the Criminal Code. Those over 18 are disposed of by the police as offenders of social orders and the habitual prostitution-involved girls(boys) may be committed to one of the two rehabilitation centres for illegal prostitutes situated in the aforementioned governmental institutions -- the KTPAI or the YLTTC.[79]

Children under 18 should, according to welfare laws, be referred to the public observation centre situated in the KTPAI. After the observation period, the competent welfare authority will choose a treatment programme for each girl. Children under 12 may be returned to the fit guardians or retained under the protection of competent welfare authorities. Adolescents aged between 12 and 18 are subjected to the categorisation process. The 'voluntary' ones are subjected to the disposition of the Juvenile Court. In the past, most girls were put on probation and returned home with the guardians. After 1989, the Court may also apply the JWL and assigns the welfare authority or a juvenile welfare organisation to take charge of the discipline of the involved child.

When a child is found to have been forced into prostitution by a person other than her\his statutory agents (normally the parents), she\he will normally be handed back to the guardians without follow-up unless there is strong evidence suggesting otherwise. On the other hand, if it is maintained that the child had been sold into prostitution by guardians and protection of the child from further exploitation is needed, then the welfare authority may choose to retain temporary custody of the child until a Court ruling is obtained to the effect that parental rights or adoptions are terminated, and the welfare authority is appointed the guardian of the child.

All children under the care of the welfare authorities are first committed to the rehabilitation centres of the KTPAI or the YLTTC. After completing the legally provided rehabilitation process for 6 months to 2 years, the authority may then arrange for her\him to be adopted, or to send her\him to the NGO long-term mid-way houses. Unlike the rehabilitation centre in which all children are subjected to strict rules, the long-term mid-way houses are to offer a home-like environment and to help these children return to schools or find appropriate jobs.

Under the present general laws, three sets of rules are applied to prostitution-involved children of different age groups: children under 12, juveniles between 12 and 18, and minors under 20. The 1993 Child Welfare Law treats all children found in prostitution as victims of sexual exploitation and provide welfare services for them. The 1989 Juvenile Welfare Law confirmed the past professional practice and draws a line between the delinquent youth (the 'voluntary'), who are the responsibility of the Juvenile Court and other victims (the 'forced'), who are entitled to welfare services. Girls over 18 are dealt with under the 1991 Social Order Maintenance Law together with other adult prostitutes. In the case of child-prostitution, parents of all minor children under 20 can be deprived of their guardianship according to the Child Welfare Law (under 12), the Juvenile Welfare Law (12 to 18) or the Civil Code (over 18) depending on the age of the involved child.

Inadequacy of Law Enforcement in the Treatment of Victims

The Classification Process

Under the 1989 Juvenile Welfare Law, the police authorities, when locating a prostituted child aged between 12 and 18, should refer the case to the welfare authorities who will observe the juvenile for two to four weeks and decide whether she\he belongs to the 'forced' or the 'voluntary' group. In practice, although the 'voluntary' ones are legally discriminated against, the label was practically favoured by the girls for three main reasons summed up from past case interviews carried out by social workers.

First, in the brothels, the girls were often threatened with the fact that their parents had borrowed a lot of money from the brothel or have actually sold them into prostitution, and therefore, a girl is warned that if she told the police that she was forced into prostitution, her parents would be prosecuted and sent into prison. Although most of the girls did not have a good relationship with their native families, they would not want to send their parents to prison.

Second, the two public rehabilitation centres are far from well equipped. Moreover, in order to avoid disturbance caused by the parents or the prostitution operators, the centres are guarded with steel windows and doors and the girls' access to the outside world is very much restricted for their protection. This gave the prostitution operators a chance to spread rumour among the girls that once they complained to have been forced into prostitution, the police would put them into a 'prison' for at least six months. Unfortunately, the rumour could easily be accepted as the truth, for many girls who had stayed in such a 'prison' for rehabilitation would make the same observation.

And third, when a rescued girl is brought to the police station, there is no specialist police assigned to handle such cases. When a police officer questions or examines a girl, it is not required by law that she/he has to be accompanied by a social worker. Many interviewed girls complained that they were questioned and examined in a manner which suggested that the officers or examiners actually regarded them as 'prostitutes'. For them, to say: 'I was voluntary' could avoid answering more humiliating questions.

It was mentioned above that, in practice, the police used to make their own decision as to whether to discharge the victim, to return her\him to the family, to refer her\him to the welfare authority or to send her\him to a rehabilitation centre. It is now mandated by the 1989 Juvenile Welfare Law and the 1993 Child Welfare Law that cases involving children under 18 should be immediately referred to welfare authorities. However, most police stations (especially those not located in *Taipei*) still follow the aforementioned pre-1989 routine in handling child prostitution cases.

This raises problems in practice. Very often, the child is unwilling to tell the truth for reasons summed up above. As a result, many children were handed back to their own parents and very soon, they would be taken back to prostitution again. Because of this ignorance or abuse of laws by the police in the very beginning of the legal process, countless perpetrators of child prostitution were set free, while their victims were deprived of available legal protection.

In addition, past experience of concerned social workers have revealed the high possibility of sold children being treated under the law as 'voluntary' ones, for during the observation period the girls refuse to tell the truth in order not to endanger their parents or for other reasons. Thus even though a juvenile may have been forced into prostitution and to remain in it, as a result of a false observation report, she\he may be labeled 'voluntary' and referred to the Juvenile Court for her\his delinquent behaviour. Although the Juvenile Court may finally mandate that the girl\boy should be treated with welfare measures, the trauma of the labeling process will not disappear.

The Juvenile Justice System

The inappropriateness of the juvenile justice system has been explored in chapter two. Basically speaking, the functions of the ROC Juvenile Court are to deal with adolescent criminals and delinquents who are in danger of committing crimes, as it is clearly specified in Article 3 of the Law Governing the Disposition of Juvenile Cases (LGDJC). As a line is drawn in the application of the Juvenile Welfare Law between the 'forced' and the 'voluntary', those prostitution-involved girls referred to the Juvenile Court either by the police or by the welfare authority are generally presumed to be 'delinquents' even before the trial.

This presumption again excludes the juvenile victims from the protection system. One of the most constant comments made in the interviews of experienced social workers was that despite the 1989 Juvenile Welfare Law's intention to empower the Juvenile Court judges to avail themselves of the welfare measures in deciding girl prostitution cases, judges still considered it appropriate to apply the LGDJC unless strong evidence proves otherwise.

Despite the label of 'delinquents', the juveniles are actually subjected to less legal restraints when the LGDJC is applied. The Juvenile Courts usually place delinquents on probation unless compulsory medical treatment is required. Prostitution-involved juveniles are no exception. The problem with probation is that the juvenile only has to report to the assigned probation officer once every month. And according to two of the leading activists of the Taipei Women Rescue Foundation *Ms HUANG Yi Chun* and *Ms HONG Wen Huey* it was not uncommon to see that every month, the juvenile was accompanied by the brothel-keeper, a brothel-employed bouncer, the parent or some other family member to report to the probation officer, and after the half-an-hour counselling, the child returned to the brothel and work as usual.

The Rehabilitation Process

Chapter three has summed up the practical difficulties for the victims to resume the 'normal' life generally expected for 'healthy' children and juveniles. Professionals have long tried to develop treatment programmes which will provide strong incentives for the child victims to stay out of prostitution. But apart from indoctrination of moral standards and religious belief which have achieved not enough success, it is almost agreed among professionals that in dealing with the problem of child prostitution, most treatment efforts are expected to end in vain.

The problems do not all lie with the rehabilitation process itself. There is no doubt that there is need for more educational programmes, more manpower and equipment, recruitment of more well-trained personnel, and for more loving and caring environment. But even if the rehabilitation is effective, it leaves the structural problems unattended. During the rehabilitation, the child is implanted with a sense of shame. She\he knows prostitution is an immoral profession and her\his earnings were 'dirty' money. So she\he is given skills-training to make a moral living. However, as soon as the child goes out of the steel door, the legal treatment is shut out. She\he is now given a lot more reasons to go back to prostitution -- the indebted parents, the intimidating brothel-keepers, the past peer friends, and the hostile society.

The Exploitation Chain

The power of exploitation is too strong to fight against under the present socio-legal environment in *Taiwan*. The huge economic gain has strengthened the exploitation chain formed around the child. The best outcome expected under the exercise of present ROC general laws is a successful rehabilitation. However, even if rehabilitation programmes can give the children enough incentives to resist the temptation of easy money, how can the child alone be expected to encounter the family and the brothel-keepers, whom they are indebted to? How can she\he refuse her mother's invitation to join the family prostitution business?

Parental rights may be terminated by law, but a Court ruling alone cannot cut off the exploitative blood tie. The perpetrators may be sentenced to prison, but as shown above, their stay in the prison is normally shorter than the duration of a rehabilitation programme. With the enormous economic gain involved, the present legal measures involving rehabilitation of the children, termination of parental rights, and imprisonment of the perpetrators seem to have offered very restricted deterrence to the power of exploitation.

Return of the Victims to Society

The paradoxical idea of protecting the healthy and innocent children from fatalistic leverage of delinquents is often invoked against prostitution-involved children. Apart from having to face the exploitation chain, the situation of the child is further worsened by the social atmosphere which has built a strong fence against accommodating the rehabilitated or reformed child back into society. All teachers and parents are afraid that these 'bad' girls and boys might poison the innocent minds of their children. Very few schools would admit a child with prostitution experience. And the label of prostitution is as harmful as a crime record in finding a job. The prospects for a girl victim to marry into a 'good family' become remote. And they may not be treated as 'women with respectable character' ever again.

Concluding Remarks

Under the ostensible prostitution policy of 'short-term regulation and long-term abolition', the ROC law has been submerged by its ineffectiveness in censoring illegal prostitution including that involving sold-daughters, whilst further preoccupied with the task of encountering new forms of the old problem. The current ROC legislators have been engaged in making new legislation intending to mitigate the social problem. However, the real problem lies in the fact that there has always been a disjunction between apparent legislative intentions and their practical implementation.

Why is the law not implemented? Obviously, its guards -- many enforcers are colluding or tolerating the 'social evil'. Administrative officials brazenly excuse themselves of their illiteracy in law. Local policemen and Council members are said to be shamelessly harbouring or even operating child prostitution. When it is perceived that the social disease is worsening, that new threatening problems have grown out of the old epidemic, the law makers are always prepared to make more laws. And these new laws serve to confuse more enforcers, to provide more loopholes for new problems to emerge, and to enhance the counter-power of the 'social evils'.

Even the judiciary takes part in this process. Criminal punishments against concerned offences of child prostitution are quite severe in law but judges have been lenient in imposing sentences, especially when the accused is a parent. The original intention of the Criminal Code (CRC) is that the parent-offender should be subjected to heavier punishment (comparing CRC:232 with CRC:231), but the discretionary power of the judge has allowed him to speak for another legal 'truth':[80] although abandoning children to prostitution is wrong, its condemnability can be mitigated if the parent was in financial difficulties, was ignorant, or the child has forgiven the abusive parent and pleaded for mercy.

Another message given in the Court decisions is that if there are other children for the convicted parents to rear, then the parents should be released to carry out their responsibilities 'under the supervision of the Court', which in practice means that, if the parents shall sell another child in the future, the Court will impose a more severe punishment with no mitigation. By doing this, the Court seems to be implying that there is very little risk of recidivism. However, the 'truth' assumed by the Court is in conflict with the 'truth' found in practice.[81]

The modern ROC law appears determined to wipe out the old evils of prostitution, but its power has been eroded in the social context of resistance manifested by the collusion of legislators, law enforcers, and the general public of all social strata in the practice of illegal prostitution. Consequently, child prostitution, though may be denounced as the most serious form of child abuse and the most heinous act of sexual exploitation, is practised without much deterrence. Further, when modern forms of illegal prostitution penetrated into all kinds of business settings, the sold daughters also started to accumulate their experiences in prostitution within the less and less censured flesh market.

The general laws for protection and treatment of prostitution-involved children have shown various legal attitudes towards different age groups of children. The law regards all such children under the age of 12 as victims of illegal prostitution. Juveniles who are sold and coerced into prostitution and remain in it are classified as 'forced' victims of sexual exploitation; while the others are labelled 'voluntary' and referred to the Juvenile Court to be dealt with as juvenile delinquents. Those who are over 18 are regarded as violators of social orders and charged with police offences.

In practice, these four categories of prostitution-involved juveniles were treated in various ways by the police, the court and the social workers/welfare officers. The experience of all children in the police station is usually humiliating, except for those very young ones. In courts, they either have to incriminate their own parents (Civil Court) or become violators of laws themselves (Juvenile Court). The welfare professionals generally prefer to sever the relationship between the child and her\his exploitative parents rather than to work for the therapy and reunification of the family. For the protection of the child in care, measures taken are to terminate parental rights through legal proceedings. The Court ruling may be effective when the child is under the physical custody of welfare authorities. But once the child is out of the protection and treatment network, she/he may be ready again to surrender to the power of exploitation.

Once any of the children, voluntary or forced, are sent to the 'Special Training Institution' according to the Social Order Maintenance Law or to the 'Special Educational Institution' according to the Juvenile/Child Welfare Laws, they are actually sent to the same institutions: either the KTPAI or the YLTTC. So in practice, no matter whether she\he is 'voluntary' or 'forced', whether the children are committed to the institution by the police or the Juvenile Court as violators of social morals, or by the welfare authorities as victims of sexual exploitation, they finally receive counselling and skill-training at the same place. When they finally complete the treatment, they become birds of the same feather -- the feather printed with their final label -- prostitutes.

Then most of the children are abandoned back to the exploitative family, to prostitution, or/and to the normative society in which the disclosure of their sex history would only make them an anathema and an embarrassment. Throughout the process of legal treatment, the girl has been made aware of the shame attached to her past experiences. But case studies have shown that the majority of these 're-educated', 'retrained', 'rehabilitated', or 'corrected' children either fell or were taken back to prostitution sooner or later (*Chen,H.N.,1992*; *TWRF,1991,1992*; *Yin,C.C. et al.,1993*). This inability of law and its enforcers to keep these children from rejoining prostitution has two implications. One, a lot of resources are wasted in rescue, emergency protection, and short-term (six months) or long-term (two years) rehabilitation. And two, all the law has done is to provide legal objects -- the victims -- for enthusiastic moralists and professionals to express their concerns and practice their expertise.

Ironically, for those children who experienced legal treatment but fall back to prostitution, the law may have exacerbated their victimisation. If the law had never intervened, and if the children had never been taken out of the sewage and fallen back again, they would not have to practice prostitution with the imposed shame, and they would keep a better (though exploitative) relationship with both their families and their exploiters. They might still believe that someday when they have earned enough money, they could leave prostitution and dress up like a good woman or a successful man. Their whole life might have been much better-off both materially and spiritually if the law and its enforcers had never enlightened but humiliated them.

Law has been designed and intended to rescue, protect and treat victims, but it turns out that the intervention of law has become a kind of disturbance in the children' lives as 'prostitutes'. During the interruption, resources have been exhausted in the name of protection and rehabilitation. Yet, in reality, the public expressed their anger and sympathy, the press got their stories, the enforcers and practitioners obtained their fame, but what became of the children?

This is not to suggest that all the past efforts are in vain. Rather it is to point out that a successful treatment programme does not end with rehabilitation of the victims. It has to envisage the structural problems encountering the child after she\he walks out of the police station, after she\he is released by the Juvenile Court, and after the gate of the rehabilitation centre shut behind her\him. Under the general-law regime, the child is made responsible to resist the power of the exploitation chain. Thus it can be well expected that further resources are to be wasted in all rehabilitation programmes. In view of the past failures, it is clear that only a structural reform can solve a structural problem.

All the above mentioned failures of the general laws were carefully collected and ayalysed during the legislative process of the 1995 Law to Suppress Sexual Transactions Involving Children and Juveniles. As the Law has only been enacted for less than two years at the completion of this book, it remains to be seen whether it can solve, or at least alleviate some problems.

NOTES

[1] Under these Orders, prostitution itself was legally banned but not criminalised. Those who violated the Orders would only be subjected to administrative fines with their raided brothels dismantled and immoral earnings confiscated.

[2] For details of those Orders/Decrees, see *Liu,Y.M.,1976:50-51*; *Shen,M.C.,1989:34*.

[3] See 'The Administration Brief of the *Taipei* Government (*shih cheng chi yao* 市政紀要)', p.307, quoted at *Shen,M.C.,1989:35*.

[4] Before 1985, the police was legally in charge of licensing and operation of all special entertainment establishments. After local governments adopted the 'Regulations Governing Prostitution' (1985), special entertainment establishments (e.g. dancing halls, girlie restaurants, American bars, hotels/motels, girlie coffee/tea houses) have been subjected to the administration of The Construction Department (*Taiwan*) / Bureau (*Taipei*, *Kaohsiung*), which are under the supervision of the ROC Ministry of Economic Affairs.

[5] In court practice, it means the woman was not a prostitute when the offence was committed against her. See Judicial Yuan (ROC),1992:406; Liu et al.,1992:1094.

[6] The Regulations only forbid brothel-keepers to admit the entrance of minor boys (under 20) and students, violating which the license of the brothel can be revoked. See *Shen,M.C.,1989:38*.

[7] The general readings for this section include: *Chuang,K.M.,1991*; *Hsieh,K.,1972,1982*; *Huang,Y.C.,1991a*; *Kao,M.,1988*; *Liu,Y.M.,1976acd*; *Shen,M.C.,1989:32-42,109-131*; *Sun,T.W.,1980*; *Wang,S.R.,1984*.

[8] The POL was abolished together with the martial law and replaced by the SOML. However, it is a general criticism that the two laws are 'same in context though different in names'. See *Tao,P.C. et al.,1991:1314-1320*.

[9] Those prostitutes who are cautioned for three or more times within a year may, after imposition of administrative punishment, be sent by the competent police authority to rehabilitation centres to receive counselling and skills-training for a period between six months and one year (SOML:80).

[10] The exchange rate of English Pounds Sterling: NT$ is approximately 1:40.

[11] There are detailed provisions governing the relationship between brothels and the employed prostitutes concerning earnings, lodging, health, hygiene and liberty. See *Shen,M.C.,1989:37-39*.

[12] It was mentioned above that under the 'abolition through taxation' policy, governments have been levying high commercial tax on special entertainment establishments since the

1970s. The rationale was followed and strengthened in the RGSEE by further charging annual license fees ranging from approximately 4,000-5,600 Pounds Sterling for the girlie restaurants to 100,000-143,000 Pounds Sterling for the dancing halls depending on the governmental estimated profits made by each establishment. See *Shen.M.C.,1989:41*.

[13] The general readings for this section include: *Chen,Y.C.,1991*; *Chuang,K.M.,1991*; *Huang,Y.C.,1991a*; *Li,T.C.,1992*; *Lin,Y.C.,1992*; Shee,A.1991,*1992:34-45*; *Shen,M.C.,1989: 118-131*, Wang,C.F.,1988,1990, *1992a,1992b*; *Wang,T.S. et al.,1989:361-366*; *Yin,C.C. et al.,1993:163-180*. For contents of relevant laws, see Shee,A.,1994:Appendix I:CRC &CCRP.

[14] See Shee,A.,1994:Appendix I: CRC: Chapter V. Punishment.

[15] Some of the offences against social morals and offences against personal liberty can only be prosecuted upon private complaint. See CRC: Articles 236, 245, which provide that prosecution against offenses specified in one of CRC:221 to 230, 238, 239, & 240(II) may be initiated only upon complaint. See also CCRP: 232-239 for information on initiation of cases upon complaint.

[16] It is mentioned in chapters two and three that the Chinese distinguished the 'good women' from the 'bad women' and in order to protect the 'good women' (or to guard the authority over them), the 'bad women' are ironically abandoned into prostitution. Such dichotomy is carried into the ROC law. The Chinese term used in CRC:231 of the CRC is '*liang cha fu nu 良家婦女*' which literally means 'women of good families'. In application, both academics and professionals agree that the '*liang cha fu nu*' referred to in CRC:231 does not necessarily have to possess a good and clean family background. As far as a female person is not accustomed to sexual promiscuity, she is protected under the Article. In other words, the '*lian cha fu nu*' of CRC:231 denotes any woman who was not in prostitution or the like when the criminal act was committed against her, no matter whether she had once been a prostitute or not. Now, both official as well as academic translations of ROC laws refer to the '*lian cha fu nu*' as 'a female person of respectable character', which is followed in the discussion of this thesis. See Judicial Yuan,ROC,1992:406; Liu,C.M. et al.,1991a:1094.

[17] Under the CRC, the legal term for sexual intercourse (*hsing chiao 性交*) is carnal relations (*chien yin 姦淫*).

[18] One '*yuan*' is equal to N.T.$10 according to the Regulation Governing the Exchange Rates of Fines.

[19] The term 'indecent act' legally means any sexual contact between two persons except heterosexual intercourse (carnal relations) as provided in CRC:231-I.

[20] This 'supervision right' legally means 'guardianship' over a minor person.

[21] In practice, forcible abduction means abduction by means of violence, threat, duress, or fraud.

[22] Under CRC:221-I, rape can only be committed if the offender, in order to have carnal relations with the victim, uses violence, threats, or administers drugs, or induces hypnosis, or invokes other means, thereby renders resistance of the victim impossible. One can see that the ROC legislators have imposed strict responsibilities on women for preventing themselves from being raped. But if the victim had not reached the age of 14 when the

sexual intercourse took place, the offender is by law guilty of statutory rape under CRC:221-II.

[23] That is to say, the age of a child below which sexual intercourse with her is an offence. For more discussions see Criminal Law Revision Committee [England],1980:24-34 & 1984:44-50; Home Office Policy Advisory Committee on Sexual Offences [England],1979.

[24] In my opinion, the law was ostensibly to protect 'the girl', but actually to protect 'the girl's virginity', the intact of which may qualify an unmarried girl as a 'good' woman.

[25] It means that the accused did not care whether the girl he had carnal relations with was under the age of consent.

[26] CRC:296 provides: (I) A person who enslaves another or places him in a position without freedom similar to slavery shall be punished with imprisonment for not less than one and not more than seven years. (II) An attempt to commit an offence specified in the preceding paragraph is punishable.

[27] CRC:286 provides: (I) A person who maltreats a male or female person who has not completed the sixteenth year of his age or who by other means impairs the natural development of the body of such male or female person shall be punished with imprisonment for not more than five years, detention, or a fine of not more than 500 yuan may be imposed. (II) A person who for the purpose of gain commits an offence specified in the preceding Section shall be punished with imprisonment for not less than five years; in addition thereto, a fine of not more than 1,000 yuan may be imposed.

[28] When CRC:296 was added to the second amendment of the CRC in 1954, the legislative intention was that '(t)here were laws against traffic in persons in the Imperial Code, and accordingly Articles 363 and 364 of the draft bill for this amendment especially provided for punishments against the acts of "selling (with or without consent) a person who is under his/her support and protection", "parents forcibly selling children", and "husband forcibly selling wife". However, these enumerated offences fail to cover all sorts of criminal acts involving traffic in persons. Therefore, the mentioned Articles 363 and 364 shall be merged into a inclusive Article 296 which penalises slavery as a whole'. See *Tao,P.C. et al., 1991:857.*

[29] Some female children may be subjected to all sorts of injection to accelerate their physical growth for prostitution purposes. In order to facilitate brothel control, many girls are made into drug abusers. Long-term contraception and inappropriate abortion often make the girls barren. Many girls also suffer from chronic sexually-transmitted diseases and uneven bodily growth.

[30] For detailed explanation of how the laws can be applied to all sorts of cases, see Shee,A.,1994:Ch.6 & Appendix III.

[31] Articles governing suspension of punishment (Chapter IX) and conditional release (Chapter X) may be availed to suspend or shorten execution of the pronounced penalty.

[32] Under the ROC judicial system, a procurator is a judicial officer whose legal functions mainly include investigating criminal cases, initiating cases of public prosecution in the Criminal Court, assisting in private prosecution, conducting the execution of a Criminal Court decision. For introduction to the ROC Procuratorial System, see Liu,J.C. et al., 1991:1911-1927.

[33] For the criminal procedure of cases which may only be instituted upon complaint, see CCRP: 232-239.

[34] The analyses are summed up from the final judgments of court cases studied in *Shen,M.C.,1989*. For a brief introduction to the studied cases, see Shee,A.,1994:Appendix IV.

[35] A typical case of CRC:240 abduction or CRC:241 forcible abduction is that a parent sells a daughter without the consent of the other parent, who objects to or has no knowledge of the body contract. In such cases, if the sold daughter is over 16 and agrees to the sale, CRC:240-III will be applied. If the offender uses violence, threats, or fraud, then he commits the offence of forcible abduction specified in CRC:241-II. But if the sold daughter is under 16, she is not legally eligible to give consent, and thus even if she volunteers to be sold, the offending parent will still be charged with forcible abduction provided in CRC:241-III.

[36] In the case No.6 (SHEN-6) studied by *Shen,M.C.* in her 1989 book (SHEN book), the offender *Tseng* was the adoptive grandparent and the sole custodian of the sold girl. *Tseng* and his friend *Lin* owned a hotel. They forced *Tseng*'s 11-year-old adopted granddaughter to receive customers in his hotel. The girl's freedom was restricted and all the profits made from her prostitution were shared between *Tseng* and *Lin*. Later they further procured a 13-year-old girl from her father *Chang* (also a sole custodian) and forcibly prostituted her. The *Tainan* District Court (final instance) applied CRC:298-II to prosecute all the three offenders.

[37] In the case No.10 of the above SHEN book (*SHEN-10)*, *Liu* and his wife agreed to sell their 13-year-old adopted daughter, 13-year-old daughter and 12-year-old daughter to a broker *Cheng*, who re-sold the girls to a brothel-keeper *Hsu*. The *Panch'iao* District Court applied CRC:298-II to prosecute the *Liu* couple. The High Court changed the application of law to CRC:232 because the case was not initiated by a private complaint and thus CRC:298(II) was not applicable. In this case, the Court applied CRC:232 to prosecute the parents who had committed the CRC:231 offence and the broker was charged with CRC:231. Suppose that before the girls were sold, they had been working in the family brothel operated by *Liu*. Then CRC:231 & 232 would not be applicable because the girls were not 'of respectable character' under the law. Thus CRC:233 would be applied instead, for the girls were under 16. It should be noticed that both CRC:231/232 and CRC:233 are applicable in *SHEN-10,* and according to CRC:56, the offenders should be punished with the more severe offence provided in CRC:233. But the Court chose to charge the offenders of a less severe offence. If the case had been appealed to the Supreme Court, the High Court judgment might have been set aside for its application of inappropriate laws.

[38] A broad definition for this 'brothel-keeper' is adopted here to include those who provide premises for use of girl prostitution.

[39] If the court find both articles applicable, then CRC:233 which provides for a heavier basic punishment should apply according to the aforementioned principle stated in CRC:56.

[40] See the case *SHEN-6* as introduced above. *Lin* was a procurer punished under CRC:298-II.

[41] Generally speaking, the brothel-keepers who buy girls from other procurers will be prosecuted under CRC:243-I & 300-I. Besides, it is generally held by the Courts that 'restricting the freedom of the girl is **the means** to commit offences of CRC:243-I & 300-I', and so according to CRC:56 as explained in section I, the offender should not be charged with the offence of illegal detention under CRC:302. See *Shen,M.C.,1989:136-137.*

[42] In the case No.9 studied by *Shen,M.C.* (*SHEN-9)*, a procurer and brothel-keeper *Ts'ai* was found guilty of the offences of CRC:298-II, 241-III,II & 233. *Ts'ai* first procured a 17-year-old girl from her father (a sole custodian) *Hsu*. For this, both *Tsai* and *Hsu* were convicted CRC:298-II upon a private complaint. Then *Ts'ai* procured a 15-year-old girl and a 13-year-old girl from their mothers whose husband did not consent to the sale. For this *Ts'ai* and both the mothers were prosecuted under CRC:241-III,II. *Ts'ai* also procured three girls under 16 from their consenting parents and for this all were punished under CRC:233.

[43] In the above mentioned case *SHEN-9*, *Ts'ai* also employed *Chiang*, *Huang*, *Lin* and *Liu* to assist in the business and to prevent the girls from escaping. The Court found all of the abettors guilty of the offence against personal liberty under CRC:302.

[44] In the case No.2 of the SHEN book (*SHEN-2)*, the *Taichung* District Court held that the offender who sold her 12-year-old daughter into prostitution had 'subjugated a person to circumstances similar to slavery' and 'should be prosecuted under CRC:296'. However, the *Taichung* High Court applied CRC:232 instead on the ground that 'it seems to be a misunderstanding of the law for the District Court to apply CRC:296 in such cases'. But the High Court did not explain the reason why it was a misunderstanding and the case was not appealed further. In the case *SHEN-9*, which was introduced in the previous two footnotes, the public prosecutor recommended in the indictment that *Ts'ai* and all her employees as well as those parents who sold daughters under 16 into prostitution should all be prosecuted by CRC:296. However, the *Kaohsiung* District Court applied CRC:298-II & 241-III,II instead on the ground that 'CRC:296 is to punish a person who enslaves others, but in the present case, the sold girls said that they were only restrained from escape and not forced to receive a certain number of customers, nor were they subjected to inhuman maltreatment'. The Court decided that since the victims were still given certain degree of freedom, the offenders should not be guilty of the offence of slavery. See further discussions at *Shen,M.C.,1989:151-152,202,204.*

[45] For introduction to the Court cases collected and studied by *Shen,M.C.,1989,* see Shee,A., 1994:Appendix IV.

[46] This case was finalised in the first instance district court (*Tainan* District Court,1988-382, summarised at *Shen,M.C.,1989:203*). My observation from studies on court cases is that if the case had been appealed to higher court, the final sentence would have been more lenient (Shee,A.,1989:Appendix IV:B). It has been a judicial tradition that a higher Court would always impose less severe punishment. The reason given by some higher Courts judges of my acquaintance is that District Court judges are normally very young both in age and in judicial experiences. They consider themselves as the guard of legal order and are inclined to impose heavier punishment on law offenders. If this observation is correct, then a primitive presumption can be made from the study of the 12 cases of the first instance provided in Shee,A.,1994:Appendix IV: B that the pronounced penalties for crimes

involving sold-daughter-prostitution are now becoming less and less severe even at the District Courts.

[47] In one case, the offender sold his 14-year-old adopted daughter to a brothel-keeper. In the other case, three parents sold daughters under 16 to a brothel-keeper. All were sentenced to 10 months' imprisonment but their punishments were suspended according to CRC:74 on the ground that the offenders were indigenous people who were 'ignorant and vulgar (*chih lu chien po 智慮淺薄*)', which means these parents were considered underdeveloped in both intelligence and consideration because of their indigenous origin.

[48] The offender sold her 13-year-old adopted daughter, 13-year-old daughter, and 12-year-old daughter to a procurer.

[49] The offender forcibly sold her elder brother's 13-year-old daughter into an illegal brothel.

[50] The offender successively sold his 13-year-old adoptive daughter, 13-year-old daughter, and 12-year-old daughter to a procurer. He was charged under CRC:232 with increased punishment for recidivism.

[51] In one case, the offender sold her 12-year-old daughter to a public brothel, and then re-sold her to another brothel. She was prosecuted under CRC:232 with recidivism. In the other case, the offender sold her 16-year-old daughter to a brothel-keeper. The pronounced punishment in this case is comparatively harsher than all other cases which did not involve recidivism.

[52] These comments are based on the analysis made by *Shen,M.C.* in chapter four of her LL.M. dissertation (*Shen,M.C.,1989:109-224*).

[53] Policemen have been reported to have permitted, fostered, harboured, or even operated and consumed illegal prostitution (*Liu,Y.M.,1976:49-51*; *Shen,M.C.,1989:119-122*). This corruption of the police has become structural in nature (*Ho,C.W.,1992:31-32*; *Pan,W.K.,1992:1-2*). Occasionally there were some 'good' police who thought of doing something about it, but very soon, they would learn not to challenge the established alliance among their colleagues, local politicians, organised mobsters, and operators of illegal prostitution.

[54] This information was obtained in interviews of concerned professionals in *Taiwan*.

[55] The three reasons are summed up from information given by concerned professionals.

[56] This information was given in interviews of professionals in *Taiwan*. However, it is worthy of mentioning that the attitude of law enforcers may be changed to some extent as the new 1995 specific law has brought them more legal duties.

[57] See CRC: 221.

[58] In practice, once a girl is sold for more than once, her victim status is lost, and no offenders will be charged under these provisions except the first procurer(s).

[59] For contents of the relevant provisions of these general laws, see Shee,A.,1994:Appendix I.

[60] See chapter five for introduction to relevant civil, criminal, and administrative laws.

[61] This number is released by the Director of the Department of Social Affairs (Ministry of the Interior), *Mr Pai, Hsiu Hsiung*. See The China Post on June 22, 1994. See also *The Central Daily* (international edition) and *The Liberty Times* on June 23, 1994.

[62] See chapter four for details.

[63] See chapter five for details.

[64] For cases concerning parent-child relationship, the welfare laws are the 'specific law' to supersede the application of the Civil Code if the involved child is under 18; while in child prostitution matters, the 1995 Law to Suppress Sexual Transactions Involving Children and Juveniles is the specific law and all other relevant laws become 'general laws'.

[65] See chapter five for general legal principles governing parent-child relationships under ROC laws.

[66] For comments on the ROC Juvenile Court, see Shee,A.,1994:Appendix VIII.

[67] For introduction to the contents and operation of the LGDJC, see Chuen,J.S.,1988; Judicial Yuan (ROC),1982ab; Lee,J.J.,1981,1986,1988; and *Chang,K.M.,1982*; *Lin,C.H., 1988*; *Shen,Y.H.,1989*; *Ting,T.Y.,1985*; *Wang,ShuNu (II),1991*; *Yang,K.S.,1991*.

[68] This 'police law' refers to the 1991 SOML which has replaced the 1954 POL.

[69] See LGDJC: 3.

[70] See LGDJC: 27.

[71] The Court may order the guardian of the girl to pay for the expenses (in part or in total) of treatment.

[72] The law does not, however, provide for the time limit of this period of protection and placement.

[73] It has long been debated as to whether this 'guardianship' is the same as that provided in the Civil Code, which covers all the legal rights and duties of a parent. In practice, most of the professionals in my interviews said that they would only exercise this guardianship for the purpose of protection and rehabilitation of the girl. However, in my observation, different groups of professionals have availed themselves of this guardianship in various ways in order to achieve their 'purpose' of protection and treatment. Some ill-equipped institutions could only afford to assume the 'physical custody' of the child, some others even found it difficult to retain a girl in the institution. The well-organised institutions would, in contrast, impose strict Christian discipline on all received girls and provide for short-term and long-term education, skills-training, and job-placement services, which even an average parent would not do.

[74] In practice, this is seldom worked out for practical difficulties and very few social workers would try to do it.

[75] Before the SOML was enacted in June 1991, a similar POL:64 applied under which all illegal prostitutes including the underage ones could be detained for maximum 7 days with a fine of not more than 50 *yuan* (about 12 Pounds Sterling).

[76] It is then their obligation to transfer every case of public prosecution to the competent procurator's office. To those who have violated police offence laws, the police may also impose administrative measures including detention and fines according to the SOML.

[77] For an introduction to the organisations of the ROC central and local governments, see Chung & Hsieh, 1989:118-158; Chiu & Fa,1984:617-625.

[78] In addition to the protection and treatment of child victims, welfare authorities are also legally empowered to impose administrative punishment on child molesters including fines, compulsory counseling education, to publish their names, and to take the perpetrators to Court.

[79] There are temporary shelters in both institutions to accommodate boys. See *Chen & Chuan et al.,1996; Chou.Y.Y.,1995.*

[80] In the book 'Feminism and the Power of Law', C. Smart adopted a Foucaultian analysis of truth/knowledge and power, and criticises that the 'Truth' articulated by Lord Denning about the natural differences between women and men is a trespass of the legal power to non-legal issues. As a result, law extends itself beyond uttering the truth of law to making claims about other areas of social life (Smart,1989:12-14). Similarly, the ROC Criminal Court extends its legal power of discretion to adapt the application of law to local customs. So by the Court's definition, it is constructed as a 'legal truth' that parents who are ignorant and in financial difficulties are prone to sell daughters into prostitution and should be less condemned.

[81] According to the estimation of experienced social workers including *Mr CHENG Yi Shih*; *Ms WANG Isa*; and *Ms WANG Yeh Hau* of GOH; *Ms LI Ming Yu* of ECPAT; and *Ms CHEN Mei Ling* of TWRF, recidivism was found in more than half of the involved families.

7 CHANGES MADE IN THE SPECIFIC LAW

Before the promulgation of the Law To Suppress Sexual Transactions Involving Children and Juveniles (the new Law), the problem of child prostitution was dealt with by general laws including the Criminal Code, the Social Order Maintenance Law, the Civil Code, the Child Welfare Law, the Juvenile Welfare Law, the Law Governing the Disposition of Juvenile Cases, and administrative regulations on prostitution control. This chapter intends to compare and contrast the contexts of the general laws and the new specific law so as to detect the changes made under the new Law.

Introduction

Legislative Policies

Punishment against forced and under-age prostitution Although the ROC legal policies of prostitution control have remained obscure, it is certain that traffic in persons, profiting from the prostitution of others, and sexual intercourse with children under the age of 16 have been penalised under the Criminal Code since its first promulgation.[1] Although crimes concerning forced or under-age prostitution have never appeared with specific provisions, research into the objectives of the Criminal Code has shown that many general offences against social morals, against the family, or against personal liberty were intended to criminalise forced prostitution, especially that involving exploitative husbands or parents (*Han,C.M.,1980:366-367*; *Shen,M.C.,1989:136*, *Tao,P.C.et al,1991:844-857*).[2]

As a result of pressure from concerned NGOs and professionals, helped by social demand expressed through the media, there is now a trend among law-makers towards criminalisation of the acts of forcing prostitution on others, profiting from under-age prostitution, and consuming illegal prostitution. Legal moralists have long tried to outlaw prostitution without substantial success, but their efforts have mounted to make forced-prostitution and under-age prostitution two distinctive social problems deserving special legal vigilance.

Except for the failure of NGOs in retaining punishment against customers of illegal prostitution in the Social Order Maintenance Law, they have made substantial achievements in more recent legal reforms. The 1989 Juvenile Welfare Law is the first triumph and it was followed by the 1993 Child Welfare Law, in both laws specific or heavier criminal as well as administrative punishments can now be imposed on child abusers and exploiters including all perpetrators of child prostitution. The 1995 Law to Suppress Sexual Transactions Involving Children and Juveniles further demonstrates a clear legislative policy against underage prostitution. Recently the draft bill for the Amendment of the Criminal Code has been completed by the Executive Yuan and sent to the Legislative Yuan for review. Concerned professionals also proposed the inclusion of specific articles in the new Criminal Code to convict abusers and exploiters of forced or under-age prostitution with more severe punishments.[3]

Treatment of prostitution involved children The first laws that were invoked to deal with prostitution-involved children were the Law Governing the Disposition of Juvenile Cases (to deal with juvenile delinquency) and the Police Offence Law (to deal with illegal pimping, prostitution, and frequenting prostitution). Both laws are punitive in nature. When the juvenile delinquency law was applied, every prostitution-involved child was treated the same as other delinquent youths who were in danger of committing a crime,[4] while older ones (aged 18 to 20) received the same administrative punishments as those for illegal prostitutes under the police offence law.

It was not until the late 1980s that the practice of forced child prostitution was finally recognised as one of the most serious social problems.[5] When concerned NGOs (mainly the Rainbow Project, the Garden of Hope Foundation, and the Taipei Women Rescue Foundation, joined later by the Good Shepherd Sisters Foundation and the End Child Prostitution Association Taiwan) got themselves more and more involved in the treatment of child prostitution problems, they began to realise and urge that the existing punishment-oriented laws could not serve the purposes of treatment (*Chen,Y.C.,1991*; *Huang,Y.C.,1991a*; *TMSWB, 1990b*; *Wang,C.F.,1990*). Their efforts ultimately resulted in specific articles in the 1989 Juvenile Welfare Law for the prevention and treatment of juvenile prostitution. Before the Juvenile Welfare Law was promulgated in response to unprecedented social demands for governmental intervention and legal reforms, it was generally conceded that the lack of specific laws was one of the vital obstacles to the prevention and treatment of child prostitution problems in *Taiwan*. Thus both preventive and therapeutic measures were included into the Juvenile Welfare Law. However, demands from the concerned specialists for legal reforms never stopped.

As the nature and prevalence of the problem of child prostitution had developed, both academics and practitioners found the Juvenile Welfare Law to be inadequate. On the other hand, as selective application of relevant general laws became intolerable at least among concerned professionals, strong urges were made to make a single specific law governing exclusively with the child prostitution issue. Numerous conferences and public hearings were held to discuss the possibility and practicability of making a 'Girl Prostitution Prevention and Treatment Law (*chu chi fang chi fa* 雛妓防治法)' (*GOH,1992:Preface*; *Shee,A.,1992: 1-5*; *TMSWB,1990:72-74*). The draft bill of this Law was widely supported by the ROC Legislature, although some male legislators strongly oppose to some of the provisions concerning punishment of the customers.[6] The basic principles of the bill included first, heavy criminal punishment for procurers, second, publication of names, imprisonment for a maximum of three years, and counselling treatment for customers, and third, establishment of a prevention and treatment network, and the compulsory counseling education for all prostitution-involved children. Besides, the Bill also mandates governmental authorities to establish a interdisciplinary supervision team in order to facilitate departmental cooperation (*Chen,C.H.,1993:4-5*; *Lin,Y.S.,1993:2-3*; *Wang,I.,1993:1*). Most of the proposed provisions in the bill concerning treatment of the involved children were accepted by the Legislative Yuan with only some technical amendments. Debates concerning the Law mainly concentrated on the degree of penalty for the customers. Some urged that the sexual intercourse committed against a girl under 14 is equivalent to statutory rape, which is publishable with imprisonment of 5 to 20 years under the Criminal Code, thus the proposed penalty of imprisonment for not more than 3 years is far too lenient. But a lot more others argued that since the customers **PAID** for the sexual service, they should not be condemned as a **RAPIST**. As a result, all customers are subjected to a maximum penalty of 3-year imprisonment even though the involved child is under the age of consent. Again, as the problem is legally defined in term of 'sexual transactions', the justification to sanction the customer as an abuser becomes legally irrelevant.

Principles of Law Application

Specific law supercedes general law The application of ROC laws is governed by the 'specific law supersedes general law' principle. For example, the 'general law' which governs parent-child relationship is the Civil Code. So in judging such family matters, the Court should basically apply the Civil Code. However, there are now specific provisions concerning custody of children after parental divorce in the Juvenile/Child Welfare Laws. Therefore, in making decisions as to such specific matters, the Welfare Law provisions have to be applied. Thus, as far as 'sexual transactions' involving children and juveniles are concerned, the new Law is the specific law, and all other laws mentioned above become the general laws. So in all child prostitution cases, application of the new Law should supercede that of other laws unless in matters that are not regulated under the specific law.

Punishments for an act under different laws For the same act, punishment may be imposed on an offender under administrative laws as well as criminal laws. Take a pimp, for instance, when he/she is arrested, the police may first impose administrative punishments of detention and fines on him/her according to the Social Order Maintenance Law. And besides being a police offence, pimping is also a criminal offence under the new specific Law, so after execution of the administrative punishments, the police may also refer the pimp to the Procurator's Office[7] of a competent district Court to institute a criminal proceeding, and in addition, the administrative authority may also oblige the pimp to attend counselling sessions.

Child Prostitution under General Laws

Relevant General Laws

Introduction The current ROC laws applicable to deal with child prostitution can be variously categorised. They include civil (and procedural) laws, criminal (and procedural) laws, and administrative laws.[8] The treatment of prostitution-involved children is provided by laws applicable to specified age groups for different purposes including punishment, rehabilitation, and retraining. Proceedings concerning parent-child relationship are governed by civil and welfare laws. The perpetrators can be subjected to the punishments of criminal or administrative laws, while the vice business is subjected to the control of various governmental regulations. The main law enforcers of civil and criminal laws are the law Courts, and those of administrative laws are governmental administrative authorities, while the police assume various duties including maintaining social order, protecting people, raiding and investigating crimes etc. as provided by law. These relevant ROC laws mainly include the Civil Code, the Criminal Code, the Law Governing the Disposition of Juvenile Cases and administrative laws which are, namely, the Child Welfare Law, the Juvenile Welfare Law, and the Social Order Maintenance Law. Laws pronounced by local governments consist of the 'Regulations Governing Prostitution' and the 'Regulations Governing Special Entertainment Establishments'.

Prostitution control regulations The main laws governing licensing and control of prostitution are the three sets of the 'Regulations Governing Prostitution' applied to the *Taiwan* Province, the *Taipei* Municipality and the *Kaohsiung* Municipality. This administrative law has undergone several amendments since their first pronouncement in 1973, although most of the changes have been trivial.[9] When the problem of illegal prostitution being practised in legal business settings was recognised, three sets of the 'Regulations Governing Special Entertainment Establishments' were made in 1986.

Laws punishing perpetrators All the perpetrators can be convicted in the Criminal Court and punished by the Criminal Code with imprisonment, detention or fines for committing criminal offences of traffic in persons, illegal detention for illicit purposes, illegal sexual relationship with children under 16, etc.. Under the Social Order Maintenance Law, the perpetrators may also be subjected to detention or fines imposed by the police for pimping or accommodating illegal prostitution; besides, competent administrative authorities are also empowered to take certain administrative measures including closing down illegal entertainment establishments, imposing fines, running counselling education, and publicising names of the customers in accordance with the Juvenile/Child Welfare Laws.

Laws governing parent-child relationship After the Juvenile/Child Welfare Laws were promulgated in 1989 and 1993, some provisions concerning deprivation of parental rights and custody after divorce and guardianship have now replaced the application of the Civil Code according to the aforementioned 'specific law supersedes general law' principle. Therefore, the exploitative parents may now be brought to the Family Court where their parental rights may be suspended or removed according to the Civil Code (when the victim has reached the age of 18 years), the Juvenile Welfare Law (when the victim is aged between 12 and 18) or the Child Welfare Law (when the victim is under 12), and the custody of child victims will be, at least in theory, reallocated to those who are able to provide proper care and control of the child until she\he reaches the age of 20.

Laws concerning rehabilitation of the children As illegal prostitution is generally regarded as an offence against the social order, prostitution-involved children were first dealt with as juvenile offenders[10] under the Law Governing the Disposition of Juvenile Cases. As more and more legislative efforts have been made in response to pressure from concerned professionals, the victimisation and needs of the prostitution-involved children are becoming legal concerns. The inclusions of specific provisions governing child prostitution in the Juvenile/Child Welfare Laws showed noticeable moves in that direction.

As a result, in the treatment of child prostitution under general laws, there is a parallel system of protection and correction to deal respectively with the 'sold-forced' and the 'unsold-voluntary' juveniles, while children under the age of 12 are indiscriminately received into the child protection system. So all prostitution-involved children under 12 are protected under the Child Welfare Law; while laws which may be applied to juveniles include the Juvenile Welfare Law[11] for the protection and care of 'sold-forced' children, and the Law Governing the Disposition of Juvenile Cases for the rehabilitation and correction of 'unsold-voluntary'. The older and habitual prostitution-involved juveniles may also be fined under the Social Order Maintenance Law for having violated good morals and thus referred to rehabilitation centres for habitual prostitution.

The Call for a Specific Law

As shown in the last chapter, the inter-actions and inter-applications of the laws are complicated and confusing both in theory and in practice.[12] Both academics and concerned decision-makers had found it difficult to agree, even among themselves, how all the general laws shall be put together and be applied to cases. Distorted elucidation and selective enforcement of laws by their enforcers, either deliberately or recklessly, have caused further confusion in practice. All these difficulties in practice accumulated the calls to make a specific law to combine and replace all the relevant provisions under the general laws.

Contents of the New Law[13]

The Law to Suppress Sexual Transactions Involving Children and Juveniles is consisted of five Chapters, namely, General Principles (Articles 1 to 5), Rescue (Articles 6 to 10), Protection and Settlement (Articles 11 to 21), Punishment (Articles 22 to 36), and Supplementary Regulations (Articles 37 to 39).

Legislative Intention

According to Article 1, the purpose of this Law is to suppress and eliminate the incidence of sexual transactions involving children and juveniles. Article 2 defines the term 'sexual transactions' as 'sexual intercourse or indecent acts committed with consideration (*tuei chia 對價*)'.

Authorities

Competent authorities According to Article 3-I, the term 'competent authority' under this Law refers to the Ministry of the Interior at the Central Government level, the Social Department (Bureau) at the Provincial (Municipal) administrative level, and the local governments at the County administrative level. The competent authorities of all levels should allocate independent budget and appoint professional personnel to handle the affairs concerning sexual transactions involving children and juveniles.
Relevant authorities According to Article 3-II, the administrative authorities responsible for justice administration, education, public health and hygiene, national defense, information, economics, and public transportation are referred to under this Law as the 'relevant authorities', who should act cooperatively with the competent authorities to deal with the affairs concerning sexual transactions involving children and juveniles. Within six months after this Law becomes effective, all the above relevant authorities should enact administrative laws governing the organisation of and operation of preventive school and social education.
Assembly of Direction and Supervision

Under Article 3-III of the Law, the Ministry of the Interior and other administrative authorities have to establish collaboratively, within six months after the Law is enforced, an 'Assembly of Direction and Supervision （*tu tou hui pao* 督導會報）', whose function is to evaluate among the authorities on the effects of enforcement in order to locate practical difficulties and to work on solutions.

Prevention Programmes

Article 4 provides that the contents of the courses and social educational programmes carried out by or under the supervision of the government concerning sexual transactions involving children and juveniles should include programmes designed to cultivate appropriate sexual psychology, to cultivate respect for the sexual liberty of others, to correct improper sexual conception, to make believe that sex must not become an object for commercial transactions, to help the public understand the miserable lives of those children and juveniles who are involved in sexual transactions, and to care for other matters concerning the prevention of sexual transactions involving children and juveniles.

Principles of Application

Article 5 makes it clear that the Law is a specific legislation as far as 'matters concerning them suppression of sexual transactions involving children and juveniles (*erh tung chi shau nien hsing chiau yi fang chi shi hsiang 兒童及少年性交易防制事項*)' is concerned; and thus its application in such cases shall supercede general laws. However, general laws shall govern when relevant matters are not regulated under this Law.

Rescue of Involved Children

Specilised Duty Squads Article 6 first mandates that, within six months after the Law becomes effective, the Ministry of Justice Administration and the Ministry of the Interior shall establish 'Specialised Duty Squads (*chuan tse jen wu pian tsu 專責任務編組*)' to take the responsibilities to detect crimes governed by the Law. Article 8 further provides that within six months after this law becomes effective, the Ministry of Justice Administration and the Ministry of the Interior shall make 'Regulations Governing Merits and Demerits (*chiang cheng pan fa 獎懲辦法*) ' in order to promote the police work of rescue and detection.

National Hot Line Article 7 then provides that after the establishment of the Specialised Duty Squads, the competent authorities shall set up or authorise voluntary organisations to set up a national hot line (*chuen kuo hsing chiou yuan chuan hsien 全國性救援專線*).

Mandatory Reporting System Article 9-I further strengthens the reporting system by making it a legal obligation for all concerned professionals including medical doctors, pharmacists, nurses, social workers, clinical psychiatrists, education professionals, policemen/women, judicial personnel or other professionals working on child or juvenile welfare who may have the knowledge of a person under eighteen being involved or at the risk of being involved in sexual transactions or a person who is suspected to have committed any crime specified in this Law, immediately report to the local authority or any of the Specialised Duty Squads. Under Article 36, violators of the report obligation may be imposed on a fine of not less than NT$6,000[14] but not more than NT$30,000. However, those doctors, nurses or other medical workers who commit such crime for the purpose of saving the children/juveniles from emergent dangers causing to their lives or bodies shall be excused from the punishment.

Special protection for children from double victimisation Article 9-II provides that the personal data of an informer who reports a case according to this Law shall be kept confidential.

Under Article 10, during the courses of investigation and Court hearings, the authority shall appoint social workers to accompany the involved children or juveniles and to express their opinions on the case. Besides, the involved children or juveniles shall not be summoned after the essential legal interrogations have completed.

Protection and Settlement

Schooling Control System According to Article 11, when a primary school or junior high school student is found to be absent from school for three or more days without informing the school authority of the reasons, or such student who is supposed to transfer from one school to another but fails to report to the new school in due course, the school authority shall immediately report the case to the competent or education authorities; and in such cases, the competent authority shall immediately appoint social workers to investigate the case and to take necessary measures. In order to regulate this schooling control system, the Law mandates the Ministry of Education to promulgate a governmental 'Order to Regulate the Schooling Control System (*chung tu chuo hsueh hsueh sheng tung pao pan fa* 中途輟學學生通報辦法)' within six months after this Law becomes effective.

Affectionate Care Centre In order to prevent run-away children or juveniles under eighteen to be involved in lust business settings, Article 12 requires that the competent authority shall, within six months after the Law becomes effective, establish or authorise voluntary organisations to establish 'Affectionate Care Centres (*kuan huai chung hsin* 關懷中心)' which will provide for emergency protection and temporary shelter for the running-away children and juveniles. The centre should also offer needed consultation, help to communicate with concerned people, and take other necessary measures.

Emergency Settlement Centre Under Articles 13, the competent authority shall temporarily locate the children or juveniles who are found or reported to have involved or to be at the risk of being involved in sexual interactions at the Emergency Settlement Centres（*chin chi shou jung chung hsin* 緊急收容中心）established by the authority. In order to fulfil this legal duty, the competent authorities at the Municipal and County levels shall, within six months after this Law becomes effective, establish these Centres and appoint specialised professionals to help the needing children and juveniles.

Temporary Settlement Centre Under Articles 13, the competent authorities at the Municipal and County levels shall, within six months after this Law becomes effective, establish Temporary Settlement Centres (*tuan chi shou jung chung hsin* 短期收容中心) to accommodate those children or juveniles who were involved in or at the risk of being involved in sexual transactions. These Centres shall also appoint specialised professionals to deal with matters concerning observation, consultation and medical treatment.

Mid-Way School Under Article 14, the Ministry of Education shall, within one year after this Law becomes effective, coordinate the competent authorities at the Provincial and the Municipal Levels to establish the specialised Mid-Way School (*chung tu hsieh hsiao* 中途學校) for the continuing education of those children or juveniles who were involved in sexual transactions. The Mid-Way school shall appoint professionals specialised in social work, psychiatry, and special education to provide for special education. In order to prevent the students being labelled, the registration/enrolment records of the Mid-Way school students shall reside with normal/general schools. When such students graduate, they shall be given certificate awarded by normal/general schools.[15]

Procedure of protection and settlement According to Articles 15-I & II, 16, 17, and 18, the legal procedure to dispose of prostitution-involved children and juveniles are as follows:

First, when judges, procurators, juris-police, units of inspectors, or members of the Specialised Duty Squads as specified in Article 6, locate or rescue children or juveniles who are involved or at the risk of being involved in sexual transactions, shall immediately inform the competent authority to appoint social workers to accompany the children or juveniles to take part in the identification of criminal suspects and in essential interrogation, and shall refer the involved children or juveniles to the Emergency Settlement Centres established by the Provincial, Municipal or County authorities. The Emergency Settlement Centres shall, within seventy-two hours after settlement, submit a report to the Law Court applying for an order.

The Court, after receiving the aforementioned application, should make an order for the competent authority to settle the involved child/juveniles at a Temporary Settlement Centre except the following two situations: First, it is clear that the child/juvenile has not been engaged in, nor at the risk of being engaged in sexual transactions. The Court should make an order to return the child/juvenile to his/her legal agent, head of the household, nearest relative or other pertinent persons. Second, there are other reasons which make the Temporary Settlement Centre inappropriate. The Court should then make an order for the competent authority to allocate the child/juvenile at an appropriate place.

After examining the case, if it is clear that the child/juvenile has not been engaged, nor at the risk of being engaged in sexual transactions, the Court should make an order to return the child/juvenile to his/her legal agent, the head of the household, the nearest relative or other pertinent persons. If the Court finds that the child/juvenile has been engaged in sexual transactions, it should render an order to settle the child/juvenile at a Mid-Way School for two-year special education. If a child/juvenile reaches his/her age of eighteen during the term of special education, the Mid-Way School may continue the special education until the two-year specified term is completed. After the special education has completed its first year, the competent authority may apply to the Court to discharge the special education. After the two-year special education is completed, the competent authority may apply to the Court to prolong the term of special education until the child/juvenile reaches the age of twenty.

Custodianship Under Article 20, the competent authority or the Ministry of Education, when settle, counsel, or protect a child/juvenile according to Articles 15 to 18 of this Law, shall exercise parental or custodian rights by proxy.

If a parent, adoptive parent or custodian commits one of the crimes specified in Articles 23 to 28 of this Law against a child or juvenile under the age of eighteen, a procurator, the nearest ascendant of the child/juvenile, the competent authority, a child/juvenile welfare institution, or any other interested person may apply to the Court to suspend the parental/custodian rights and appoint a new guardian. An application may also be made against an adoptive parent to terminate the adoption.

The Court, when appointing the guardian according to Article 20, is not restricted by Article 1094 of the Civil Code. The Court may appoint a person who is in charge of the competent authority or a child/juvenile welfare institution, or any other pertinent person to be the custodian of the involved child/juvenile. The Court may also order custody rules and require the parent(s) or adoptive parent(s) to pay expenses to the appointed guardian.

Children and juveniles who report for themselves According to Article 15-III, the competent authority shall render necessary protection, settlement or other assistance to the child or juvenile engaged in or at the risk of being engaged in sexual transactions who reports to the authority and requires for help.

Cases involving delinquency Under Article 19, a child or a juvenile who is engaged in or is at the risk of being engaged in sexual transactions without committing other crimes should not be treated under the Law Governing the Disposition of Juveniles Cases or Social Order Maintenance Law. However, if a child or a juvenile is engaged in or is at the risk of being engaged in sexual transactions, and at the same time commits a crime, the case should first be decided according to Articles 16 to 18 of this Law for treatment before the Law Governing the Disposition of Juveniles Cases applies to deal with the misbehaviour.

Application of the Law in cases involving forced prostitution Article 21 specifically provides that, a person of the age of eighteen or over who is forced by coercion, threat, enticement, trafficking or any other illegal ways to be involved in sexual transactions may require for settlement and protection according to this Law.

Punishment

Promotion of police work According to Article 8, within six months after this law becomes effective, the Ministry of Justice Administration and the Ministry of the Interior shall make a governmental Order to govern the merits and demerits in the enforcement of this Law in order to promote the police work of rescue and detection.

The customer Under Article 22, those who conduct sexual transactions with a person under the age of sixteen shall be punished with imprisonment of not more than three years, alternatively coupled with a fine of not more than NT$100,000. In comparison, those who conduct sexual transactions with a person aged between sixteen and eighteen will only have imposed a fine of not more than NT$ 100,000 without imprisonment.

The pimp and the brothel-keeper The criminal punishment for the pimp or the brothel keeper is provided by Articles 23 and 24. Article 23 penalised the acts of enticement, accommodation, mediation, assistance and other ways of involvement in the operation of child prostitution; while Article 24 provides for heavier penalties for the Articles 23 acts which are committed with coercion, threats, drugs, fraud, hypnotism or other methods which are against the victim's will.

Under the provisions, those who entice, accommodate, mediate, assist or by other ways to involve a person under the age of eighteen in sexual transactions (the act) shall be punished with imprisonment of not less than one year but not more than seven years, and alternatively coupled with a fine of not more than NT$1,000,000. If the act further involves coercion, threats, drugs, fraud, hypnotism or other methods which are against the victim's will, the penalty shall be imprisonment of at least five years, and the alternative fine may be doubled

If the act is committed with the intention to make profits, the punishment will be imprisonment of not less than three years but not more than ten years, coupled with a fine of not more than NT$5,000,000; if the act further involves coercion, threats, drugs, fraud, hypnotism or other methods that are against the victim's will, the penalty shall be imprisonment of at least seven years, and the alternative fine may be increased up to NT$7,000,000. If such profit making is habitual, then the punishment will be imprisonment of not less than five years with the fine doubled; and if this habitual commitment further involves coercion, threats, drugs, fraud, hypnotism or other methods which are against the victim's will, the penalty shall be no less than ten-year or life imprisonment, and the coupled fine may be up to NT$10,000,000.

Those who receive or shield the victims of the crimes specified in Articles 23 and 24, or who make the victims hide or to mediate in such acts shall be punished with imprisonment of not less than one year but not more than seven years, and alternatively coupled with a fine of not more than NT$300,000. If the act further involves coercion, threats, drugs, fraud, hypnotism or other methods that are against the victim's will, the penalty shall be imprisonment of at least five years, and the alternative fine may be up to NT$500,000.

The trafficker According to Article 25, those who intend to make profits and involve a person under the age of eighteen in sexual transactions by trafficking, pawning or other means of the same nature or those who receive or shield the victims of such crime shall be punished with imprisonment of not less than five years, coupled with NT$7,000,000. Those who use coercion, threats, drugs, fraud, hypnotism or other methods which are against the victim's will and commit the above crime shall be punished with imprisonment of not less than seven years, coupled with a fine of not more than NT$7,000,000. If the victim dies as a result, the death penalty shall be imposed and if serious bodily harm is caused to the victim, the penalty shall be life imprisonment. Those who act as the mediator of the crimes specified above shall be punished with imprisonment of not less than five years, coupled with not more than NT$5,000,000.

Those who habitually commit the crimes specified in the preceding paragraph shall be punished with life imprisonment or imprisonment of not less than ten years, coupled with a fine of not more than NT$20,000,000.

The Media Advertiser Article 29 provides that those who utilise propaganda, publications, television or other media to publish or broadcast advertisements in order to induce, mediate, imply or by other means cause others to be involved in sexual transactions shall be punished with imprisonment of not less than one year but not more than seven years, and alternatively coupled with a fine of not more than NT$1,000.000. In addition, those publishers who print advertising messages to induce, mediate, imply or by other ways to involve others in sexual transactions may be sanctioned by the Government Information Office and have imposed an administrative fine of not less than NT$30,000 but not more than NT $400,000 under Article 33. Should payment of the fine specified above be delayed, a petition may be made to the Court for its enforcement.

Pornography Under Article 27, those who film or make paintings, video tapes, film pictures, CD ROM, electrical signals or other products showing conducts of indecency or sexual interaction involving a person under the age of eighteen shall be punished with imprisonment of not less than six months but not more than five years, and alternatively coupled with a fine of not more than NT$500,000.

Those who commit the act with the intention to make profits shall be punished with imprisonment of not less than one year but not more than seven years, coupled with a fine of not more than NT$5,000,000. Those who induce, mediate or use other means to involve a person under the age of eighteen in the filming or making of paintings, vedio tapes, film pictures, CD ROM, electrical signals or other product showing conducts of indecency or sexual intercourse shall be punished with imprisonment of not less than one year but not more than seven years, and alternatively coupled with a fine of not more than NT$1,000,000. Those who use coercion, threats, drugs, fraud, hypnotism or other methods that are against the victim's will and commit the above crimes shall be punished with imprisonment of not less than five years, and alternatively coupled with a fine of not more than NT$3,000,000.

Those who habitually commits the crimes specified in Article 27 shall be punished with imprisonment of not less than seven years, coupled with a fine of not more than NT$10,000,000. The pornographic products specified above shall all be confiscated despite their ownership.

According to Article 28, those who distribute or sell the paintings, video tapes, film pictures, CD ROM, electrical signals or other products specified above, or display such products to the public, shall be punished with imprisonment of not more than three years, and alternatively coupled with a fine of not more than NT$5,000,000. The pornographic products shall all be confiscated despite their ownership.

Heavier penalty for public servants and elected officials Under Article 30, those public servants or elected officials who commit any crime specified in this Law or patron others to commit crimes specified under this Law shall receive punishment increased up to one half of the original provision for imprisonment.

Heavier penalty for international trafficking Those who intend to commit the crimes specified in Articles 23 to 27 of this Law, transport the victims out of this country shall receive punishment increased up to one half of the original provision for imprisonment.

Decreased penalty for parents Those parents who commit a crime specified in this Law against their children may be sanctioned with leniency on two occasions: first, any other involved offender is captured owing to the parent's information or testimony, and second, the parent informs on oneself and makes a confession and thus helps to capture other offenders of the case.

Publication of the name and photograph of the offender and the ratio decidendi of the case Article 34 mandates the competent authority to inform in public the names and photographs of the offenders, and the *ratio decidendi* of the finalised judgments, but not those of or involving customers. Also, if the offender is under the age of eighteen, the provision of public notice shall not apply.

Counselling education course for the offenders Article 35 mandates the competent authority to impose counselling education on all involved offenders under this Law. To those who refuse to attend the counselling education programme as provided or who does not finish the imposed counselling hours, the competent authority may impose on a fine of not less than NT$6,000 but not more than NT$30,000. Such fine may be continuously imposed for every refusal to comply with the counselling requirement.

Application of the Law in cases involving forced prostitution Article 37 extends the application of this Law to punish all offenders involved in forced prostitution despite the age of the victim.

Prominent Changes Written by the Law

A Specific Law to Respond to Practical Needs

The Law to Suppress Sexual Transactions Involving Children and Juveniles (the Law) is the first specific law to govern a certain social problem 'owned' by NGOs. Before the promulgation of the Law, the issue of child prostitution as a whole was never a main concern for legislation. So when a child prostitution case was at stake, relevant provisions in general laws have to be applied for protection and punishment. As the legislative purposes and governing matters of each law were distinctive and different, selective application of similar provisions of various laws became unavoidable. These practical problems in law enforcement were widely criticised by those NGO experts who were socially responsible to manage the child prostitution issue. The criticisms finally amounted to the proposal for a piece of specific legislation. A NGO draft bill was then proposed to and supported by some leading legislators, which was then joined by two bills of other legislators, though there was never a governmental draft bill. It was the first time in the history of ROC social legislation that the government chose to play an unconditionally passive role law-making. As a result, the Law is comparatively idealistic to those laws in which the government intervened in or actually led the legislative process.

A Legal Definition for the Child Prostitution Problem

Under the new Law, the child prostitution problem is for the first time legally defined as 'sexual transactions involving children and juveniles (*erh tung chi shau nien hsing chiao yi 兒童及少年性交易)*'. Despite the fact that the Law sets up a thorough routine of protection and treatment for all involved children and juveniles, to define their acts as 'sexual transactions' may cast doubts on their victim status. Now that it is the 'sexual transactions' that the Law governs, it becomes debatable in law enforcement as to whether children or a juveniles are legally eligible to make 'sexual transactions' by themselves since sexual intercourse or other indecent acts committed with a person under 16 is not legally permissible.

Specified Legal Duties for Administrative Authorities

The new Law imposes on relevant administrative authorities including the Ministry of the Interior, the Department of Justice Administration, the Department of Education, the Department of Public Health and Hygiene, the Department of National Defence, the Department of Economics, the

Department of Public Transportation and the Government Information Office to conduct certain legal duties within a prescribed period of time. As a result, the 'Assembly of Direction and Supervision', the 'Specialised Duty Squads' of the police and the procurators, the ' Affectionate Care Centre(s)', the 'Emergency Settlement Centre(s)' and the 'Temporary Settlement Centre(s)' shall all be established within six months after the Law is promulgated; and the 'Mid-Way School(s)' has to be set up no later than one year after the Law becomes active. In addition, relevant administrative regulations or orders concerning preventive education and censorship of police law enforcement have to be made within six months after the Law is enacted. This is the first piece of social legislation to mandate relevant authorities to complete something within a certain period of time.

One Treatment Routine for All Involved Children and Juveniles

Before the Law was made, all prostitution-involved children and juveniles were classified as 'voluntary' and 'forced' in order to decide whether he or she should be protected under welfare laws or be corrected under delinquency laws. The classification system finally became the technical mechanism to help in the selective application of laws by their enforcers. Many involved juveniles were classified as 'voluntary' because the police were much more familiar with delinquency laws, and on the other hand, the process for referral to the welfare system was considered time-consuming and thus was avoided more than approached. In order to redress this problem, the specific Law treats equally all children and juveniles under 18 who are involved in sexual transactions. In fact, the Law further protects all victims of forced prostitution disregarding their age.

Specified and Heavy Punishments for All Perpetrators

Under the general laws, as child prostitution or prostitution itself is not a specific legal concern, and thus perpetrators have been punished under relevant provisions in the Criminal Code or the Social Order Maintenance Law governing offences against social morals, offences against the family, offences against personal liberty, and so forth. In addition, Juvenile Welfare Law and Child Welfare Law also provide for administrative punishments for perpetrators who involve a person under 18 or 12 in commercial sex deals. So in practice, if the law enforcers have vigorously applied relevant laws to punish child prostitution perpetrators, every one of the brothel-keepers, the pimps, the traffickers, and their abettors could have been sanctioned with both criminal and administrative punishments. But it was by far the case, so perpetrators always escaped from legal loopholes. The new Law not only specifies and criminalises all kinds of perpetrators but also imposes much heavier penalties (imprisonment and fines).

Concluding Remarks

The making of a specific law to deal with a social problem is generally intended to redress practical problems in the enforcement of general laws. The social problem has to be recognised as distinctive and serious enough to deserve a single piece of legislation. Also, it has to be agreed that existing laws cannot deal with the social problem properly. The Law to Suppress Sexual Transactions Involving Children and Juveniles was made with all these qualifications, and it was celebrated as the triumph of NGO lobbying for a law to empower them in their work. However, as the aim was to obtain a specific law quickly, substantial compromises were made for exchange. In order to push the legislative process and to avoid long discussions and debates, the legislators who supported the GOH bill were ready to give way. As a result, the urge to define the problem as 'child abuse and sexual exploitation' was sacrificed, and the penalty for the customers was reduced to the minimum. The impacts of these concessions were not envisaged during the legislative process. But in practice, the intended functions of the new specific law have been limited.

NOTES

[1] See chapter six on the punishments against perpetrators of child prostitution.

[2] See relevant discussions in chapter six.

[3] The proposal was made as part of the interim report of the Taipei Bar Association (TBA) research project on 'The Physical Security of Women in *Taiwan*' carried out during 1991 and 1992. According to the report submitted the TBA on March 8, 1991, five specific crimes concerning child prostitution were enumerated to be included into the Criminal Code amendment. They include: (1) encourage and/or profit from prostitution; (2) involvement in the operation of girl prostitution; (3) traffic in persons; (4) force prostitution on others; (5) abuse supervision authority and force prostitution on others. It was also recommended that all such cases should be initiated upon public prosecution.

[4] See relevant discussions in chapter six.

[5] It was not until the recent couple of years did NGOs begin to involve themselves in the rehabilitation of the so-called 'voluntary child prostitutes'.

[6] These legislators, led by *Mr TING Shou Chung and Ms HUANG Chau Shuen respectively*, proposed another two draft bills in order to encounter the GOH bill. One controversial provision of the GOH bill was to publish the name, address and photograph of customers on well-sold newspapers. The TING bill not only rejected the idea, but also suggested that punishment should also be imposed upon those juveniles who got involved in illegal prostitution voluntarily.

[7] For definition and legal status of a 'procurator' under the ROC justice system, see Liu, J.C. et al.,1991bc; Yang,C.S.,1987.

[8] Civil laws deal with private matters including obligations, rights over things, family relations and succession. Criminal laws deal with crimes, and offenders may be imposed on criminal penalties including death, imprisonment, detention and fines. Administrative laws are those laws governing governmental administration and the relationship between government and people including, for the purpose of this thesis, the Social Order Maintenance Law, Prostitution Control Regulations, and Welfare Laws. It has to be noticed that individual administrative laws often contain articles or sections providing for civil remedies for certain infringements of rights or criminal penalties for certain offences, which are referred to as 'specific laws'. As will be explained later, these specific laws should be applied in relevant cases disregarding the general provisions of civil or criminal laws.

[9] As this book is only concerned with important principles of the Regulations, the articles referred to and the years of amendments will not be specified.

[10] The general principle of the CRC concerning criminal responsibilities is that an act committed by a person who is under the age of 14 is not punishable and the punishment imposed on a convicted person aged between 14 and 18 may be reduced under the discretion of the judge (CRC:18). The same principle also applies to administrative measures under the SOML: 8 & 9. On July 1, 1971, a LGDJC was enforced to deal with juvenile criminal cases and to impose reformatory measures on juvenile offenders (LGDJC:1). Since then, adolescents aged between 12 and 18 who violate criminal laws or who are considered under the law to be in danger of committing a crime have been subjected to the jurisdiction of this law (LGDJC: 2 & 3). See Shee,A.,1994:Appendix I for the text of relevant provisions.

[11] Before the CWL was promulgated on February 5, 1993, the law did not provide for appropriate welfare or protection measures for children under the age of 12, let alone child prostitution in particular. Thus, since the JWL was put into practice in January 1989, it has also been invoked to deal with cases, though very few in number, involving children under 12.

[12] For detailed explanation concerning law enforcement, see Shee,A.,1994:Chs 6 & 7.

[13] For a general introduction to the new Law, See *Chi,H.J.,1995a; Chou,Y.Y.,1995; ECPAT,1995ab;. et al.,1996; Shee,A.,1996b*.

[14] The exchange rate of English Pound Sterling: NT$ is approximately 1:40.

[15] For detailed plans for the establishment of the Mid-Way School, see *Chen & Chuan et al.,1996; Chou,Y.Y.,1995; Wang,I.,1995*.

8 PROSPECTS AND LIMITS OF THE NEW LAW

The new Law to Suppress Sexual Transactions Involving Children and Juveniles seems to have induced substantial changes not only in black letters, but also in action. But how far the new law may achieve depends on many factors. It is clear from past experiences that the existing general laws have not dealt with the child prostitution problem properly. Many perpetrators evaded from the loopholes of law because the enforcers tended to find relevant laws inapplicable. So no customer has ever been reported to be punished for statutory rape, because they PAID for the 'service'. On the other hand, many victims were legally treated as 'delinquents', because they appeared to the law enforcers to deserve correction instead of protection. It is convenient to assume that if there is a law to provide for specific punishment for every legally defined crimes of child prostitution, no perpetrator can escape from legal sanctions; and if there is a legally provided treatment programme for all prostitution-involved children, no victims will be misjudged or double-victimised. NGOs have been fuelled with hope for the success of the new Law. However, will and can the Law be properly implemented within current socio-legal environment? How far can the Law accomplish to influence the thinking and behaviour of concerned authorities? Does the Law create new loopholes in practice and why? The following discussion tries to give answers to these questions.

PROBLEMS OF SOCIO-LEGAL MEASURES UNDER THE GENERAL LAWS

Several problems under the old socio-legal circumstances may be summed up from the examination of previous chapters. Vulnerabilities of children from the disadvantaged families, patronage of the exploitation chain by powerful people, selective application of law by the enforcers, refusal on the part of the exploited children to enter treatment programmes, and improper disposition of child prostitution cases in the Juvenile Courts, all have contributed to the deterioration of the problem.

The Disadvantaged Family

Certain aspects of Chinese culture and traditional teachings have in many ways led to the exploitation of young children by parents. The customary practice of sacrificing female children (especially the adoptive ones) for family survival perpetuates in its modern form -- children are sold into prostitution to repay family debts or to rebuild family house and satisfy family vanity. The Confucian teaching of filial piety and the Chinese ethic of self-sacrifice further helps tolerate the practice or even encourage some children to surrender themselves to exploitation. The good/bad dichotomy of the patriarchal family is also responsible for pushing 'bad girls' into prostitution. All these factors have contributed to cause the 'dysfunction' of the families involved in child prostitution.

Moreover, the unrestrained free-market culture in *Taiwan* leads to a pervasive social climate among some aboriginal tribes and certain economically deprived groups which makes people think it is all right to prostitute children for good money. Many children will not resist being sold, because they believe this is their fate. And besides, their inexperienced minds are deceived and corrupted by the neighbourhood, which is obsessed by the power that money generates. This social learning process gradually wipes out the children's identification as 'the forced victim' that our law is to protect. Furthermore, it makes the child a scapegoat for the practice of illegal prostitution, while exempts all others from the social condemnation and the legal punishment for having maltreated them.

The Exploitation Chain

The huge economic gains generated from the operation of child prostitution has formulated and strengthened an exploitation chain around the disadvantaged family. There is a lucrative flesh market fuelled by lavish male demand for clean and tender children. Children of disadvantaged families thus become objects used to satisfy adults' sexual and economic gratification. The wealth derived from a child's body contract has been used to rebuild the family house as well as family pride. A sold child might be rescued or may escape from prostitution before the contract obligation was fulfilled. But it would mean that the family had to repay the socially enforceable debts by sending the daughter back or by giving out another child for replacement. The lucrative business is operated by law breakers, patronised by patriarchal customers, and guarded by law enforcers. Legal restraints against the perpetrators and the exploitation chain are either easy to break or loosely imposed. The large economic gains coupled with prospects of very limited punishments under the general laws has accelerated the growth of the power of exploitation against the power of law.

Selective Application of Law by the Police

Under present ROC general laws, there is a well-established legal process for the disposal of child prostitution cases.[1] Under the Child and Juvenile Welfare Laws, the police are legally required to act immediately upon information, and every child found in prostitution has to be sent to the KTPAI for observation before a decision is made as to whether to refer her\him to the Juvenile Court or to commit her\him to a rehabilitation centre or an educational institution. In practice, however, the children were subjected to disparate treatment under the discretion of law enforcers. There were substantial differences between one police jurisdiction and another in the ways that a case was processed. Apart from the *Taipei* Police Squad for Juvenile Cases and certain police stations which have been incorporated into NGO-organised rescue and protection networks, a due legal process is seldom followed.

Speaking from past experiences, before police action actually took place, the owner of a sex-related business was often informed of the raid and given time to transfer the underage ones to other places. Perpetrators were often charged with minor police offences involving illegal prostitution and released. Only certain police stations would take further steps to refer criminal suspects to the procurator's office. On the other hand, after the involved children were taken to the police station, they were questioned and filed as illegal prostitutes. Coupled with the common police prejudice towards these 'bad' children and the children's loyalty towards their exploitative parents, their victimisation was hardly disclosed. These children were thus returned to their parents without follow-up services, or referred to the Juvenile Court if the police officers chose to do so. Only those police stations which were incorporated into the 'rescue and protection network' by concerned NGOs would be expected to apply welfare laws and refer every involved child under 18 to the KTPAI Observation Centre.

Alienation of the Child Victims from Legal Treatment

Efforts have been made both in the general law (welfare laws) and in practice to divert the sold children from the Juvenile Court into the welfare system. Unfortunately, the distorted enforcement of law made a group of victims resist legal protection. The moral judgments exercised by law enforcers subjected all children to humiliation and degradation. By presuming the children to be 'bad' before they prove themselves to be 'good', the law actually pushes the children to the side of the exploiters. Many children also defied legal intervention because both the criminal justice system and the welfare agencies were antagonistic to their parents. The do-gooders were keen to bring the parents to the Civil Court for their parental rights to be legally severed and to the Criminal Court for their heinous offences to be punished. But the support given to the children was not enough for them to appreciate all these efforts more than a legally obliged betrayal of their parents.

Besides, the care and treatment offered for the child by the welfare state is limited both in scale and in time. Legally speaking, all sold children will be dealt with by welfare authorities who are responsible for their rehabilitation. For the purpose of protection, they were taken away from the family and severed from all family relations during the treatment. The rehabilitation programmes were designed and set up (though some having undergone modifications recently) first to impose on the child a strong anti-prostitution moral sense by harshly condemning the immoral practice of prostitution and the parental misbehaviour of committing her to such immoral profession. Generally speaking, the child was made aware of the social and legal repugnance towards prostitutes during legal proceedings and treatment.

However, after the child was finally released after rehabilitation and skill-training, no follow-ups will be made to meet their special needs. They may have to return to the family whose vulnerability in the exploitative social framework remains. Shadowed by their past experiences, there always appear more incentives for the child to return to prostitution than to make a new living in society. Now the welfare state has ceased its service, so the child is abandoned back to the exploitation chain. Only this time a responsibility is imposed on the child to protect herself\himself and resist all temptation and intimidation. After rehabilitation, she was supposed to be aware of all the illegality and immorality involved in prostitution. She was provided with a sense of shame to say 'no' as well as the skills to earn a 'decent' living. However, she was also left alone to bear all the undesirable results caused by law's impotence.

Unprofessional Disposal of Child Prostitution Cases by the Juvenile Court

The Juvenile Court has not developed special expertise to deal with child prostitution cases. Juvenile Court judges were accustomed to apply juvenile delinquency laws -- the Law Governing the Disposition of Juvenile Cases. Although the Juvenile Welfare Law requires the Juvenile Court to consider the appropriateness of diverting prostitution-involved juveniles under its jurisdiction to the welfare system, most cases were still given a probation decision. The probation officers do not normally have the knowledge to deal with specific circumstances of child prostitution cases. So the child was simply required to report to the probation officer as general delinquents. Unavoidably, a child might be taken back to prostitution as soon as she\he left the Juvenile Court without being noticed by the probation officer.

The New Law Versus the Old Problems

The Defined Problem

The very first mistake made in the definition of the social problem of child prostitution in *Taiwan* was to name the involved children 'the girl prostitutes'. In recent years, however, NGOs have constantly reminded the public to refer to these involved children as 'the unfortunate girls\boys' or the 'victims'. Nevertheless, since the new Law defines the problem as 'sexual transactions involving children and juveniles', the element of 'child abuse and sexual exploitation' becomes invisible (*Lin,J.P.,1994*). Nevertheless, such legislative definition is not fully understood by certain law enforcers who restrict the application of the new Law to cases of 'sexual transactions involving children and juveniles', and to return cases of 'statutory rape and criminal indecency' to the jurisdiction of the Criminal Code (*Tsai,P.Y.,1996*). On the other hand, this legislative definition does not affect NGO practice at all. They keep treating all prostitution-involved children and juveniles as 'victims' to be protected under the Law disregarding the judicial opinion on what constitute 'sexual transactions'.

Punishment

One of the most distinctive changes made by the new Law is, for the first time in ROC legislation, to provide for both criminal and administrative punishments for all specified crimes involving child prostitution. In chapter four (Articles 22 to 36) of the Law, the 'constituent elements' of criminal acts of the customers, the pimps, the brothel-keepers, the traffickers, the pornography operators, and the media who put on lust advertisements. Those elected officials or public servants who operate or patron the child prostitution industry are imposed on much heavier criminal penalties; while leniency is offered to the abusive parents who would assist in prosecution. A concession was made in the penalty for customers to the legislators who insisted that **PAID** sex is much less condemnable than statutory rape and criminal indecency. All provided crimes are subject to public prosecution. All penalties can be imposed coupled with substantial amount of fines. And all perpetrators have to attend counselling programmes. Generally speaking, the Law is not only clear in what acts may invoke what sanctions, but also impose definite and harsh punishments. Nevertheless, harsh punishment in black letters will not work as a deterrence if it is not enforced continuously and vigorously. Both the police and the prosecution authorities have made orders and establish specialist squads to show their intention to enforce the Law properly (*Huang,F.Y.,1996; Li,T.C.,1996bc; Tsai,P.Y.,1996*). The Government Information Office also works hard to impose a duty of self-restraint on the media (*Chi & Yang, 1996; GIO,1996ab*). Before the time comes for their performance to be reviewed, we can only keep our fingers crossed.

Treatment

The total triumph of NGO lobbying recorded in the new Law is chapter three which governs protection and settlement. (Articles 11 to 21) Under the Law, treatment starts early with those who play truancy and those who run away from their families. A schooling control system will be operated to locate all children absent from the school for more than three days. The Affectionate Care Centre will offer needed help for run-away children. If they both work well, it is expected that a considerable number of 'high-risk' cases will not end up in prostitution. For the victims, there are the

Emergency Settlement Centre and the Temporary Settlement Centre for short-term treatment, and the Mid-Way School will provide for long-term education, counselling, and skill-training. There seems to be a thorough plan for treatment, at least in black letters. In fact, if the authorities could effectively coordinate existing NGO establishments and render financial help in their improvements, the Law might have been enforced properly (*GSS, 1996; GOH. 1997; Su,H.T.,1997; Wang,Y.H.,1997; Wu,F.F.,1996*). However, the authorities choose to make some new plastic tags with the words 'Affectionate Care Centre', 'Emergency Settlement Centre', and 'Temporary Settlement Centre', then put them on to doors of the old treatment shelters located in KTPAI and YLTCC. On the other hand, all authorities reported that they were trying to allocate budget for the establishment of brand new Centres and a Mid-Way School, though the administration process towards that end would, as it has been urged, 'take time' (*Chou,Y.Y.,1995; Yang,T.H.,1996*).

Prevention

One of the most important findings from NGO experiences is that prevention programmes must be strengthened to tackle the above mentioned structural problems. So when NGOs proposed the draft Bill for legislation, they included a chapter two entitled 'Prevention, Education and Propagation' (Articles 6 to 16)[2], which mandate concerned authorities to conduct constant research on the problem and carry on wide-range educational programmes based on research findings not only for school children and the public but also for law enforcers. However, the detailed provisions were finally compressed to become Article 4 of the Law which simply give a legal guideline for certain enumerated educational programmes to be held.[3] So in practice now, NGOs are still responsible for most of the preventive work.

Enforcement

One distinctive attribute of the new Law is that all concerned authorities are under the legal mandate to take specified affirmative actions including to allocate an independent budget, to congregate the Assembly of Direction and Supervision, to establish the Specialised Duty Squads, to enact administrative regulations and to reinforce law enforcement, to install a National Hot Line, to organise centres for protection and settlement, to build the Mid-Way School, and so on. However, it may be concluded from NGO reviews that most authorities respond to the law passively (*Chi & Yang,1996; Han,I.T.,1996ab; Yang,T.H.,1996*). All sorts of official documents report that certain actions have been taken to work 'towards' the full implementation of the Law, though the authorities need a 'transition period' to complete their work (*Chou,Y.Y.,1995; GIO,1996ab*) and this administration delay is expected to be met with one of the most distinctive Chinese ethics -- patience (*GOH,1996a; Li,T.C.,1996a; Tsai,P.Y.,1996*). On the other hand, major NGOs in this field seem to be switching their attention from child prostitution alone to child sexual abuse or forced prostitution as a whole.[4] This reorientation of NGO work seems to contradict with the legislative rationale of the Law, namely, child prostitution is a distinctive and unique social problem demanding sepcialised and exclusive socio-legal attention.

Conflicting Application of the General Law and the Specific Law

The Law to Suppress Sexual Transactions Involving Children and Juveniles is a specific law as far as the matter of child prostitution is concerned. Therefore, in a child prostitution case, all enforcers should apply applicable provisions of the Law. It is only when a certain matter is not governed in the Law that relevant provisions of general laws will be considered applicable. However, problems arise in practice as to whether 'sexual transactions involving children and juveniles' will cover all sorts of child prostitution cases. In those cases in which the enforcers disagree as to whether a 'sexual transaction' is present, the applicability of the Law will also be doubted.

The Legislative Purposes of a Specific Law

If we look into the legislative purposes of the Law, we may presume that the Legislature wanted to make a specific law to govern the child prostitution problem as an entity. The draft bill proposed by NGOs was entitled 'The Law to Treat and Prevent Girl Prostitution (*chu chi fang chi fa 雛妓防治法*)', though the word 'prostitution' could have various definitions:

it could be confined to 'sexual deals in brothels', while it could also be broadened to mean 'all sorts of sex-related services provided in exchange for money or the kind'. Thus it was agreed among NGOs that a better title should be in place, though they never insisted on a certain title as far as the Law could be passed in due course. Disregarding the fact that the nature of the child prostitution problem is shifting, the Legislature had their own definition for it -- sexual transactions involving children and juveniles (*erh tung chi shau nien hsing chiao yi* 兒童及少年性交易). It was once raised that 'sexual exploitation' would be a more appropriate definition, because the term 'sexual transactions' implied that the nature of child prostitution was identical with adult prostitution and would undermine thc law's purpose for child protection. However, the Legislature considered the term 'exploitation' excessive and also it was not a legal term. So finally 'sexual transactions' were used to give the problem its legal definition instead of 'sexual exploitation' without much resistance.

The Law Enforcers

One of the main arguments for the making of the specific was that no child prostitution customers were punished for statutory rape or indecency committed against children under 16 under the Criminal Code. Now by Article 22 of the Law, those who conduct sexual transactions with a person under the age of 16 can be punished with imprisonment for not more than three years. One important impact of the new Law in practice is that at least one assigned procurator in each District and High Court is trained to apply the Law to child prostitution cases. When they prosecute the customers applying Article 22 of the Law, many started to realise that Articles 221, 224 and 227 of the Criminal Code could have been applied to punish the customers. However, the Law is a specific law to deal with child prostitution cases and shall supersede the application of the Criminal Code. So those who prefer to apply the Criminal Code will have to evade the Law by judicial interpretation. They find a way out by interpreting the term 'sexual transactions': there must be a child prostitution operator who negotiates the deal with the customer so that 'sexual transactions' can be conducted. In other words, if a customer offers money or the like directly to a child under 16 in exchange of sexual intercourse or indecent acts as defined in Article 221, 224 or 227 of the Criminal Code, it is argued that, a child under 16 cannot consent to sexual intercourse or indecent acts, so there cannot be 'sexual transactions' constituted in such cases. In short, the Law will not apply in such cases, so the customers shall be prosecuted under the Criminal Code.

The application of the Criminal Code on customers by procurators is generally welcomed by concerned professionals and NGOs, because it involved much harsher penalties. However, its possible backfires have to be attended, too. Despite this *de facto* selective application of law under the disguise of the *de jure* judicial interpretation, the principle of equity in imposing punishment will also be sacrifised: if a man pays a 13-year-old child and has sexual intercourse with her, his penalty under Article 221-II of the Criminal Code is imprisonment for not less than five years; while if the money is paid to the brothel-keeper instead, then his penalty under Article 22 of the Law is reduced to imprisonment for not more than three years. On the other hand, if children under 16 are not eligible to conduct the 'sexual transactions' under the Law, can provisions concerning protection and treatment be applied for the benefit of the involved children or juveniles? Apparently if the judicial rationale is employed to answer this question, general laws will have to be applied instead, which means that these involved children and juveniles will have to be referred to the Juvenile Court to deal with their delinquency.

Concluding Remarks

Twenty-two months of enforcement is not long enough to judge the credit of a newly enacted law. However, if a premature evaluation has to be made by observing what have been done so far to implement the Law to Suppress Sexual Transactions Involving Children and Juveniles, one shall not be too optimistic. If the authorities keep finding ways out of their legal duties, and if concerned NGOs continue to divert their attention to other social problems, the Law will be at most a new bottle filled with old wine. The structural problems are left unattended. The need for prevention work is ignored. The victim status of the involved children is not secured. The power of the exploitative chain is not curtailed. And the vulnerabilities of children and their families in consumerism are left unattended. The specific law has been made, but we need more socio-institutional changes.

NOTES

[1] See chapter six for details.

[2] For detailed introduction to the draft Bill, see *Lin, Y.S., 1995*.

[3] Article 4 provides that the contents of the courses and social educational programmes concerning sexual transactions involving children and juveniles include: (1) to cultivate appropriate sexual psychology, (2) to cultivate respect for the sexual liberty of others, (3) to correct improper sexual conception, (4) to make believe that sex must not become an object for commercial transactions, (5) to make known the miserable lives of those children and juveniles who are involved in sexual transactions, and (6) other matters concerning the prevention of sexual transactions involving children and juveniles.

[4] See chapter four for details.

9 CONCLUSION

This book has been criticising the existence, recognition, and reactions to the problem of child prostitution in *Taiwan*, but it does not intend to end with negative statements. Some suggestions will thus be presented as a contribution to the efforts of those who have endeavoured to eradicate the social epidemic by employing legal measures.

The child prostitution problem has become a central concern in Taiwanese society in the 1990s. It has attracted substantial public and government attention, which, helped by a recent pro-child protection socio-legal climate, has prompted considerable changes to legislation, policing matters and welfare intervention. Government administration has recognised the social problems caused by illegal prostitution and police corruption, so certain reform programmes, though passive in manner and limited in scale, are initiated to offset them. The welfare authorities are willing to support, with their restricted budget and personnel, the implementation of NGO treatment and prevention projects both in finance and in publicity. Legislative changes are made towards imposing specific and heavier punishments on all perpetrators including the customers on the one hand, and towards rendering more supportive and welfare services to the children and their families on the other. Through the years of concerted efforts of people with various responsibilities, we have witnessed some socio-ideological changes, too. There is a social consensus that child prostitution is wrong and an inclination to restrain the customary patriarchal 'entitlement' to all forms of prostitution.

Concerned NGOs have developed expertise and are becoming influential as organised pressure groups. The aboriginal groups protest against structural inequality suffered by the indigenous people, which make them vulnerable to all sorts of exploitation. These groups are working for the enlightenment of aboriginal people and protest against inappropriate governmental policies towards aboriginal development. Owing to their efforts, it is generally recognised that aboriginal people are particularly vulnerable to the exploitation of child prostitution and socio-educational programmes have been organised by concerned groups for better prevention.

The welfare professionals maintain that it is nearly impossible to achieve their goal of rehabilitation with the existing resources. Many further argue that it is extremely difficult to cure the trauma of prostitution experiences. So besides seeking for more available resources, they also redirect their attention to prevention. In their proposals for the making of welfare laws and the recent specific law, social workers have strongly articulated their practical needs for strengthening treatment programmes. They also emphasise the importance of social and legal preventive measures. Backed by their professional knowledge, the social workers are assuming more and more legal power under welfare laws.

Recently, feminists started to attack the patriarchal men and the sexually pervert men for creating huge demand for child prostitution. They urge that more social and legal restraints and punishments should be imposed on child prostitution customers. Compared to welfare professionals, the feminists encountered much more challenges, not only from the legislators but also from society. However, owing to their persistent efforts, slow progress has been made towards the criminalisation of child prostitution customers.

The 'law and order' advocates attribute the deterioration of the problem to the lack of appropriate law and the corruption and incapability of law enforcers. They have concentrated their efforts on lobbying for legislation and calling for a thorough moral reform of law enforcement agencies. This group is organised by philanthropic female lawyers, who believe that law has the power to right wrongs. They appeal with their legal knowledge to the government authorities, the legislators, and the public. They involve themselves enthusiastically in the rescue, protection and treatment of prostitution-involved children as well as the prosecution of perpetrators. Their altruism, humanitarianism and legal discipline not only win social respect but also obtain for them a dominant role in the socio-legal construction of child prostitution.

The constructive socio-legal climate is, however, offset by some limitations. The alliance between law enforcers and law breakers in the lucrative flesh market is not easy to break up by means of short-term and punitive reform programmes. The implementation of treatment and prevention projects are often hindered by insufficient budget and resources. The children who have been deprived of their childhood innocence are suffering from double-victimisation caused by the societal value complex of humanitarian and antagonism towards prostitution-involved children. NGO efforts have resulted in certain administrative and legal reforms, but no policy changes have been made to prostitution control or aboriginal development. In view of the resources and limitations, suggestions may be made as to how child prostitution should be tackled.

Approach

Stereotypes and misinformation about child prostitution in *Taiwan* have significantly hampered our overall approach. In the past under the practice of the general laws, we tended to approach the problem as if it always involved a forcible sale of the children by exploitative parents. So we expected child victims to 'act traumatized' and discounted the possibility of their victimisation if they acted otherwise. Moreover, our legal system required the child to prove her innocence by giving evidence against her own parents. As a result, although a legal process was well-established to divert the treatment of sold children to the welfare system, many victims were still referred to the Juvenile Court as delinquents. The new specific law regards all involved children and juveniles under 18 as victims to be protected, but whether or not it can change the old practice just as it is written remains questionable. In addition, we still approach most cases of child prostitution as if they were capricious and catastrophic one-time-only events, yet many of these cases actually reflect a continuum of family dysfunction over time. The traditional approach to a social problem at the individual level ignores the structural situations which induce individual misbehaviour and deviance.

We continue to concentrate our efforts on intensifying control over the supply and the operation of child prostitution, but neglect the fact that the lucrative business cannot prosper without inputs from the demand side. The over-reliance on new laws to redress the loopholes of old laws not only reduces the attentions on proper law enforcement but also overlooks the importance of corresponding social measures. On the other hand, socio-legal measures are mainly created for treatment and punishment for everyday cases. However, more child victims continue to pay the penalty for the lack of effective prevention.

The understanding of child prostitution based on individual misbehaviour and deviance also hinders the development of appropriate reform projects. One of the lingering issues is how to define and explain child prostitution as a social problem. This book proposes that it should be defined as a problem of child maltreatment caused by the structural inequality generated in the Taiwanese capitalist-patriarchy. So individual cases have to be dealt with in their structural situation, and longer term strategies are needed to tackle the whole problem at not only the individual but also the institutional and societal level.

Redefine the Problem and Refocus the Attention in Policy and Practice

Child prostitution is defined as a problem of family dysfunction, of illegal prostitution and of juvenile delinquency under the general laws on the one hand, and referred to as 'sexual transactions involving child and juveniles' under the specific law on the other. Due to the fragmentary and misfocused definition of the problem, there has been a lack of a comprehensive measure to respond to it. This book suggests that child prostitution is actually a problem of child maltreatment happening in an overall exploitative social framework. Therefore, when measures are designed to prevent or manage the involved problem, attention should be focused on reducing the possibility and redressing the results of child maltreatment.

Moreover, it is very important to reconstruct the problem so that the focus on the 'victim' is balanced by a focus on the 'consumer'. It may be urged that in a civil society, every individual has the liberty to purchase sexual services. However, such a liberty should not impede the legal right of children to be protected against sexual exploitation. Therefore, the customers of child prostitution should be punished because they have infringed a child's legal right. The illegality of frequenting child prostitution has become an important legislative issue in *Taiwan*. But the issue is often confused with debates over the legality of prostitution. Society as a whole still tolerate more than condemn the consumers. It is recommended that activities of legislators, media and pressure groups should be effectively directed to control the *demand*. Coupled with appropriate social educational programmes and lobbying for laws against customers and effective enforcement, the problem caused by the 'demand' side will be mitigated.

Some development issues also deserve serious attention. The growing economic maturity of *Taiwan* is generating a climate in which social change is possible if tackled properly. However, it needs realisation that significant pockets of underdevelopment within a context of overdevelopment of society as a whole can produce social costs for the whole society. The economic prosperity has generally improved the lives of children with more legal protection and welfare services made available to them. However, the resulting consumerism also subjects children of disadvantaged families to exploitation. Therefore, in reforming policy and practice, the uneven development between disadvantaged socio-economic groups and other parts of society should be given proper consideration.

Ensure Effective Enforcement of Current Laws and Avoid Over-Reliance on Law

In dealing with child prostitution in *Taiwan*, a regime of positive laws is in place but it is not enforced satisfactorily. Under the current general and specific laws, the whole process of rescue and protection may be impeded because of distorted and selective application of laws which may also results in the contempt of the perpetrators towards law and the resistance of the child victims against legal protection. One crucial task is thus to improve the accountability of law in society by vigorous and proper enforcement. On the other hand, the limits of law have to be recognised to avoid over-reliance on law.

In fact, one of the biggest problem in the contemporary law of *Taiwan* is the over-emphasis on the instrumentality of law. Past failures in practice were primarily caused by three myths attached to the law. One, *Taiwan* is a modern, Westernised, capitalist society, so whenever a social problem is identified, solutions can be found in related positive laws of more advanced countries without referring to the socio-cultural roots of the problem. Two, when old laws have failed their tasks, new laws must be made to redress the failures. And three, laws can be made to deal with a problem without reviewing relative socio-legal policies (prostitution, family and welfare policies, for example). However, this study of child prostitution in *Taiwan* has shown that law alone is incapable of mitigating a problem with cultural, social and economic roots. So we must review our over-dependence on law as the sole instrument of solving this social problem. In order to achieve the goal of law making and enforcement, the support and coordination of other institutions are essential and available resources should be reshuffled to make a proper mix of law and non-law measures.

This does not mean that law is less important than it is expected to be. To make relevant laws and to ensure their efficient enforcement are both crucial in the management of the problem. However, it is also important to ensure that law making is not seen as the beginning and end of the issue. For achieving this, efforts should be devoted in two directions. On the one hand, law enforcers should be given appropriate professional training in order to acquire up-to-date legal knowledge and specific techniques for dealing with all kinds of child prostitution cases. Administrative projects should be initiated to reduce police discretion and corruption. Specialised child protection units should be established in the police which will adopt a broad sympathetic approach to the problem and work on effective coordination with other governmental agencies and concerned NGOs. Welfare personnel should be given more resources and abilities to provide follow-up services for the children and their families. Legal education and training for future judges, procurators, and lawyers should be broadened to view the law in a pluralist society. On the other hand, social policies have to be strengthened to work against the vulnerabilities of disadvantaged families and help children of troubled families acquire a healthy childhood. In doing these, current socio-legal measures have to be reviewed and coordinated. Government agencies should be encouraged to take an active role in all treatment and prevention programmes. Concerned NGOs should share their experiences, expertise and resources. The existing rescue, protection and treatment networks must be widened and reinforced.

Strengthen Treatment Programmes and Emphasise Prevention Measures

To seriously face the problem of child prostitution in *Taiwan*, the point to re-start is to treat child victims as respectable individuals, as ordinary people. Their needs should be met in terms of their backgrounds, but the backgrounds would not be used against them. In both the processes of punishment and treatment, the prostitution experiences should stop being a parameter for judging the children. And the sexually exploited child should enjoy the same right under the law as that shared by other abused children. Just as special needs of child victims of incest are recognised and dealt with under the child protection system, the treatment of all prostitution-involved children can also be incorporated into the same system. In other words, the victims should be treated as maltreated children with specific resulting traumas and problems, and so specific programmes should be designed for their treatment. Once the problem of child prostitution is reconceptualised and reconstructed into law and legal measures, the perpetrators will be punished because they have impeded the healthy development of children, and the children can be treated as victims of abuse and exploitation.

In view of the present legal policy that the involvement of prostitution before adulthood is prohibited as well as the fact that once involved in prostitution, successful rehabilitation of the children is highly impossible, efforts should be concentrated more on prevention than on punishment and treatment. Under the ROC welfare system, the family is still vested with the primary responsibility of child upbringing and discipline. In order to prevent the dysfunction of the family, general social services in the form of financial and educational supports provided for disadvantaged families will be more appropriate than the present coercive intervention in the form of legal severance of the maltreated child from her\his family. In doing so, the criticism against the 'tutelage state' as addressed in chapter two may become unavoidable. The civil rights of certain parents may have to be subjected to constant restraints. Therefore, a cautious balance should be found between these restraints and the risks of abandoning young children and their families to structural exploitation.

The construction of modern childhood has been through schooling and the ROC law mandates a Nine-Year compulsory school education for all children aged between 6 and 15. Case studies have shown that a majority of children were recruited into prostitution after graduating from primary school (aged 12). However, those children should have stayed in high school for three more years had the law of national compulsory education been truly enforced. In fact, school curriculums also include constant family visits paid by school teachers and counsellors to the parents, especially for a student who is absent from the school or who has not performed well in school works. If the present education system as provided by the law can be strengthened in its enforcement with proper surveillance from the authorities, the children at risk may be identified earlier before the flesh contract actually takes place.

Apart from strengthening the education system, welfare services should also be made more available to children in poor or troubled families to help eradicate the practical difficulties impeding schooling. There is now a mandatory reporting system provided by the 1989 Juvenile Welfare Law, the 1993 Child Welfare Law, and the 1995 Law to Suppress Sexual

Transactions Involving Children and Juveniles. Under the system, school teachers as well as welfare officers have a legal duty to report possible cases of child abuse, neglect, and exploitation. Coupled by the sensitive police response required by the same Laws, and more professional assistance in the coordination of police actions, a prevention network can be set up. Within this network, all efforts should be given to supporting the family and encouraging caring parent-child relationship.

In implementing prevention programmes, special attention has to be paid to socially and economically disadvantaged groups -- the poor and the aboriginal. Careful studies must be made in order to develop specific and client-amicable programmes in order to meet their needs and to cure their vulnerabilities. Generally speaking, school education has to accommodate social reality. Children have to be taught good Chinese ethics and traditional morals, but they also have to be warned of the possibilities of their abuse and be taught the ways to protect themselves from maltreatment and exploitation.

Work on Long-Term Moral Transformation

In order to achieve the final goals of treatment and prevention, a reform of the moral and value systems of the law enforcers and of society as a whole is essential. With the present involvement and patronage of police officers and local politicians in the operation of child prostitution, the power of law will never defeat the power of exploitation. On the other hand, if the professionals hold their hatred towards prostitutes and try to save all prostitution-involved children from their 'heinous' parents and from the 'immoral' profession, they will keep encountering children who resent the legal intervention.

The problems of child prostitution in *Taiwan* are perpetuated as a result of social conspiracy in the practice of prostitution involving children. But humiliation is imposed on the child. In order to achieve the final goal of a structural reform, a long-term rebuilding of social values is crucial. The exploitation of the powerless by the powerful may have been manifested in the operation of the patriarchal family system and the capitalist economic system, but the real cause of the exploitation relationship lies in the corruptive use of power over others. It is only when human beings learn to respect the existence of one another will the ownership of power not result in exploitation.

Final Words

Looking back to those years when I was fully involved in anti-child-prostitution activities, there are things I wish I had done and things I wish I had avoided. The final words of this book are thus a reminder to myself as well as my expert friends in the field to make up our mistakes in the past. As a group, we must realise our power as well as our limits. Within the group, we must coordinate available resources, cultivate mutual respect and work out differences among responsible experts, especially between the legal and the social professionals, between the law makers and the law enforcers, between government officials and the idealist do-gooders. For the children, we must create a client-amicable treatment system. To the parents, we must withhold our condemnations and approach them with understanding and constructive assistance. Holding the power as professional experts, we have the responsibilities to appeal forcefully to the government and the Legislature to render more budget and resources for disadvantaged socio-economic groups and to reinforce the training and discipline of law enforcers. We should also incorporate and make use of available social resources to redress our limits in improving law making and enforcement. We must be realistic in tackling the social problem, while conveying our ideal to society that there is no excuse for the existence of child prostitution in a civilised and modernised country like *Taiwan*.

BIBLIOGRAPHY I : General English References

I. BOOKS, ARTICLES, DISSERTATIONS, REPORTS

Adams, N. (1993) 'Prostitution Women, Justice and the Law', Women: A Cultural Review, 4(3): Gender, Law and Justice -- Writing Legal Difference

Adelman, S. & Paliwala, A. (1993) Law and Crisis in the Third World (eds.) (Hans Zell, London)

Adler, R.M. (1985) Taking Juvenile Justice Seriously (Scottish Academic Press, Edinburgh)

Alcock, P. & Horris, P. (1982) Welfare Law and Order: A Critical Introduction to Law for Social Workers (Macmillan, London)

Alder, C. (1993) 'Police, Youth and Violence', Gale, F.; Naffine, N. & Wundersitz, J. (eds.) -- Juvenile Justice: Debating the Issues:78-87

Allen, N. (1990) Making Sense of the Children Act 1989 (Longman, London)

Allott, A.N. (1980) The Limits of Law (Butterworth, London)

Alston, P.; Parker, S.; & Seymour, J. (1992) Children, Rights and the Law (eds.) (Clarendon Press, Oxford)

Anderson, M. (1979) 'The Relevance of Family History', Harris, C. (ed.) -- The Sociology of the Family: New Directions for Britain (Sociological Review Monograph, No.28.)

Ansell, J. (1984) 'Problems of Prostitution', a paper presented to the 28th Congress of the International Abolitionist Federation, Vienna.

Anti-Slavery International(1997) Enslaved Peoples in the 1990s (Anti-Slavery & IWGIA, U.K. & Denmark)

Aries, P. (1962) Centuries of Childhood (Jonathan Cape, London; Alfred Knopf, New York 1973; Penguin, Harmondsworth, 1986)

Asian Church Women's Conference [ACAC] (1986) Report of the Consultation on Tourism and Prostitution (Catholic Publishing House)

Asian Women's Liberation [AWL] (1980) Prostitution Tourism (Asian Women's Liberation, No.3, Japan)

Asian Women's Liberation [AWL](1984) Sex Tourism and Military Occupation (Asian Women's Liberation, No.6, Japan)

Asquith, S. (1983) 'Justice, Retribution and Children', Morris, A. & Giller, H. (eds.) -- Providing Criminal Justice for Children:7-18

Athamesara, A.R. (1991) 'Tourism and Child Prostitution: A Buddhist Perspective', Srisang,K. (ed.) -- Caught in Modern Slavery:91-93

Atkins, S. & Hoggett, B. (1984) Women and the Law (Basil Blackwell, Oxford)

Atkinson, L. (1993a) 'Welfare and Justice', Gale, F., Naffine, N. & Wundersitz, J. (eds.) -- Juvenile Justice: Debating the Issues:70-77

Atkinson, L. (1993b) 'Police Action', Gale, F., Naffine, N. & Wundersitz, J. (eds.) -- Juvenile Justice: Debating the Issues:96-105

Atkinson, L. (1993c) 'Alternatives to Court', Gale, F., Naffine, N. & Wundersitz, J. (eds.) -- Juvenile Justice: Debating the Issues:122-129

Atkinson, L. (1993d) 'Court Outcomes and Processes', Gale, F., Naffine, N. & Wundersitz, J. (eds.) -- Juvenile Justice: Debating the Issues:154-160

Bagley, C. (1983) 'Childhood Sexuality and the Sexual Abuse of Children', Journal of Child Care, 1(3):105-27

Bainham, A. (1988) Children, Parents and the State (Sweet & Maxwell, London)

Baker, C.D. (1980) 'Preying on Playgrounds: The Sexploitation of Children in Pornography and Prostitution', in Schultz, L.D. (ed.) -- The Sexual Victimology of Youth: 292-334

Bane, M.J. (1983) 'Is the Welfare State Replacing the Family?', The Public Interest, 70:91-101

Bangkok Post (1992) 'The Number of Prostitutes in Thailand. The Debate', Bangkok Post: 29th, August, 1992; quoted at ECPAT, Newsletter,6:7-8

Barber, R. (1977) 'The Criminal Law Amendment Act of 1891 and the Age of Consent', Australian and New Zealand Journal of Criminology, 10:95-113

Barret, M. & McIntosh, M. (1987) The Anti-Social Family (NLB, London)

Barry, K. (1979) Female Sexual Slavery (Prentice-Hall, New York)

Barry, M. (1993) 'Informal Processing: the South Australian Experience', Gale, F.; Naffine, N. & Wundersitz, J. (eds.) -- Juvenile Justice: Debating the Issues:116-121

Baxter, I.F.G. & Eberts, M.A. (1978) The Child and the Courts (Sweet & Maxwell, London)

Bazell, C (1980) 'Evidential and Procedural Problems in Child Abuse Cases', Family Law, 19:35-38

Benjamin, H. & Masters, R.E.L. (1965) Prostitution and Morality: A Report on the Prostitute in Contemporary Society and An Analysis of the Causes and Effects of the Suppression of Prostitution (Souvenir, New York)

Bevan, H.K. (1989) Child Law (Butterworths, London)

Blackmore, R. (1993) 'Influences in Reform of Juvenile Courts', Gale, F., Naffine, N. & Wundersitz, J. (eds.) -- Juvenile Justice: Debating the Issues:103-138

Blagg, H. & Stubbs, P. (1987) A Child Centered Practice? Multi-agency Approaches to Child Sexual Abuse', Practice, 2(1):12-19

Bottomley, A. (1987) 'Feminism in Law Schools', Mclaughlin, S. (ed.) -- Women and the Law (University College London, Faculty of Law, Working Paper No.5.)

Boyd, N. (1986) The Social Dimensions of Law (Parentice-Hall Canada, Ontario)

Bradley, D. (1990) 'Children, Family and the State in Sweden', Journal of Law and Society, 17(4):427-444

Bridel, R. (1982) 'Traffic of Children', MSS in files of Defense for Children International, Switzerland

Bridge, J., Bridge,S., & Luke,S. (1990) Blackstone's Guide to the Children Act 1989 (Blackstone)

Bristow, E.J. (1977) Vice and Vigilance: Purity Movements in Britain since 1700 (Gill & Macmillan, Dublin)

Brown, B. (1992) 'Reassessing the Critique of Biologism', Gelsthorpe,L. & Morris, A. (eds.) -- Feminist Perspectives in Criminology: 41-56

Brown, P. (1981a) 'A Daughter: A Thing to Be Given Away', The Cambridge Women's Studies Group (eds.) -- Women in Society: Interdisciplinary Essays:126-145 (Virago, London)

Brown, P. (1981b) 'Universals and Particulars in the Position of Women', The Cambridge Women's Studies Group (eds.) -- Women in Society: Interdisciplinary Essays:242-256 (Virago, London)

Bruce, F. (1991) 'The International Catholic Child Bureau (ICCB)', Srisang,K. (ed.) -- Caught in Modern Slavery:29-36

Bryan, J.H. (1967) 'Apprenticeships in Prostitution', Gagnon, J.H. & Simon, W. (eds.) -- Sexual Deviance:146-164

Bullough, V. & Bullough, B. (1987) Women and Prostitution: A Social History (Prometheus Books, New York)

Bulmberg, G.G. (1993) 'Who Should Do the Work of Family Law?' Family Law Quarterly, 27(2):213-227

Burgess, A.W., Groth, A.N., Holstrom, L.L., & Sgrol, S.M. (1978) Sexual Assault on Children and Adolescent (Lexington, Toronto)

Butler-Sloss, Lord Justice [England] (1988) Report of the Inquiry into Child Abuse in Cleveland 1987 (HMSO:Cm 412, London)

Cabinet Office and Ministries (1996) Seminar on Sexual Exploitation of Children and Adolescents in the Americas (Printing Works of The Cabinet Office and Ministries ,Stockholm)

Cain, M. (1992) 'Realist Philosophy and Standpoint Epistemologies or Feminist Criminology As A Successor Science', Gelsthorpe,L. & Morris, A. (eds.) -- Feminist Perspectives in Criminology: 124-140

Campagna, D. (1985) 'The Economic of Juvenile Prostitution in the USA', International Children's Rights Monitor,2(1)

Campbell, T.D. (1985) 'Philosophy, Ideology and Rights', Legal Studies, 5:10-20

Campbell, T.D. (1992) 'The Rights of the Minor: As Person, As Child, As Juvenile, As Future Adult', Alston, P. et al. (eds.) -- Children, Rights and the Law:1-23

Caplan, G.M. (1984) 'The Facts of Life about Teenage Prostitution', Crime and Delinquency, 30(1):69-74

Carlsson, B. (1984) 'The Sexual Exploitation of Children', unpublished draft manuscript for the Anti-Slavery Society, London.

Carney, T. (1992) 'Reconciling the 'Irreconcilable'?: A Rights or Interests Based Approach to Controllability? A Comment on Seymour', Alston, P. et al (eds.) -- Children, Rights and the Law:119-125

Chambliss, W.J. & Seidman, R.B. (1971) Law, Order and Power (Addison-Wesley, Reading/Massachusetts)

Chisholm, L. et al. (1990) Childhood, Youth and Social Change: A Comparative Perspective (eds.) (Falmer, London)

Christiane, F. (1980) Autobiography of a Child Prostitute and Heroin Addict (Corgi Books, UK)

Chutikul, S. (1991) 'Psychological Perspectives on Child Prostitution', Srisang,K. (ed.) -- Caught in Modern Slavery:83-86

Chutikul, S. (1992) 'The Sex Industry Must Be Ended', O'Grady,R. (ed.) -- Children in Prostitution :1-3

Clair, R. & Cottingham, J. (1984) 'Migration and Tourism: An Overview', Women and Development, ISIS, Switzerland

Clarke, M. (1975) 'Social Problem Ideologies', British Journal of Sociology, 26:406-416

Coady, C.A.J. (1992) 'Theory, Rights and Children: A Comment on O'Neill and Campbell', Alston, P. et al. (eds.) -- Children, Rights and the Law:43-51

Cohen, S. (1972) Folk Devils and Moral Panics (MacGibbon & Kee, London; 1973, Paladin)

Comment (1976) 'Do Children Have the Legal Right to Be Incorrigible?', Brigham Young University Law Review, 1976:659-691

Committee on Sexual Offences against Children and Youth [appointed by the Minister of Justice and Attorney General of Canada, the Minister of National Health and Welfare] (1984) Summary of Sexual Offences against Children in Canada (Government of Canada)

Constantine, L.L. (1979) 'The Sexual Rights of Children: Implications of a Radical Perspective', Cook, M. & Wilson, G. (eds.) -- Love and Attraction: An International Conference (Pergamon Press, Oxford)

Constantine, L.L. & Martinson, F.M. (1981) Children and Sex: New Findings, New Perspectives (eds.) (Little, Brown, Boston)

Conway, A. (1977) 'Sexual Delinquency', Crime and Delinquency, 1977(April):39-40

Coombs, N.R. (1974) 'Male Prostitution: A Psychological View of Behaviour', American Journal of Orthopsychiatry, 44,5(October):782-789

Cotterell, R. (1984) The Sociology of Law: An Introduction (Butterworths, London)

Council of Europe (1988) 'Sexual Exploitation, Pornography and Prostitution of, and Trafficking in, Children and Young Women', report submitted by the Norwegian delegation to the 16th Conference of European Ministers of Justice, Lisbon, 21-22 June, 1988

Cretney, S.M. (1990) 'Defining the Limits of State Intervention: the Child and the Courts', Freeston, D. (ed.) -- Children and the Law:58-74

Criminal Law Revision Committee [England] (1980) Working Paper on Sexual Offenses (H.M.S.O., London)

Criminal Law Revision Committee [England] (1982) Working Paper on Offenses Relating to Prostitution (H.M.S.O., London)

Criminal Law Revision Committee [England] (1984) Fifteenth Report: Sexual Offenses Cmnd 9213 (H.M.S.O., London)

Cullen, S. (1992) 'Persistence Will Win', O'Grady, R. (ed.) -- Children in Prostitution: 22-26

Cullen, S., Smith, D., & Parry, N. (1992) Street Children in the Philippines (eds.) (Jubilee Campaign, Surrey)

Cutright, P. (1972) 'Teenage Sexual Revolution and the Myth of an Abstinent Past', Family Planning Perspectives, 4:24-31

Dahl, R.A. (1968) 'Power', Sills, D.L. (ed.) -- International Encyclopedia of the Social Sciences, Vol.12:405-415 (Macmillan & Free Press)

Das, M.S. & Bardis, P.D. (1979) The Family in Asia (George Allen & Unwin, London)

Davidson, H.A. (1982) 'Sexual Exploitation of Children in the United States' paper presented to the 4th International Congress on Child Abuse and Neglect, Paris, 1982

Davidson, S. (1982) 'Lust City in the Far East', Time, May 10

Davis, K. (1971) 'Sexual Behaviour', Merton, R.K. & Nisbert, R. (eds.) -- Contemporary Social Problems (Harcourt Brace Jovanovich, New York)

Davis, N.J. (1971) 'The Prostitute: Developing a Deviant Identity', in Henslin,J.M. (ed.) -- Studies in the Sociology of Sex:297-324 (Appleton-Century-Crofts, New York)

Deisher, R.W., Eisner, V., & Sulzbacher, S. (1969) 'The Young Male Prostitute', Paediatrics, 43,6(Junc):936-941

De Leon, A. (1991) 'Economic, Political, Legal, Cultural and Psychological Aspects: A Philippine Perspective', Srisang, K. (ed.) -- Caught in Modern Slavery:87-88

De Leon, A., Contor, E., & Abueva, A. (1991) 'Tourism and Child Prostitution in the Philippines', Srisang, K. (ed.) -- Caught in Modern Slavery:53-59

De Mause, L. (1992) 'The Evolution of Childhood', Jenks, C. (ed.) -- The Sociology of Childhood:48-59

De Sousa, D. (1991) 'Images of Tourism and Child Prostitution', Srisang, K. (ed.) -- Caught in Modern Slavery: 94-95

Dense-Gerber, J. & Hutchinson, S.F. (1978) 'Medical-legal and Societal Problems involving Children -- Child Prostitution, Child Pornography and Drug-related Abuse; Recommended Legislation', Smith, S.M. (ed.) -- The Maltreatment of Children: 317-49 (M.T.P. Press, Lancaster)

Derrett, J.D.M. (1968) An Introduction to Legal Systems (ed.) (Sweet & Maxwell, London)

Detrick, S. (1992) The United Nations Convention on the Rights of the Child: A Guide to the "Travaux Preparatoires" (ed.) (Martinus Nijhoff, Dordrecht / Boston / London)

Dewar, J. (1989) Law and the Family (Butterworth, London)

Dickens, B.M. (1981) 'The Modern Function and Limits of Parental Rights', Law Quarterly Review, 97:462-485

Dickson, D.T. (1968) 'Bureaucracy and Morality', Social Problems, 16(2):143-156

Dingwall, R. & Eekelaar, J. (1984) 'Rethinking Child Protection', Freeman, M.D.A.(ed.) -- State, Law and the Family: 93-114

Dingwall, R., Eekelaar, J., & Murray, T. (1983) The Protection of Children: State Intervention and Family Life (eds.) (Blackwell, Oxford)

Dingwall, R., Eekelaar, J., & Murray, T. (1984) 'Childhood as a Social Problem: A Survey of the History of Legal Regulation', Journal of Law and Society, 1984: 207-32

Donzelot, J. (1980) The Policing of Families: Welfare versus the State (Hutchinson, London)

Douglas, G. (1988) 'The Family and the State under the European Convention on Human Rights', International Journal of Law and the Family, 2:76-105

Douglas, G. (1990) 'Family Law under the Thatcher Government', Journal of Law and Society, 17(4):411-426

Doyle, C. (1987) Sexual Abuse: Giving Help to Children (National Children's Bureau, Whiting and Birch, London)

Durkheim, E. (1992) 'Childhood', Jenks, C. (ed.) -- The Sociology of Childhood:146-150

Dworkin, R. (1977) Taking Rights Seriously (Duckworth, London)

ECOSOC (1984) 'Review of Developments in the Field of Slavery and the Slave Trade in all their Practices and Manifestations', Reports by States concerning the Convention for the Suppression of the Traffic in Persons and the Exploitation of the Prostitution of Others. Note by the Secretary General E/CN.4/Sub.2/AC.2/1984/5, May 17, Geneva

ECPAT [The International Campaign to End Child Prostitution in Asian Tourism] (1991a) 'An International Campaign Aimed at the Asian Tourist Industry: To End Child Prostitution', Srisang, K. (ed.) -- Caught in Modern Slavery:13-16

ECPAT (1991b) 'Children Caught in Modern Slavery: Conclusions of the Chiang Mai Consultation on Tourism and Child Prostitution', Srisang, K. (ed.) -- Caught in Modern Slavery:19-23

ECPAT (1992a) 'Good News from the Philippines: New Law Protects Children', ECPAT Newsletter, 6(October):2

ECPAT (1992b) 'Reports of ECPAT National Campaigns', ECPAT Newsletter, 6(October):4-10

ECPAT (1992c) 'Reports from National Groups', O'Grady, R. (ed.) -- Children in Prostitution:56-63

ECPAT (1996) Enforcing The Law: Against the Commercial Sexual Exploitation of Children (ECPAT, Thailand)

Edwards, S. (1981) Female Sexuality and the Law: A Study of Constructs of Female Sexuality as They Inform Statute and Legal Procedure (Robertson, Oxford)

Edwards, S. (1985) Gender, Sex and Law (ed.) (Croom Helm, London)

Edwards, S. (1987) 'Prostitutes: Victims of Law, Social Policy and Organised Crime', Carler, P. & Warrall, A. (eds.) -- Gender, Crime and Justice:43-56 (Open University Press, Milton Keynes/Philadelphia)

Edwards, S. (1992) 'Violence Against Women: Feminism and the Law', Gelsthorpe, L. & Morris, A. (eds.) -- Feminist Perspectives in Criminology: 145-159

Eekelaar, J.M. (1973) 'What Are Parental Rights?', Law Quarterly Review, 89:210

Eekelaar, J.M. (1984) Family Law and Social Policy (Weildenfeld & Nicolson, London)

Eekelaar, J.M. (1986a) 'The Emergence of Children's Rights', Oxford Journal of Legal Studies, 6:161-182

Eekelaar, J.M. (1986b) 'The Eclipse of Parental Rights', Law Quarterly Review, 102:4ff

Eekelaar, J.M. (1989) 'What is 'Critical' Family Law?', Law Quarterly Review, 105:244-261

Eekelaar, J.M. (1992) 'The Importance of Thinking that Children Have Rights', Alston, P. et al. (eds.) -- Children, Rights and the Law:221-235

Eekelaar, J.M. & Dingwall, R. (1990) The Reform of Child Care Law: A Practical Guide to the Children Act 1989 (Routledge, London)

Eiduson, B.T. & Alexander, J.W. (1978) 'The Role of Children in Alternative Family Styles', Journal of Social Issues, 34(2)

Elliot, F.R. (1989) 'The Family: Private Arena or Adjunct of the State', Journal of Law and Society, 16(4):443-463

Elliott, D. (1988) Gender, Delinquency and Society: A Comparative Study of Male and Female Offenders and Juvenile Justice in Britain (Avebury, Aldershot)

Ely, P. & Stanley, C. (1990) The French Alternative: Delinquency Prevention and Child Protection in France (NACRO)

ECPAT (1994) End Child Prostitution: Report of An International Consultation on Child Prostitution (ECPAT, Bangkok)

Ennew, J. (1986) The Sexual Exploitation of Children (Polity, Cambridge)

Evan, W.M. (1980) The Sociology of Law (ed.) (Free Press, New York)

Farson, R. (1978) Birthrights (Penguin, Harmondsworth)

Feinberg, J. (1984) The Moral Limits of the Criminal Law (Vol.I): Harm to Others (Oxford University Press, Oxford)

Feinberg, J. (1985) The Moral Limits of the Criminal Law (Vol.II): Offence to Others (Oxford University Press, Oxford)

Feinberg, J. (1986) The Moral Limits of the Criminal Law (Vol.III): Harm to Self (Oxford University Press, Oxford)

Feinberg, J. (1987) The Moral Limits of the Criminal Law (Vol.IV): Harmless Wrongdoing (Oxford University Press, Oxford)

Fernand-Laurent, J. (1983) 'Report of the Special Rapporteur on the Suppression of the Traffic in Persons and the Exploitation of the Prostitution of Others', ECOSOC, E/1983/7, March 13, United Nations, Geneva

Fernandez-Magno, S. (1987) 'Child Prostitution: Image of a Decadent Society', Essays on Women (St Scholastica, Manila)

Field Responses (1991) The Sexual Exploitation of Children (International Catholic Child Bureau,Geneva)

Finkelhor, D. (1979) Sexually Victimised Children (Free Press, New York)

Finkelhor, D. (1979) 'What's Wrong with Sex between Adults and Children? Ethics and the Problem of Sexual Abuse', American Journal of Orthopsychiatry, 29(4):692-697

Finkelhor, D., Gelles, R.J., Hotlaing, G.T., & Strauss, M.A. (1983) The Dark Side of the Family (Sage, Beverly Hills)

Flammang, C.J. (1980) 'Interviewing Child Victims of Sex Offenders', in Schultz, L.G. (ed.) -- The Sexual Victimology of Youth:175-186

Flandrin, J. (1977) 'Repression and Change in the Sexual Life of Young People', Journal of Family History, 2:196-210

Fletcher, R. (1966) Family and Marriage in Britain, An Analysis and Moral Assessment (Penguin, Harmonsworth)

Ford, D. (1978) 'The Emergence of the Child as a Legal Entity', in Smith, S.M. (ed.) -- The Maltreatment of Children: 393-413 (M.T.P. Press)

Foucault, M. (1973) The Order of Things (Vintage, New York)

Foucault, M. (1977) Discipline and Punish: the Birth of Prison (trans. A. Sheridan) (Penguin, Harmondsworth)

Foucault, M. (1979) The History of Sexuality (Vol.I): An Introduction (trans. R. Hurley) (Penguin, Harmondsworth; Vintage, New York, 1978)
Foucault, M. (1980) Power/Knowledge (Brighton)
Foucault, M. (1990) The History of Sexuality (Vol.III): The Care of the Self (translated by R. Hurley) (Penguin, Harmondsworth)
Foucault, M. (1992) The History of Sexuality (Vol.II): The Use of Pleasure (translated by R. Hurley) (Penguin, Harmondsworth; Pantheon, New York, 1985)
Fox, G. (1977) 'Nice Girl: Social Control of Women through a Value Construct', Signs: Journal of Women in Culture and Society, 2:805-817
Franklin, B. (1986) The Rights of Children (ed.) (Basil Blackwell, Oxford)
Freedman, E. (1987) 'Uncontrolled Desires: the Response to the Sexual Psychopath, 1920-1960', Journal of American History, 74(1):83-106
Freeman, M.D.A. (1980a) Violence in the Home: A Socio-Legal Study (Gower, Hampshire)
Freeman, M.D.A. (1980b) 'The Rights of Children in the International Year of the Child', Current Legal Problems, 1980:1-31
Freeman, M.D.A. (1983a) The Rights and Wrongs of Children (Frances Printer, London)
Freeman, M.D.A. (1983b) 'Freedom and the Welfare State: Child Rearing, Parental Autonomy and State Intervention', Journal of Social Welfare Law, 1983:70-91
Freeman, M.D.A. (1983c) 'The Concept of Children's Rights', Geach, H. & Szwed, E. (eds.) -- Providing Civil Justice for Children (Edward Arnold, London)
Freeman, M.D.A. (1984) The State, the Law and the Family (Tavistock, London)
Freeman, M.D.A. (1985) 'Towards A Critical Theory of Family Law', Current Legal Problems, 38:153-162
Freeman, M.D.A. (1992a) Children, Their Families and the Law: Working with the Children Act (Macmillan, Hampshire)
Freeman, M.D.A. (1992b) 'Taking Children's Rights More Seriously', Alston, P. et al. (eds.) -- Children, Rights and the Law:52-71
Freestone, D. (1990) Children and the Law (ed.) (Hull University Press, Hull)
Friedmann, W. (1964) Law in a Changing Society (Stevens & Sons, London)
Frug, M.J. (1992) Postmodern Legal Feminism (Poutledge, London)
Fuller, R.C. & Myers, R.D., (1941) 'The Natural History of A Social Problem', American Sociological Review,6:320
Gagnon, J.H. & Simon, W. (1967) Sexual Deviance (eds.) (Happer & Row, New York)
Gale, F.; Naffine, N. & Wundersitz, J. (1993) Juvenile Justice: Debating the Issues (Allen & Unwin, Australia)
Galiher, J.F. & Walker, A. (1977) 'The Puzzle of the Social Origins of the Marihuana Tax Act of 1937', Social Problems, 24(3):367-377
Garland, D. (1981) 'The Birth of the Welfare Sanction', British Journal of Law and Society, 9:29-45
Garland, D. (1985) Punishment and Welfare: A History of Penal Strategies (Milton Keynes)
Geach, H. & Szwed, E. (1983) Providing Civil Justice for Children (eds.) (Edward Arnold, London)

Gelles, R.J. (1978) 'Violence toward Children in the United States', American Orthopsychiat, 48(4):580-592

Gelsthorpe, L. (1992) 'Feminist Methodologies in Criminology: A New Approach or Old Wine in New Bottles?', Gelsthorpe,L. & Morris, A. (eds.) -- Feminist Perspectives in Criminology: 89-106

Gelsthorpe, L. & Morris, A. (1992a) Feminist Perspectives in Criminology (eds.) (Open University, Milton Keynes / Philadelphia)

Gelsthorpe, L. & Morris, A. (1992b) 'Introduction: Transforming and Transgressing Criminology', Feminist Perspectives in Criminology: 1-6

Gersen, R.L. (1979) The Hidden Victims: the Sexual Abuse of Children (Beacon, Boston)

Gil, D.G. (1975) 'Unraveling Child Abuse', American Journal of Orthopsychiatry, 45(3):346-356

Gil, D.G. (1978) 'Societal Violence and Violence in Families'. Eekelaar, M. & Katz, S.N. (eds.) -- Family Violence -- An International and Interdisciplinary Study (Butterworth, London)

Giller, H. (1986) 'Is There a Role for a Juvenile Court?', Howard Journal, 25:161-171

Giovannoni, J.M. & Becerra, R.M. (1979) Defining Child Abuse (Free Press, New York)

Glaster, D. & Spencer, J.R. (1990) 'Sentencing, Children's Evidence and Children's Trauma', Criminal Law Review:371-382

Goldstein, J., Freud, A., & Solnit, A.J. (1973) Beyond the Best Interest of the Child (Free Press, New York)

Goldstein, J., Freud, A., & Solnit, A.J. (1980) Before the Best Interest of the Child (Burnett Books, Andre Deutsch, London)

Goode, W.J. (1963) World Revolution and Family Patterns (Free Press, New York)

Goode, W.J. (1972) The Family (Prentice-Hall, Inc., New York)

Gordon, C. (1980) Michel Foucault Power/Knowledge (Harvester, Brighton)

Gordon, L. (1987) 'Feminism and Social Control: the Case of Child Abuse', Mitchell, J. & Oakley, A. (eds.) -- What is Feminism? (Blackwell, Oxford)

Gordon, L. (1988) 'The Politics and child Sexual Abuse: Notes from American History' Feminist Review, 28:56-64

Gorham, D. (1978) 'The 'Maiden Tribute of Modern Babylon' Re-examined', Victorian Studies, 21(3):353-379

Gough, K. (1975) 'The Origin of the Family', Rieter, R.R. -- Toward an Anthropology of Women (Monthly Review Press)

Goverment of the United Kingdom (1996) Action against the Commercial Sexual Exploitation of Children (Home Office,London)

Gray, D. (1973) 'Turning Out: Teenage Prostitution', Urban Life and Culture, 1:401-442

Greene, N. & Esselstyn, T. (1972) 'The Beyond Control Girl', Juvenile Justice, 23:13-19

Grey, A. (1975) 'Civilising Our Sex Laws', Journal of the Society of Teachers of Law, 13:106-112

Gusfield, J. (1975) 'Categories of Ownership and Responsibility in Social Issues: Alcohol Abuse and Automobile Use', Journal of Drug Issues, 5:290

Hafen, B. (1976) 'Children's Liberation and the New Egalitarianism: Reservations about Abandoning Youth to Their Rights', Brigham Young University Law Review, 1976:605-658

Hafen, B. (1977) 'Puberty, Privacy and Protection: the Risks of Children's Rights', American Bar Association Journal, 63:1383

Halberg, M. (1989) 'Feminist Epistemology: An Impossible Project?', Radical Philosophy, 53:3-7

Hall, J.C. (1972) 'The Waning of Parental Rights', Cambridge Law Journal, 31(1):248-265

Hall, J.G. & Martin, D. (1987) Child Abuse Procedure and Evidence in Juvenile Courts (2nd Barry Rose Books, London)

Hall, S. (1980) 'Reformism and the Legislation of Consent', National Deviancy Conference (eds.) -- Permissiveness and Control -- the Fate of the Sixties Legislation (Macmillan, London)

Halsey, A.H. (1993) 'Individualism and the Decline of the Family', Family Law, 23:152-153

Hammel, E.A. & Laslett, P. (1974) Comparing Household Structure over Time and between Cultures', Comparative Studies in Society and History, 16(1):73-109

Hancock, L. (1993) 'Issues of Juvenile Justice and Police', Gale, F.; Naffine, N. & Wundersitz, J. (eds.) -- Juvenile Justice: Debating the Issues:88-95

Hardin, M. (1987) '*Guardian ad Litem* for Child Victims in Criminal Proceedings', Journal of Family Law, 25(4):687-728

Harris, J.W. (1980) Legal Philosophies (Butterworth, London)

Harris, O. & Young, K. (1976) 'The Subordination of Women in Cross-cultural Perspective', Patriarchy Papers, 1976

Harris, R. & Webb, D. (1987) Welfare, Power and Juvenile Justice: the Social Control of Delinquent Youth (Tavistock, London)

Hart, H. (1982) 'Legal Rights', Hart, H. (ed.) -- Essays on Bentham: Studies in Jurisprudence and Political Theory:162-193 (Clarendon Press, Oxford)

Healy, M.A(1996) Child Sex Tourism--Does Legislation in Western Industrialized Nations Effectively Safeguard the Rights of Child which are Mandated by International Law? (Draft JD Dissertation, Fordham University)

Heid Bracey, D. (1979) Baby-Pros, Preliminary Profiles of Juvenile Prostitutes (John Jay Press, New York)

Helfer, R.E. & Kempe, C.H. (1968) The Battered Child (University of Chicago Press, Chicago, London)

Heywood, J.S. (1978) Children in Care: the Development of the Service for the Deprived Child (Routledge & Kegan Paul)

Hiew, C. (1992) 'Child Prostitutes as Victims of Tourism', O'Grady, R. (ed.) -- Children in Prostitution:27-33

Hilton, D.G. (1971) Turning Out: A Study of Teen-age Prostitution (University of Washington Press, Seattle)

Hofman, A. & Pilpel, H. (1973) 'The Legal Rights of Minors', Paediatric Clinics of North America, 20:989-1004

Hogan, M. (1993) 'Children's Court: To Be or What To Be?', Gale, F.; Naffine, N. & Wundersitz, J. (eds.) -- Juvenile Justice: Debating the Issues:139-148

Holt, J. (1975) Escape from Childhood (Penguin, Harmondsworth)

Home Office Policy Advisory Committee on Sexual Offenses [England] (1979) Working Paper on the Age of Consent in Relation to Sexual Offenses (H.M.S,O., London)

Home Office Policy Advisory Committee on Sexual Offenses [England] (1981) Report on the Age of Consent in Relation to Sexual Offenses. Cmnd 8216 (H.M.S.O., London)

Honore, T. (1978) Sex Law (Duckworth, London)

Host Committee (1996a) Report of The World Congress: Part 1 (The Host Committee for the World Congress against Commercial Sexual Exploitation of Children, Stockholm)

Host Committee (1996b) Statements by Heads of Delegation:Part 2 (The Host Committee for the World Congress against Commercial Sexual Exploitation of Children, Stockholm)

Houlgate, L.D. (1980) The Child and the State: A Normative Theory of Juvenile Rights (The Johns Hopkins University Press, London)

Howard League for Legal Reform (1985) Unlawful Sex -- Offenses, Victims and Offenders in the Criminal Justice System of England and Wales, the Report of a Howard League Working Party (Waterlow, London)

Hoyles, M. (1979) Changing Childhood (Writers and Readers, London)

Hudson, A. (1992) 'Elusive Subjects': Researching Young Women in Trouble', Gelsthorpe, L. & Morris, A. (eds.) -- Feminist Perspectives in Criminology: 115-123

Hughes, G. (1967) 'Consent in Sexual Offenses', Modern Law Review, 25:672-686

Humphries, S. (1981) Hooligans or Rebels? An Oral History of Working-Class Childhood and Youth 1889-1939 (Basil Blackwell, Oxford)

Hunt, D. (1970) Parents and Children in History (Basic Books, New York)

Hutter, B. & Williams, C. (1981) Controlling Women, the Normal and Deviant (eds.) (Croom Helm, London)

ICCB [The International Catholic Child Bureau] (1991) The Sexual Exploitation of Children -- Field Responses (ICCB, Geneva)

ICCB (1992) Children Worldwide: Children Sexually Exploited (ICCB, Geneva)

Illinois Legislative Investigation Commission [USA] (1980) Sexual Exploitation of Children (Illinois General Assembly, State of Illinois, USA)

Ives, R. (1986) 'Children's Sexual Rights', Franklin, B. (ed.) -- The Rights of Children:143-162

Jackman, N.R.; O'Toole, R.; & Geis, G. (1967) 'The Self Image of the Prostitute', Gagnon, J.H. & Simon, W. (eds.) -- Sexual Deviance:133-146

Jackson, S. (1982) Childhood and Sexuality (Blackwell, Oxford)

James, J. (1977) 'Early Sexual Experience and Prostitution', American Journal of Psychiatry, 134:1381-1385

James, J. (1978) Juvenile Female Prostitution: Final Report (University of Washington, Seatle)

James, J. (1980) 'Self Destructive behaviour and Adaptive Strategies in Female Prostitute', in James, J. (ed.) -- The Many Faces of Suicide: Indirect Self Destructive Behaviours:341-359

James, J. & Boyer, D. (1982) Intervention with Female Prostitutes (Research Paper, University of Washington, Seattle)

James, J. & Davis, N.J. (1982) 'Contingencies in Female Sexual Role Deviance: the Case of Prostitution', Human Organisation, 41(4):345-350

James, T. (1960) 'The Age of Majority', American Journal of Legal History, 4:21-33

Janus, S.S. & Heid Bracey, D.H. (1980) Runaways: Pornography and Prostitution (Mimeo, New York)

Jarvinen, M. (1993) Of Vice and Women: Shades of Prostitution (trans. K. Leander) (Scandinavian Studies in Criminology, Vol.13; The Scandinavian Research Council for Criminology, Scandinavian University Press)

Jenkins, I. (1980) Social Order and the Limits of Law: A Theoretical Essay (Princeton University Press, New Jersey)

Jenks, C. (1992) The Sociology of Childhood, Essential Readings (ed.) (Gregg Revivals, Hampshire)

Jenks, C. (1992) 'Introduction: Constituting the Child', Jenks, C. (ed.) -- The Sociology of Childhood:9-26

Jennings, M.A. (1976) 'The Victim as Criminal: A Consideration of California's Prostitution Law', California Law Review, 64:1248

John Pasion, M. (1992) 'Helping Rehabilitate Young Prostitutes: the Role of Education', a paper delivered by Sister John Pasion and translated into Mandarin by Amy Shee in the Consultation on Prevention and Treatment of Youth Prostitution, June 13, 1992, Taipei, Taiwan (Garden of Hope, Taipei, Taiwan, ROC)

Justice, B. & Justice, R. (1990) The Abusing Family (Useful Books, California)

Kadushin, A. (1974) Child Welfare Services (Collier Macmillian, New York, London)

Kamchedzera, G.S. (1991) 'The Rights of the Child in Malawi: An Agenda for Research on the Impact of the United Nations Convention in a Poor Country', International Journal of Law and the Family, 5:241-257

Kapur, P. (1978) The Life and World of Call-Girls in India: A Sociopsychological Study of Aristocratic Prostitutes (Vikas Publishing House PVT Ltd, New Delhi)

Karunatilleke, K. (1981) 'Recent Trends in the Fight against the Traffic in Human Beings and the Exploitation of Prostitution', paper submitted on behalf of INTERPOL to the 27th Congress of the International Abolitionist Federation, Nice, France.

Kelly, L. (1992) 'Journeying in Reverse: Possibilities and Problems in Feminist Research on Sexual Violence', Gelsthorpe, L. & Morris, A. (eds.) -- Feminist Perspectives in Criminology: 107-114

Kent, G. (1991) 'Our Children, Our Future', Srisang, K. (ed.) -- Caught in Modern Slavery:71-82

Khalaf, S. (1966) Prostitution in A Changing Society (Khalfats, Beirut)

Khan, H., Seng, C.F., & Cheong, W.K. (1990) 'The Social Impact of Tourism on Singapore', Service Industries Journal, 10(3):541-548

Kilpatrick, A.C. (1986) 'Some Correlates of Women's Childhood Sexual Experiences: A Retrospective Study', The Journal of Sex Research, 22(2):221-242

Kilpatrick, A.C. (1987) 'Childhood Sexual Experiences: Problems and Issues in Studying Long-Range Effects', The Journal of Sex Research, 23(2):173-196

King, M. (1981a) Childhood, Welfare and Justice: A Critical Examination of Children in the Legal and Childcare Systems (ed.) (Batsford Academic and Educational Ltd., London)

King, M. (1981b) 'Welfare and Justice', (ed.) -- Childhood, Welfare and Justice

King, M. (1984) 'Child Protection and the Search for Justice for Parents and Families in England and France', Freeman, M.D.A. (ed.) -- The Law, the State and the Family

King, M. (1991) 'Child Welfare Within Law: the Emergence of a Hybrid Discourse', Journal of Law and Society, 18(3):303-322

King, M. & Piper, C. (1990) How the Law Thinks about Children (Gower, Aldershot, England)

King, M. & Trowell, J. (1992) Children's Welfare and the Law: The Limits of Legal Intervention (Sage, London)

Kitzinger, J. (1988) 'Defining Innocence: Ideologies of Childhood', Feminist Review, 28:77-87

Koh, K. (1968) 'Consent and Responsibility in Sex Offenses', Criminal Law Review, 1968:81-84

Koltain, M. & Lin, Y. M-J (1989) 'Summary Record', Lin,Y.M-R (ed.) -- Asian Consultation on Tourism and Aboriginal Peoples:16-36

Konopka, G. (1976) 'The Needs, Rights, and Responsibilities of Youth', Child Welfare, 55:173-182

Korbin, J.E. (1979) 'A Cross-Cultural Perspective on the Role of the Community in Child Abuse and Neglect', Child Abuse and Neglect, 3:9-18

Korbin, J.E. (1980) 'The Cultural Context of Child Abuse and Neglect', Child Abuse and Neglect, 4:3-13

Korbin, J.E. (1981) Child Abuse and Neglect: Cross-Cultural Perspectives (University of California Press, California)

Lacey, N., Wells, C., & Meure, D. (1990) Reconstructing Criminal Law: Text and Materials (Weidenfeld & Nicolson, London)

Lasch, C. (1977) Heaven in A Heartless World: the Family Besieged (Basic Books, New York)

Laslett, P. (1972) The Household and Family in Past Time (Cambridge University Press, Cambridge)

Laslett, P. (1977) Family Life and Illicit Love in Earlier Generations, Essays in Historical Sociology (Cambridge University Press, Cambridge)

Laster, K. (1993) 'Juvenile Justice Reform and the Symbol of the Child', Gale, F., Naffine, N. & Wundersitz, J. (eds.) -- Juvenile Justice: Debating the Issues:57-69

Lazar, R.J. (1979) 'Asian Family and Society -- A Theoretical Overview', Das M.S. & Bardis, P.D. (eds.) -- The Family in Asia:1-15

Lebra, J. & Paulson, J. (1980) Chinese Women in South East Asia (Times Books International, Singapore)

Lees, S. & Mellor, J. (1986) 'Girls' Rights', Franklin, B. (ed.) -- The Rights of Children:164-185

Levy, A., QC (1991) 'Comment: Child Witnesses', Family Law, 21:285

Levy, R.J. (1993) 'Rights and Responsibilities for Extended Family Members?', Family Law Quarterly, 27(2):191-212

Libai, D. (1980) 'The Protection of the Child Victim of a Sexual Offence in the Criminal Justice System', Schultz, L.G. (ed.) -- The Sexual Victimology of Youth: 187-245 (Ill: C.C. Thomas, Springfield)

Lieberman, F. (1973) 'Sex and the Adolescent Girl: Liberation or Exploitation', Clinical Social Work Journal, 1:224-243

Lin, Y. M-J (1989a) Asian Consultation on Tourism and Aboriginal Peoples: Community Control, Cultural Dignity & Economic Value (ed.), A consultation held between November 11-16, 1989 at Wulai, Taiwan (Huadong Community Development Centre, Taidong, Taiwan, ROC)

Lin, Y. M-J (1989b) 'Preface: The Assault of Tourism', Lin,Y.M-J (ed.) -- Asian Consultation on Tourism and Aboriginal Peoples: i-iii

Lindsay, N. (1938) Age of Consent (An Angus & Robertson Book)

Lloyd, R. (1979) Playground: A Study of Human Exploitation (Blond and Briggs, London)

Los, M. (1992) 'Feminism and Rape Law Reform', Gelsthorpe, L. & Morris, A. (eds.) -- Feminist Perspectives in Criminology: 160-171

Lowen, J. (1978) 'Juvenile Prostitution and Child Pornography', a research paper prepared under Grant No. 77JN990017 from the National Institute for Juvenile Justice and Delinquency Prevention, Law Enforcement Assistance Administration, U.S. Department of Justice (Carter for Law and Justice, University of Washington)

Lowy, C. (1992) 'Autonomy and the Appropriate Projects of Children: A Comment on Freeman', Alston, P. et al. (eds.) -- Children, Rights and the Law:53-71

Luke, G. (1993) 'Theory vs Practice: a Case Study', Gale, F., Naffine, N. & Wundersitz, J. (eds.) -- Juvenile Justice: Debating the Issues:149-153

Lukes, S. (1976) Power: A Radical View (Macmillan, London)

Lurigio, A.J., Skogan, W.G., & Davis, R.C. (1990) Victims of Crime: Problems, Policies, and Programmes (eds,) (Sage, California)

Lystad, M.H. (1975) 'Violence at Home: A Review of the Literature', American Journal of Orthopsychiatry, 45(3):328-345

MacDougall, D.J. (1978) 'Children and the Law: the Limited Effectiveness of Legal Process', Baxter & Eberts (eds.) -- The Child and the Courts:185-202

Mackey, T.C. (1984) Red Lights Out: A Legal History of Prostitution, Disorderly Houses, and Vice Districts, 1870-1917 (PH.D. Thesis, Rice University, U.S.A.)

MacKinnon, C. (1987) Feminism Unmodified, Discourses on Life and Law (Harvard University Press, London)

MacLeod, M. & Saraga, E. (1988) 'Challenging the Orthodoxy: Towards A Feminist Theory and Practice', Feminist Review, 28:26-55

Maidment, S. (1981) 'The Fragmentation of Parental Rights', Cambridge Law Journal, 40(1):135-158

Majgull, A.(1996) Rosario is Dead (Raben Prisma,Swedish)
Majchrzak, A. (1984) Methods for Policy Research (Sage, Beverly Hills, London, New Delhi)
Manazan, Sr. M.J. (1982) 'Sexual Exploitation in a Third World Setting', MSS in Files of Defense for Children International, Switzerland.
Mann, A. (1977) 'Society's Obligation to the Family', Franklin, A.W. (ed.) -- The Challenge of Child Abuse (Proceedings of a Conference sponsored by the Royal Society of Medicine 2-4 June 1976):206-218
Margolin, C. (1978) 'Salvation Versus Liberation: The Movement for Children's Rights in a Historical Context', Social Problems, 22:441
Matsui, Y. (1980) 'Economy and Psychology of Prostitution and Tourism', Asian Women's Liberation, 1980
Matsui, Y. (1991) 'Asian Migrant Women Working at Sex Industry in Japan Victimised by International Trafficking', Srisang, K. (ed.) -- Caught in Modern Slavery:100-102
Marsh, C. & Arber, S. (1992) Families and Households: Divisions and Change (eds.) (Macmillan, London)
Maurer, M. (1991) 'Tourism, Prostitution and Aids', Srisang, K. (ed.) -- Caught in Modern Slavery:96-99
Mawby, R.I. (1979) 'Policing the Age of Consent', Journal of Adolescence, 2:41-49
Mawby, R.I. & Walklate, S. (1994) Critical Victimology: International Perspectives (Sage, London)
May, M. (1973) 'Innocence and Experience: The Evolution of the Concept of Juvenile Delinquency in Mid-nineteenth Century', Victorian Studies, 17:7-29
McCaghy, C.H. & Hou, C. (1989) 'Career Onset of Taiwanese Prostitutes'. paper presented in the Annual Meeting of the Society for the Study of Social Problem, August 6-8, California, U.S.A.
McEwan, J. (1988) 'Child Evidence: More Proposals for Reform', Criminal Law Review, 1988:813-822
McIntosh, M. (1978) 'Who Needs Prostitutes? The Ideology of Male Sexual Needs', Smart,C. & Smart, B. (eds.) -- Women, Sexuality and Social Control (Routledge & Kegan Paul, London)
McIntosh, M. (1988) 'Introduction to An Issue: Family Secrets as Public Drama', Feminist Review, 28:6-15
McLeod, E. (1978) 'Working with Prostitutes: Probation Officers' Aims and Strategies', British Journal of Social Work, 9(4):453-469
McLeod, E. (1982) Women Working: Prostitution Now (Croom Helm, London)
McNay, L. (1992) Foucault and Feminism: Power, Gender and the Self (Polity Press, Cambridge)
Mcmullen, R.J. (1987) 'Youth Prostitution: A Balance of Power', Journal of Adolescence, 10:35-43
Millett, K. (1977) Sexual Politics (Virago, London)
Mitra, C. (1987) 'Judicial Discourse in Father-Daughter Incest Appeal Cases', International Journal of the Sociology of Law, 15(2):121-148

Mohr, J.V. (1986) The Future of the Family, the Law and the State (Canada), Landau, B. (ed.) -- Children's Rights in the Practice of Family Law
Montgomery, J. (1988) 'Children as Property?', Modern Law Review, 51:323-342
Morgan, D.H.J. (1975) Social Theory and the Family (Routledge & Kegan Paul, London)
Morgan, D.H.J. (1985) The Family, Politics and Social Theory (Routledge & Kegan Paul, London)
Morgan, J. & Zedner, L. (1992) Child Victims: Crime, Impact, and Criminal Justice (Clarendon, Oxford)
Morris, A. (1987) Women, Crime and Criminal Justice (Basil Blackwell, Oxford)
Morris, A., Giller, H., Szwed, E., & Geach, H. (1980) Justice for Children (Macmillan, London)
Morris, A. & Giller, H. (1983) Providing Criminal Justice for Children (Edward Arnold, London)
Morris, A. & Giller, H. (1987) Understanding Juvenile Justice (Croom Helm, London)
Moselina, L. (1978) 'Rest and Recreation: the US Naval Base at Subic Bay', ISIS, 13:17-20 (Switzerland)
Mott, J. (1983) 'Police Decisions for Dealing with Juvenile Offenders', British Journal of Criminology, 23(3):249-262
Mount, F. (1982) The Subversive Family, An Alternative History of Love and Marriage (Cape, London)
Mulligan, L.W. (1972) 'Wives, Women and Wife Role Behaviour: An Alternative Cross-Cultural Perspective', International Journal of Contemporary Society, 13(1):36-47
Muntarbhorn, V. (1991) 'Perspectives on Prostitution', Srisang, K. (ed.) -- Caught in Modern Slavery:68-70
Muntarbhorn, V. (1992a) 'To and From Asia and Beyond', O'Grady, R. (ed.) -- Children in Prostitution:8-15
Muntarbhorn, V. (1992b) 'Report of the Special Rapporteur on the Sale of Children', Report submitted to the United Nations Commission on Human Rights, 48th session, E/CN.4/1992/55, Geneva.
Mutukumara, N. (1992) 'The Buddhist Tradition', O'Grady, R. (ed.) -- Children in Prostitution:46-50
Naffine, N. (1990) Law and the Sexes: Explorations in Feminist Jurisprudence (Allen & Unwin, Sydney)
Naffine, N. (1992) 'Children in the Children's Court: Can There Be Rights without Remedy?', Alston, P. et al. (eds.) -- Children, Rights and the Law:76-97
Naffine, N. (1993) 'Philosophies of Juvenile Justice', Gale, F., Naffine, N. & Wundersitz, J. (eds.) -- Juvenile Justice: Debating the Issues:2-17
Naffine, N. (1994) 'Possession: Erotic Love in the Law of Rape', The Modern Law Review, 57(1):10-37
Nagel, S.S. (1970) Law and Social Change (ed.) (Sage, California/London)
Nava, M. (1988) 'Cleveland and the Press: Outrage and Anxiety in the Reporting of Child Sexual Abuse', Feminist Review, 28:103-121
Nelson, S. (1982) Incest: Fact and Myth (Stramullion, Edinburgh)

Newell, P. (1991) The UN Convention and Children's Rights in the UK (The National Children's Bureau, London)

Noble, S.M. (1978) 'The Contributions of the Social Agencies and the Social Worker', in Smith, S.M. (ed.) -- The Maltreatment of Children: 351-391

Nontawasee, P.A. (1991) 'Biblical Justice', Srisang,K. (ed.) -- Caught in Modern Slavery:89-90

O'Donovan, K. (1985) Sexual Divisions in the Law (Weidenfeld & Nicolson)

O'Donovan, K. (1993) Family Law Matters (Pluto, Colorado)

O'Grady, R. (1980) 'Third World Tourism', Report of a Workshop on Tourism held in Manila, September 12-25, Christian Conference of Asia.

O'Grady, R. (1991) 'Preface', Srisang, K. (ed.) -- Caught in Modern Slavery:3

O'Grady, R. (1992a) The Child and the Tourist (ECPAT, Bangkok)

O'Grady, R. (1992b) Children in Prostitution: Victims of Tourism in Asia -- Report of the International Conference held at Sukhothai Thammathirat Open University, Bangkok, Thailand, March 31 - April 3, 1992 (ed.) (ECPAT, Bangkok)

O'Grady, R. (1992c) 'Foreword', O'Grady, R. (ed.) -- Children in Prostitution

O'Neill, M. (1994) 'Prostitution and the State: Towards a Feminist Practice', Lupton, C. & Gillespie, T. (eds.) -- Working with Violence (Macmillan, Hampshire/London)

Ohse, U. (1984) Forced Prostitution and Traffic in Women in West Germany (Human Rights Group, Edinburgh)

Olsen, F.E. (1984) 'The Politics of Family Law', Law and Inequality, 2:1

Olsen, F.E. (1985) 'The Myth of State Intervention in the Family', University of Michigan Journal of Law Reform, 18(4):835-864

Olsen, F.E. (1992) 'Children's Rights: Some Feminist Approaches to the United Nations Convention on the Rights of the Child', Alston, P. et al. (eds.) -- Children, Rights and the Law:192-220

Otaganonta, W. (1990) 'Child Prostitution in Thailand', Bangkok Post, August 1, 1990

Parker, H., Casburn, M., & Turnbull, D. (1981) Receiving Juvenile Justice: Adolescents and State Care and Control (Oxford)

Parliament by the Secretary of State for Social Services by Command of Her Majesty (1988) Report of The Inquiry into Child Abuse in Cleveland 1987 (Her Majesty Stationery Office, London)

Parsloe, P. (1978) Juvenile Justice in Britain and the United States, the Balance of Needs and Rights (Routledge & Kegan Paul, London)

Parton,N. (1979) 'The Natural History of Child Abuse: A Study in Social Problem definition', British Journal of Social Work,9(4):431-451

Parton, N. (1985) The Politics of Child Abuse (Macmillan, Basignstoke)

Parton, N. (1991) Governing the Family, Child Care, Child Protection and the State (Macmillan, London)

Patrikios, T. (1973) 'Age 16, Civil Majority 18, Voting Age 21, Why?', UNESCO COURIER, 26:24-31

Pearl, D. & Gray, K. (1981) Social Welfare Law (Croom Helm, London)

Pearson, M. (1972) The Age of Consent: Victorian Prostitution and Its Enemies (David & Charles, Newton Abbot)
Perpignan, Sr. M-S (1983) Philippine Women in the Service and Entertainment Sector (TWMAEW, Singapore)
Pescattello, A. (1980) Female and Male in Latin America (ed.) (University of Pittsburg Press, Pittsburg)
Pheterson, G. (1989) A Vindication of the Rights of Whores (ed.) (Seal Press, Seattle)
Philp, M. (1985) 'Power', Kuper, A. & Kuper, J. (eds.) -- The Social Science Encyclopedia: 635-639 (Routledge & Kegan Paul, London)
Pinchbeck, I. & Hewitt, M. (1973) Children in English Society, I & II (Routledge & Kegan Paul, London)
Platt, A.M. (1969) 'The Rise of the Child-Saving Movement', Annals of the American Academy, 381:21-38. Also in Jenks, C. (ed.) -- The Sociology of Childhood: 151-170 (1982,1992)
Platt, A.M. (1977) The Child Savers, the Invention of Delinquency (University of Chicago Press, Chicago)
Polan,D. (1982) 'Towards A Theory of Law and Patriarchy', Kairys, D. (ed.) -- The Politics of Law
Polk, K. (1993) 'The Search for Alternatives to Coercive Justice', Gale, F., Naffine, N. & Wundersitz, J. (eds.) -- Juvenile Justice: Debating the Issues:106-115
Poster, N. (1984) Critical Theory of the Family (Seabury Press, New York)
Poster, N. (1989) Critical Theory and Poststructualism, in Search of A Context (Cornell University Press, Ithaca, New York)
Potterat, J.J., Phillips, L., Rothenberg, R.B., & Darrow, W.W. (1984) 'On Becoming A Prostitute: An Exploratory Case-Comparison Study', Brief Reports, 1984(March 20):329-335
Power, D. (1977) 'Paedophilia', Practitioner, 218:805-811
Pratt, J. (1993) 'Welfare and Justice: Incompatible Philosophies', Gale, F., Naffine, N. & Wundersitz, J. (eds.) -- Juvenile Justice: Debating the Issues:38-51
Pratt, M.A. (1970) 'A Model for Social Welfare and National Development', International Social Work, 13(1):2 (January 1970)
Prison Reform Trust (1987) 'Comparisons in Juvenile Justice', Juvenile Justice, Project Report No.1
Rae, M. (1986) Children and the Law, Young People and Their Rights (Longman, London)
Rawls, J. (1972) A Theory of Justice (Clarendon, Oxford)
Raz, J. (1979) The Authority of Law: Essays on Law and Morality (Clarendon Press, Oxford)
Raz, J. (1984) 'Legal Rights', Oxford Journal of Legal Studies, 4:1-21
Redley, S. (1984) 'Harrow of Sex for Sale Boys', Northamptonshire Post, October 25:5
Reiss, A. (1961) 'The Sexual Integration of Peers and Queers', Social Problems, 9:102-120
Riback, L. (1971) 'Juvenile Delinquency: Juvenile Women and the Double Standard of Morality', University of California (Los Angeles) Law Review, 19:313-342

Rice, M. (1992) 'Challenging Orthodoxy in Feminist Theory: A Black Feminist Critique', Gelsthorpe, L. & Morris, A. (eds.) -- Feminist Perspectives in Criminology: 57-69

Richards, D.A.J. (1979) 'Commercial Sex and the Rights of the Person: A Moral Argument for the Decriminalisation of Prostitution', University of Pennsylvania Law Review, 127:1233

Richards, D.A.J. (1982) Sex, Drugs, Death, and the Law: An Essay on Human Rights and Overcriminalisation (Rowman & Littlefield, New Jersey)

Riley, D. (1981) 'Left Critiques of the Family', The Cambridge Women's Studies Group -- Women in Society: Interdisciplinary Essays:75-92 (Virago, London)

Ritchie, D. (1994) Legal Considerations of Proposed Legislation to Prosecute New Zealanders Who Sexually Exploit/Abuse Children Overseas(LL.B. Dissertation, University of Auckland, Auckland)

Roe, C. (1911) The Great War on White Slavery (reprinted in 1979 by Garland Publishing Inc., New York)

Rogers, J.R. (1991) 'Introduction to the Consultation', Srisang, K. (ed.) -- Caught in Modern Slavery:24-25

Rogers, M. & Wrightsman, L.S. (1978) 'Attitudes Towards Children's Rights: Nurturance or Self-Determination?', Journal of Social Issues, 34(2)

Rose, N. (1987) 'Beyond the Public and the Private Division: Law, Power and the Family', [British] Journal of Law and Society, 14:61

Rosen, R. (1982) The Lost Sisterhood: Prostitution in America 1900-1918 (Johns Hopkins, Baltimore / London)

Rosenbleet, C. & Puriente, B.J. (1973) 'The Prostitution of the Criminal Law', American Criminal Law Review, 11:373

Rossman, P. (1979) Sexual Experience between Men and Boys (Maurice, Temple Smith Ltd., London)

Rossman, P. (1980) 'The Pederasts', in Schultz, L.G. (ed.) -- The Sexual Victimology of Youth:335-49

Rubington, E. & Weinberg, M.S. (1977) The Study of Social Problems: Five Perspectives (eds.) (Oxford University Press, Oxford)

Ruff, H. (1992) 'Action for Change', O'Grady, R. (ed.) -- Children in Prostitution:34-42

Russell, B. (1929) Marriage and Morals (George Allen & Unwin, London)

Russell, B. (1938) Power: A New Social Analysis (George Allen & Unwin, London)

Russell, D.E.H. (1984) Sexual Exploitation, Rape, Child Sexual Abuse, and Workplace Harassment (Sage, Beverly Hill, London)

Rutter, M. & Giler, H. (1983) Juvenile Delinquency -- Trends and Perspectives (Penguin, Harmondsworth)

Sachs, C. (1973) 'Children's Rights', Bridge, J.W., Lasok, D., Perrot, D.L., & Plender, R.O. (eds.) -- Fundamental Rights:31-42

Saffady, W. (1975) 'Fears of Sexual Licence in the English Reformation', History of Childhood Quarterly, 8:18-37

Sanday, P.R. (1981) 'The Social-Cultural Context of Rape: A Cross-Cultural Study', Journal of Social Issues, 37(4):5-27

Sarri, R. (1983) 'Paradigms and Pitfalls in Juvenile Justice Diversion', Morris, A. & Giller, H. (eds.) -- Providing Criminal Justice for Children:52-73

Schaffer, B. & DeBlassie, R.R. (1984) 'Adolescent Prostitution', Adolescence, 19(75):689-696

Schechter, M.D. & Roberg, L. (1986) 'Sexual Exploitation', Helfer, R.E. & Kempe, C.H. (eds.) -- Child Abuse and Neglect: the Family and the Community

Schlossman, S. & Wallach, S. (1978) 'The Crime of Precocious Sexuality: Female Juvenile Delinquency in the Progressive Era', Harvard Educational Review, 48(1):65-94

Schrag, F. (1973) 'Rights over Children', Journal of Value Inquiry, 7:96-105

Schrag, F. (1977) 'The Child in the Moral Order', Philosophy, 52:126-135

Schultz, L.G. (1980a) The Sexual Victimology of Youth (ed.) (C.C. Thomas, Springfield, Illinois)

Schultz, L.G. (1980b) 'The Sexual Abuse of Children and Minors: a Short History of Legal Control Efforts', in. (ed.) -- The Sexual Victimology of Youth: 3-17

Schultz, L.G. (1980c) 'Incest Policy Recommendations', in. (ed.) -- The Sexual Victimology of Youth: 163-167

Schultz, L.G. (1980d) 'The Victim and the Justice System -- An Introduction', in. (ed.) -- The Sexual Victimology of Youth: 171-174

Schultz, L.G. (1980e) 'Policy Recommendations on Child Pornography Control', in. (ed.) -- Policy Recommendations on Child Pornography Control: 350-351

Schultz, L.G. (1980f) 'Sexual Emancipation -- An Introduction', in. (ed.) -- The Sexual Victimology of Youth: 355-356

Schultz, L.G. (1980g) 'The Age of Sexual Consent: Fault, Fraction, Freedom'. (ed.) -- The Sexual Victimology of Youth: 357-377

Scraton, P. (1992) 'Scientific Knowledge or Masculine Discourses? Challenging Patriarchy in Criminology', Gelsthorpe, L. & Morris, A. (eds.) -- Feminist Perspectives in Criminology: 10-25

Searle, G. (1971)The Quest for National Efficiency (Oxford University Press)

Seneviratne, M. & Peiris, S.J.S. (1991) 'Tourism and Child Prostitution in Sri Lanka', Srisang, K. (ed.) -- Caught in Modern Slavery:47-52

Seng, M.J. (1989) 'Child Sexual Abuse and Adolescent Prostitution: A Comparative Analysis', Adolescence, 24(85):665-675

Sereny, G. (1984) The Invisible Children: A Study of Child Prostitution (Andre Deutsch, London)

Sexual Assault Centre, Harborview Medical Centre, Seattle, Washington (1980) 'Sexual Assault Centre Emergency Room Protocol: Child/Adolescent Patients', in Schultz, L.G. (ed.) -- The Sexual Victimology of Youth: 83-90

Seymour, J. (1992) 'An 'Uncontrollable' Child: A Case Study in Children's and Parents' Rights', Alston, P. et al (eds.) -- Children, Rights and the Law: 98-118

Seymour, J. (1993) 'Australia's Juvenile Justice Systems: A Comment', Gale, F., Naffine, N. & Wundersitz, J. (eds.) -- Juvenile Justice: Debating the Issues:52-56

Shapland, J. & Cohen, D. (1987) 'Facilities for Victims: the Role of the police and the Courts', Criminal Law review, 1987:28-38

Shorter, E. (1976) The Making of the Modern Family (ed.) (Collins, London)

Shubert, C. (1992) 'A Symptom of Deeper Problems', O'Grady, R. (ed.) -- Children in Prostitution:20-21

Sion, A.A. (1977) Prostitution and the Law (Farber, London)

Skogan, W., Lurigio, A.J., & Davis, R.C. (1990) 'Criminal Victimisation'. (eds.) -- Victims of Crime: Problems, Policies, and Programmes: 7-22

Slogvolk (1852) 'The Rights of Children', Knickerbocker, 36

Smart, B. (1985) Michel Foucault (Ellis Horwood, Sussex / Tavistock, London)

Smart, C. (1976) Women, Crime and Criminology: A Feminist Critique (Routledge & Kegan Paul, London)

Smart, C. (1981) 'Law and the Control of Female Sexuality: the Case of the 1950s', Hutter, B. & Williams, G. (eds.) -- Controlling Women, the Normal and the Deviant (Croom Helm, London)

Smart, C. (1982) 'Regulating Families or Legitimating Patriarchy? Family Law in Britain', International Journal of the Sociology of Law, 10:129-148

Smart, C. (1985) 'Legal Subjects and Sexual Objects: Ideology, Law and Female Sexuality', Brophy, J. & Smart, C. (eds.) -- Women in Law: Exploitations in Law, Family and Sexuality:50-70

Smart, C. (1989) Feminism and the Power of Law (Routledge, London)

Smart, C. (1992) 'Feminist Approaches to Criminology or Postmodern Women Meets Atavistic Man', Gelsthorpe, L. & Morris, A. (eds.) -- Feminist Perspectives in Criminology: 70-84

Smart, C. & Smart, B. (1978) Women, Sexuality and Social Control (eds.) (Routledge & Kegan Paul, London)

Smelser, N. (1982) 'The Victorian Family', Rapport, R.N. et al. (eds.) -- Families in Britain (Routledge & Kegan Paul, London)

Smith, B.E. (1990) 'The Adjudication of Child Sexual Abuse Cases', Lurigio, A.J. Skogan, W.G., & Davis, R.C. (eds.) -- Victims of Crime: Problems, Policies, and Programmes: 104-119

Smith, J.C. & Hogan, B. (1986) Criminal Law: Cases and Materials (Butterworths, London)

Snare, A. (1993) 'Forward', Jarvinen, M. -- Of Vice and Women:9-12

Song, K.H. (1989) 'In Recognition of the Cultural Dignity and Tourist Industry Sovereignty of the indigenous People', Lin,Y.M-J (ed.) -- Asian Consultation on Tourism and Aboriginal Peoples: iv-vi

Soothill, K. & Walby, S. (1991) Sex Crime in the News (Routledge, London / New York)

Sorn-Aw, B. & Klanprasert, T. (1992) 'The Challenge from Children', O'Grady, R. (ed.) -- Children in Prostitution:4-7

Spencer, J.R. & Flin, R.H. (1990) The Evidence of Children: the Law and the Psychology (Blackstone, London)

Spencer, J.R., Nicholson, G., Flin, R., & Bull, R. (1990) Children's Evidence in Legal Proceedings: An International Perspective (eds.) (University of Cambridge, Cambridge)

Srisang, K. (1989) 'Tourism and Cultural Dignity', Lin,Y.M-J (ed.) -- Asian Consultation on Tourism and Aboriginal Peoples: 95-103

Srisang, K. (1991a) Caught in Modern Slavery: Tourism and Child Prostitution in Asia -- International Campaign to End Child Prostitution in Asian Tourism (ECPAT): Report and Proceedings of the Chiang Mai Consultation, May 1-5, 1990 (ed.) (ECTWT: The Ecumenical Coalition on the Third World Tourism, Bangkok)

Srisang, K. (1991b) 'Introduction -- The Child: The Greatest Who Suffers the Most'. (ed.) -- Caught in Modern Slavery:4-8

Srisang, S. (1991) 'Tourism and Child Prostitution in Thailand', Srisang, K. (ed.) -- Caught in Modern Slavery:37-46

Stafford, A. (1964) The Age of Consent (Hodder and Stoughton, London)

Stainton, M. (1989a) 'Evaluation Report', Lin,Y.M-J (ed.) -- Asian Consultation on Tourism and Aboriginal Peoples: 9-15

Stainton, M. (1989b) 'Summary Presentation', Lin,Y.M-J (ed.) -- Asian Consultation on Tourism and Aboriginal Peoples: 104-110

Stanko, E. (1992) 'When Precaution Is Normal: A Feminist Critique of Crime Prevention', Gelsthorpe, L. & Morris, A. (eds.) -- Feminist Perspectives in Criminology: 173-183

Stevens, D. & Berliner, L. (1980) 'Special Techniques for Child Witnesses', in Schultz, L.G. (ed.) -- The Sexual Victimology of Youth: 246-256

Steward, A. (1993) 'The Dilemmas of Law in Women's Development', Andelman, S. & Paliwala, A . (eds.) -- Law and Crisis in the Third World:219-242

Stone, L. (1977) The Family, Sex and Marriage in England, 1500-1800 (Penguin, Harmondsworth)

Su, J.E. (1995) Universal Human Rights vs. Cultural and Sovereignty Rights :The Case of Forced Prostitution in Asia (California State University, Long Beach)

Sumner, C. (1992) 'Foucault, Gender and the Censure of Deviance', Gelsthorpe, L. & Morris, A. (eds.) -- Feminist Perspectives in Criminology: 26-40

Suresh, K.T. (1991) 'Child Prostitution and Tourism in India', Srisang, K. (ed.) -- Caught in Modern Slavery:63-67

Sutton, J. (1985) 'The Juvenile Court and Social Welfare: Dynamics of Progressive Reform', Law and Society Review, 19(1):107

Swift, C. (1980) 'Sexual Victimisation of Children: An Urban Mental Health Centre Survey', in Schultz, L.G. (ed.) -- The Sexual Victimology of Youth: 18-24

Taliercio Co (1996) International Law and Legal Aspects of Child Sex Tourism in Asia-A Contemporary Form of Slavery? (Children's Ombudsman, Sweden)

Tannahill, R. (1981) Sex in History (Abacus, London)

Tappan, P.W. (1969) Delinquent Girls in Court: A Study of the Wayward Minor Court of New York (Patterson Smith, New Jersey)

Taylor, C. (1986) 'Foucault on Freedom and Truth', Couzens Hoy, D. (ed.) -- Foucault: A Critical Reader (Blackwell, Oxford)

Temkin, J. (1987) Rape and the Legal Process (Sweet & Maxwell, London)

Temkin, J. (1990) 'Child Sexual Abuse and Criminal Justice: 1 & 2', New Law Journal, 140(6447):352-355 & 140(6448:410-411

Teubner, G. (1988) Autopoietic Law: A New Approach to Law and Society (ed.) (De Gruyter)

Thane, P. (1981) 'Childhood in History', King, M. (ed.) -- Childhood, Welfare and Justice

Tomlinson, M., Varley, T., & McCullagh, C. (1988) Whose Law and Order? Aspects of Crime and Social Control in Irish Society (eds.) (Sociological Association of Ireland, Belfast)

Tong, R. (1984) Women, Sex and the Law (Rowman & Little Field, U.S.A.)

Turner, L. & Ash, J. [England] (1975) The Golden Hordes: International Tourism and the Pleasure Periphery (Constable, London)

United Nations Expert Group Meeting (1994) Children and Juveniles in Detention: Application of Human Rights Standards (United Nations Expert Group Meeting, Austria)

URSA (1981) 'Adolescent Male Prostitution: A Study of Sexual Exploitation, Etiological Factors and Runaway Behaviour', Draft of Executive Summary, California, October, 1981.

Usman, H.B. (1989) The Consequences of Family Breakdown in Post-Independence Nigeria: A Case Study of Borno State (Ph.D. Thesis, School of Law, University of Warwick, U.K.)

Veevers, J. (1989) 'Pre-court Diversion for Juvenile Offenders', Wright, M. & Galaway, B. -- Mediation and Criminal Justice (Sage, London)

Vice Commission of Chicago [USA] (1911) 'The Social Evil in Chicago: A Study of Existing Conditions with Recommendations', Gunthrop Warren, Chicago.

Victorian Law Reform Commission (1988) Sexual Offenses Against Children; Report No.18

Vitaliano, P.P., Boyer, D. & James, J. (1981) 'Perceptions of Juvenile Experience: Females Involved in Prostitution Versus Property Offenses', Criminal Justice and Behaviour, 8(3):325-342

Wald, M.S. (1979) 'Children's Rights: A Framework for Analysis', Davis Law Review, 12:255-282

Walker, H. & Beaumont, B. (1981) Probation Work: Critical Theory and Social Practice (Blackwell, Oxford)

Walkowitz, J.R. (1980) Prostitution and Victorian Society: Women, Class and the State (Cambridge University Press, Cambridge)

Waller, I. (1990) 'The Police: First in Aid?', Lurigio, A.J.; Skogan, W.G.; & Davis, R.C. (eds.) -- Victims of Crime: Problems, Policies, and Programmes:139-156

Waller,W., (1936) 'Social Problems and Mores', American Sociological Review,1:922-933

Walz, I. (1992) 'We Demanded Political Action', O'Grady, R. (ed.) -- Children in Prostitution:16-19

Warburton J. & Maria Teresa Camacho de la Crue (1996) A Right to Happiness : Approaches to the Prevention & Psycho-social Recovery of Child Victims of Commercial Sexual Exploitation (NGO Group for the Convention on the Right of the Child)

Wasi, P. (1991) 'Tourism and Child Prostitution', Srisang, K. (ed.) -- Caught in Modern Slavery:26-28

Watson, A. (1985) The Evolution of Law (Basil Blackwell, Oxford)

Weeks, J. (1981) Sex, Politics and Society (Longman, London)

Weeks, J. (1985) Sexuality and Its Discontents: Meanings. Myths and Modern Sexuality (Routledge, London)

Weeks, R. (1976) 'The Sexually Exploited Child', Southern Medical Journal, 69:848-850

Weisberg, D.K. (1985) Children of the Night (Lexington, MA:DC.Health)

White, R. , Carr, P., & Lowe, N. (1990) A Guide to the Children Act 1989 (Butterworth, London)

Wihtol, R. (1982) 'Hospitality Girls in the Manila Tourist Belt', Philippine Journal of Industrial Relations, 6(1-2)

Williams, J. (1988) 'Family Courts: Justice for Children?', Social Work Today, 1988 (Nov.10):17-19

Wilson, J. & Tomlinson, M. (1986) Wilson: Children and the Law (2nd ed., Butterworth, Toronto)

Wolfenden Committee [England] (1957) Report of the Committee on Homosexual Offenses and Prostitution, Cmnd 247 (HMSO, London)

Wundersitz, J. (1993) 'Some Statistics on Youth Offending: An Inter-Jurisdictional Comparison', Gale, F., Naffine, N. & Wundersitz, J. (eds.) -- Juvenile Justice: Debating the Issues:18-36

Yayori, M. & Park, S.A. (1983) 'Theoretical Reflections on the Prostitution Industry', CTC Bulletin, 4(3):7 (Bangkok)

Yondorf, B. (1979) 'Prostitution As A Legal Activity -- the West Germany Experience', Policy Analysis, 5(4):417-433

Young, M. de (1982) The Sexual Victimisation of Children (Jefferson, N.C.: MacFarland)

Zaretsky, E. (1982) 'The Place of the Family in the Origins of the Welfare State', Thorne, B. (ed.) -- Rethinking the Family, Some Feminist Questions:188-224 (Longman, New York, London)

Zuckerman, M. (1976) 'Children's Rights: The Failure of Reform', Policy Analysis, 2:371-383

II. CONVENTIONS AND LAWS

[The United Nations]

* Convention for the Suppression of the Traffic in Persons and of the Exploitation of the Prostitution of Others [opened for signature at Lake Success, New York, on March 21, 1950; for text, see United Nations Treaty Series, Vol.96(I), No.1342, pp.272-289]

* Declaration of the Rights of the Child [adopted by the UN General Assembly on November 20, 1959; for text, see Newell, P.,1991:182-183 (Appendix III)]

* Convention on the Rights of the Child [adopted by the UN General Assembly on November 20, 1989; for text, see Newell, P.,1991:158-180 (Appendix I)]

[National Laws]

* Republic of Philippines, Republic Act No. 7610, 1993 [An Act Providing for Stronger Deterrence and Special Protection against Child Abuse, Exploitation and Discrimination, Providing Penalties for its Violation, and for other Purposes]

* United Kingdom, Sexual Offences Act 1956 and Sexual Offences (Amendment) Act 1976

* United Kingdom, Children Act 1989

III. STATEMENTS OF INTERNATIONAL CONSULTATION MEETINGS AND CONFERENCES

* Statement of The Asian Consultation on Tourism and Aboriginal Peoples [Asian Consultation on Tourism and Aboriginal Peoples, November 11-16, 1989, Wulai, Taiwan, ROC. See Lin, Y.M-J,1989a:37-39]

* An International Campaign aimed at the Asian Tourist Industry: To End Child Prostitution: Statement [International Consultation on Tourism and Child Prostitution in Asia, May 1-5, 1990, Ching Mai, Thailand. See Srisang, K. 1991:13-16]

* Conference Statement [International Conference on Children in Prostitution, March 31-April 3, 1992, Sukhothai Thammathirat Open University, Bangkok, Thailand. See O'Grady, R., 1992:53-54]

* Declaration and Agenda for Action [World Congress Against Commercial Sexual Exploitation of Children, August 27-31, 1996, Stockholm, Sweden. See Host Committee, 1996a:9-22]

BIBLIOGRAPHY II : English References on China and Taiwan

I. BOOKS, ARTICLES, DISSERTATIONS, REPORTS

Baker, H.D.R. (1979) Chinese Family and Kinship (Columbia University Press, New York)

Belton, D. (1992) 'The Socio-Political Dimensions of AIDS', a paper presented to the NASW Symposium on AIDS, April 24, 1992, National Taiwan University, Taipei

Bodde, D. & Morris, C. (1973) Law in Imperial China (University of Pennsylvania Press, Philadelphia)

Branegan, J. (1990) 'Island of Greed, A Wave of Wild Wealth Washes Over Taiwan', Time, March 19:50-51

Burkhardt, V.R. (1953) Chinese Creeds & Customs (The South China Morning Post, Hong Kong)

Buxbaum, D.C. (1978a) Chinese Family Law and Social Change in Historical and Comparative Perspective (ed.) (University of Washington Press, Seattle)

Buxbaum, D.C. (1978b) 'Family Law and Social Change: A Theoretical Introduction', (ed.) -- Chinese Family Law and Social Change in Historical and Comparative Perspective:3-20

Buxbaum, D.C. (1978c) 'A Case Study of the Dynamics of Family Law and Social Change in Rural China', (ed.) -- Chinese Family Law and Social Change in Historical and Comparative Perspective:217-260

Chang, M.C., Freedman, R., & Sun, T.H. (1981) 'Trends in Fertility, Family Size Preferences, and Family Planning Practice: Taiwan, 1961-1980', Studies in Family Planning, 12(5):211-228

Chang, M.C. (1988) 'Changing Relations between Traditional and State Social Security in Taiwan', von Bende-Beckman, F. et al. (eds.) -- Between Kinship and the State: Social Security and Law in Developing Countries (Foris Publications)

Chang, M.C. (1987) 'Changing Familial Network and Social Welfare in Taiwan', Conference on Economic Development and Social Welfare in Taiwan: 459-482

Chao, Y.T. (1987) 'Social Security and Resource Allocation', Industry of Free China, 68(6):1-6

Chen, C.L. (1968) 'The Taiwanese Family', Journal of the China Society, 7:64-79

Chen, C.Y. (1957) 'The Foster-daughter-in-law System in Formosa', American Journal of Comparative Law, 6(3):302-314

Chen, H.H. (1986) 'Taiwan Situation Report', ACWC -- Report of the Consultation on Tourism and Prostitution:126-139

Chen, K.C. (1986) 'Culture, Morality and Sexuality in Late Nineteenth Century China', Bulletin of the Institute of Ethnology, Academic Sinica, 62:205-33 (Academic Sinica, Taipei, Taiwan)

Chen, K.J. (1987) 'On the Change of Household Composition in Taiwan', Sociological Journal of China, 11:171-183

Chen, L.F. & Hou, C.M. (1990) 'Confucianism, Education, and Economic Development in Taiwan (I) & (II)', Industry of Free China, 68(5):1-11, & 68(6):7-20

Chen, L.H. (1963) 'Literary Formosa', The China Quarterly, 15:75-85

Chen, P.M. (1973) Law and Justice: the Legal System in China, 2400 B.C. to 1960 A.D. (Dunellen Publishing Company, New York)

Chen, S.H. (1956) 'Social Change in Taiwan', Studia Taiwanica, 1:1-20

Cheng, C.K. (1939) 'The Chinese Large Family System and Its Disorganisation', Social Forces, 17:538-545

Cheng, C.K. (1944) 'Familism the Foundation of Chinese Social Organisation', Social Forces, 20(1):50-59

Cheng, C.K. (1946) 'Characteristic Traits of the Chinese People', Social Forces, 25(2):146-155

Chiu, H.D. (1984) 'Legal Development in the Republic of China 1949-1981', Chiu, H.D. & Leng, S.C. (eds.) -- China Seventy Years after the 1911 Hsin-hai Revolution:287-330 (University Press of Virginia, Charlottesville)

Chiu, H.D. & Fa, J.P. (1984) 'The Legal System of the Republic of China in Taiwan', Redden, K.R. (ed.) -- Modern Legal Systems Cyclopedia (II):Pacific Basin:605-691 (William S.H., Buffalo, New York)

Chiu, H.D. & Fa, J.P. (1988) 'Republic of China: Editorial Note', Beer, L.W. (ed.) -- Constitutionalism in Asia: Asian View of the American influence:35-38 (University of Maryland Press, Maryland)

Chiu, V.Y. (1966) Marriage Laws and Customs of China (University of Hong Kong, Hong Kong)

Chu, S.C.; Clark, L.L.; Lo. J.P.; & Wu. Y.L. (1959) China, Its People, Its Society, Its Culture (Mayflower, London)

Chuen, J.S. (1988) 'Juvenile Delinquency in the Republic of China: A Chinese Empirical Study of Social Control Theory', International Journal of Comparative and Applied Criminal Justice, 12(1):59-71

Clark, C. (1987) 'Economic Development in Taiwan: A Model of a Political Economy', Journal of Asian and African Studies, 22(1-2):1-16

Cohen, J.A. (1970) Contemporary Chinese Law: Research Problems and Perspectives (Harvard University Press, Cambridge)

Cohen, J.A., Edwards, R.R., & Chen, F.F. Chang (1980) Essays on China's Legal Tradition (eds.) (Princeton University Press, New Jersey)

Cohen, M.L. (1976) House United, House Divided: the Chinese Family in Taiwan (Columbia University Press, New York, London)

Cohen, M.L. (1978) 'Developmental Process in the Chinese Domestic Group', Wolf, A.P. (ed.) -- Studies in Chinese Society:183-360

Croizier, R., Chen, C.S., & Ho, S.P.S. (1975) 'Symposium: Taiwan in Chinese History', Journal of Asian Studies, 34(2)

Davis, D. (1989) 'Chinese Social Welfare: Policies and Outcomes', China Quarterly, 119:577-597

De Vos, G.A. & Hsu, M.T. (1985) Minority Status and Coping Strategies: An Illustration from Korean, Japanese and Taiwanese Aborigines, Symposium on the Minorities on Chinese Border Area, 1365-1392. (National Chengchi University Press, Taipei)

Diamond, N.(1975) 'Women Under Kuomingtang Rule, Variations on the Feminine Mystique', Modern China, 1(1):3-45

Diamond, N. (1979) 'Women and Industry in Taiwan', Modern China, 5(3):317-340

Dutton, M. (1988) 'Policing the Chinese Household: A Comparison of Ancient and Modern Forms', Economy and Society, 17(2):195-224

Economics, The (1988) 'Taiwan: Transition on Trial', The Economist (Survey), 1988(March 5):3-18

Freedman, M. (1961) 'The Family in China, Past and Present', Pacific Affairs, 34:223-236

Freedman, M. (1970) Family and Kinship in Chinese Society (ed.) (Standford, University Press, Standford)

Freedman, R.A., Chang, M.C., & Sun, T.H. (1982) 'Household Composition, Extended Kinship and Reproduction in Taiwan, 1973-1980', Population Studies, 36(3):395-411

Furth, C. (1987) 'Concepts of Pregnancy, Childbirth and Infancy in Ch'ing Dynasty China', Journal of Asian Studies, 46(1):7-36

Gallin, B. (1966) Hsin Hsing, Taiwan: A Village in Change (University of California Press, Berkeley) (ed.) -- Chinese Family Law and Social Change in Historical and Comparative Perspective:261-282

Greenhalgh, S. (1984) 'Networks and their Nodes: Urban Society on Taiwan', The China Quarterly, 99:529-552

Greiff, T.E. (1985) 'The Principle of Human Rights in Nationalist China', in China Quarterly, 1985:101-104, 441-461

Gronewold, S. (1982) Beautiful Merchandise: Prostitution in China 1860-1936 (Haworth Press, New York)

Hsieh, C.C. (1985) Strategy for Survival: the Foreign Policy and External Relations of the Republic of China on Taiwan, 1949-79 (The Sherwood Press, London)

Hsieh, J.C. (1982) 'The Impact of Urbanisation on Chinese Family Organisation in Taiwan', Bulletin of the Institute of Ethnology, Academic Sinica, 54:47-70

Hsiung, J.C. et al. (1981) Contemporary Republic of China: the Taiwan Experience 1950-1980 (Praeger, New York)

Hsu, F.L.K. (1943) 'The Myth of Chinese Family Size', American Journal of Sociology, 48(5):555-562

Hsu, F.L.K. (1944) 'Some Problems of Chinese Law in Operation Today', Far Eastern Quarterly, 3:211-221

Hsu, M.T. (1982) 'Ethnic Identity and Intercultural Interaction in Taiwan', Wu, D.Y.H. (ed.) -- Ethnicity and Interpersonal Interaction: A Cross-cultural Study:199-211 (Maruzen Asia, Hong Kong)

Hsu, M.T. (1987) 'Psychological Adaption of Two Malayo-Polynesian Cultures in Taiwan', Ph.D. Dissertation, University of California, Berkeley

Hsu, M.T. (1991) Culture, Self, and Adaptation: the Psychological Anthropology of Two Malayo-Polynesian Groups in Taiwan (Institute of Ethnology, Academia Sinica, Taipei)

Hwang, K.K. (1987) 'Face and Favour: the Chinese Power Game', American Journal of Sociology, 92:944-974

Jejeebhoy, S.J. (1981) 'Cohort Consistency in Family Size Preferences: Taiwan, 1965-1973', Studies in Family Planning, 12(5):229-232

Judd, E.R. (1989) 'Chinese Women and Their Natal Families', The Journal of Asian Studies, 48(3):525-544

Judicial Yuan, Republic of China (1982a) 'A Brief Introduction to the Juvenile Court System of the Republic of China', Juvenile Courts of the Republic of China:1-5 (Judicial Yuan, ROC)

Judicial Yuan, Republic of China (1982b) 'A Brief Introduction to the Probation System of Juvenile Case of the Republic of China', Juvenile Courts of the Republic of China:6-11 (Judicial Yuan, ROC)

Judicial Yuan, Republic of China (1992) Major Statutes of the Republic of China: Volume II: Civil and Criminal Statutes (Judicial Yuan, ROC)

Kao, R. (1988) 'Taiwan', Report of the International Seminar on Women and Tourism, April 20-23, 1988, Seoul and Cheju Island, Korea

Kao, R. (1991) 'Child Prostitution and Tourism in Taiwan', Srisang, K. (ed.) -- Caught in Modern Slavery:60-62

Kesson, W (1975) Childhood in China (Yale University Press)

Kim, H.I. (1981) Fundamental Legal Concepts of China and the West: A Comparative Study (Kennikat Press, Port Washington, New York)

Kulp, D.H. (1925) Country Life in South China (Teachers College, Columbia University, New York)

Lang, O. (1946) Chinese Family and Society (Yale University Press, New Haven)

Law Revision Planning Group, the Executive Yuan, Republic of China (1961) Laws of the Republic of China: Major Laws

Lee, J.J. (1986) 'Preventing Juvenile Delinquency in Taiwan', International Journal of Comparative and Applied Criminal Justice, 10(2):205-213

Lee, J.J. (1988) 'Corrections in Taiwan (Republic of China)', International Journal of Comparative and Applied Criminal Justice, 12(1):95-100

Lee, K.T. (1988) 'Population Policy and Family Planning', The Evaluation of Policy behind Taiwan's Development Success:66-82 (Yale University Press)

Lee, L.T. & Lai, W.W. (1984) 'The Chinese Concepts of Law: Confucian, Legalist, and Buddhist', Redden, K.R. (eds) -- Modern Legal Systems Cyclopedia, 2:585-601

Leslie, G.R. (1973) 'The Family System of China'. -- The Family in Social Context:80-121

Levy, M.J. (1949) The Family Revolution in Modern China (Harvard University Press, Cambridge)

Li, K.T. (1985) 'Contributions of Women in the Labour Force to Economic Development in Taiwan, the Republic of China', Industry of Free China, 1985 (August):1-8

Li, K.T. (1988a) 'Urban and Population Decentralisation Policies: The Experience of Taiwan', Industry of Free China, 1988 (January):1-14

Li, K.T. (1988b) 'Basic Consideration in Social Welfare Planning for the ROC', Industry of Free China, 1988 (February):1-6

Li, V.H. (1978) Law Without Lawyers: A Comparative View of Law in China and the United States (Westview Press/Boulder, Colorado)

Lin, Y.J. (1975) Morality and Chinese Traditional Law (National Chung-hsiung University, Taipei)

Liu, A.P.L. (1982) Social Change on Mainland China and Taiwan, 1949-1980 (School of Law, University of Maryland, Maryland)

Liu, C.M. & Shih, M.L. (1992) Major Laws of the Republic of China on Taiwan I & II (eds.) (Magnificent Publishing Company, Tainan, Taiwan, ROC)

Liu, J.A. (1976) Sino-American Juvenile Justice System (San Min Book Company, Taipei, Taiwan)

Liu, J.C., Lo, A.M., Lan, F.H., & Lin, F. (1991a) Major Laws of the Republic of China (Ta Wei Book Company, Taiwan)

Liu, J.C., Lo, A.M., Lan, F.H., & Lin, F. (1991b) 'A Brief Introduction in Outline Form to the Taipei District Court', Liu, J.C. et al. -- Major Laws of the Republic of China:1886-1910

Liu, J.C., Lo, A.M., Lan, F.H., & Lin, F. (1991c) 'A Brief Introduction to the Procuratorial System of the Republic of China', Liu, J.C. et al. -- Major Laws of the Republic of China: 1911-1927

Ma, H.H.P. (1985) 'General Features of the Law and Legal System of the Republic of China', (ed.) -- Trade and Investment in Taiwan:1-53

Ma, H.H.P. (1988) American Influence on the Formation of the Constitution and Constitutional Law of the Republic of China: Past History and Future Prospects', Beer, L.W. (ed.) -- Constitutionalism in Asia: Asian View of the American Influence:39-55 (University of Maryland Press, Maryland)

Martin, R. (1975) 'The Socialisation of Children in China and on Taiwan: An Analysis of Elementary School Textbooks', China Quarterly, 62:242-262

McAleavy, H. (1968) 'Chinese Law' in Derrett, J.M.D. (ed.) -- An Introduction to Legal Systems (Sweet & Maxwell)

McCaghy, C.M. & Hou, C. (1989) Career Onset of Taiwanese Prostitutes (a paper presented to the annual meeting of the Society for the Study of Social Problems, August 6-8, 1989, Berkeley, California

McCaghy, C.M. & Hou, C. (1990) 'Female Prostitution in the Republic of China (Taiwan)', Davis, N. (ed.) -- International Prostitution (Greenwood, Westport)

Meyer, J.E. (1988) 'Teaching Morality in Taiwan Schools: The Message of the Textbooks', The China Quarterly, 114:267-284

Michael, F. (1962) 'The Role of Law in Traditional, Nationalist and Communist China', The China Quarterly:124-148

Myers, R.H. (1972) 'Taiwan under Ch'ing Rule, 1684-1895: the Traditional Society', Journal of the Institute of Chinese Studies of the Chinese University of Hong Kong, 5:413-451

Netting, R., Wilk, R.R. & Arnould, E.J. (1984) Households (eds.) (University of California Press, Los Angeles)

Newton, L. & Wang, J. (1989) 'A Research Guide to Taiwan (ROC) Law', Journal of Chinese Law, 3(2):257-315

Ng, V.V. (1987) 'Ideology and Sexuality: Rape Laws in Qing China', Journal of Asian Studies, 46(1):57-70

Parish, W.L. (1978) 'Modernisation and Household Composition in Taiwan', Buxbaum, D.C. (ed.) -- Chinese Family Law and Social Change in Historical and Comparative Perspective:283-320

Pound, R. (1948a) 'Comparative Law and History as Bases for Chinese Law', Harvard Law Review, 61:749-962

Rainbow Project [RP] (1990) Research on Tourism and Prostitution in Taiwan in 1990 (unpublished paper, Rainbow Project, Taipei)

Shee, A. (1991) 'Report on Legal Problems Concerning Child Prostitution in Taiwan', a paper prepared for the ECPAT Hong Kong Lawyers Meeting held on November 11-15, 1991 (Association for the Campaign to End Child Prostitution in Taiwan, Taipei)

Shee, A. (1992) 'Model Legislation on Child Prostitution for Asian Countries: the Taiwan Report', a paper prepared for the ECPAT Bangkok International Conference to Report on the Campaign to End Child Prostitution in Asian Tourism held on March 31 - April 3, 1992 (Association for the Campaign to End Child Prostitution in Taiwan, Taipei)

Shee, A. (1994) Sold-Daughter-Prostitution and Child Protection in Taiwan: A socio-Legal Study Ph.D. Thesis, School of Law, University of Warwick, U.K.

Shiga, S. (1967) 'Some Remarks on the Judicial System in China: Historical Development and Characteristics', Journal of Asian and African Studies, 2:44-53

Speare, A. Jr. (1974) 'Migration and Family Change in Central Taiwan', Elvin, M. & Skinner, G.W. (eds.) -- The Chinese City between Two Worlds:303-330

Stacy, J. (1983) Patriarchy and Socialist Revolution in China (University of California Press, Berkeley, London)

Stainton, M. (1989) 'Taiwan / Tourism and Taiwan Aboriginal People', Lin,Y.M-J (ed.) -- Asian Consultation on Tourism and Aboriginal Peoples:43-56

Taipei Women's Rescue Foundation [TWRF] (1991) Project Lily -- Rescue Taiwan's Native Taiwanese Girls: Final Report (TWRF, Taipei)

Tao, L.S. (1971) 'Reform of the Criminal Process in Nationalist China', The American Journal of Comparative Law, 19:747-765

The Europa Year Book 1986 [A World Survey] (1986) 'China(Taiwan): Introductory Survey', The Europa Year Book 1986, 1:740-741

Thompson, S.E. (1984) 'Taiwan: Rural Society', China Quarterly, 97-100:553-568

Thornton, A., Chang, M.C.,& Sun, T.H. (1984) 'Social and Economic Change, Intergenerational Relationships and Family Formation in Taiwan', Demography, 21(4):475-499

Thornton, A., Yang, L.S., & Fricke,T. (1989) 'Weakening the Linkage between the Ancestors, the Living, and Future Generations', unpublished paper, University of Michigan

Tozer, W. (1970) 'Taiwan's 'Cultural Renaissance': A Preliminary View', China Quarterly, 43:81-99

Tsao, W.Y. (1953) The Law in China as Seen by Roscoe Pound (ed.) (China Culture Publishing Foundation, Taipei, Taiwan)

Tsay, C.H. (1989) 'Community Control from the Perspectives of National Policy and Self-Rule of Aboriginal Territories', Lin,Y.M-J (ed.) -- Asian Consultation on Tourism and Aboriginal Peoples:87-88

Tseng, S.C. (1989) 'Community Control in the Context of National Park Planning', Lin,Y.M-J (ed.) -- Asian Consultation on Tourism and Aboriginal Peoples:89-94

Tseng, W.S. & Hsu, J. (1972) 'The Chinese Attitude Toward Parental Authority as Expressed in Chinese Children's Stories', Archives of General Psychiatry, 26:28-34

Tu, E.J.C., Liang, J.S., & Li, S.M. (1989) 'Mortality Decline and Chinese Family Structure: Implications for Old Age Support', Journal of Gerontology: Social Science, 44(4): 157-168

Wang, C.F. (1988) The Status Quo and Proposed Cures for Child Prostitutes in Taiwan (unpublished paper)

Wang, C.F. (1990) A Probe into Rape, Sexual Harassment, Marital Violence, Women-mongering and Forced Prostitution in a Legal Point of View: Introduction (unpublished paper of the Female Affairs Committee, Taipei Bar Association, Taipei, Taiwan, ROC)

Wang, D.T.C. (1977) 'The Family Court System of Taiwan', International and Comparative Law Quarterly, 26:202-207

Wang, I. (1992) 'Giving Help to the Victims', ECPAT -- Children in Prostitution: 43-45

Wang, I. (1996) Give Her a Piece of Land to Grow (ECPAT,Taiwan)

Wang, I.S. (1980) 'Cultural Contact and the Migration of Taiwan's Aborigines: A Historical Perspective', Knapp, R.G. (ed.) -- China's Island Frontier: Studies in the Historical Geography of Taiwan:31-43 (University Press of Hawaii, Honolulu)

Wang, S.H. (1977) 'Family Structure and Economic Development in Taiwan', Bulletin of the Institute of Ethnology, Academic Sinica, 44:1-11

Wang, S.H. (1985) 'On the Household and Family in Chinese Society', Hsieh, J.C. & Chuang, T.C. (eds.) -- The Chinese Family and Its Ritual Behaviour (Institute of Ethnology, Academia Sinica, ROC)

Wang, S.N. (1988) Testing Criminological Theories in An Oriental Society (Bou-Win Tang Publishing Company, Taipei)

Wang, T.C. (1927) The Youth Movement in China (New Republic Inc., New York)

Ward, B.E. (1984) Through Other Eyes (The Chinese University Press, Hong Kong)

Wen, Y.T. (1966) 'The Chinese Family from Customary Law to Positive Law', in Hasting Law Journal, 17:727-765

Winckler, S.S. (1975) Family and Community in Urban Taiwan: Social Status and Demographic Strategy among Taipei Households, 1885-1935 (Ph.D. Thesis in Sociology and East Asian Languages, Harvard University, Cambridge, Massachusetts)

Wolf, A.P. (1966) 'Childhood Association, Sexual Attraction, and the Incest Taboo: A Chinese Case', American Anthropologist, 68:833-898

Wolf, A.P. (1968) 'Adopt a Daughter-in-law, Marry a Sister: A Chinese Solution to the Problem of the Incest Taboo', American Anthropologist, 70(5)

Wolf, A.P. (1970) 'Childhood Association and Sexual Attraction: A Further Test of the Westermark Hypothesis', American Anthropologist, 72(3)

Wolf, A.P. (1974) 'Marriage and Adoption in Northern Taiwan', Smith, R.J. (ed.) -- Social Organisation and the Applications of Anthropology

Wolf, A.P. (1985) 'Chinese Family Size: A Myth Revitalised', Hsieh, J.C. & Chung, Y.C. (eds.) -- The Chinese Family and Its Ritual Behaviour (Institute of Ethnology, Academic Sinica, Taipei, Taiwan, ROC)

Wong, A.K. (1979) 'The Modern Chinese Family -- Ideology, Revolution and Residues', Das, M.S. & Bardis, P.D. (eds.) -- The Family in Asia: 245-276

Wu, D.Y.H. (1981) 'Child Abuse in Taiwan', Korbin, J.E. (ed.) -- Child Abuse and Neglect, Cross-Cultural Perspectives:138-165

Wu, Y.L. (1985) Becoming An Industrialised Nation, ROC's Development on Taiwan (Eastbourne, New York)

Yang, C.S. (1987) 'Career Judiciary in the Republic of China', Cheng-Chi University Law Review:122-159

Yang, K.S. (1988) 'Three Normal and Deviant Syndromes of Chinese Youth: Quantitative Differentiation and Psychological Profiles', a paper presented in the International Conference between Taiwan and the United States of America on Social and Psychological Factors in Juvenile Delinquency, August 1-5, 1988, Taipei

Yang, M.M.C. (1962) 'Changes in Family Life in Rural Taiwan', Journal of Chinese Society, 2:68-79

Zeng, Y. (1986) 'Changes in Family Structure in China: A Simulation Study', Population and Development Review, 12(4):675-703

II. LAWS OF THE REPUBLIC OF CHINA

A. Basic Laws/ General Laws

* Constitution of the Republic of China 1947/Additional Articles of the ROC Constitution 1992

* Civil Code (Book I) 1982 (Amendment)

* Civil Code (Book IV) 1985 (Amendment), 1996 (Amendment)

* The Code of Civil Procedure 1990 (Amendment)
* Criminal Code 1969 (Amendment)
* The Code of Criminal Procedure 1990 (Amendment)
* Law Governing the Disposition of Juvenile Cases 1980 (Amendment)

B. Administrative Laws

* Child Welfare Act 1973 & 1993 (Amendment)
* Juvenile Welfare Act 1989
* Social Order Maintenance Law 1991 (replace Police Offence Law 1954)

C. Specific Law

* Law to Suppress Sexual Transactions Involving Children and Juveniles

III. NEWSPAPERS IN TAIWAN

* The China Post

BIBLIOGRAPHY III : Chinese References

I. BOOKS, ARTICLES, DISSERTATIONS, REPORTS

Chang, K.M. 張甘妹 (1982)

'Problems of the Probation System in Taiwan, the Republic of China',
我國觀護制度上之諸問題。刑事法雜誌，第30卷，第5期，1-17頁。

Chang, W.Z. 張偉仁 (1987)

'Traditional Ethics and the Modern Chinese Legal System -- Why Learn Chinese Legal History',
傳統觀念與現行法制 -- 「為什麼要學中國法制史」一解 --。台大法學論叢，第17卷，第1期，1-64頁。

Chao, K.C. 趙貴忠 (1988)

Tears and Blood of Girl Prostitutes -- Extreme Sorrows in Silence (ed.)
雛妓血淚 -- 無聲的悲情。台北：彩虹婦女事工中心。

Chao, Y.S. 趙雍生 (1989)

'Influence of Family Factors on Juvenile Delinquency',
家庭因素對青少年偏差行為的影響。社區發展季刊，第45期，85-87頁。

Chen, B.C. 陳伯璋 (1991)

'Problems of Education',
教育問題。楊國樞、葉啓政主編：台灣的社會問題。台北：巨流。

Chen, C. 陳貞 (1988)

'Are Children in Taiwan Worthless? Children's Rights Report in Taiwan',
台灣的小孩不值錢？ 台灣兒童人權報告。台灣人權，第6期，20-24頁。

Chen, C.H. 陳志宏 (1993)

'My Opinions on the Girl Prostitution Prevention and Treatment Law',
雛妓防治法之我見。勵馨園雜誌，第31期，4-5頁。

Chen, C.L. & Cheng, F.W. 陳政亮、鄭斐文 (1994)

'A Brief Description of the Girl Prostitution Rescue Work',
雛妓救援側寫（摘錄）, 婦女救援基金會會訊, 第11期, 13-15頁。

Chen, C.M. 陳皎眉 (1995)

'A Discussion of the Family and Personal Factors of Girl Prostitution and the Strategies to Deal With It',
雛妓的家庭與個人因素及其對策之探討, 律師通訊, 第187期, 12-19頁。

Chen, C.T. 陳志東 (1996)

Why do We Need to Rescue the Girl Prostitutes?',
為什麼要救援從娼少女？ 婦女救援基金會會訊, 第17期, 第19頁。

Chen, C.Y. 陳棋炎 (1984)

'The Family System under the ROC Civil Code',
論吾國民法上之家制。台大法學論叢，第13卷，第2期，151-173頁。

Chen, H.C. 陳煥生 (1983)

A Practical Textbook on the Special Provisions of the ROC Criminal Code (San Min, Taipei)

刑法分則實用。台北：三民。

Chen, H.N. 陳慧女 (1992)

'An Analysis on the Personal and Family Backgrounds of Girl Prostitutes and Their Run-away Behaviour',
從娼少女之各人及家庭特質與其逃家行爲之分析。東吳大學社會學研究所社會工作組碩士論文。

Chen, K.C, Wang, T.M, Chen, W.L. 陳寬政、王德睦、陳文玲 (1986)

'Causes and Results of Population Changes in Taiwan',
台灣地區人口變遷的原因與結果。台灣大學人口學刊，第9期，1-23頁。

Chen,K.C., Wang T.M., Chen, W.L. 陳寬政、王德睦、陳文玲 (1991)

'The Population Problems',
人口問題。楊國樞、葉啓政主編：台灣的社會問題。台北：巨流。

Chen, M.L. 陳美鈴 (1991a)

'The Customer of Illegal Prostitution Should Also Be Punished',
罰娼亦應罰嫖。婦援會訊，第6期，13-19頁。

Chen, M.L. 陳美鈴 (1991d)

'Be Aware of the Lust Trap. It May Destroy Your Beautiful Life -- The TWRF Preventive Social Educational Activities: The Introductory Report',
小心色情陷阱，毀掉美麗一生：預防宣導系列活動說明報告。婦援會訊，第 7 期，17-22頁。

Chen, M.L. 陳美鈴 (1992)

'A Life Description of GOP-A Midway Home',
「勵馨園-中途之家」生活點滴, 勵馨園雜誌, 第26期, 第4頁。

Chen, M.L. 陳美鈴 (1995)

'It is Said That She Is Voluntary',
聽說她是自願的, 勵馨園雜誌, 第1期, 第10-11頁。

Chen, M.L. 陳美鈴 (1996)

'A Behavioural Study on The Unfortunate Girls Who Got Involved in Girl Prostitution',
不幸少女淪落色情行業之行爲研究--以省立雲林教養院收容對象爲例,社會福利, 第124期,第55-56頁

Chen, P.C. 陳樸生 (1981)

'The 'Rechts Gut' of the Victims of Sex Crimes',
性犯罪之被害法益。法令月刊，第63期，63-67頁。

Chen, P.H. 陳炳宏 (1970)

'A Study of State Control over Prostitution: Suggestions for Making Improvements',
如何改進社會風化管制問題之研究。政治大學公共行政研究所碩士論文。

Chen, YiChen 陳怡真 (1989)

God Pity the Helpless
天意憐孤草。台北：台北市婦女救援基金會。

Cheng, C.T. 鄭健才 (1981)

General Principles of the ROC Criminal Code
刑法總則。台北：三民。

Cheng, I.S. 鄭怡世 (1993)

'Child, I'll Bring You Towards Sunshine',
孩子, 我帶你走向陽光, 勵馨園雜誌, 第33期, 第10-11頁。

Cheng, R.L. 鄭瑞隆 (1986)
'An Assessment of the Seriousness of the Problem of Child Abuse in Taiwan',
我國兒童被虐待嚴重性之評估研究。文化大學兒童福利研究所碩士論文。

Cheng, S.Y. 鄭淑燕 (1990)
'A Proposal for the Amendment of the ROC Child Welfare Law',
我國兒童福利法修訂取向。社區發展季刊，第50期，140-144頁。

Chi, H.J. 紀惠容 (1993)
'The Call for the "Anti Girl Prostitution Campaign" is Ringing',
「反雛妓」的號角正響起, 勵馨園雜誌, 第33期, 第4-5頁。

Chi, H.J. 紀惠容 (1995a)
'Law Itself Is Not Enough: Prevention and Treatment of Girl Prostitution Still Needs Hard Work',
徒法不足以自行,雛妓防治仍待努力, 勵馨園雜誌, 第3期, 第1頁.

Chi, H.J. 紀惠容 (1995b)
'A Study on the News Reports About Girl Prostitution ',
雛妓新聞處理之探討, 台大新聞論壇, 第3期, 第1卷, 第22-51頁。

Chi, H.J. 紀惠容 (1995c)
'The Public Relations Princess-The Poison With Sugar-coat ',
毒藥糖衣--公關公主, 勵馨園雜誌, 第1期, 第3頁。

Chi, H.J. 紀惠容 (1995d)
'Public Interests Groups vs. Social Movements',
公益團體 vs 社會運動, 勵馨園雜誌, 第1期, 第2頁。

Chi, H.J. 紀惠容 (1996a)
'Is the Media a Killer or a Contributor?',
媒體是殺手還是功臣, 勵馨園雜誌, 第8期第2卷, 第2頁。

Chi, H.J. 紀惠容 (1996b)
'When "Watching(the People)" is Staring At "Doing(the Government)"',
當Watching 盯上Doing, 勵馨園雜誌, 第9期第2卷, 第2頁。

Chi, H.J. 紀惠容 (1996c)
'The Advertisement Traps Are Looking Less and Less Dangerous',
陷阱廣告越來越不「陷阱」, 勵馨園雜誌, 第10期, 第5頁。

Chi, H.J. 紀惠容 (1996d)
'Preventive Education and Human Value',
預防教育與人性價值, 終止童妓雙月刊, 第8-9期, 第24頁。

Chi, H.J. 紀惠容 (1996e)
' "It is Said That She is Voluntary"-Making A Film About Girls' Protection',
「聽說她是自願的」少女保護短片推出, 勵馨園雜誌, 第6期, 第9-11頁。

Chi, H.J. 紀惠容 (1996f)
'Applauding for the Law Enforcers to Challenge the Lust Industry',
爲公權力挑戰色情工業喝采！ 勵馨園雜誌, 第10期, 第2頁。

Chi, H.J. 紀惠容 (1996g)
' "Bad" Girl, You Aren't In Fault!',

「壞」女孩, 錯不在你！勵馨園雜誌, 第11期, 第2頁。

Chi, H.J. 紀惠容 (1996h)

'Anti-Girl-Prostitution Campaign Steps Into Another Strategic Point',
「反雛妓」運動跨向另一「關」, 勵馨園雜誌, 第6期, 第2頁。

Chi, H.J. 紀惠容 (1997)

'Calling for the Birth of the "Child Sexual Abuse Treatment Centre" ',
爲「兒童性侵害治療中心」催生, 勵馨園雜誌, 第13期, 第2頁。

Chi, L. 齊力 (1990)

'A Study of the Trend of Nuclearisation of Family Households in Taiwan Over the Past Twenty Years',
台灣地區近二十年來家戶核心化趨勢的研究。國立台灣大學社會學刊， 第20期，41-83頁。

Chiang, H.S. 江漢聲 (1994)

'Consuming Girl Prostitution: A Pitiful and Immature Conception of Sex',
嫖雛妓--是幼稚可悲的性觀念--採陰補陽的文化考證, 勵馨園雜誌, 第34期, 第6頁。

Child Welfare League Foundation (CWLF) 兒童福利聯盟文教基金會 (1991)

A Proposal for the Amendment of Child Welfare Law
兒童福利法修正案。台北：兒童福利聯盟文教基金會。

Chinese Children's Foundation (CCF) 中華兒童福利基金會 (1990)

Child Protection Annual Report July 1989 - June 1990
兒童保護年報。中華兒童福利基金會。

Ching, W. 井雯 (1992)

'My Encountering',
我的遭遇, 勵馨園雜誌, 第26期, 第4頁。

Chou, C.C. 周建卿 (1986)

'Evolution and Prospects of the Child Welfare Policy and Legislation in Taiwan, the Republic of China',
我國兒童福利政策及立法的演進和展望。社區發展季刊，第33期，26-35頁。

Chou, C.I. 周晴燕 (1994)

'Oh! They Are All Just Children',
啊！都是孩子呀！婦女救援基金會會訊, 第11期, 第4頁。

Chou, C.O. 周震歐 (1991)

Child Welfare
兒童福利。台北：巨流。

Chou, J.T. 周瑞德 (1996a)

'Why Don't They Go Home? Caring About The Run-Away and Street Juveniles is Our Common Duty',
他們爲什麼不回家？關懷街頭遊蕩青少年不分你我, 終止童妓雙月刊, 第6期, 第6-7頁。

Chou, J.T. 周瑞德 (1996b)

'My Accounts on the Investigative Journey to NGOs in Hong-Kong and Macao',
港澳機構考察團隨行見聞, 終止童妓雙月刊, 第7期, 第12-14頁。

Chou, P.E. 周碧娥 (1991)
'Women Issues',
婦女問題。楊國樞、葉啓政主編：台灣的社會問題。台北：巨流。
Chou, P.J. 周佩蓉 (1996)
'The Implementation Report on the Law to Suppress Sexual Transactions Involving Children And Juveniles',
兒童及少年性交易防制條例實施現況, 勵馨園雜誌, 第6期,第7-8頁。
Chou, P.J. 周佩蓉 (1996a)
'Record of the Public Hearing on the Examination of Rescue Work',
救援總體檢公聽會紀實, 勵馨園雜誌, 第10期第6卷, 第6頁。
Chou, P.J. 周佩蓉 (1996b)
'Wear It , Then You Are The Guardian of Children--The Spreading Daisy Activity',
戴上它, 您就是孩子的守護神-雛菊散播行動, 勵馨園雜誌, 第8期, 第20-21頁。
Chou, P.J. 周佩蓉 (1996c)
'Petition to Government on September the Nineteenth',
九一九中央部會請願, 勵馨園雜誌, 第10期 ,第10-11頁。
Chou, Y.Y. 邱月雲 (1995)
'Responses of the Taipei City Social Welfare Bureau to the Law to Suppress Sexual Transactions Involving Children and Juveniles ',
談「兒童及少年性交易防制條例」通過後台北市政府社會局之因應措施,福利社會雙月刊, 第51期, 第26-35頁.
Chu, H.Y. 瞿海源 (1991a)
'Problems of Lust and Prostitution',
色情與娼妓問題。楊國樞、葉啓政主編：台灣的社會問題。台北：巨流。
Chu, H.Y. 瞿海源 (1991b)
'The Problems of Gambling and Speculation',
賭博與投機問題。楊國樞、葉啓政主編：台灣的社會問題。台北：巨流。
Chu, H.Y. 瞿海源 (1996)
'Preventive Education and Human Value',
預防教育與人性價值, 終止童妓雙月刊, 第8-9期, 第22-23頁。
Chu, M.L. 褚玫玲 (1990)
'Welfare State and Legal System ',
福利國家與法律體系。社會建設，第62期，4-10頁。
Chueh, H.C. 闕漢中 (1995)
'A Brief Introduction to the Palm Assessment on the "Little Daisy Hope Network" '
簡介「雛菊希望網路」計劃評估, 勵馨園雜誌, 第2期, 第15頁。
Chiou, C.J. 邱嘉蓉 (1996)
'Is It Really Her Fault?',
真是她的錯？ 勵馨園雜誌, 第6期, 第19頁。
Chiou, I.N. 丘彥南 (1993)
'Who Can Give Her A Hand?-the Need for Long-lasting Treatment of the Girl Prostitutes',
誰來拉她一把?--談雛妓漫長的心裡復建歷程和需要, 勵馨園雜誌, 第31期, 第6-7頁。

Chiou, Y.C. 邱玉珍 (1995)

'He Is Only Sixteen , and He Is for Sale',
他只有16歲, 他可以賣, 自立早報, 第5版。

Chu, H.Y. 瞿海源 (1993)

'Sincerely Facing The Phenomenon and Problems of Girl Prostitution',
誠心面對雛妓現象及問題, 勵馨園雜誌, 第33期, 第6頁。

Good Shepherd Sisters Foundation(GSS) 天主教善牧基金會 (1996)

'Experiences of GSS in Taiwan: Report to the International Congress Against Commercial Sexual Exploitation of Children',
善牧的台灣經驗: 致「反對兒童商業化性剝削世界大會」報告書。 台北:善牧基金會。

Han, C.M. 韓忠謨 (1967)

'Legislative Problems of Laws Concerning Offences Against Social Morals and Offences Against Marriage and the Family',
關於妨害風化及婚姻家庭罪立法問題之商榷。刑事法雜誌，第11卷，第2期，11-25頁。

Han, C.M. 韓忠謨 (1980)

The ROC Criminal Code: Special Provisions
刑法各論。台北：自版。

Hong, W.H. 洪文惠 (1995)

'A Study on the Causes of Girl Prostitution',
未成年少女從娼原因之探討, 律師通訊, 第187期, 第20-23頁。

Hsia, C.C. 夏鑄九 (1991)

'The Urban Problems',
都市問題。楊國樞、葉啓政主編：台灣的社會問題。台北：巨流。

Hsieh, K. 謝 康 (1972)

The Commercial Sex Institution and the Prostitution Problem in Taiwan
賣淫制度與台灣娼妓問題。台北：古風。

Hsien, K. 謝 康 (1982)

'A Comparative Study of Chinese and Foreign Prostitutes',
中外娼妓問題比較研究。中外社會問題比較研究。台北：中央文物。

Hsien, K. 謝 康 (1987)

'Prostitution and Sex Crimes',
論性犯罪與娼妓問題。政治評論，第45卷，第9期，43-48頁。

Hsieh, K.C. 謝高橋 (1980a)

'Movements of Urban Population in Taiwan： the Migration Model of Kaohsiung City and the Life Adjustments of Migrants',
台灣地區城市人口遷移之研究--高雄市人口遷移模式與移動者的生活適應。 台北：政大民社系人口調查研究室。

Hsieh, K.C. 謝高橋 (1980b)

'Composition, Structure and Breeds of Family Households',
家戶組成、結構與生育。台北：政大民社系人口調查研究室。

Hsieh, M.E. 謝美娥 (1990)

'The U.S. Family Support Act 1988 -- A Milestone towards Social Welfare',

美國一九八八年的家庭維持法 -- 社會福利的新里程碑。美國月刊，第5卷， 第7期，111-118頁。

Hsieh, Y.N. 謝永年 (1977a)
'A Brief History of Prostitution (I)',
煙花滄桑（一）娼妓制度小史。中外雜誌，第22卷，第1期。

Hsieh, Y.N. 謝永年 (1977b)
'A Brief History of Prostitution (II)',
煙花滄桑（二）娼妓制度小史。中外雜誌，第22卷，第2期。

Hsieh, Y.W. 謝友文 (1987)
ROC Policy and Laws Concerning Child and Juvenile Welfare
青少年兒童福利政策與法規彙編。台北：桂冠。

Hsieh, Y.W. 謝友文 (1991a)
A Proposal for the Amendment of the ROC Child Welfare Law
修正我國兒童福利法之芻議。台北：兒福聯盟。

Hsieh, Y.W. 謝友文 (1991b)
'What Are Children's Rights?',
兒童福利知多少？--別讓童權睡著了。謝文友：給孩子一個安全童年， 22-27頁。台北：牛頓。

Hsieh, Y.W. 謝友文 (1993)
'The Newly Amended Child Welfare Law Will Work Together with You for Child Protection',
兒童福利法與您一起保護孩子。學前教育，1993年3月，56頁。

Hsu, C.L. 許金鈴 (1988)
'A Study of Institutional Correction of Illegal Prostitutes',
台北市廣慈博愛院輔導違警私娼之研究。台北市廣慈博愛院七十七年度研 究報告。

Hsu, C.L. 許金鈴 (1989)
'A Study of the Guidance and Counselling Services for Girl Prostitutes under the Juvenile Welfare Law',
從少年福利法談從娼少女輔導工作。社區發展季刊，第46期，82-84頁。

Hsu, C.Y. 徐朝陽 (1968)
The Origins of Chinese Family Law
中國親屬法溯源。台北：商務。

Hsu, M.C. 許木柱 (1991a)
'Problems of the Inferior People',
弱勢族群問題。楊國樞、葉啓政主編：台灣的社會問題。台北：巨流。

Hsiao, H.C. 蕭宏祺 (1996)
'Sexual Tourists-Does the New Law Really Protect Children's Rights?',
起訴「性觀光客」-新法真的保障了兒童的權益嗎？ 終止童妓雙月刊, 第5期, 第15-17頁。

Huang, F.Y. 黃富源 (1996)
'Punishment of the Perpetrators Under the Law to Suppress Sexual Transactions Involving Children and Juveniles ',
「兒童及少年性交易防治條例」執行現況與加害者之處罰, 終止童妓雙月刊, 第

8-9期,第10-11頁。

Huang, K.K. 黃光國 (1991)

'The Corruption Problems',

貪污問題。楊國樞、葉啓政主編：台灣的社會問題。台北：巨流。

Huang, S.L. 黃淑玲 (1990)

'A Study of the Prostitution Problems and the State Policies (I & II)',

娼妓問題與政策的探討（上、下）。婦女新知，第100期，11-13頁，第101期, 27-29頁。

Huang, Y.C. 黃怡君 (1991a)

The Girl Prostitution Problem, and the Rescue, Protection, Care Settlement of Girl Prostitutes in Taiwan: Evaluation and Suggestions

台灣雛妓問題現況及救援、保護安置成效之檢討與建議。台北市婦女救援 基金會報告。

Huang, S.L. 黃淑玲 (1995)

'A Study on The Causes of Girl Prostitution and the Living Conditions of the Minor Girls Who Work in the Sex Industry--The Distinctions between "Voluntary" and "Sold", "Aborigines" and "The Han People" ',

未成年少女從事色情行業的原因與生活狀況之探討--「自願」與「被賣」、原住民與漢人的差異, 律師通訊, 第187期, 第8-11頁。

Hu, S.H. 胡昇華 (1996)

'Observing the Girl Prostitution Problem in Terms of "Cost" ',

從「成本」看雛妓問題, 勵馨園雜誌, 第9期, 第19頁。

Jen, I.A. 任一安 (1996)

'Health and Settlement',

健康與安置, 終止童妓雙月刊, 第8-9期, 第25-26頁。

Kao, D.L., Wang, M.J., Wong, H.Y., Ho, S.C. 高迪理、王明仁、翁慧圓、何素秋 (1991)

A Study of the Recognition, Attitude and Willingness of the Paediatrician in the Management of the Child Abuse Problem

小兒科醫生對「兒童虐待問題」的認知、態度、意願之研究。中華兒童福利基金會。

Kao, M. 高 邁 (1988)

'Historical Studies on Chinese Prostitution Institutions',

中國娼妓制度之歷史的搜究，118-127 頁。中國婦女史論集。台北：稻香。

Kao, R. 高李麗珍 (1993)

'Human Rights of the Child and Child Prostitution',

兒童人權與童妓, 終止童妓雙月刊, 第8期,第2-3頁。

Kao, R. 高李麗珍 (1995a)

'Past、Present , and Future',

過去、現在、未來, 終止童妓雙月刊, 第1期, 第2頁。

Kao, R. 高李麗珍 (1995b)

'The End of the Year',

歲暮, 終止童妓雙月刊, 第4期, 第2-4頁。

Kuo, C.C. 郭振昌 (1990)

'Reviews and Prospects: Dr. Sun, Yat Sen's 'The Principle of Livelihood', Welfare

State and Welfare Policy', 民生主義，福利國家及福利政策之反省與展望。中山社會科學季刊， 第5卷，第3期，148-158頁。

Lai, W.C. 賴文珍 (1995)

'Fruits of the Counselling Programmes',
輔導會談心得, 勵馨園雜誌, 第2期, 第9頁。

Lai, W.C. 賴文珍 (1996)

'In the "Hope" Network',
在「希望」中, 勵馨園雜誌, 第9期, 第6頁。

Li, C.C. 李清泉 (1995)

'The Context and Traits of the "Law to Suppress Sexual Transactions Involving Children and Juveniles" ',
「兒童及少年性交易防治條例」內容與特色初探, 社區發展季刊第72期,第189-195頁.

Li, C.W. 李佳玟 (1995)

'An Analysis on Child Prostitution: Strategies for Prevention and Treatment',
未成年從娼制度之初步分析-兼論防治策略, 法律學刊, 第25期, 第43-63頁。

Li, C.Y. 李欽勇 (1988)

'Develop A Welfare State System in the Post Chiang, Ching Kuo Era',
開展「後蔣經國時代」福利國家體制。社會福利，第298期，52-56頁。

Li, L.F. 李麗芬 (1995a)

'Lobbying for Legislation To Punish the Child Sex Tourists',
促修法嚴懲出國嫖童妓之人, 終止童妓雙月刊,第8、9期, 第4頁.

Li, L.F. 李麗芬 (1995b)

'Will Your Child Stay At Home Tonight?',
你的孩子今晚會在家嗎？ 終止童妓雙月刊, 第1期, 第3頁。

Li, L.F. 李麗芬 (1995c)

'About ECPAT',
關於終止童妓協會的大小事, 終止童妓雙月刊, 第4期, 第5-6頁。

Li, L.F. 李麗芬 (1996a)

'Sex Tourism And Trafficking',
性觀光業與運輸, 終止童妓雙月刊, 第8-9期, 第20-21頁。

Li, L.F. 李麗芬 (1996b)

'Children Have Become the Victims of the Internet Sex Industry',
兒童已淪爲色情網路的犧牲品, 終止童妓雙月刊, 第7期, 第10頁。

Li, L.F. 李麗芬 (1996c)

'The Perfect Tourists--Refuse The Sex Adventure',
完全旅行家--拒絕粉味冒險, 終止童妓雙月刊, 第8-9期, 第40頁。

Li, M.C. 李美琴 (1992)

'A Study of the Girl Prostitution Problem in Taiwan (I)&(II)',
雛妓問題之研究（上）（下）。法務通訊，1992 年，6 月。

Li, M.L. 李玫玲 (1995)

'An Analysis On The Annual Review on the Work of the Dandelion Centre',
蒲公英週年成果分析, 勵馨園雜誌, 第2期, 第3-4頁。

Li, M.L. 李玫玲 (1996)

'How Should The Dandelion Centre Work In The Future?',
蒲公英未來怎麼走？勵馨園雜誌, ;第2期, 第5頁。

Li, M.Y. 李明玉 (1993)
'Let The Dreams of The Mountain Girls Come True',
圓山中小女孩的夢, 終止童妓雙月刊, 第8期, 第10-11頁。

Li, T.C. 李子春 (1996a)
'A Review on The Specialist Squads of the Police and the Procurators' Office ',
「兒童及少年性交易防治條例」規定成立「檢警方專責任務編組」平議, 婦女救援基金會會訊, 第17期, 第20-21頁.

Li, T.C. 李子春 (1996b)
'The Executive Condition of The 'Child And Juvenile Sexual Trade Prevention and Treatment Law' and The Punishment to The Perpetrators',
「兒童及少年性交易防制條例」執行現況與加害者處罰, 終止童妓雙月刊, 第8-9期, 第6-9頁。

Li, T.C. 李子春 (1996c)
'Punishment of the Perpetrators and the "Law to Suppress Sexual Transactions Involving Children and Juveniles" ',
「兒童及少年性交易防制條例」犯罪行爲法律執行探討。

Li, Y.C. 李易駿 (1990)
'A Thorny Path to Social Welfare: the Case of the ROC on Taiwan',
荊棘中的台灣福利之路。中國論壇。第359期，66-69頁。

Liao, C.H. 廖正宏 (1991)
'Problems of Farm Villages',
農村問題。楊國樞、葉啓政主編：台灣的社會問題。台北：巨流。

Liao, B.Y. 廖碧英 (1996)
'Do They Deserve It?!--An Analysis on Sex Perpetrators',
他們是自找的？！-剖析性侵害者, 勵馨園雜誌, 第10期, 第12頁。

Lin, C.C., Yeh, C.L. & Hsieh, C.T. 林志嘉、葉菊蘭、謝啓大 (1996)
'A Discussion on the "Law to Suppress Sexual Transactions Involving Children and Juveniles" by Legislators of The Three Political Parties ',
三黨立委談「兒童少年性交易防制條例」, 勵馨園雜誌, 第11期, 第11-13頁。

Lin, C.H. 林清祥 (1988)
Protection and Punishment of Delinquent Juveniles
少年行爲保護與處罰。台北：書泉。

Lin, C.Y. 林振裕 (1990)
'Social Welfare Policy and Social Development in Taiwan, the Republic of China',
我國社會福利政策與社會發展。社會建設，第62期，11-16頁。

Lin, F.M. 林芳玫 (1996)
'Media Ethics And Lust Advertisement',
媒體倫理與色情廣告, 終止童妓雙月刊, 第8-9期, 第16-17頁。

Lin, I.C. 林羿君 (1995)
'The Role of Preventive Education in Handling the Problem of Child Prostitution',
預防教育在兒童賣淫問題上的角色, 終止童妓雙月刊, 第2期, 第14-16頁。

Lin, J.P. 林瑞彬 (1994)

'Is the Title of 'Girl Prostitution Prevention And Treatment Law' Appropriate?',
「雛妓防治法」名稱好不好,勵馨園雜誌,第34期,第三卷,第三頁.

Lin, S.F. 林聖芬 (1996)
'Media Ethics And Lust Advertisement',
媒體倫理與色情廣告, 終止童妓雙月刊, 第8-9期, 第14-15頁。

Lin, S.L. 林松齡 (1991)
'The Poverty Problems',
貧窮問題。楊國樞、葉啓政主編：台灣的社會問題。台北：巨流。

Lin, S.T. 林山田 (1976)
'Offences of Rape',
論強姦罪與輪姦罪。刑事法雜誌，第23卷，第1期，7-20頁。

Lin, S.Y. 林勝義 (1988)
Child Welfare Administration
兒童福利行政。台北：五南。

Lin, W.Y. 林萬億 (1990)
'Charity and Gambling -- the Pitfalls of Social Welfare',
愛心與賭博 -- 社會福利的困境。自立晚報，民國79年年11月八日，第5版。

Lin, Y.C. 林毓君 (1995)
'How to Prevent And Treat the Trauma of Sexual Abuse for Children',
如何預防及處遇孩子受到性傷害, 終止童妓雙月刊, 第3期, 第17-18頁

Lin, Y.H. 林益厚 (1989)
'Relations between Population Changes and Family Household Composition： the Taiwan Model',
人口變遷與家戶組成之關係：台灣地區之模擬分析。私立東海大學社會學研 究所博士論文。

Lin, Y.R. 林永榮 (1982)
A Comparative Study of Customary Chinese Law and Modern Western Law
中國固有法律與西洋現代法律之比較。台北：中央文物供應社。

Lin, Y.S, 林永頌 (1993a)
Why Do We Need A 'Girl Prostitution Prevention and Treatment Law' ?
爲什麼要制定「雛妓防治法」? 台北市勵馨福利事業基金會。

Lin, Y.S, 林永頌 (1993b)
'A Brief Introduction to the Girl Prostitution Prevention and Treatment Law',
雛妓防治法之簡介。勵馨園雜誌，第31期，2-3頁。

Lin, Y.S, 林永頌 (1993c)
'Legal Problems of Girl Prostitution',
雛妓的法律問題,勵馨園雜誌, 第31期, 4-5頁.

Lin, Y.S, 林永頌 (1995)
'A Brief Introduction to the Girl Prostitution Prevention And Treatment Law',
雛妓防治法簡介,律師通訊, 第187期, 第37-44頁.

Lin, Y.T. 林詒彤 (1978)
'Parent-Child Relationship and Juvenile Crimes',
親子關係與少年犯罪。警學叢刊, 第8卷, 第3期, 91-96頁。

Liu, I.C. 劉怡君 (1995)

'A Public Hearing for the Promotion of Children's Rights: the Ministry of Foreign Affairs Declares The Intention of ROC To Be Abided by the UN Convention of the Rights of the Child',
促進兒童權利公聽會-外交部對外發表聲明我國遵守聯合國兒童權利公約的意願, 終止童妓雙月刊, 第3期, 第4-5頁。

Liu, L.C. 劉良純 (1977)
A Study of the Legal Status of Women under the Chinese Laws
婦女法律地位之研究。台北:商務。

Liu, Y.M. 呂英敏 (1976a)
'A Study of the Prostitution Problem in Taiwan',
台灣娼妓問題之研究。中央警官學校警政研究所碩士論文。

Liu, Y.M. 呂英敏 (1976b)
'Origins and Evolution of Chinese Prostitution Institution',
中國娼妓制度之起源及演變。今日中國，第60期，19-22頁。

Liu, Y.M. 呂英敏 (1976c)
'Regulation of Prostitution in Taiwan',
台灣娼妓之管理。今日中國，第60期，49-65頁。

Liu, Y.M. 呂英敏 (1976d)
'The Pros and Cons of Regulating Prostitution in Taiwan',
台灣娼妓之存廢。警光，第236期，22-25頁。

Lu, Y.H. 呂又慧 (1995a)
'Give the Little Daisy New Hopes',
給雛菊新希望, 勵馨園雜誌 ,第1期, 第7頁。

Lu, Y.H. 呂又慧 (1995b)
'Our Needs--A Letter To The People Who Care About The Girl Prostitutes' Hope Net ',
我們的需要--給關心「雛菊希望網路」的人的一封信, 勵馨園雜誌, 第2期, 第13-14頁。

Lyu, Y.H. 呂又慧 (1996)
'Let's Be Dream Builders',
作一個築夢的人, 勵馨園雜誌, 第9期, 第3頁。

Luo, C.Y. 羅志淵 (1976)
Evolution of Modern Chinese Legal History
近代中國法制演變研究。台北：正中。

Luo, Y. 洛陽 (1992)
Administrative Law
行政法。台北：雙榜。

Ma, H.P 馬漢寶 (1987)
'Relations between Law and Social Changes Over the Past Thirty Years in Taiwan',
近三十年法律與社會變遷之關係。社會科學論叢，第35期，1-8 頁。

Pai, H.H. 白秀雄 (1973)
'Some Suggestions to the Reform of the Social Welfare System in Taiwan, the Republic of China',
對我國社會福利措施幾點革新意見。勞工保險，第21期，4-6頁。

Shang, C.T. 商正宗 (1993)

'Is The Prize Award A Joyfulness or a Worry for GOH?',
得獎是喜？是憂？勵馨園雜誌, 第33期, 第3頁。

Shee, A. 施慧玲 (1995)
'A Brief Introduction to the International Campaign to End Child Prostitution in Asian Tourism ',
國際終止亞洲觀光事業童妓運動簡介,台大婦女研究室「婦女與兩性研究通訊」,第35期,第18-19頁

Shen, M.C. 沈美真 (1989)
'The Victimised Women in Commercial Prostitution and the Problems of Criminal Law Legislation in Taiwan', 台灣娼妓營業的被害婦女與刑事立法諸問題之研究。國立台灣大學法律學研 究所碩士論文。

Shen, M.C. 沈美真 (1990)
Victimised Prostitutes and Prostitution Control Policy in Taiwan
台灣被害娼妓與娼妓政策。台北：前衛。

Shen, M.C. 沈美真 (1995)
'We Should Improve Our Criminal Law To Protect Girl Prostitutes',
爲保護雛妓應改進刑事立法,律師通訊, 第187期, 第24-26頁.

Shen, Y.H. 沈銀和 (1989)
'Protection and Control of Juveniles under the ROC Laws',
我國少年保護管束立法結購之檢討。刑事法雜誌，第33卷，第1期,1-28頁。

Su, H.T. 蘇希宗 (1997)
'There is Still A Long Way to Go for GOH',
勵馨的路還很長, 勵馨園雜誌, 第12期, 第3頁。

Sun, T.W. 孫定渥 (1980)
Prostitution and the Law
娼妓與法律。民眾日報。

Tai, Y.H. 戴炎輝 (1982)
Chinese Family Law
中國親屬法。台北：國立台灣大學。

Tai, Y.H.; Tai, T.H. 戴炎輝、戴東雄 (1987)
Chinese Family Law
中國親屬法。台北：自版。

Taipei Bar Association (TBA) 台北律師公會 (1992)
A Proposal for the Amendment of Child (and Juvenile) Welfare Law
兒童（少年）福利法修正草案。台北律師公會。

Taipei Women Rescue Foundation (TWRF) 台北市婦女救援基金會 (1989a)
Mainland Chinese Girls Selling Sex in Taiwan
大陸女子在台賣淫現狀。未出版。

Tang, L.C. 湯麗珍 (1996)
'An Introduction of Child Protective Measures(III)--Girl Prostitution',
兒童保護措施介紹之三-雛妓篇, 靖娟, 第17期, 第3頁。

Tao, H.S. 陶希聖 (1966)
Chinese Marriage, Family and Kinship
婚姻與家族。台北:商務。

Tao, P.C., Wang, T.C., Liu, T.J., Ko, K.C. 陶百川、王澤鑑、劉宗榮、葛克昌 (1991)
A Reviewed Reference Book of the Major Laws of the Republic of China (eds.)
最新綜合六法全書。台北：三民。

Ting, P.Y. 丁碧雲 (1987)
A General Introduction to Chinese Child Welfare Measures
兒童福利通論。台北：正中書局。

Ting, T.Y. 丁道源 (1985)
Juvenile Law
少年法。台北：自版。

Tsai, H.C. 蔡宏昭 (1990)
'A Proposal for the ROC Social Welfare Policy and Legislation in Taiwan',
現階段我國社會福利政策與法制的提案。社區發展季刊，第50期，134-140頁

Tsai, W.H. 蔡文輝 (1964)
'Evolution of the Chinese Family System',
中國家庭制度之演變。思與言，第11卷，第1期，211-219頁

Tsai, W.H. 蔡文輝 (1987)
The Sociology of the Family
家庭社會學。台北：五南圖書出版公司。

Tsai, W.H. 蔡文輝 (1990)
'A Review of the ROC Social Welfare System in Taiwan',
中華民國社會福利之檢討與展望。今日財經，第308期，7-8頁。

Tsai, Y.Y. 蔡鶯鶯 (1992)
'Legal Status of the KTPAI Vocational Training and Counselling Centre for Distressed Women',
從法律看婦職所的地位。張老師，第10卷，第6期，454-457頁。

Wang, I. 梁望惠 (1993)
'We Need A Consolidated 'Girl Prostitution Prevention And Treatment Law' ',
我們需要一部完整的「雛妓防治法」,勵馨園雜誌, 第31期, 1頁.

Wang, I. 梁望惠 (1995)
'What is the "Midway School"?',
何謂中途學校？ 律師通訊, 第187期, 第23-24頁。

Wang, I. & Wang, Y.H. 梁望惠、王玥好 (1992)
An Estimation of the Scale of the Girl Prostitution Problem in Taiwan
雛妓問題大小之推估。台北市勵馨福利事業基金會。

Wang, J.H. 王仁雄 (1983)
Adoption and Replacement Services and Social Work
領養安置服務與社會工作。中華兒童福利基金會。

Wang, Shu Nu (I) 王書奴 (1971)
A History of Chinese Prostitution
中國娼妓史。台北：仙人掌。

Wang, Shu Nu (II) 王淑女 (1991)
'The Crime Problems',
犯罪問題。楊國樞、葉啓政主編：台灣的社會問題。台北：巨流。

Wang, S.R. 王秀絨 (1984)

'A Study of Illegal Prostitution in Taiwan',
台灣私娼之研究。東海大學社會學研究所社工組碩士論文。

Wang, Y.H. 王玥好 (1992)
'Her Tragedy',
她的悲劇, 勵馨園雜誌, 第26期, 第6-7頁。

Wang, Y.H. 王玥好 (1993a)
'Girl Prostitution and AIDS',
雛妓與AIDS, 勵馨園雜誌, 第33期, 第12-13頁。

Wang, Y.H. 王玥好 (1993b)
'The Family Ethics Ruined In the Dark',
黑暗中被毀滅的親情, 勵馨園雜誌, 第32期, 第3-4頁。

Wang, Y.H. 王玥好 (1995)
'To Testify or Not--Choices of the Victimised Child during the Process of Litigation',
要不要作證--談被害少女訴訟過程中面臨之問題, 勵馨園雜誌, 第1期, 第8-9頁。

Wang, Y.H. 王玥好 (1996a)
'Keep Them Company in their Wounds and Recovery',
陪她們走過生命中的創傷與復原, 勵馨園雜誌, 第6期, 第5-6頁。

Wang, Y.H. 王玥好 (1996b)
'At the Back of The "Voluntary" ',
「自願」的背後, 勵馨園雜誌, 第6期, 第18頁。

Wang, Y.H. 王玥好 (1996c)
'What Settlement Organisations Do We Need?'
我們需要怎樣的安置機構？勵馨園雜誌, 第10期, 第8-9頁。

Wang, Y.H. 王玥好 (1997)
'A Review Report on the Work of the GOH Midway House in the Past Five Years',
勵馨中途之家近五年收容分析報告, 勵馨園雜誌, 第12期, 第8頁。

Wei, H.C. 魏賢政 (1996)
'Sex Tourism And Trafficking',
性觀光業與運輸, 終止童妓雙月刊, 第8-9期, 第18-19頁。

Wu, F.F. 吳方芳 (1996)
'Health and Care Settlement',
健康與安置, 終止童妓雙月刊, 第8-9期, 第26-28頁。

Wu, T.L. 伍翠蓮 (1987)
'Why Do They Become Girl Prostitutes?',
她們爲甚麼淪爲雛妓？聯合月刊，第66期，70-73頁。

Wu, T.S. 吳自甦 (1968)
The Chinese Family System
中國家庭制度。台北:商務。

Yang, K.C. 楊國樞 (1991)
'An Analysis of the Contemporary Social Problems in Taiwan'
當前台灣社會問題的剖析。楊國樞、葉啓政主編：台灣的社會問題。台北：巨流。

Yang, K.S. 楊國樞 (1991)
'Introduction (Taiwan Social Problem)',

緒論。楊國樞、葉啓政主編：台灣的社會問題。台北：巨流。
Yang, K.S. & Yeh, C.C. 楊國樞、葉啓政主編 (1991)
Taiwan Social Problems
台灣的社會問題。台北：巨流。
Yang, M.C. 楊懋春 (1955)
'Changes in the Chinese Family Over the Past Fifty Years'
近五十年來中國家庭的變化。學術季刊，第3卷，第4期，40-50頁。
Yang, M.C. 楊懋春 (1981)
A cross-cultural Study on Chinese and Foreign Family Relationships
中外文化與親屬關係。台北：中央文物供應社。
Yeh, T.H. 葉大華 (1993)
'What Makes Us Get Together Is Love'
是愛, 使我們相聚一起, 勵馨園雜誌, 第33期, 第8-9頁。
Yeh, T.H. 葉大華 (1996)
'The Problems of Minor Commercial Sex In Japan'
未成年賣春問題在日本, 勵馨園雜誌, 第11期, 第15-16頁。
Yin, C.C. 伊慶春 (1987)
'Social Problems Resulting from Girl Prostitution'
雛妓問題引伸出來的另一些社會問題。中國論壇, 第280期, 30-32頁。
Yin, C.C. 伊慶春 (1991)
'The Family Problems',
家庭問題。楊國樞、葉啓政主編：台灣的社會問題。台北：巨流。
Yin, C.C. 伊慶春 (1993)
'The Structural Causes of Girl Prostitution',
雛妓問題結構根源之探討。勵馨園雜誌，第32期，1-2頁。

II. PAPERS, RECORDS, HANDBOOKS

Chen, C.D. 陳志東 (1996)
'An Examination on the Implementation of the "Law to Suppress Sexual Transactions Involving Children and Juveniles". One Year After Its Promulgation: Rescue'
「兒童及少年性交易防制條例」施行一週年總體檢: 救援監督報告。 台北市婦女救援社會福利事業基金會。
Chen, K.T. 陳國慈 (1989)
'Is There Legal Discrimination against Women in Taiwan?',
法律真的歧視婦女嗎？「當今婦女角色與定位」研討會論文。台北：崇她三社。
Chen, M.L. 陳美鈴 (1991b)
'The Number of Non-Sold Girl Prostitutes Is Increasing; The Problem of Lured Girl Prostitution Is Deteriorating',
從非被賣從娼少女日益增加，誤蹈色情陷阱為雛妓者日趨嚴重。台北市婦女救援基金會：百合計劃 -- 搶救原住民少女研習營手冊。
Chen, M.L. 陳美鈴 (1991c)

'Formation of the Protection and Rescue Network',
救援網絡之形成。台北市婦女救援基金會：百合計劃 -- 搶救原住民少女 研習營手冊。

Chen, M.L. 陳美鈴 (1992)
'Social Work Management and the Utilisation of Resources',
社工安置與資源運用。台北市婦女救援基金會：百合計劃 -- 預防少女誤蹈 色情陷阱研討會手冊。

Chen, M.Y. 陳孟瑩 (1990)
'An Analysis of the Juvenile Welfare Act',
解析少年福利法。台北市政府社會局：輔導雛妓面面觀座談會手冊。

Chen, W.C, Chuan, K.C., Huang, C.H, Huang, Y.J. 陳維智、全國成、黃正雄、黃韻如 (1996)'An Examination on the Implementation of the "Law to Suppress Sexual Transactions Involving Children and Juveniles" One Year After Its Promulgation: Protection and Settlement',
「兒童及少年性交易防制條例」施行一週年總體檢,安置保護小組公聽會,總召集-台灣世界展望會。

Chen, YiChen 陳怡真(1991)
'The Causes and Characteristics of Girl Prostitution',
雛妓的形成原因與特質。台北市婦女救援基金會：百合計劃 -- 搶救原住民 少女研習營手冊。

Chen, YingChen 陳映真(1992)
'Girl Prostitution As a Modern Slavery Institution',
做爲一種現代奴隸制度的雛妓問題。台北市勵馨社會福利事業基金會：雛妓防治公聽研討會手冊。

Chi, H.J., Chou, P.J., Han, I.T. 紀惠容、周佩蓉、韓意慈 (1996)
'An Examination on the Implementation of the "Law to Suppress Sexual Transactions Involving Children and Juveniles" One Year After Its Promulgation: Policy',
「兒童及少年性交易防治條例」施行一週年總體檢監督報告, 政策監督小組總召集-勵馨基金會。

Chi, H.J, & Yang, T.H. 紀惠容、楊泰興 (1996)
'An Examination on the Implementation of the "Law to Suppress Sexual Transactions Involving Children and Juveniles" One Year After Its Promulgation: Media'
「兒童及少年性交易防制條例」施行一週年總體檢監督報告, 媒體監督小組總召集-勵馨基金會。

Chu, H.Y. 瞿海源 (1992)
'The Girl Prostitution Problem in Taiwan -- A Sociological Analysis',
台灣雛妓問題的社會學解析。台北市勵馨社會福利事業基金會：雛妓防治公 聽研討會手冊。

Chung, K.M. 莊國明 (1991)
'Legal Punishment and Collection of Evidence in Girl Prostitution Cases',
法律制裁與證據蒐集。台北市婦女救援基金會：百合計劃 -- 搶救原住民少 女研習營手冊。

Chung, K.M. 莊國明 (1992)
'The Rescue of Shih, Huey Tze',

雛妓李ｘｘ救援記。台北市婦女救援基金會：百合計劃 -- 預防少女誤蹈色情陷阱研討會手冊。

ECPAT 中華民國終止童妓協會 (1991)

'A Brief Introduction of Taiwan Commission of International End Asian Child Prostitution Activity',

國際終止亞洲童妓運動台灣委員會簡介, 終止童妓雙月刊, 第1期,第2頁。

ECPAT 中華民國終止童妓協會 (1994)

'A Summary of Foreign News',

國外新聞集錦, 終止童妓雙月刊, 第12期, 第20頁。

ECPAT 中華民國終止童妓協會 (1995a)

'The Characteristics of the Law to Suppress Sexual Transactions Involving Children and Juveniles ',

「兒童及少年性交易防治條例」三讀通過條文之特點, 終止童妓協會雙月刊, 第2期,第11-12頁。

ECPAT 中華民國終止童妓協會 (1995b)

'What Should the Administrative System Do After the Promulgation of the Law to Suppress Sexual Transactions Involving Children and Juveniles',

「兒童及少年性交易防制條例」公佈後,行政體系要做什麼, 終止童妓協會雙月刊,第2期,第13頁。

ECPAT 中華民國終止童妓協會 (1995c)

'A Record of Important Events In 1994',

一九九四年大事記, 終止童妓雙月刊, 第1期, 第17頁。

ECPAT 中華民國終止童妓協會 (1995d)

'A Swedish Man Was Convicted And Put In Prison by the Swedish Court for Engaging in Boy Prostitution In Thailand',

在泰國嫖男童妓, 瑞典男子返國後被判刑入獄, 終止童妓雙月刊, 第2期, 第17頁。

ECPAT 中華民國終止童妓協會 (1995e)

'A Report of ECPAT Events in Every Country',

各國ECPAT之消息報導, 終止童妓雙月刊, 第4期, 第16-17頁。

ECPAT 中華民國終止童妓協會 (1997a)

'An Introduction to the Organisation of ECPAT-International',

國際終止童妓組織介紹, 終止童妓雙月刊, 第11期, 第4-5頁。

ECPAT 中華民國終止童妓協會 (1997b)

'An Introduction to ECPAT-Taiwan',

國際終止童妓協會台灣委員會介紹, 終止童妓雙月刊, 第11期, 第2-3頁。

Garden of Hope (GOH) 台北市勵馨福利事業基金會 (1992a)

'Prevention and Treatment of Girl Prostitution',

雛妓防治公聽研討會手冊。台北市勵馨福利事業基金會。

Garden of Hope (GOH) 台北市勵馨福利事業基金會 (1992b)

'Anti-Girl Prostitution Is A National Campaign',

做為一種全民運動的反雛妓行動, 勵馨園雜誌, 第26期, 第1頁。

Garden of Hope (GOH) 台北市勵馨福利事業基金會 (1992c)

'The Anti-Girl-Prostitution Convention',

反雛妓公約, 勵馨園雜誌, 第26期, 第2頁。

Garden of Hope (GOH) 台北市勵馨福利事業基金會 (1992d)

'Guidelines for the Campaign',
行動綱領, 勵馨園雜誌, 第26期, 第3頁。

Garden of Hope (GOH) 台北市勵馨福利事業基金會 (1993)

'A Declaration on the Estimation of the Girl Prostitution Population',
我們對雛妓人數推估的聲明, 勵馨園雜誌, 第33期, 第7頁。

Garden of Hope (GOH) 台北市勵馨福利事業基金會 (1995)

'A Chart of the GOH Organisation',
勵馨社會福利事業基金會組織圖。

Garden of Hope (GOH) 台北市勵馨福利事業基金會 (1996a)

'Appeals to and Reactions for the Enforcement of the Law to Suppress Sexual Transactions Involving Children and Juveniles ',
我們對「兒童及少年性交易防制條例」的訴求與回應, 台北市勵馨福利事業基金會--搶救少女雛菊行動。

Garden of Hope (GOH) 台北市勵馨福利事業基金會 (1996b)

'My Adoptive Mother and I',
我和我的養母, 勵馨園雜誌, 第6期, 第21頁。

Garden of Hope (GOH) 台北市勵馨福利事業基金會 (1996c)

'The "Reason" and "Power" of Social Reform',
社會改造的「理」與「力」, 勵馨園雜誌, 第6期, 第3頁。

Garden of Hope (GOH) 台北市勵馨福利事業基金會 (1996d)

'The Working Report of the Dandelion Centre',
蒲公英關懷輔導中心服務成果報告, 勵馨園雜誌, 第8期, 第3-5頁。

Garden of Hope (GOH) 台北市勵馨福利事業基金會 (1996e)

'Our Steps Are More And More Stable',
腳步：漸行漸穩, 勵馨園雜誌, 第9期, 第10頁。

Garden of Hope (GOH) 台北市勵馨福利事業基金會 (1997)

'A Working Report of the Dandelion Centre',
蒲公英關懷輔導中心成果報告, 勵馨園雜誌, 第12期, 第9頁。

Han, I.T. 韓意慈 (1996a)

'An Annual Examination of the Law to Suppress Sexual Transactions Involving Children and Juveniles Public Hearing Record',
「兒童及少年性交易防制條例」週年總體檢公聽會紀實, 勵馨園雜誌, 第10期, 第3頁。

Han, I.T. 韓意慈 (1996b)

'A Public Hearing Record of the Examination on Settlement and Protection',
安置保護總體檢公聽會紀實, 勵馨園雜誌, 第10卷, 第7頁。

Ho, C.W. 侯崇文 (1988)

'Contemporary Prostitution Problems in Taiwan',
當代台灣娼妓問題。彩虹婦女事工中心：預防國際婦女運輸研討會報告書。

Ho, C.W. 侯崇文 (1992)

'The Girl Prostitution Problem -- A Sociological Point of View',
從社會學的觀點看雛妓問題。台北市勵馨社會福利事業基金會：雛妓防治公聽

研討會手冊。

Hong, W.W. 洪文惠 (1991b)

'General Discussions on the Guidance and Counselling of Girl Prostitutes',
淺談雛妓輔導。台北市婦女救援基金會：百合計劃 -- 搶救原住民少女研習營手冊。

Hong, W.W. 洪文惠 (1992)

'Treatment of Girl Prostitutes -- Working Towards Inter-Agency Cooperation',
從不同體制互相搭配的觀點談雛妓處遇。台北市勵馨福利事業基金會：雛妓 防治公聽研討會手冊。

Hsu, M.C. 許木柱 (1991b)

'The Culture Traits of Aboriginal People in Taiwan',
原住民的文化特質。台北市婦女救援基金會：百合計劃 -- 搶救原住民少 女研習營手冊。

Huang, Y.C. 黃怡君 (1991b)

'How to Discover and Prevent Girl Prostitution Problems',
如何發現與預防問題。台北市婦女救援基金會：百合計劃 -- 搶救原住民 少女研習營手冊。

Kang, W.L. & Shee, H.L. 康雯莉、施慧玲 (1995)

'A News Summary of the International Campaign to End Child Prostitution',
國際終止童妓行動新聞集錦, 終止童妓雙月刊, 第1期, 第16頁。

Kao, LL.C. 高李麗珍 (1991)

'The Opening Speech on the Children's Right Day Celebration',
「兒童人權日聯歡會」致詞, 終止童妓雙月刊, 第2期,第2卷, 第1頁。

Li, T.C. 李子春 (1992)

'Treatment of Girl Prostitution: A Judicial Point of View',
從司法的觀點談雛妓處遇。台北市勵馨社會福利事業基金會：雛妓防治公聽 研討會手冊。

Li, Y.N. 李又寧 (1987)

'Dr. Sun, Yat Sen and Women's Movements in Early Republican China',
孫中山先生與民元後的婦女運動。「孫中山先生與中國現代化」國際學術會議論文集。珠海學報，第15期。香港珠海學院。

Liau, B.Y. 廖碧英 (1985)

'Contemporary Lust Problems in Taiwan',
色情問題：現狀報告。亞洲教會婦女大會：觀光與賣春研討會宣讀論文。

Lin, M.J. 林美瑢 (1989)

Asian Consultation on Tourism and Aboriginal People (ed.)
原住民與觀光。台灣基督教長老教會花東社區發展中心。

Lin, Y.S. 林永頌 (1992)

'The Juvenile Prostitution Problem: A Legal Point of View',
回應從法律之觀點談雛妓問題。台北市勵馨社會福利事業基金會：雛妓防治 公聽研討會手冊。

Pai, H.H. 白秀雄 (1992)

'Treatment of Girl Prostitutes: A Social Welfare Point of View',
從社會福利的觀點談雛妓處遇。台北市勵馨社會福利事業基金會：雛妓防治

公聽研討會手冊。

Pan, W.K. 潘維剛 (1992)

'Crashed Roses, Twisted Lives: A Girl Prostitute's Right of Existence',

壓扁的玫瑰, 扭曲的人生 -- 論雛妓生存權。台北市勵馨社會福利事業基金會：雛妓防治公聽研討會手冊。

Rainbow Project (RP) 彩虹婦女事工中心 (1988)

Prevention of International Trafficking of Women. Reports of A Seminar held on November 15-16, 1988, Taipei.

預防國際婦女運輸研討會報告書。

Shee, A. 施慧玲 (1992)

Research Materials for the 'Statement for the Campaign to End Child Prostitution in Taiwan',

終止童妓運動聲明參考資料手冊。

Shee, A. 施慧玲 (1995)

'A Proposal for the Amendment to Articles 9,22 & 34 of the Law to Suppress Sexual Transactions Involving Children and Juveniles',

兒童及少年性交易防制條例第九條、第二十二條、第三十四條之修正,勵馨園雜誌,第11期,第13-14頁。

Shee, A. 施慧玲 (1996a)

'The Feasible Directions of Amendments to the Law to Punish Child Sex Tourists ',

處罰出國嫖童妓者：修法可行方向。 終止童妓協會。

Shee, A. 施慧玲 (1996b)

'The Meaning And Contents of the Law to Suppress Sexual Transaction Involving Children and Juveniles',

兒童及少年性交易防制條例之意義及規範內容, 終止童妓雙月刊, 第5期, 第6-11頁。

Taipei Municipal Social Bureau (TMSB) 台北市政府社會局 (1990a)

'Providing Guidance and Counselling for Girl Prostitutes',

輔導雛妓面面觀手冊。

Taipei Women Rescue Foundation (TWRF) 台北市婦女救援基金會 (1989)

'Mainland Chinese Girls Forced into Prostitution: A Reflection',

大陸少女在台賣淫之省思座談會記錄。未出版。

Taipei Women Rescue Foundation (TWRF) 台北市婦女救援基金會 (1990)

'Lust Problems in Taiwan',

色情問題系列座談會記錄。未出版。

Taipei Women Rescue Foundation (TWRF) 台北市婦女救援基金會 (1991)

'The Lily Project (I): Rescuing the Aboriginal Girls',

百合計劃 -- 搶救原住民少女研習營手冊。

Taipei Women Rescue Foundation (TWRF) 台北市婦女救援基金會 (1992)(1993)

'The Lily Project (II): Prevention of Lured Girl Prostitution',

百合計劃 -- 預防少女誤蹈色情陷阱研討會手冊。

Taipei Women Rescue Foundation (TWRF) 台北市婦女救援基金會 (1994a)

'A Chart of Rescue/Information Record',

救援/檢舉 資料表, 婦援會訊, 第11期, 第6-7頁。

Taipei Women Rescue Foundation (TWRF) 台北市婦女救援基金會 (1995a)
'An Information Form to Report Against Advertisements of Lust Traps',
色情陷阱廣告檢舉函, 終止童妓雙月刊, 第4期, 第19-22頁。

Taipei Women Rescue Foundation (TWRF) 台北市婦女救援基金會 (1996)
'A Monthly Report Chart of Informed Cases',
檢舉個案月報表（84年12月至85年1月）, 婦女救援基金會會訊, 第7期, 第31-34頁。

Tsai, P.Y. 蔡碧玉 (1996)
'A Discussion on the Law to Suppress Sexual Transactions Involving Children and Juveniles',
關於「兒童及少年性交易防治條例」的討論與回應, 終止童妓雙月刊, 第8-9期, 第12-13頁。

Tseng, S.M., Chun, S. 曾淑美、俊陞 (1987)
'The Girl Prostitutes Are Beseeching Heaven for Mercy',
雛妓籲天錄。台北市勵馨社會福利事業基金會：雛妓防治公聽研討會手冊。

Wang, C.F. 王清峰 (1992a)
'Child Prostitution, Juvenile Prostitution, and Legal Protection',
兒童少年賣淫與法律保護。台北市婦女救援基金會：百合計劃 -- 預防少女誤蹈色情陷阱研討會手冊。

Wang, C.F. 王清峰 (1992b)
'The Girl Prostitution Problem: A Legal Point of View',
從法律的觀點談雛妓問題。台北市勵馨社會福利事業基金會：雛妓防治公聽研討會手冊。

Wang, C.F. & Shen M.C. 王清峰，沈美真 (1991)
'Child Welfare Law, Juvenile Welfare Law, and Legal Protection',
兒福法、少福法與法律保護。台北市婦女救援基金會：百合計劃 -- 搶救原住民少女研習營手冊。

Wang, I. 梁望惠 (1992a)
'Guidance and Counselling Services for Unfortunate Girls in Hong Kong',
香港如何輔導不幸少女。台北市勵馨社會福利事業基金會：雛妓防治公聽研討會手冊。

Wang, I. 梁望惠 (1992b)
'Juvenile Welfare Law and the Protection, Guidance and Counselling Services for Girl Prostitutes',
少年福利法與雛妓保護輔導。台北市勵馨社會福利事業基金會：雛妓防治公聽研討會手冊。

Wang, I. 梁望惠 (1992c)
'A General Account of the Present Guidance and Counselling Services for Victims of Juvenile Prostitution and Sexual Abuse in Taiwan',
雛妓，性虐待個案之輔導概況。台北市婦女救援基金會：百合計劃 -- 預防少女誤蹈色情陷阱研討會手冊。

Wu, H.Y. 吳惠櫻 (1990)
'Taipei Municipal Kuang Tzu Po Ai Institution, Vocational Training and Counselling Centre for Distressed Women: Working Report',

台北市立廣慈博愛院婦女職業輔導所輔導工作報告。台北市政府社會局：輔 導雛妓面面觀手冊。

Wu, H.Y. 吳惠櫻 (1991)

'Social Work Management and Utilisation of Social Resources',

社工安置與社會資源之運用。台北市婦女救援基金會：百合計劃 -- 搶救原 住民少女研習營手冊。

Wuei, C.M. 魏京梅 (1996a)

'A Review on the Enforcement of the Law to Suppress Sexual Transactions Involving Children and Juveniles',

「兒童及少年性交易防制條例」施行狀況, 勵馨園雜誌, 第9期, 第13頁。

Wuei, C.M. 魏京梅 (1996b)

'Policy and Activities on the Law to Suppress Sexual Transactions Involving Children and Juveniles',

「兒童及少年性交易防制條例」相關活動及政策, 勵馨園雜誌, 第9期, 第14頁。

Yang, T.H. 楊泰興 (1996)

'A Public Hearing Record of the Examination on the Media',

媒體總體檢公聽會紀實, 勵馨園雜誌, 第10期第4卷, 第4頁。

III. OFFICIAL PUBLICATIONS

Chan, H.S. et al. 詹火生 等 (1991)

A Study of the ROC Social Welfare Legislation in Taiwan

我國社會福利法制之研究。行政院經濟建設委員會建全經社法規工作小組。

Cheng, Z.H., Fan-Chang, H. 鄭榮豪、范姜迴 (1990)

A Study of the Girl Prostitution Problem

雛妓問題之研究。台灣台北少年觀護所七十九年度專題研究。

Feng, Y. 馮燕 (1992)

An Assessment of the Effectiveness of the Child Welfare Law in Implementation

兒童福利法執行成效之評估。行政院研究發展考核委員會。

Government Information Office(GIO), Executive Yuan, ROC 行政院新聞局 (1996a)

'A Report on the Enforcement of the Law to Suppress Sexual Transactions Involving Children and Juveniles',

執行「兒童及少年性交易防制工作」宣導成果報告表。

Government Information Office(GIO), Executive Yuan, ROC 行政院新聞局 (1996b)

'The Conditions of Executing the Thirty-third Provision of the 'Child and Juvenile Sexual Trade Prevention and Treatment Law',

執行「兒童及少年性交易防制條例」第33條情形。

Hong, W.H. 洪文惠 (1991)

'Women Working in the Sex Industry',

從事色情工作的婦女。婦女福利工作手冊。臺灣省政府社會處編印。

Hsiao, H.H. & Chang, L.Y. 蕭新煌、張苙雲 (1988)

'Construction of the Facts of a Social Problem: An Analysis of the Recognition of A Social Problem by the Public',

社會問題的事實建構：民眾對社會問題認知的分析。楊國樞、瞿海源編：變遷中的台灣社會。中央研究院民族學研究所。

Hsu, M.C. & Chu, H.Y. et. al. 許木柱、瞿海源 等 (1992)

An Assessment of the Results of Governmental Guidance and Counselling Measures for Aboriginal People in Taiwan.

山胞輔導措施積效之檢討。行政院研究發展考核委員會。

Lai, T.H. 賴澤涵 (1982)

'Composition of the Chinese Family and Evolution of Its Power Structure',

我國家庭的組成及權力結構之變遷。中央研究院三民主義研究所編，社會科 學整合論文集。

Li, Y.Y. et. al. 李亦園 等 (1983)

Research and Evaluation Report on the ROC Administrative Policies for Aboriginal Development

山地行政政策之研究與評估報告書。中央研究院民族學研究所。

Ministry of the Interior, ROC 內政部 (1987-1996)

Important Statistics of Interior Affairs.

內政統計提要。1987-1996 年。

Ministry of Justice, ROC 法務部 (1987)

An Official Report of the Civil Customs in Taiwan

台灣民事習慣調查報告。台北：法務通訊雜誌社。

National Police Administration, ROC 警政署 (1987-1996)

Statistics of Criminal Cases in Taiwan

台灣刑案統計。1987-1996年。

Research Centre for Crime Issues, Ministry of Judicial Administration, ROC 司法行政部犯罪問題研究中心 (1967)

A Study of Issues Concerning Offences Against Social Morals

妨害風化罪問題之研究。司法行政部犯罪問題研究中心

Taipei Municipal Kuang Tzu Po Ai Institution (KTPAI) 台北市立廣慈博愛院 (1990)

Taipei Municipal Kuang Tzu Po Ai Institution: 20th Anniversary Special Edition

台北市立廣慈博愛院二十週年院慶特刊。

Taipei Municipal Social Bureau (TMSB) 台北市政府社會局 (1990b)

'Definitions of Child Abuse',

兒童虐待的定義。福利社會，第20期，10-13頁。

Taipei Municipal Social Bureau (TMSB) 台北市政府社會局 (1991)

Juvenile Welfare Laws and Regulations

少年福利法規。台北市政府社會局。

Tang, S.P. et.al. 唐學斌 等 (1983)

'A Study on the Prevention of Lust "Floods" in Taipei',

台北市遏止色情氾濫途徑之研究。 台北市政府研究發展考核委員會委託研 究計劃, 中國文化大學社會工作學系。

Wang, T.S. et. al. 王添盛 等 (1989)

A Study of the Aboriginal Girl Prostitution

山地雛妓之研究。 台灣台中地方法院檢察處。

Yang, K.S. et. al. 楊國樞 等 (1991)

Juvenile Problems and Juvenile Welfare Legislation
少年問題與少年福利法法制之研究。行政院經濟建設委員會健全經社法規工 作小組。

Yin, C.C. et. al. 尹慶春 等 (1993)
A Study of the Prevention and Treatment of Girl Prostitution in Taiwan
雛妓問題防治途徑之研究。行政院研究發展考核委員會。

IV. NEWSPAPERS

* *The Central Daily [International Edition] (Chung Yang Jih Pao Hai Wai Pan) 中央日報（海外版）*
* *The Central Daily (Chung Yang Jih Pao) 中央日報*
* *The China Times (Chung Kuo Shih Pao) 中國時晚*
* *The China Evenings (Chung Shih Wan Pao) 中時晚報*
* *The Independent Daily (Tsu Li Tzao Pao) 自立早報*
* *The Independent Evenings (Tsu Li Wan Pao) 自立晚報*
* *The United Daily (Lian He Tzao Pao) 聯合早報*
* *The United Evenings (Lian He Wan Pao) 聯合晚報*
* *The Liberty Times (Tzu Yiu Shih Pao) 自由時報*
* *The People's Livelihood Daily (Min Sheng Pao) 民生報*

Index

For Product Safety Concerns and Information please contact our EU representative GPSR@taylorandfrancis.com Taylor & Francis Verlag GmbH, Kaufingerstraße 24, 80331 München, Germany

Batch number: 10725991

Printed by Printforce, the Netherlands